Table of Contents

Preface

As the title promises, this book will introduce you to one of the world's most popular programming languages: Python. It's aimed at beginning programmers as well as more experienced programmers who want to add Python to the languages they already know.

In most cases, it's easier to learn a computer language than a human language. There's less ambiguity and fewer exceptions to keep in your head. Python is one of the most consistent and clear computer languages. It balances ease of learning, ease of use, and expressive power.

Computer languages are made of *data* (like nouns in spoken languages) and *instructions* or *code* (like verbs). You need both. In alternating chapters, you'll be introduced to Python's basic code and data structures, learn how to combine them, and build up to more advanced ones. The programs that you read and write will get longer and more complex. Using a woodworking analogy, we'll start with a hammer, nails, and scraps of wood. Over the first half of this book, we'll introduce more specialized components, up to the equivalents of lathes and other power tools.

You'll not only learn the language, but also what to do with it. We'll begin with the Python language and its "batteries included" standard library, but I'll also show you how to find, download, install, and use some good third-party packages. My emphasis is on whatever I've actually found useful in more than 10 years of production Python development, rather than fringe topics or complex hacks.

Although this is an introduction, some advanced topics are included because I want to expose them to you. Areas like databases and the web are still covered, but technology changes fast. A Python programmer might now be expected to know something about cloud computing, machine learning, or event streaming. You'll find something here on all of these.

Python has some special features that work better than adapting styles from other languages that you may know. For example, using for and *iterators* is a more direct way of making a loop than manually incrementing some counter variable.

When you're learning something new, it's hard to tell which terms are specific instead of colloquial, and which concepts are actually important. In other words, "Is this on the test?" I'll highlight terms and ideas that have specific meaning or importance in Python, but not too many at once. Real Python code is included early and often.

 I'll include a note such as this when something might be confusing, or if there's a more appropriate *Pythonic* way to do it.

Python isn't perfect. I'll show you things that seem odd or that should be avoided—and offer alternatives you can use, instead.

Now and then, my opinions on some subjects (such as object inheritance, or MVC and REST designs for the web) may vary a bit from the common wisdom. See what you think.

Audience

This book is for anybody interested in learning one of the world's most popular computing languages, regardless of whether you have previously learned any programming.

Changes in the Second Edition

What's changed since the first edition?

- About a hundred more pages, including cat pictures.
- Twice the chapters, each shorter now.
- An early chapter devoted to data types, variables, and names.
- New standard Python features like *f-strings*.
- New or improved third-party packages.
- New code examples throughout.
- An appendix on basic hardware and software, for new programmers.
- An appendix on *asyncio*, for not-so-new programmers.
- "New stack" coverage: containers, clouds, data science, and machine learning.

- Hints on getting a job programming in Python.

What hasn't changed? Examples using bad poetry and ducks. These are evergreen.

Outline

Part I (Chapters 1–11) explains Python's basics. You should read these chapters in order. I work up from the simplest data and code structures, combining them on the way into more detailed and realistic programs. Part II (Chapters 12–22) shows how Python is used in specific application areas such as the web, databases, networks, and so on; read these chapters in any order you like.

Here's a brief preview of the chapters and appendixes, including some of the terms that you'll run into there:

Chapter 1, A Taste of Py
> Computer programs are not that different from directions that you see every day. Some little Python programs give you a glimpse of the language's looks, capabilities, and uses in the real world. You'll see how to run a Python program within its *interactive interpreter* (or *shell*), or from a text *file* saved on your computer.

Chapter 2, Data: Types, Values, Variables, and Names
> Computer languages mix data and instructions. Different *types* of data are stored and treated differently by the computer. They may allow their values to be changed (*mutable*) or not (*immutable*). In a Python program, data can be *literal* (numbers like 78, text *strings* like "waffle") or represented by named *variables*. Python treats variables like *names*, which is different from many other languages and has some important consequences.

Chapter 3, Numbers
> This chapter shows Python's simplest data types: *booleans*, *integers*, and *floating-point* numbers. You'll also learn the basic math operations. The examples use Python's interactive interpreter like a calculator.

Chapter 4, Choose with if
> We'll bounce between Python's nouns (data types) and verbs (program structures) for a few chapters. Python code normally runs a line at a time, from the start to the end of a program. The if code structure lets you run different lines of code, depending on some data comparison.

Chapter 5, Text Strings
> Back to nouns, and the world of text *strings*. Learn how to create, combine, change, retrieve, and print strings.

Chapter 6, Loop with while and for

Verbs again, and two ways to make a *loop*: `for` and `while`. You'll be introduced to a core Python concept: *iterators*.

Chapter 7, Tuples and Lists

It's time for the first of Python's higher-level built-in data structures: `lists` and `tuples`. These are sequences of values, like LEGO for building much more complex data structures. Step through them with *iterators*, and build lists quickly with *comprehensions*.

Chapter 8, Dictionaries and Sets

Dictionaries (aka *dicts*) and *sets* let you save data by their values rather than their position. This turns out to be very handy and will be among your favorite Python features.

Chapter 9, Functions

Weave the data and code structures of the previous chapters to compare, choose, or repeat. Package code in *functions* and handle errors with *exceptions*.

Chapter 10, Oh Oh: Objects and Classes

The word *object* is a bit fuzzy, but important in many computer languages, including Python. If you've done *object-oriented programming* in other languages, Python is a bit more relaxed. This chapter explains how to use objects and classes, and when it's better to use alternatives.

Chapter 11, Modules, Packages, and Goodies

This chapter demonstrates how to scale out to larger code structures: *modules*, *packages*, and *programs*. You'll see where to put code and data, how to get data in and out, handle options, tour the Python Standard Library, and take a glance at what lies beyond.

Chapter 12, Wrangle and Mangle Data

Learn to manage (or mangle) data like a pro. This chapter is all about text and binary data, joy with Unicode characters, and *regex* text searching. It also introduces the data types *bytes* and *bytearray*, counterparts of strings that contain raw binary values instead of text characters.

Chapter 13, Calendars and Clocks

Dates and times can be messy to handle. This chapter shows common problems and useful solutions.

Chapter 14, Files and Directories

Basic data storage uses *files* and *directories*. This chapter shows you how to create and use them.

Chapter 15, Data in Time: Processes and Concurrency
> This is the first hard-core system chapter. Its theme is data in time—how to use *programs*, *processes*, and *threads* to do more things at a time (*concurrency*). Python's recent *async* additions are mentioned, with details in Appendix C.

Chapter 16, Data in a Box: Persistent Storage
> Data can be stored and retrieved with basic flat files and directories within filesystems. They gain some structure with common text formats such as CSV, JSON, and XML. As data get larger and more complex, they need the services of *databases*—traditional *relational* ones, and some newer *NoSQL* data stores.

Chapter 17, Data in Space: Networks
> Send your code and data through space in *networks* with *services*, *protocols*, and *APIs*. Examples range from low-level TCP *sockets*, to *messaging* libraries and queuing systems, to *cloud* deployment.

Chapter 18, The Web, Untangled
> The *web* gets its own chapter—clients, servers, APIs, and frameworks. You'll *crawl* and *scrape* websites, and then build real websites with *request* parameters and *templates*.

Chapter 19, Be a Pythonista
> This chapter contains tips for Python developers—installation with pip and virtualenv, using IDEs, testing, debugging, logging, source control, and documentation. It also helps you to find and install useful third-party packages, package your own code for reuse, and learn where to get more information.

Chapter 20, Py Art
> People are doing cool things with Python in the arts: graphics, music, animation, and games.

Chapter 21, Py at Work
> Python has specific applications for business: data visualization (plots, graphs, and maps), security, and regulation.

Chapter 22, Py Sci
> In the past few years, Python has emerged as a top language for science: math and statistics, physical science, bioscience, and medicine. *Data science* and *machine learning* are notable strengths. This chapter touches on NumPy, SciPy, and Pandas.

Appendix A, Hardware and Software for Beginning Programmers
> If you're fairly new to programming, this describes how hardware and software actually work. It introduces some terms that you'll keep running into.

Appendix B, Install Python 3

If you don't already have Python 3 on your computer, this appendix shows you how to install it, whether you're running Windows, macOS, Linux, or some other variant of Unix.

Appendix C, Something Completely Different: Async

Python has been adding asynchronous features in different releases, and they're not easy to understand. I mention them as they come up in various chapters, but save a detailed discussion for this appendix.

Appendix D, Answers to Exercises

This has the answers to the end-of-chapter exercises. Don't peek here until you've tried the exercises yourself, or you might be turned into a newt.

Appendix E, Cheat Sheets

This appendix contains cheat sheets to use as a quick reference.

Python Versions

Computer languages change over time as developers add features and fix mistakes. The examples in this book were written and tested while running Python version 3.7. Version 3.7 was the most current as this book was being edited, and I'll talk about its notable additions. Version 3.8 is scheduled for general release in late 2019, and I'll include a few things to expect from it. If you want to know what was added to Python and when, try the What's New in Python page (*https://docs.python.org/3/whatsnew*). It's a technical reference; a bit heavy when you're just starting with Python, but may be useful in the future if you ever have to get programs to work on computers with different Python versions.

Conventions Used in This Book

The following typographical conventions are used in this book:

Italic

Indicates new terms, URLs, email addresses, filenames, and file extensions.

`Constant width`

Used for program listings, as well as within paragraphs to refer to program elements such as variables, functions, and data types.

`Constant width bold`

Shows commands or other text that should be typed literally by the user.

Constant width italic

Shows text that should be replaced with user-supplied values or by values determined by context.

 This icon signifies a tip, suggestion, or general note.

 This icon indicates a warning or caution.

Using Code Examples

The substantial code examples and exercises in this book are available online for you to download (*https://github.com/madscheme/introducing-python*). This book is here to help you get your job done. In general, you may use the code in this book in your programs and documentation. You do not need to contact us for permission unless you're reproducing a significant portion of the code. For example, writing a program that uses several chunks of code from this book does not require permission. Selling or distributing examples from O'Reilly books does require permission. Answering a question by citing this book and quoting example code does not require permission. Incorporating a significant amount of example code from this book into your product's documentation does require permission.

We appreciate, but do not require, attribution. An attribution usually includes the title, author, publisher, and ISBN. For example: "*Introducing Python* by Bill Lubanovic (O'Reilly). Copyright 2020 Bill Lubanovic, 978-1-492-05136-7."

If you feel your use of code examples falls outside fair use or the permission given here, feel free to contact us at *permissions@oreilly.com*.

O'Reilly Online Learning

 For over 40 years, *O'Reilly Media* has provided technology and business training, knowledge, and insight to help companies succeed.

Our unique network of experts and innovators share their knowledge and expertise through books, articles, conferences, and our online learning platform. O'Reilly's online learning platform gives you on-demand access to live training courses, in-depth learning paths, interactive coding environments, and a vast collection of text and video from O'Reilly and 200+ other publishers. For more information, please visit *http://oreilly.com*.

How to Contact Us

Please address comments and questions concerning this book to the publisher:

O'Reilly Media, Inc.
1005 Gravenstein Highway North
Sebastopol, CA 95472
800-998-9938 (in the United States or Canada)
707-829-0515 (international or local)
707-829-0104 (fax)

We have a web page for this book, where we list errata, examples, and any additional information. You can access this page at *https://oreil.ly/introducing-python-2e*.

To comment or ask technical questions about this book, send an email to *bookquestions@oreilly.com*.

For more information about our books, courses, conferences, and news, see our website at *http://www.oreilly.com*.

Find us on Facebook: *http://facebook.com/oreilly*

Follow us on Twitter: *http://twitter.com/oreillymedia*

Watch us on YouTube: *http://www.youtube.com/oreillymedia*

Acknowledgments

My sincere thanks to the reviewers and readers who helped make this better:

Corbin Collins, Charles Givre, Nathan Stocks, Dave George, and Mike James

Python Basics

CHAPTER 1

A Taste of Py

Only ugly languages become popular. Python is the one exception.

—Don Knuth

Mysteries

Let's begin with two mini-mysteries and their solutions. What do you think the following two lines mean?

```
(Row 1): (RS) K18,ssk,k1,turn work.
(Row 2): (WS) Sl 1 pwise,p5,p2tog,p1,turn.
```

It looks technical, like some kind of computer program. Actually, it's a *knitting pattern*; specifically, a fragment describing how to turn the heel of a sock, like the one in Figure 1-1.

Figure 1-1. Knitted socks

This makes as much sense to me as a Sudoku puzzle does to one of my cats, but my wife understands it perfectly. If you're a knitter, you do, too.

Let's try another mysterious text, found on an index card. You'll figure out its purpose right away, although you might not know its final product:

```
1/2 c. butter or margarine
1/2 c. cream
2 1/2 c. flour
1 t. salt
1 T. sugar
4 c. riced potatoes (cold)

Be sure all ingredients are cold before adding flour.
Mix all ingredients.
Knead thoroughly.
Form into 20 balls.  Store cold until the next step.
For each ball:
  Spread flour on cloth.
  Roll ball into a circle with a grooved rolling pin.
  Fry on griddle until brown spots appear.
  Turn over and fry other side.
```

Even if you don't cook, you probably recognized that it's a *recipe*[1]: a list of food ingredients followed by directions for preparation. But what does it make? It's *lefse*, a Norwegian delicacy that resembles a tortilla (Figure 1-2). Slather on some butter and jam or whatever you like, roll it up, and enjoy.

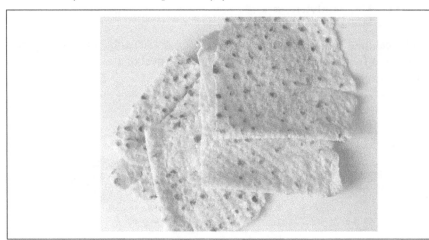

Figure 1-2. Lefse

---

1 Usually only found in cookbooks and cozy mysteries.

The knitting pattern and the recipe share some features:

- A regular *vocabulary* of words, abbreviations, and symbols. Some might be familiar, others mystifying.

- Rules about what can be said, and where—*syntax.*

- A *sequence of operations* to be performed in order.

- Sometimes, a repetition of some operations (a *loop*), such as the method for frying each piece of lefse.

- Sometimes, a reference to another sequence of operations (in computer terms, a *function*). In the recipe, you might need to refer to another recipe for ricing potatoes.

- Assumed knowledge about the *context*. The recipe assumes you that know what water is and how to boil it. The knitting pattern assumes that you can knit and purl without stabbing yourself too often.

- Some *data* to be used, created, or modified—potatoes and yarn.

- The *tools* used to work with the data—pots, mixers, ovens, knitting sticks.

- An expected *result*. In our examples, something for your feet and something for your stomach. Just don't mix them up.

Whatever you call them—idioms, jargon, little languages—you see examples of them everywhere. The lingo saves time for people who know it, while mystifying the rest of us. Try deciphering a newspaper column about bridge if you don't play the game, or a scientific paper if you're not a scientist (or even if you are, but in a different field).

Little Programs

You'll see all of these ideas in computer programs, which are themselves like little languages, specialized for humans to tell computers what to do. I used the knitting pattern and recipe to demonstrate that programming isn't that mysterious. It's largely a matter of learning the right words and the rules.

Now, it helps greatly if there aren't too many words and rules, and if you don't need to learn too many of them at once. Our brains can hold only so much at one time.

Let's finally see a real computer program (Example 1-1). What do you think this does?

Example 1-1. countdown.py

```
for countdown in 5, 4, 3, 2, 1, "hey!":
    print(countdown)
```

If you guessed that it's a Python program that prints the lines

```
5
4
3
2
1
hey!
```

then you know that Python can be easier to learn than a recipe or knitting pattern. And you can practice writing Python programs from the comfort and safety of your desk, far from the hazards of hot water and pointy sticks.

The Python program has some special words and symbols—for, in, print, commas, colons, parentheses, and so on—that are important parts of the language's *syntax* (rules). The good news is that Python has a nicer syntax, and less of it to remember, than most computer languages. It seems more natural—almost like a recipe.

Example 1-2 is another tiny Python program; it selects one Harry Potter spell from a Python *list* and prints it.

Example 1-2. spells.py

```
spells = [
    "Riddikulus!",
    "Wingardium Leviosa!",
    "Avada Kedavra!",
    "Expecto Patronum!",
    "Nox!",
    "Lumos!",
    ]
print(spells[3])
```

The individual spells are Python *strings* (sequences of text characters, enclosed in quotes). They're separated by commas and enclosed in a Python *list* that's defined by enclosing square brackets ([and]). The word spells is a *variable* that gives the list a name so that we can do things with it. In this case, the program would print the fourth spell:

```
Expecto Patronum!
```

Why did we say 3 if we wanted the fourth? A Python list such as spells is a sequence of values, accessed by their *offset* from the beginning of the list. The first value is at offset 0, and the fourth value is at offset 3.

People count from 1, so it might seem weird to count from 0. It helps to think in terms of offsets instead of positions. Yes, this is an example of how computer programs sometimes differ from common language usage.

Lists are very common *data structures* in Python, and Chapter 7 shows how to use them.

The program in Example 1-3 prints a quote from one of the Three Stooges, but referenced by who said it rather than its position in a list.

Example 1-3. quotes.py

```python
quotes = {
    "Moe": "A wise guy, huh?",
    "Larry": "Ow!",
    "Curly": "Nyuk nyuk!",
    }
stooge = "Curly"
print(stooge, "says:", quotes[stooge])
```

If you were to run this little program, it would print the following:

```
Curly says: Nyuk nyuk!
```

quotes is a variable that names a Python *dictionary*—a collection of unique *keys* (in this example, the name of the Stooge) and associated *values* (here, a notable saying of that Stooge). Using a dictionary, you can store and look up things by name, which is often a useful alternative to a list.

The spells example used square brackets ([and]) to make a Python list, and the quotes example uses curly brackets ({ and }, which are no relation to Curly), to make a Python dictionary. Also, a colon (:) is used to associate each key in the dictionary with its value. You can read much more about dictionaries in Chapter 8.

That wasn't too much syntax at once, I hope. In the next few chapters, you'll encounter more of these little rules, a bit at a time.

A Bigger Program

And now for something completely different: Example 1-4 presents a Python program performing a more complex series of tasks. Don't expect to understand how the program works yet; that's what this book is for! The intent is to introduce you to the look and feel of a typical nontrivial Python program. If you know other computer languages, evaluate how Python compares. Even without knowing Python yet, can you roughly figure out what each line does before reading the explanation after the program? You've already seen examples of a Python list and a dictionary, and this throws in a few more features.

In earlier printings of this book, the sample program connected to a YouTube website and retrieved information on its most highly rated videos, like "Charlie Bit My Finger." It worked well until shortly after the ink was dry on the second printing. That's when Google dropped support for this service and the marquee sample program stopped working. Our new Example 1-4 goes to another site which should be around longer—the *Wayback Machine* at the Internet Archive (*http://archive.org*), a free service that has saved billions of web pages (and movies, TV shows, music, games, and other digital artifacts) over 20 years. You'll see more examples of such *web APIs* in Chapter 18.

The program will ask you to type a URL and a date. Then, it asks the Wayback Machine if it has a copy of that website around that date. If it found one, it returns the information to this Python program, which prints the URL and displays it in your web browser. The point is to show how Python handles a variety of tasks—get your typed input, communicate across the internet to a website, get back some content, extract a URL from it, and convince your web browser to display that URL.

If we got back a normal web page full of HTML-formatted text, we would need to figure out how to display it, which is a lot of work that we happily entrust to web browsers. We could also try to extract the parts that we want (see more details about *web scraping* in Chapter 18). Either choice would be more work and a larger program. Instead, the Wayback Machine returns data in *JSON* format. JSON (JavaScript Object Notation) is a human-readable text format that describes the types, values, and order of the data within it. It's another little language, and it has become a popular way to exchange data among different computer languages and systems. You'll read more about JSON in Chapter 12.

Python programs can translate JSON text into Python *data structures*—the kind you'll see in the next few chapters—as though you wrote a program to create them yourself. Our little program just selects one piece (the URL of the old page from the Internet Archive website). Again, this is a complete Python program that you can run yourself. We've included only a little error-checking, just to keep the example short. The line numbers are not part of the program; they are included to help you follow the description that we provide after the program.

Example 1-4. archive.py

```
1 import webbrowser
2 import json
3 from urllib.request import urlopen
4
5 print("Let's find an old website.")
6 site = input("Type a website URL: ")
```

```
7 era = input("Type a year, month, and day, like 20150613: ")
8 url = "http://archive.org/wayback/available?url=%s&timestamp=%s" % (site, era)
9 response = urlopen(url)
10 contents = response.read()
11 text = contents.decode("utf-8")
12 data = json.loads(text)
13 try:
14     old_site = data["archived_snapshots"]["closest"]["url"]
15     print("Found this copy: ", old_site)
16     print("It should appear in your browser now.")
17     webbrowser.open(old_site)
18 except:
19     print("Sorry, no luck finding", site)
```

This little Python program did a lot in a few fairly readable lines. You don't know all these terms yet, but you will within the next few chapters. Here's what's going on in each line:

1. *Import* (make available to this program) all the code from the Python *standard library* module called webbrowser.

2. Import all the code from the Python standard library module called json.

3. Import only the urlopen *function* from the standard library module urllib.request.

4. A blank line, because we don't want to feel crowded.

5. Print some initial text to your display.

6. Print a question about a URL, read what you type, and save it in a program *variable* called site.

7. Print another question, this time reading a year, month, and day, and then save it in a variable called era.

8. Construct a string variable called url to make the Wayback Machine look up its copy of the site and date that you typed.

9. Connect to the web server at that URL and request a particular *web service*.

10. Get the response data and assign to the variable contents.

11. *Decode* contents to a text string in JSON format, and assign to the variable text.

12. Convert text to data—Python data structures.

13. Error-checking: try to run the next four lines, and if any fail, run the last line of the program (after the except).

14. If we got back a match for this site and date, extract its value from a three-level Python *dictionary*. Notice that this line and the next two are indented. That's how Python knows that they go with the preceding try line.

15. Print the URL that we found.

16. Print what will happen after the next line executes.

17. Display the URL we found in your web browser.

18. If anything failed in the previous four lines, Python jumps down to here.

19. If it failed, print a message and the site that we were looking for. This is indented because it should be run only if the preceding except line runs.

When I ran this in a terminal window, I typed a site URL and a date, and got this text output:

```
$ python archive.py
Let's find an old website.
Type a website URL: lolcats.com
Type a year, month, and day, like 20150613: 20151022
Found this copy: http://web.archive.org/web/20151102055938/http://www.lolcats.com/
It should appear in your browser now.
```

And Figure 1-3 shows what appeared in my browser.

Figure 1-3. From the Wayback Machine

In the previous example, we used some of Python's *standard library* modules (programs that are included with Python when it's installed), but there's nothing sacred about them. Python has a trove of excellent third-party software. Example 1-5 is a rewrite that accesses the Internet Archive website with an external Python software package called requests.

Example 1-5. archive2.py

```
1 import webbrowser
2 import requests
3
4 print("Let's find an old website.")
5 site = input("Type a website URL: ")
6 era = input("Type a year, month, and day, like 20150613: ")
7 url = "http://archive.org/wayback/available?url=%s&timestamp=%s" % (site, era)
8 response = requests.get(url)
9 data = response.json()
10 try:
11     old_site = data["archived_snapshots"]["closest"]["url"]
12     print("Found this copy: ", old_site)
13     print("It should appear in your browser now.")
14     webbrowser.open(old_site)
15 except:
16     print("Sorry, no luck finding", site)
```

The new version is shorter, and I'd guess it's more readable for most people. You'll read more about requests in Chapter 18, and externally authored Python software in general in Chapter 11.

Python in the Real World

So, is learning Python worth the time and effort? Python has been around since 1991 (older than Java, younger than C), and is consistently in the top five most popular computing languages. People are paid to write Python programs—serious stuff that you use every day, such as Google, YouTube, Instagram, Netflix, and Hulu. I've used it for production applications in many areas. Python has a reputation for productivity that appeals to fast-moving organizations.

You'll find Python in many computing environments, including these:

- The command line in a monitor or terminal window
- Graphical user interfaces (GUIs), including the web
- The web, on the client and server sides
- Backend servers supporting large popular sites
- The *cloud* (servers managed by third parties)
- Mobile devices

- Embedded devices

Python programs range from one-off *scripts*—such as those you've seen so far in this chapter—to million-line systems.

The 2018 Python Developers' Survey (*https://oreil.ly/8vK7y*) has numbers and graphs on Python's current place in the computing world.

We'll look at its uses in websites, system administration, and data manipulation. In the final chapters, we'll see specific uses of Python in the arts, science, and business.

Python Versus the Language from Planet X

How does Python compare against other languages? Where and when would you choose one over the other? In this section, I show code samples from other languages, just so you can see what the competition looks like. You are *not* expected to understand these if you haven't worked with them. (By the time you get to the final Python sample, you might be relieved that you haven't had to work with some of the others.)

Each program is supposed to print a number and say a little about the language.

If you use a terminal or terminal window, the program that reads what you type, runs it, and displays the results is called the *shell* program. The Windows shell is called `cmd` (*https://en.wikipedia.org/wiki/Cmd.exe*); it runs *batch* files with the suffix `.bat`. Linux and other Unix-like systems (including macOS) have many shell programs. The most popular is called `bash` (*https://www.gnu.org/software/bash*) or `sh`. The shell has simple abilities, such as simple logic and expanding wildcard symbols such as `*` into filenames. You can save commands in files called *shell scripts* and run them later. These might be the first programs you encountered as a programmer. The problem is that shell scripts don't scale well beyond a few hundred lines, and they are much slower than the alternative languages. The next snippet shows a little shell program:

```
#!/bin/sh
language=0
echo "Language $language: I am the shell. So there."
```

If you saved this in a file as `test.sh` and ran it with `sh test.sh`, you would see the following on your display:

```
Language 0: I am the shell. So there.
```

Old stalwarts C (*https://oreil.ly/7QKsf*) and C++ (*https://oreil.ly/iOJPN*) are fairly low-level languages, used when speed is most important. Your operating system and many of its programs (including the `python` program on your computer) are probably written in C or C++.

These two are harder to learn and maintain. You need to keep track of many details like *memory management*, which can lead to program crashes and problems that are difficult to diagnose. Here's a little C program:

```
#include <stdio.h>
int main(int argc, char *argv[]) {
    int language = 1;
    printf("Language %d: I am C! See? Si!\n", language);
    return 0;
}
```

C++ has the C family resemblance but has evolved some distinctive features:

```
#include <iostream>
using namespace std;
int main() {
    int language = 2;
    cout << "Language " << language << \
        ": I am C++!  Pay no attention to my little brother!" << \
        endl;
    return(0);
}
```

Java (*https://www.java.com*) and C# (*https://oreil.ly/1wo5A*) are successors to C and C++ that avoid some of their forebears' problems—especially memory management—but can be somewhat verbose. The example that follows shows some Java:

```
public class Anecdote {
    public static void main (String[] args) {
        int language = 3;
        System.out.format("Language %d: I am Java! So there!\n", language);
    }
}
```

If you haven't written programs in any of these languages, you might wonder: what is all that *stuff*? We only wanted to print a simple line. Some languages carry substantial syntactic baggage. You'll learn more about this in Chapter 2.

C, C++, and Java are examples of *static languages*. They require you to specify some low-level details like data types for the computer. Appendix A shows how a data type like an integer has a specific number of bits in your computer, and can only do integer-ey things. In contrast, *dynamic languages* (also called *scripting languages*) do not force you to declare variable types before using them.

The all-purpose dynamic language for many years was Perl (*http://www.perl.org*). Perl is very powerful and has extensive libraries. Yet, its syntax can be awkward, and the language seems to have lost momentum in the past few years to Python and Ruby. This example regales you with a Perl bon mot:

```
my $language = 4;
print "Language $language: I am Perl, the camel of languages.\n";
```

Ruby (*http://www.ruby-lang.org*) is a more recent language. It borrows a little from Perl, and is popular mostly because of *Ruby on Rails*, a web development framework. It's used in many of the same areas as Python, and the choice of one or the other might boil down to a matter of taste, or available libraries for your particular application. Here's a Ruby snippet:

```
language = 5
puts "Language #{language}: I am Ruby, ready and aglow."
```

PHP (*http://www.php.net*), which you can see in the example that follows, is very popular for web development because it makes it easy to combine HTML and code. However, the PHP language itself has a number of gotchas, and PHP has not caught on as a general language outside of the web. Here's what it looks like:

```
<?PHP
$language = 6;
echo "Language $language: I am PHP, a language and palindrome.\n";
?>
```

Go (*https://golang.org*) (or *Golang*, if you're trying to Google it) is a recent language that tries to be both efficient and friendly:

```
package main

import "fmt"

func main() {
    language := 7
    fmt.Printf("Language %d: Hey, ho, let's Go!\n", language)
}
```

Another modern alternative to C and C++ is Rust (*https://doc.rust-lang.org*):

```
fn main() {
    println!("Language {}: Rust here!", 8)
```

Who's left? Oh yes, Python (*https://python.org*):

```
language = 9
print(f"Language {language}: I am Python. What's for supper?")
```

Why Python?

One reason, not necessarily the most important, is popularity. By various measures, Python is:

- The fastest-growing (*https://oreil.ly/YHqqD*) major programming language, as you can see in Figure 1-4.

- The editors of the June 2019 TIOBE Index (*https://www.tiobe.com/tiobe-index*) say: "This month Python has reached again an all time high in TIOBE index of

8.5%. If Python can keep this pace, it will probably replace C and Java in 3 to 4 years time, thus becoming the most popular programming language of the world."

- Programming language of the year for 2018 (TIOBE), and top ranking by IEEE Spectrum (*https://oreil.ly/saRgb*) and PyPL (*http://pypl.github.io/PYPL.html*).

- The most popular language for introductory computer science courses at the top American colleges (*http://bit.ly/popular-py*).

- The official teaching language for high schools in France.

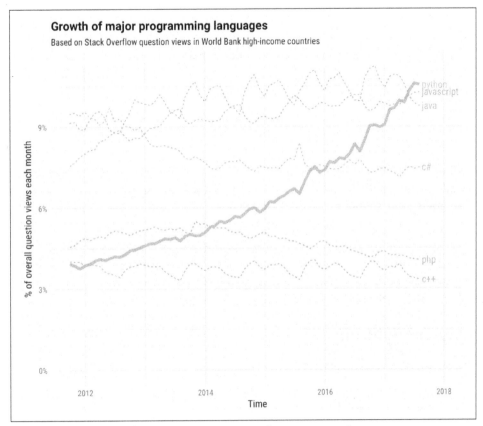

Figure 1-4. Python leads in major programming language growth

More recently, it's become extremely popular in the data science and machine learning worlds. If you want to land a well-paying programming job in an interesting area, Python is a good choice now. And if you're hiring, there's a growing pool of experienced Python developers.

But *why* is it popular? Programming languages don't exactly exude charisma. What are some underlying reasons?

Python is a good general-purpose, high-level language. Its design makes it very *readable*, which is more important than it sounds. Every computer program is written only once, but read and revised many times, often by many people. Being readable also makes it easier to learn and remember; hence, more *writable*. Compared with other popular languages, Python has a gentle learning curve that makes you productive sooner, yet it has depths that you can explore as you gain expertise.

Python's relative terseness makes it possible for you to write programs that are smaller than their equivalents in a static language. Studies have shown that programmers tend to produce roughly the same number of lines of code per day—regardless of the language—so, halving the lines of code doubles your productivity, just like that. Python is the not-so-secret weapon of many companies that think this is important.

And of course, Python is free, as in beer (price) and speech (liberty). Write anything you want with Python, and use it anywhere, freely. No one can read your Python program and say, "That's a nice little program you have there. It would be a shame if something happened to it."

Python runs almost everywhere and has "batteries included"—a metric boatload of useful software in its standard library. This book presents many examples of the standard library and useful third-party Python code.

But, maybe the best reason to use Python is an unexpected one: people generally *enjoy* programming with it rather than seeing it as a necessary evil to get stuff done. It doesn't get in the way. A familiar quote is that it "fits your brain." Often, developers will say that they miss some Python design when they need to work in another language. And that separates Python from most of its peers.

Why Not Python?

Python isn't the best language for every situation.

It is not installed everywhere by default. Appendix B shows you how to install Python if you don't already have it on your computer.

It's fast enough for most applications, but it might not be fast enough for some of the more demanding ones. If your program spends most of its time calculating things (the technical term is *CPU-bound*), a program written in C, C++, C#, Java, Rust, or Go will generally run faster than its Python equivalent. But not always!

Here are some solutions:

- Sometimes a better *algorithm* (a stepwise solution) in Python beats an inefficient one in C. The greater speed of development in Python gives you more time to experiment with alternatives.

- In many applications (notably, the web), a program twiddles its gossamer thumbs while awaiting a response from some server across a network. The CPU (central processing unit, the computer's *chip* that does all the calculating) is barely involved; consequently, end-to-end times between static and dynamic programs will be close.

- The standard Python interpreter is written in C and can be extended with C code. I discuss this a little in Chapter 19.

- Python interpreters are becoming faster. Java was terribly slow in its infancy, and a lot of research and money went into speeding it up. Python is not owned by a corporation, so its enhancements have been more gradual. In "PyPy" on page 444, I talk about the *PyPy* project and its implications.

- You might have an extremely demanding application, and no matter what you do, Python doesn't meet your needs. The usual alternatives are C, C++, and Java. Go (*http://golang.org*) (which feels like Python but performs like C) or Rust could also be worth a look.

Python 2 Versus Python 3

One medium-sized complication is that there are two versions of Python out there. Python 2 has been around forever and is preinstalled on Linux and Apple computers. It has been an excellent language, but nothing's perfect. In computer languages, as in many other areas, some mistakes are cosmetic and easy to fix, whereas others are hard. Hard fixes are *incompatible*: new programs written with them will not work on the old Python system, and old programs written before the fix will not work on the new system.

Python's creator (Guido van Rossum (*https://www.python.org/~guido*)) and others decided to bundle the hard fixes together, and introduced them as Python 3 in 2008. Python 2 is the past, and Python 3 is the future. The final version of Python 2 is 2.7, and it will be around for while, but it's the end of the line; there will be no Python 2.8. The end of Python 2 language support is in January of 2020. Security and other fixes will no longer be made, and many prominent Python packages will drop support (*https://python3statement.org*) for Python 2 by then. Operating systems will soon either drop Python 2 or make 3 their new default. Conversion of popular Python software to Python 3 had been gradual, but we're now well past the tipping point. All new development will be in Python 3.

This book is about Python 3. It looks almost identical to Python 2. The most obvious change is that `print` is a function in Python 3, so you need to call it with parentheses surrounding its arguments. The most important change is the handling of *Unicode* characters, which is covered in Chapter 12. I point out other significant differences as they come up.

Installing Python

Rather than cluttering this chapter, you can find the details on how to install Python 3 in Appendix B. If you don't have Python 3, or aren't sure, go there and see what you need to do for your computer. Yes, this is a pain in the wazoo (specifically, the right-anterior wazoo), but you'll need to do it only once.

Running Python

After you have installed a working copy of Python 3, you can use it to run the Python programs in this book as well as your own Python code. How do you actually run a Python program? There are two main ways:

- Python's built-in *interactive interpreter* (also called its *shell*) is the easy way to experiment with small programs. You type commands line by line and see the results immediately. With the tight coupling between typing and seeing, you can experiment faster. I'll use the interactive interpreter to demonstrate language features, and you can type the same commands in your own Python environment.

- For everything else, store your Python programs in text files, normally with the *.py* extension, and run them by typing `python` followed by those filenames.

Let's try both methods now.

Using the Interactive Interpreter

Most of the code examples in this book use the built-in interactive interpreter. When you type the same commands as you see in the examples and get the same results, you'll know you're on the right track.

You start the interpreter by typing just the name of the main Python program on your computer: it should be `python`, `python3`, or something similar. For the rest of this book, we assume it's called `python`; if yours has a different name, type that wherever you see `python` in a code example.

The interactive interpreter works almost exactly the same as Python works on files, with one exception: when you type something that has a value, the interactive interpreter prints its value for you automatically. This isn't a part of the Python language, just a feature of the interpreter to save you from typing `print()` all the time. For example, if you start Python and type the number 27 in the interpreter, it will be echoed to your terminal (if you have the line 27 in a file, Python won't get upset, but you won't see anything print when you run the program):

```
$ python
Python 3.7.2 (v3.7.2:9a3ffc0492, Dec 24 2018, 02:44:43)
[Clang 6.0 (clang-600.0.57)] on darwin
Type "help", "copyright", "credits" or "license" for more information.
>>> 27
27
```

In the preceding example, $ is a sample system *prompt* for you to type a command like python in the terminal window. We use it for the code examples in this book, although your prompt might be different.

By the way, print() also works within the interpreter whenever you want to print something:

```
>>> print(27)
27
```

If you tried these examples with the interactive interpreter and saw the same results, you just ran some real (though tiny) Python code. In the next few chapters, you'll graduate from one-liners to longer Python programs.

Using Python Files

If you put 27 in a file by itself and run it through Python, it will run, but it won't print anything. In normal noninteractive Python programs, you need to call the print function to print things:

```
print(27)
```

Let's make a Python program file and run it:

1. Open your text editor.
2. Type the line print(27), as it appears here.
3. Save this to a file called *test.py*. Make sure you save it as plain text rather than a "rich" format such as RTF or Word. You don't need to use the *.py* suffix for your Python program files, but it does help you remember what they are.
4. If you're using a GUI—that's almost everyone—open a terminal window.[2]

---

2 If you're not sure what this means, see Appendix B for details for different operating systems.

5. Run your program by typing the following:

```
$ python test.py
```

You should see a single line of output:

```
27
```

Did that work? If it did, congratulations on running your first standalone Python program.

What's Next?

You'll be typing commands to an actual Python system, and they need to follow legal Python syntax. Rather than dumping the syntax rules on you all at once, we stroll through them over the next few chapters.

The basic way to develop Python programs is by using a plain-text editor and a terminal window. I use plain-text displays in this book, sometimes showing interactive terminal sessions and sometimes pieces of Python files. You should know that there are also many good *integrated development environments* (IDEs) for Python. These may feature GUIs with advanced text editing and help displays. You can learn about details for some of these in Chapter 19.

Your Moment of Zen

Each computing language has its own style. In the Preface, I mentioned that there is often a *Pythonic* way to express yourself. Embedded in Python is a bit of free verse that expresses the Python philosophy succinctly (as far as I know, Python is the only language to include such an Easter egg). Just type import this into your interactive interpreter and then press the Enter key whenever you need this moment of Zen:

```
>>> import this
The Zen of Python, by Tim Peters

Beautiful is better than ugly.
Explicit is better than implicit.
Simple is better than complex.
Complex is better than complicated.
Flat is better than nested.
Sparse is better than dense.
Readability counts.
Special cases aren't special enough to break the rules.
Although practicality beats purity.
Errors should never pass silently.
Unless explicitly silenced.
In the face of ambiguity, refuse the temptation to guess.
There should be one--and preferably only one--obvious way to do it.
Although that way may not be obvious at first unless you're Dutch.
```

```
Now is better than never.
Although never is often better than *right* now.
If the implementation is hard to explain, it's a bad idea.
If the implementation is easy to explain, it may be a good idea.
Namespaces are one honking great idea--let's do more of those!
```

I'll bring up examples of these sentiments throughout the book.

Coming Up

The next chapter talks about Python data types and variables. This will prepare you for the following chapters, which delve into Python's data types and code structures in detail.

Things to Do

This chapter was an introduction to the Python language—what it does, how it looks, and where it fits in the computing world. At the end of each chapter, I suggest some mini-projects to help you remember what you just read and prepare you for what's to come.

1.1 If you don't already have Python 3 installed on your computer, do it now. Read Appendix B for the details for your computer system.

1.2 Start the Python 3 interactive interpreter. Again, details are in Appendix B. It should print a few lines about itself and then a single line starting with >>>. That's your prompt to type Python commands.

1.3 Play with the interpreter a little. Use it like a calculator and type this: 8 * 9. Press the Enter key to see the result. Python should print 72.

1.4 Type the number 47 and press the Enter key. Did it print 47 for you on the next line?

1.5 Now, type `print(47)` and press Enter. Did that also print 47 for you on the next line?

CHAPTER 2

Data: Types, Values, Variables, and Names

A good name is rather to be chosen than great riches.

—Proverbs 22:1

Under the hood, everything in your computer is just a sequence of *bits* (see Appendix A). One of the insights of computing is that we can interpret those bits any way we want—as data of various sizes and types (numbers, text characters) or even as computer code itself. We use Python to define chunks of these bits for different purposes, and to get them to and from the CPU.

We begin with Python's data *types* and the *values* that they can contain. Then we see how to represent data as *literal* values and *variables*.

Python Data Are Objects

You can visualize your computer's memory as a long series of shelves. Each slot on one of those memory shelves is one byte wide (eight bits), and slots are numbered from 0 (the first) to the end. Modern computers have billions of bytes of memory (gigabytes), so the shelves would fill a huge imaginary warehouse.

A Python program is given access to some of your computer's memory by your operating system. That memory is used for the code of the program itself, and the data that it uses. The operating system ensures that the program cannot read or write other memory locations without somehow getting permission.

Programs keep track of *where* (memory location) their bits are, and *what* (data type) they are. To your computer, it's all just bits. The same bits mean different things, depending on what type we say they are. The same bit pattern might stand for the integer 65 or the text character A.

Different types may use different numbers of bits. When you read about a "64-bit machine," this means that an integer uses 64 bits (8 bytes).

Some languages plunk and pluck these raw values in memory, keeping track of their sizes and types. Instead of handling such raw data values directly, Python wraps each data value—booleans, integers, floats, strings, even large data structures, functions, and programs—in memory as an *object*. There's a whole chapter (Chapter 10) on how to define your own objects in Python. For now, we're just talking about objects that handle the basic built-in data types.

Using the memory shelves analogy, you can think of objects as variable-sized boxes occupying spaces on those shelves, as shown in Figure 2-1. Python makes these object boxes, puts them in empty spaces on the shelves, and removes them when they're no longer used.

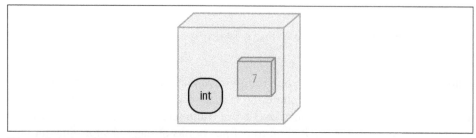

Figure 2-1. An object is like a box; this one is an integer with value 7

In Python, an object is a chunk of data that contains at least the following:

- A *type* that defines what it can do (see the next section)
- A unique *id* to distinguish it from other objects
- A *value* consistent with its type
- A *reference count* that tracks how often this object is used

Its *id* is like its location on the shelf, a unique identifier. Its *type* is like a factory stamp on the box, saying what it can do. If a Python object is an integer, it has the type int, and could (among other things, which you'll see in Chapter 3) be added to another int. If we picture the box as being made of clear plastic, we can see the *value* inside. You'll learn the use of the *reference count* a few sections from now, when we talk about variables and names.

Types

Table 2-1 shows the basic data types in Python. The second column (Type) contains the Python name of that type. The third column (Mutable?) indicates whether the value can be changed after creation, which I explain more in the next section. Examples shows one or more literal examples of that type. And the final column (Chapter) points you to the chapter in this book with the most details on this type.

Table 2-1. Python's basic data types

Name	Type	Mutable?	Examples	Chapter
Boolean	bool	no	True, False	Chapter 3
Integer	int	no	47, 25000, 25_000	Chapter 3
Floating point	float	no	3.14, 2.7e5	Chapter 3
Complex	complex	no	3j, 5 + 9j	Chapter 22
Text string	str	no	'alas', "alack", '''a verse attack'''	Chapter 5
List	list	yes	['Winken', 'Blinken', 'Nod']	Chapter 7
Tuple	tuple	no	(2, 4, 8)	Chapter 7
Bytes	bytes	no	b'ab\xff'	Chapter 12
ByteArray	bytearray	yes	bytearray(...)	Chapter 12
Set	set	yes	set([3, 5, 7])	Chapter 8
Frozen set	frozenset	no	frozenset(['Elsa', 'Otto'])	Chapter 8
Dictionary	dict	yes	{'game': 'bingo', 'dog': 'dingo', 'drummer': 'Ringo'}	Chapter 8

After the chapters on these basic data types, you'll see how to make new types in Chapter 10.

Mutability

> Nought may endure but Mutability.
>
> —Percy Shelley

The type also determines whether the data *value* contained by the box can be changed (*mutable*) or is constant (*immutable*). Think of an immutable object as a sealed box, but with clear sides, like Figure 2-1; you can see the value but you can't change it. By the same analogy, a mutable object is like a box with a lid: not only can you see the value inside, you can also change it; however, you can't change its type.

Python is *strongly typed*, which means that the type of an object does not change, even if its value is mutable (Figure 2-2).

Figure 2-2. Strong typing does not mean push the keys harder

Literal Values

There are two ways of specifying data values in Python:

- *Literal*
- *Variable*

In coming chapters, you'll see the details on how to specify literal values for different data types—integers are a sequence of digits, floats contain a decimal point, text strings are surrounded by quotes, and so on. But, for the rest of this chapter, to avoid calloused fingertips, our examples will use only short decimal integers and a Python list or two. Decimal integers are just like integers in math: a sequence of digits from 0 to 9. There are a few extra integer details (like signs and nondecimal bases) that we look at in Chapter 3.

Variables

Now, we've arrived at a key concept in computing languages.

Python, like most computer languages, lets you define *variables*—names for values in your computer's memory that you want to use in a program.

Python variable names have some rules:

- They can contain only these characters:
  - Lowercase letters (a through z)
  - Uppercase letters (A through Z)
  - Digits (0 through 9)
  - Underscore (_)
- They are *case-sensitive*: thing, Thing, and THING are different names.
- They must begin with a letter or an underscore, not a digit.
- Names that begin with an underscore are treated specially (which you can read about in Chapter 9).
- They cannot be one of Python's *reserved words* (also known as *keywords*).

The reserved words[1] are:

```
False     await     else      import    pass
None      break     except    in        raise
True      class     finally   is        return
and       continue  for       lambda    try
as        def       from      nonlocal  while
assert    del       global    not       with
async     elif      if        or        yield
```

Within a Python program, you can find the reserved words with

```
>>> help("keywords")
```

or:

```
>>> import keyword
>>> keyword.kwlist
```

These are valid names:

- a
- a1
- a_b_c___95
- _abc
- _1a

---

1 async and await are new in Python 3.7.

These names, however, are not valid:

- `1`
- `1a`
- `1_`
- `name!`
- `another-name`

Assignment

In Python, you use = to *assign* a value to a variable.

 We all learned in grade school arithmetic that = means *equal to*. So why do many computer languages, including Python, use = for assignment? One reason is that standard keyboards lack logical alternatives such as a left arrow key, and = didn't seem too confusing. Also, in computer programs you use assignment much more than you test for equality.

Programs are *not* like algebra. When you learned math in school, you saw equations like this:

```
y = x + 12
```

You would solve the equation by "plugging in" a value for x. If you gave x the value 5, 5 + 12 is 17, so the value of y would be 17. Plug in 6 for x to get 18 for y, and so on.

Computer program lines may look like equations, but their meaning is different. In Python and other computer languages, x and y are *variables*. Python knows that a bare sequence of digits like 12 or 5 is a literal integer. So here's a tiny Python program that mimics this equation, printing the resulting value of y:

```
>>> x = 5
>>> y = x + 12
>>> y
17
```

Here's the big difference between math and programs: in math, = means *equality* of both sides, but in programs it means *assignment*: *assign the value on the right side to the variable on the left side.*

Also in programs, everything on the right side needs to have a value (this is called being *initialized*). The right side can be a literal value, or a variable that has already been assigned a value, or a combination. Python knows that 5 and 12 are literal integers. The first line assigns the integer value 5 to the variable x. Now we can use the variable x in the next line. When Python reads y = x + 12, it does the following:

- Sees the = in the middle
- Knows that this is an assignment
- Calculates the right side (gets the value of the object referred to by x and adds it to 12)
- Assigns the result to the left-side variable, y

Then typing the name of the variable y (in the interactive interpreter) will print its new value.

If you started your program with the line y = x + 12, Python would generate an *exception* (an error), because the variable x doesn't have a value yet:

```
>>> y = x + 12
Traceback (most recent call last):
  File "<stdin>", line 1, in <module>
NameError: name 'x' is not defined
```

You'll get the full rundown on exceptions in Chapter 9. In computerese, we'd say that this x was *uninitialized*.

In algebra, you can work backward, and assign a value to y to calculate x. To do this in Python, you'd need to get the literal values and initialized variables on the right side before assigning to x on the left:

```
>>> y = 5
>>> x = 12 - y
>>> x
7
```

Variables Are Names, Not Places

Now it's time to make a crucial point about variables in Python: *variables are just names*. This is different from many other computer languages, and a key thing to know about Python, especially when we get to *mutable* objects like lists. Assignment *does not copy* a value; it just *attaches a name* to the object that contains the data. The name is a *reference* to a thing rather than the thing itself. Visualize a name as a tag with a string attached to the object box somewhere else in the computer's memory (Figure 2-3).

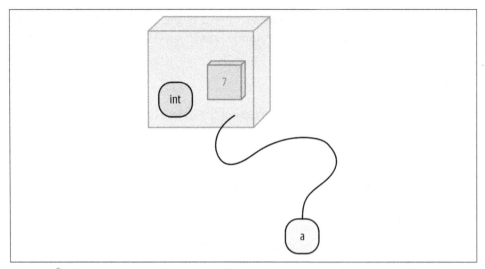

Figure 2-3. Names point to objects (variable a points to an integer object with value 7)

In other languages, the variable itself has a type, and binds to a memory location. You can change the value at that location, but it needs to be of the same type. This is why *static* languages make you declare the types of variables. Python doesn't, because a name can refer to anything, and we get the value and type by "following the string" to the data object itself. This saves time, but there are some downsides:

- You may misspell a variable and get an exception because it doesn't refer to anything, and Python doesn't automatically check this as static languages do. Chapter 19 shows ways of checking your variables ahead of time to avoid this.
- Python's raw speed is slower than a language like C. It makes the computer do more work so you don't have to.

Try this with the interactive interpreter (visualized in Figure 2-4):

1. As before, assign the value 7 to the name a. This creates an object box containing the integer value 7.

2. Print the value of a.

3. Assign a to b, making b also point to the object box containing 7.

4. Print the value of b:

```
>>> a = 7
>>> print(a)
7
>>> b = a
```

```
>>> print(b)
7
```

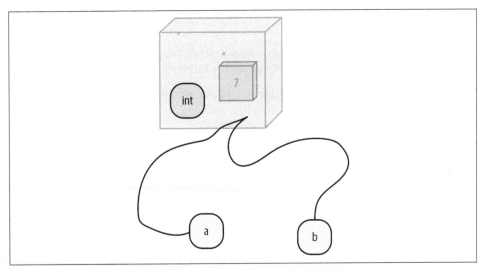

Figure 2-4. Copying a name (now variable b also points to the same integer object)

In Python, if you want to know the type of anything (a variable or a literal value), you can use type(*thing*). type() is one of Python's built-in functions. If you want to check whether a variable points to an object of a specific type, use isinstance(*type*):

```
>>> type(7)
<class 'int'>
>>> type(7) == int
True
>>> isinstance(7, int)
True
```

When I mention a function, I'll put parentheses (()) after it to emphasize that it's a function rather than a variable name or something else.

Let's try it with more literal values (58, 99.9, 'abc') and variables (a, b):

```
>>> a = 7
>>> b = a
>>> type(a)
<class 'int'>
>>> type(b)
<class 'int'>
>>> type(58)
```

```
<class 'int'>
>>> type(99.9)
<class 'float'>
>>> type('abc')
<class 'str'>
```

A *class* is the definition of an object; Chapter 10 covers classes in greater detail. In Python, "class" and "type" mean pretty much the same thing.

As you've seen, when you use a variable in Python, it looks up the object that it refers to. Behind the scenes, Python is busy, often creating temporary objects that will be discarded a line or two later.

Let's repeat an earlier example:

```
>>> y = 5
>>> x = 12 - y
>>> x
7
```

In this code snippet, Python did the following:

- Created an integer object with the value 5
- Made a variable y point to that 5 object
- Incremented the reference count of the object with value 5
- Created another integer object with the value 12
- Subtracted the value of the object that y points to (5) from the value 12 in the (anonymous) object with that value
- Assigned this value (7) to a new (so far, unnamed) integer object
- Made the variable x point to this new object
- Incremented the reference count of this new object that x points to
- Looked up the value of the object that x points to (7) and printed it

When an object's reference count reaches zero, no names are pointing to it, so it doesn't need to stick around. Python has a charmingly named *garbage collector* that reuses the memory of things that are no longer needed. Picture someone behind those memory shelves, yanking obsolete boxes for recycling.

In this case, we no longer need the objects with the values 5, 12, or 7, or the variables x and y. The Python garbage collector may choose to send them to object heaven,[2] or

---

2 Or the Island of Misfit Objects.

keep some around for performance reasons given that small integers tend to be used a lot.

Assigning to Multiple Names

You can assign a value to more than one variable name at the same time:

```
>>> two = deux = zwei = 2
>>> two
2
>>> deux
2
>>> zwei
2
```

Reassigning a Name

Because names point to objects, changing the value assigned to a name just makes the name point to a new object. The reference count of the old object is decremented, and the new one's is incremented.

Copying

As you saw in Figure 2-4, assigning an existing variable a to a new variable named b just makes b point to the same object that a does. If you pick up either the a or b tag and follow their strings, you'll get to the same object.

If the object is immutable (like an integer), its value can't be changed, so both names are essentially read-only. Try this:

```
>>> x = 5
>>> x
5
>>> y = x
>>> y
5
>>> x = 29
>>> x
29
>>> y
5
```

When we assigned x to y, that made the name y point to the integer object with value 5 that x was also pointing to. Changing x made it point to a new integer object with value 29. It did not change the one containing 5, which y still points to.

But if both names point to a *mutable* object, you can change the object's value via either name, and you'll see the changed value when you use either name. If you didn't know this first, it could surprise you.

A *list* is a mutable array of values, and Chapter 7 covers them in gruesome detail. For this example, a and b each point to a list with three integer members:

```
>>> a = [2, 4, 6]
>>> b = a
>>> a
[2, 4, 6]
>>> b
[2, 4, 6]
```

These list members (a[0], a[1], and a[2]) are themselves like names, pointing to integer objects with the values 2, 4, and 6. The list object keeps its members in order.

Now change the first list element, through the name a, and see that b also changed:

```
>>> a[0] = 99
>>> a
[99, 4, 6]
>>> b
[99, 4, 6]
```

When the first list element is changed, it no longer points to the object with value 2, but a new object with value 99. The list is still of type list, but its value (the list elements and their order) is mutable.

Choose Good Variable Names

> He said true things, but called them by wrong names.
>
> —Elizabeth Barrett Browning

It's surprising how important it is to choose good names for your variables. In many of the code examples so far, I've been using throwaway names like a and x. In real programs, you'll have many more variables to keep track of at once, and you'll need to balance brevity and clarity. For example, it's faster to type num_loons rather than number_of_loons or gaviidae_inventory, but it's more explanatory than n.

Coming Up

Numbers! They're as exciting as you expect. Well, maybe not that bad.[3] You'll see how to use Python as a calculator and how a cat founded a digital system.

Things to Do

2.1 Assign the integer value 99 to the variable `prince`, and print it.

2.2 What type is the value 5?

2.3 What type is the value `2.0`?

2.4 What type is the expression `5 + 2.0`?

---

3 8 looks like a snowman!

CHAPTER 3

Numbers

That action is best which procures the greatest happiness for the greatest numbers.

—Francis Hutcheson

In this chapter we begin by looking at Python's simplest built-in data types:

- *Booleans* (which have the value `True` or `False`)
- *Integers* (whole numbers such as `42` and `100000000`)
- *Floats* (numbers with decimal points such as `3.14159`, or sometimes exponents like `1.0e8`, which means *one times ten to the eighth power*, or `100000000.0`)

In a way, they're like atoms. We use them individually in this chapter, and in later chapters you'll see how to combine them into larger "molecules" like lists and dictionaries.

Each type has specific rules for its usage and is handled differently by the computer. I also show how to use *literal* values like `97` and `3.1416`, and the *variables* that I mentioned in Chapter 2.

The code examples in this chapter are all valid Python, but they're snippets. We'll be using the Python interactive interpreter, typing these snippets and seeing the results immediately. Try running them yourself with the version of Python on your computer. You'll recognize these examples by the `>>>` prompt.

Booleans

In Python, the only values for the boolean data type are `True` and `False`. Sometimes, you'll use these directly; other times you'll evaluate the "truthiness" of other types from their values. The special Python function `bool()` can convert any Python data type to a boolean.

Functions get their own chapter in Chapter 9, but for now you just need to know that a function has a name, zero or more comma-separated input *arguments* surrounded by parentheses, and zero or more *return values*. The `bool()` function takes any value as its argument and returns the boolean equivalent.

Nonzero numbers are considered `True`:

```
>>> bool(True)
True
>>> bool(1)
True
>>> bool(45)
True
>>> bool(-45)
True
```

And zero-valued ones are considered `False`:

```
>>> bool(False)
False
>>> bool(0)
False
>>> bool(0.0)
False
```

You'll see the usefulness of booleans in Chapter 4. In later chapters, you'll see how lists, dictionaries, and other types can be considered `True` or `False`.

Integers

Integers are whole numbers—no fractions, no decimal points, nothing fancy. Well, aside from a possible initial sign. And bases, if you want to express numbers in other ways than the usual decimal (base 10).

Literal Integers

Any sequence of digits in Python represents a *literal integer*:

```
>>> 5
5
```

A plain zero (0) is valid:

```
>>> 0
0
```

But you can't have an initial 0 followed by a digit between 1 and 9:

```
>>> 05
  File "<stdin>", line 1
    05
     ^
SyntaxError: invalid token
```

 This Python *exception* warns that you typed something that breaks Python's rules. I explain what this means in "Bases" on page 44. You'll see many more examples of exceptions in this book because they're Python's main error handling mechanism.

You can start an integer with 0b, 0o, or 0x. See "Bases" on page 44.

A sequence of digits specifies a positive integer. If you put a + sign before the digits, the number stays the same:

```
>>> 123
123
>>> +123
123
```

To specify a negative integer, insert a – before the digits:

```
>>> -123
-123
```

You can't have any commas in the integer:

```
>>> 1,000,000
(1, 0, 0)
```

Instead of a million, you'd get a *tuple* (see Chapter 7 for more information on tuples) with three values. But you *can* use the underscore (_) character as a digit separator:[1]

```
>>> million = 1_000_000
>>> million
1000000
```

---

1 For Python 3.6 and newer.

Actually, you can put underscores anywhere after the first digit; they're just ignored:

```
>>> 1_2_3
123
```

Integer Operations

For the next few pages, I show examples of Python acting as a simple calculator. You can do normal arithmetic with Python by using the math *operators* in this table:

Operator	Description	Example	Result
+	Addition	5 + 8	13
-	Subtraction	90 - 10	80
*	Multiplication	4 * 7	28
/	Floating-point division	7 / 2	3.5
//	Integer (truncating) division	7 // 2	3
%	Modulus (remainder)	7 % 3	1
**	Exponentiation	3 ** 4	81

Addition and subtraction work as you'd expect:

```
>>> 5 + 9
14
>>> 100 - 7
93
>>> 4 - 10
-6
```

You can include as many numbers and operators as you'd like:

```
>>> 5 + 9 + 3
17
>>> 4 + 3 - 2 - 1 + 6
10
```

Note that you're not required to have a space between each number and operator:

```
>>> 5+9    +      3
17
```

It just looks better stylewise and is easier to read.

Multiplication is also straightforward:

```
>>> 6 * 7
42
>>> 7 * 6
42
```

```
>>> 6 * 7 * 2 * 3
252
```

Division is a little more interesting because it comes in two flavors:

- / carries out *floating-point* (decimal) division
- // performs *integer* (truncating) division

Even if you're dividing an integer by an integer, using a / will give you a floating-point result (*floats* are coming later in this chapter):

```
>>> 9 / 5
1.8
```

Truncating integer division returns an integer answer, throwing away any remainder:

```
>>> 9 // 5
1
```

Instead of tearing a hole in the space-time continuum, dividing by zero with either kind of division causes a Python exception:

```
>>> 5 / 0
Traceback (most recent call last):
  File "<stdin>", line 1, in <module>
ZeroDivisionError: division by zero
>>> 7 // 0
Traceback (most recent call last):
  File "<stdin>", line 1, in <module>
ZeroDivisionError: integer division or modulo by z
```

Integers and Variables

All of the preceding examples used literal integers. You can mix literal integers and variables that have been assigned integer values:

```
>>> a = 95
>>> a
95
>>> a - 3
92
```

You'll remember from Chapter 2 that a is a name that points to an integer object. When I said a - 3, I didn't assign the result back to a, so the value of a did not change:

```
>>> a
95
```

If you wanted to change a, you would do this:

```
>>> a = a - 3
>>> a
92
```

Again, this would not be a legal math equation, but it's how you reassign a value to a variable in Python. In Python, the expression on the right side of the = is calculated first, and then assigned to the variable on the left side.

If it helps, think of it this way:

- Subtract 3 from a
- Assign the result of that subtraction to a temporary variable
- Assign the value of the temporary variable to a:

```
>>> a = 95
>>> temp = a - 3
>>> a = temp
```

So, when you say

```
>>> a = a - 3
```

Python is calculating the subtraction on the righthand side, remembering the result, and then assigning it to a on the left side of the + sign. It's faster and neater than using a temporary variable.

You can combine the arithmetic operators with assignment by putting the operator before the =. Here, a -= 3 is like saying a = a - 3:

```
>>> a = 95
>>> a -= 3
>>> a
92
```

This is like a = a + 8:

```
>>> a = 92
>>> a += 8
>>> a
100
```

And this is like a = a * 2:

```
>>> a = 100
>>> a *= 2
>>> a
200
```

Here's a floating-point division example, like a = a / 3:

```
>>> a = 200
>>> a /= 3
>>> a
66.66666666666667
```

Now let's try the shorthand for a = a // 4 (truncating integer division):

```
>>> a = 13
>>> a //= 4
>>> a
3
```

The % character has multiple uses in Python. When it's between two numbers, it produces the remainder when the first number is divided by the second:

```
>>> 9 % 5
4
```

Here's how to get both the (truncated) quotient and remainder at once:

```
>>> divmod(9,5)
(1, 4)
```

Otherwise, you could have calculated them separately:

```
>>> 9 // 5
1
>>> 9 % 5
4
```

You just saw some new things here: a *function* named divmod is given the integers 9 and 5 and returns a two-item *tuple*. As I mentioned earlier, tuples will take a bow in Chapter 7; functions debut in Chapter 9.

One last math feature is exponentiation with **, which also lets you mix integers and floats:

```
>>> 2**3
8
>>> 2.0 ** 3
8.0
>>> 2 ** 3.0
8.0
>>> 0 ** 3
0
```

Precedence

What would you get if you typed the following?

```
>>> 2 + 3 * 4
```

If you do the addition first, 2 + 3 is 5, and 5 * 4 is 20. But if you do the multiplication first, 3 * 4 is 12, and 2 + 12 is 14. In Python, as in most languages, multiplication has higher *precedence* than addition, so the second version is what you'd see:

```
>>> 2 + 3 * 4
14
```

How do you know the precedence rules? There's a big table in Appendix E that lists them all, but I've found that in practice I never look up these rules. It's much easier to just add parentheses to group your code as you intend the calculation to be carried out:

```
>>> 2 + (3 * 4)
14
```

This example with exponents

```
>>> -5 ** 2
-25
```

is the same as

```
>>> - (5 ** 2)
-25
```

and probably not what you wanted. Parentheses make it clear:

```
>>> (-5) ** 2
25
```

This way, anyone reading the code doesn't need to guess its intent or look up precedence rules.

Bases

Integers are assumed to be decimal (base 10) unless you use a prefix to specify another *base*. You might never need to use these other bases, but you'll probably see them in Python code somewhere, sometime.

We generally have 10 fingers and 10 toes, so we count 0, 1, 2, 3, 4, 5, 6, 7, 8, 9. Next, we run out of single digits and carry the one to the "ten's place" and put a 0 in the one's place: 10 means "1 ten and 0 ones." Unlike Roman numerals, Arabic numbers don't have a single character that represents "10" Then, it's 11, 12, up to 19, carry the one to make 20 (2 tens and 0 ones), and so on.

A base is how many digits you can use until you need to "carry the one." In base 2 (binary), the only digits are 0 and 1. This is the famous *bit*. 0 is the same as a plain old decimal 0, and 1 is the same as a decimal 1. However, in base 2, if you add a 1 to a 1, you get 10 (1 decimal two plus 0 decimal ones).

In Python, you can express literal integers in three bases besides decimal with these integer prefixes:

- `0b` or `0B` for *binary* (base 2).
- `0o` or `0O` for *octal* (base 8).
- `0x` or `0X` for *hex* (base 16).

These bases are all powers of two, and are handy in some cases, although you may never need to use anything other than good old decimal integers.

The interpreter prints these for you as decimal integers. Let's try each of these bases. First, a plain old decimal `10`, which means *1 ten and 0 ones*:

```
>>> 10
10
```

Now, a binary (base two) `0b10`, which means *1 (decimal) two and 0 ones*:

```
>>> 0b10
2
```

Octal (base 8) `0o10` stands for *1 (decimal) eight and 0 ones*:

```
>>> 0o10
8
```

Hexadecimal (base 16) `0x10` means *1 (decimal) sixteen and 0 ones*:

```
>>> 0x10
16
```

You can go the other direction, converting an integer to a string with any of these bases:

```
>>> value = 65
>>> bin(value)
'0b1000001'
>>> oct(value)
'0o101'
>>> hex(value)
'0x41'
```

The `chr()` function converts an integer to its single-character string equivalent:

```
>>> chr(65)
'A'
```

And `ord()` goes the other way:

```
>>> ord('A')
65
```

In case you're wondering what "digits" base 16 uses, they are: 0, 1, 2, 3, 4, 5, 6, 7, 8, 9, a, b, c, d, e, and f. 0xa is a decimal 10, and 0xf is a decimal 15. Add 1 to 0xf and you get 0x10 (decimal 16).

Why use different bases from 10? They're useful in *bit-level* operations, which are described in Chapter 12, along with more details about converting numbers from one base to another.

Cats normally have five digits on each forepaw and four on each hindpaw, for a total of 18. If you ever encounter cat scientists in their lab coats, they're often discussing base-18 arithmetic. My cat Chester, seen lounging about in Figure 3-1, is a *polydactyl*, giving him a total of 22 or so (they're hard to distinguish) toes. If he wanted to use all of them to count food fragments surrounding his bowl, he would likely use a base-22 system (hereafter, the *chesterdigital* system), using 0 through 9 and a through l.

Figure 3-1. Chester—a fine furry fellow, and inventor of the chesterdigital system

Type Conversions

To change other Python data types to an integer, use the int() function.

The int() function takes one input argument and returns one value, the integer-ized equivalent of the input argument. This will keep the whole number and discard any fractional part.

As you saw at the start of this chapter, Python's simplest data type is the *boolean*, which has only the values True and False. When converted to integers, they represent the values 1 and 0:

```
>>> int(True)
1
>>> int(False)
0
```

Turning this around, the bool() function returns the boolean equivalent of an integer:

```
>>> bool(1)
True
>>> bool(0)
False
```

Converting a floating-point number to an integer just lops off everything after the decimal point:

```
>>> int(98.6)
98
>>> int(1.0e4)
10000
```

Converting a float to a boolean is no surprise:

```
>>> bool(1.0)
True
>>> bool(0.0)
False
```

Finally, here's an example of getting the integer value from a text string (Chapter 5) that contains only digits, possibly with _ digit separators or an initial + or - sign:

```
>>> int('99')
99
>>> int('-23')
-23
>>> int('+12')
12
>>> int('1_000_000')
1000000
```

If the string represents a nondecimal integer, you can include the base:

```
>>> int('10', 2) # binary
2
>>> int('10', 8) # octal
8
>>> int('10', 16) # hexadecimal
16
>>> int('10', 22) # chesterdigital
22
```

Converting an integer to an integer doesn't change anything, but doesn't hurt either:

```
>>> int(12345)
12345
```

If you try to convert something that doesn't look like a number, you'll get an *exception*:

```
>>> int('99 bottles of beer on the wall')
Traceback (most recent call last):
  File "<stdin>", line 1, in <module>
ValueError: invalid literal for int() with base 10: '99 bottles of beer on the wall'
>>> int('')
Traceback (most recent call last):
  File "<stdin>", line 1, in <module>
ValueError: invalid literal for int() with base 10: ''
```

The preceding text string started with valid digit characters (99), but it kept on going with others that the int() function just wouldn't stand for.

int() will make integers from floats or strings of digits, but it won't handle strings containing decimal points or exponents:

```
>>> int('98.6')
Traceback (most recent call last):
  File "<stdin>", line 1, in <module>
ValueError: invalid literal for int() with base 10: '98.6'
>>> int('1.0e4')
Traceback (most recent call last):
  File "<stdin>", line 1, in <module>
ValueError: invalid literal for int() with base 10: '1.0e4'
```

If you mix numeric types, Python will sometimes try to automatically convert them for you:

```
>>> 4 + 7.0
11.0
```

The boolean value False is treated as 0 or 0.0 when mixed with integers or floats, and True is treated as 1 or 1.0:

```
>>> True + 2
3
```

```
>>> False + 5.0
5.0
```

How Big Is an int?

In Python 2, the size of an int could be limited to 32 or 64 bits, depending on your CPU; 32 bits can store store any integer from –2,147,483,648 to 2,147,483,647.

A long had 64 bits, allowing values from –9,223,372,036,854,775,808 to 9,223,372,036,854,775,807. In Python 3, the long type is long gone, and an int can be *any* size—even greater than 64 bits. You can play with big numbers like a *googol* (one followed by a hundred zeroes, named (*https://oreil.ly/6ibo_*) in 1920 by a nine-year-old boy):

```
>>>
>>> googol = 10**100
>>> googol
10000000000000000000000000000000000000000000000000000000000000000000000000
0000000000000000000000000
>>> googol * googol
100000000000000000000000000000000000000000000000000000000000000000000000000
00000000000000000000000000000000000000000000000000000000000000000000000000000
0000000000000000000000000000000000000000000000000
```

A *googolplex* is 10**googol (a thousand zeroes, if you want to try it yourself). This was a suggested name for Google (*https://oreil.ly/IQfer*) before they decided on *googol*, but didn't check its spelling before registering the domain name google.com.

In many languages, trying this would cause something called *integer overflow*, where the number would need more space than the computer allowed for it, with various bad effects. Python handles googoly integers with no problem.

Floats

Integers are whole numbers, but *floating-point* numbers (called *floats* in Python) have decimal points:

```
>>> 5.
5.0
>>> 5.0
5.0
>>> 05.0
5.0
```

Floats can include a decimal integer exponent after the letter e:

```
>>> 5e0
5.0
>>> 5e1
50.0
```

```
>>> 5.0e1
50.0
>>> 5.0 * (10 ** 1)
50.0
```

You can use underscore (_) to separate digits for clarity, as you can for integers:

```
>>> million = 1_000_000.0
>>> million
1000000.0
>>> 1.0_0_1
1.001
```

Floats are handled similarly to integers: you can use the operators (+, -, *, /, //, **, and %) and the divmod() function.

To convert other types to floats, you use the float() function. As before, booleans act like tiny integers:

```
>>> float(True)
1.0
>>> float(False)
0.0
```

Converting an integer to a float just makes it the proud possessor of a decimal point:

```
>>> float(98)
98.0
>>> float('99')
99.0
```

And you can convert a string containing characters that would be a valid float (digits, signs, decimal point, or an e followed by an exponent) to a real float:

```
>>> float('98.6')
98.6
>>> float('-1.5')
-1.5
>>> float('1.0e4')
10000.0
```

When you mix integers and floats, Python automatically *promotes* the integer values to float values:

```
>>> 43 + 2.
45.0
```

Python also promotes booleans to integers or floats:

```
>>> False + 0
0
>>> False + 0.
0.0
>>> True + 0
1
```

```
>>> True + 0.
1.0
```

Math Functions

Python supports complex numbers and has the usual math functions such as square roots, cosines, and so on. Let's save them for Chapter 22, in which we also discuss using Python in science contexts.

Coming Up

In the next chapter, you finally graduate from one-line Python examples. With the `if` statement, you'll learn how to make decisions with code.

Things to Do

This chapter introduced the atoms of Python: numbers, booleans, and variables. Let's try a few small exercises with them in the interactive interpreter.

3.1 How many seconds are in an hour? Use the interactive interpreter as a calculator and multiply the number of seconds in a minute (`60`) by the number of minutes in an hour (also `60`).

3.2 Assign the result from the previous task (seconds in an hour) to a variable called `seconds_per_hour`.

3.3 How many seconds are in a day? Use your `seconds_per_hour` variable.

3.4 Calculate seconds per day again, but this time save the result in a variable called `seconds_per_day`.

3.5 Divide `seconds_per_day` by `seconds_per_hour`. Use floating-point (`/`) division.

3.6 Divide `seconds_per_day` by `seconds_per_hour`, using integer (`//`) division. Did this number agree with the floating-point value from the previous question, aside from the final `.0`?

CHAPTER 4

Choose with if

If you can keep your head when all about you
Are losing theirs and blaming it on you, ...

—Rudyard Kipling, *If—*

In the previous chapters, you've seen many examples of data but haven't done much with them. Most of the code examples used the interactive interpreter and were short. In this chapter, you learn how to structure Python *code*, not just data.

Many computer languages use characters such as curly braces ({ and }) or keywords such as `begin` and `end` to mark off sections of code. In those languages, it's good practice to use consistent indentation to make your program more readable for yourself and others. There are even tools to make your code line up nicely.

When he was designing the language that became Python, Guido van Rossum decided that the indentation itself was enough to define a program's structure, and avoided typing all those parentheses and curly braces. Python is unusual in this use of *white space* to define program structure. It's one of the first aspects that newcomers notice, and it can seem odd to those who have experience with other languages. It turns out that after writing Python for a little while, it feels natural, and you stop noticing it. You even get used to doing more while typing less.

Our initial code examples have been one-liners. Let's first see how to make comments and multiple-line commands.

Comment with

A *comment* is a piece of text in your program that is ignored by the Python interpreter. You might use comments to clarify nearby Python code, make notes to yourself to fix something someday, or for whatever purpose you like. You mark a comment by using the # character; everything from that point on to the end of the current line is part of the comment. You'll usually see a comment on a line by itself, as shown here:

```
>>> # 60 sec/min * 60 min/hr * 24 hr/day
>>> seconds_per_day = 86400
```

Or, on the same line as the code it's commenting:

```
>>> seconds_per_day = 86400 # 60 sec/min * 60 min/hr * 24 hr/day
```

The # character has many names: *hash*, *sharp*, *pound*, or the sinister-sounding *octo-thorpe*.[1] Whatever you call it,[2] its effect lasts only to the end of the line on which it appears.

Python does not have a multiline comment. You need to explicitly begin each comment line or section with a #:

```
>>> # I can say anything here, even if Python doesn't like it,
... # because I'm protected by the awesome
... # octothorpe.
...
>>>
```

However, if it's in a text string, the mighty octothorpe reverts back to its role as a plain old # character:

```
>>> print("No comment: quotes make the # harmless.")
No comment: quotes make the # harmless.
```

Continue Lines with \

Programs are more readable when lines are reasonably short. The recommended (not required) maximum line length is 80 characters. If you can't say everything you want to say in that length, you can use the *continuation character*: \ (backslash). Just put \ at the end of a line, and Python will suddenly act as though you're still on the same line.

For example, if I wanted to add the first five digits, I could do it a line at a time:

```
>>> sum = 0
>>> sum += 1
>>> sum += 2
>>> sum += 3
>>> sum += 4
```

---

1 Like that eight-legged green *thing* that's *right behind you!*

2 Please don't call it. It might come back.

```
>>> sum
10
```

Or, I could do it in one step, using the continuation character:

```
>>> sum = 1 + \
...       2 + \
...       3 + \
...       4
>>> sum
10
```

If we skipped the backslash in the middle of an expression, we'd get an exception:

```
>>> sum = 1 +
  File "<stdin>", line 1
    sum = 1 +
            ^
SyntaxError: invalid syntax
```

Here's a little trick—if you're in the middle of paired parentheses (or square or curly brackets), Python doesn't squawk about line endings:

```
>>> sum = (
...       1 +
...       2 +
...       3 +
...       4)
>>>
>>> sum
10
```

You'll also see in Chapter 5 that paired triple quotes let you make multiline strings.

Compare with if, elif, and else

Now, we finally take our first step into the *code structures* that weave data into programs. Our first example is this tiny Python program that checks the value of the boolean variable `disaster` and prints an appropriate comment:

```
>>> disaster = True
>>> if disaster:
...     print("Woe!")
... else:
...     print("Whee!")
...
Woe!
>>>
```

The `if` and `else` lines are Python *statements* that check whether a condition (here, the value of `disaster`) is a boolean `True` value, or can be evaluated as `True`. Remember, `print()` is Python's built-in *function* to print things, normally to your screen.

 If you've programmed in other languages, note that you don't need parentheses for the `if` test. For example, don't say something such as `if (disaster == True)` (the equality operator `==` is described in a few paragraphs). You do need the colon (`:`) at the end. If, like me, you forget to type the colon at times, Python will display an error message.

Each `print()` line is indented under its test. I used four spaces to indent each subsection. Although you can use any indentation you like, Python expects you to be consistent with code within a section—the lines need to be indented the same amount, lined up on the left. The recommended style, called *PEP-8* (*http://bit.ly/pep-8*), is to use four spaces. Don't use tabs, or mix tabs and spaces; it messes up the indent count.

We did a number of things here, which I explain more fully as the chapter progresses:

- Assigned the boolean value `True` to the variable named `disaster`
- Performed a *conditional comparison* by using `if` and `else`, executing different code depending on the value of `disaster`
- *Called* the `print()` *function* to print some text

You can have tests within tests, as many levels deep as needed:

```
>>> furry = True
>>> large = True
>>> if furry:
...     if large:
...         print("It's a yeti.")
...     else:
...         print("It's a cat!")
... else:
...     if large:
...         print("It's a whale!")
...     else:
...         print("It's a human. Or a hairless cat.")
...
It's a yeti.
```

In Python, indentation determines how the `if` and `else` sections are paired. Our first test was to check `furry`. Because `furry` is `True`, Python goes to the indented `if large` test. Because we had set `large` to `True`, `if large` is evaluated as `True`, and the following `else` line is ignored. This makes Python run the line indented under `if large:` and print `It's a yeti`.

If there are more than two possibilities to test, use `if` for the first, `elif` (meaning *else if*) for the middle ones, and `else` for the last:

```
>>> color = "mauve"
>>> if color == "red":
...     print("It's a tomato")
... elif color == "green":
...     print("It's a green pepper")
... elif color == "bee purple":
...     print("I don't know what it is, but only bees can see it")
... else:
...     print("I've never heard of the color", color)
...
I've never heard of the color mauve
```

In the preceding example, we tested for equality by using the `==` operator. Here are Python's *comparison operators*:

equality	==
inequality	!=
less than	<
less than or equal	<=
greater than	>
greater than or equal	>=

These return the boolean values `True` or `False`. Let's see how these all work, but first, assign a value to x:

```
>>> x = 7
```

Now, let's try some tests:

```
>>> x == 5
False
>>> x == 7
True
>>> 5 < x
True
>>> x < 10
True
```

Note that two equals signs (`==`) are used to *test equality*; remember, a single equals sign (`=`) is what you use to assign a value to a variable.

If you need to make multiple comparisons at the same time, you use the *logical* (or *boolean*) *operators* and, or, and not to determine the final boolean result.

Logical operators have lower *precedence* than the chunks of code that they're comparing. This means that the chunks are calculated first, and then compared. In this example, because we set x to 7, 5 < x is calculated to be True and x < 10 is also True, so we finally end up with True and True:

```
>>> 5 < x and x < 10
True
```

As "Precedence" on page 43 points out, the easiest way to avoid confusion about precedence is to add parentheses:

```
>>> (5 < x) and (x < 10)
True
```

Here are some other tests:

```
>>> 5 < x or x < 10
True
>>> 5 < x and x > 10
False
>>> 5 < x and not x > 10
True
```

If you're and-ing multiple comparisons with one variable, Python lets you do this:

```
>>> 5 < x < 10
True
```

It's the same as 5 < x and x < 10. You can also write longer comparisons:

```
>>> 5 < x < 10 < 999
True
```

What Is True?

What if the element we're checking isn't a boolean? What does Python consider True and False?

A false value doesn't necessarily need to explicitly be a boolean False. For example, these are all considered False:

boolean	False
null	None
zero integer	0
zero float	0.0

empty string	`''`
empty list	`[]`
empty tuple	`()`
empty dict	`{}`
empty set	`set()`

Anything else is considered `True`. Python programs use these definitions of "truthi-ness" and "falsiness" to check for empty data structures as well as `False` conditions:

```
>>> some_list = []
>>> if some_list:
...     print("There's something in here")
... else:
...     print("Hey, it's empty!")
...
Hey, it's empty!
```

If what you're testing is an expression rather than a simple variable, Python evaluates the expression and returns a boolean result. So, if you type:

```
if color == "red":
```

Python evaluates `color == "red"`. In our earlier example, we assigned the string `"mauve"` to color, so `color == "red"` is `False`, and Python moves on to the next test:

```
elif color == "green":
```

Do Multiple Comparisons with in

Suppose that you have a letter and want to know whether it's a vowel. One way would be to write a long `if` statement:

```
>>> letter = 'o'
>>> if letter == 'a' or letter == 'e' or letter == 'i' \
...     or letter == 'o' or letter == 'u':
...     print(letter, 'is a vowel')
... else:
...     print(letter, 'is not a vowel')
...
o is a vowel
>>>
```

Whenever you need to make a lot of comparisons like that, separated by `or`, use Python's *membership operator* `in`, instead. Here's how to check vowel-ness more Pythonically, using `in` with a string made of vowel characters:

```
>>> vowels = 'aeiou'
>>> letter = 'o'
>>> letter in vowels
True
```

```
>>> if letter in vowels:
...     print(letter, 'is a vowel')
...
o is a vowel
```

Here's a preview of how to use `in` with some data types that you'll read about in detail in the next few chapters:

```
>>> letter = 'o'
>>> vowel_set = {'a', 'e', 'i', 'o', 'u'}
>>> letter in vowel_set
True
>>> vowel_list = ['a', 'e', 'i', 'o', 'u']
>>> letter in vowel_list
True
>>> vowel_tuple = ('a', 'e', 'i', 'o', 'u')
>>> letter in vowel_tuple
True
>>> vowel_dict = {'a': 'apple', 'e': 'elephant',
...               'i': 'impala', 'o': 'ocelot', 'u': 'unicorn'}
>>> letter in vowel_dict
True
>>> vowel_string = "aeiou"
>>> letter in vowel_string
True
```

For the dictionary, `in` looks at the keys (the lefthand side of the :) instead of their values.

New: I Am the Walrus

Arriving in Python 3.8 is the *walrus operator*, which looks like this:

```
name := expression
```

See the walrus? (Like a smiley, but tuskier.)

Normally, an assignment and test take two steps:

```
>>> tweet_limit = 280
>>> tweet_string = "Blah" * 50
>>> diff = tweet_limit - len(tweet_string)
>>> if diff >= 0:
...     print("A fitting tweet")
... else:
...     print("Went over by", abs(diff))
...
A fitting tweet
```

With our new tusk power (aka assignment expressions (*https://oreil.ly/fHPtL*)) we can combine these into one step:

```
>>> tweet_limit = 280
>>> tweet_string = "Blah" * 50
>>> if diff := tweet_limit - len(tweet_string) >= 0:
...     print("A fitting tweet")
... else:
...     print("Went over by", abs(diff))
...
A fitting tweet
```

The walrus also gets on swimmingly with `for` and `while`, which we look at in Chapter 6.

Coming Up

Play with strings, and meet interesting characters.

Things to Do

4.1 Choose a number between 1 and 10 and assign it to the variable `secret`. Then, select another number between 1 and 10 and assign it to the variable `guess`. Next, write the conditional tests (`if`, `else`, and `elif`) to print the string `'too low'` if `guess` is less than `secret`, `'too high'` if greater than `secret`, and `'just right'` if equal to `secret`.

4.2 Assign `True` or `False` to the variables `small` and `green`. Write some `if/else` statements to print which of these matches those choices: cherry, pea, watermelon, pumpkin.

CHAPTER 5

Text Strings

I always liked strange characters.

—Tim Burton

Computer books often give the impression that programming is all about math. Actually, most programmers work with *strings* of text more often than numbers. Logical (and creative!) thinking is often more important than math skills.

Strings are our first example of a Python *sequence*. In this case, they're a sequence of *characters*. But what's a character? It's the smallest unit in a writing system, and includes letters, digits, symbols, punctuation, and even white space or directives like linefeeds. A character is defined by its meaning (how it's used), not how it looks. It can have more than one visual representation (in different *fonts*), and more than one character can have the same appearance (such as the visual H, which means the H sound in the Latin alphabet but the Latin N sound in Cyrillic).

This chapter concentrates on how to make and format simple text strings, using ASCII (basic character set) examples. Two important text topics are deferred to Chapter 12: *Unicode* characters (like the H and N issue I just mentioned) and *regular expressions* (pattern matching).

Unlike other languages, strings in Python are *immutable*. You can't change a string in place, but you can copy parts of strings to another string to get the same effect. We look at how to do this shortly.

Create with Quotes

You make a Python string by enclosing characters in matching single or double quotes:

```
>>> 'Snap'
'Snap'
>>> "Crackle"
'Crackle'
```

The interactive interpreter echoes strings with a single quote, but all are treated exactly the same by Python.

 Python has a few special types of strings, indicated by a letter before the first quote. f or F starts an *f string*, used for formatting, and described near the end of this chapter. r or R starts a *raw string*, used to prevent *escape sequences* in the string (see "Escape with \" on page 66 and Chapter 12 for its use in string pattern matching). Then, there's the combination fr (or FR, Fr, or fR) that starts a raw f-string. A u starts a Unicode string, which is the same as a plain string. And a b starts a value of type bytes (Chapter 12). Unless I mention one of these special types, I'm always talking about plain old Python Unicode text strings.

Why have two kinds of quote characters? The main purpose is to create strings containing quote characters. You can have single quotes inside double-quoted strings, or double quotes inside single-quoted strings:

```
>>> "'Nay!' said the naysayer. 'Neigh?' said the horse."
"'Nay!' said the naysayer. 'Neigh?' said the horse."
>>> 'The rare double quote in captivity: ".'
'The rare double quote in captivity: ".'
>>> 'A "two by four" is actually 1 1/2" × 3 1/2".'
'A "two by four" is actually 1 1/2" × 3 1/2".'
>>> "'There's the man that shot my paw!' cried the limping hound."
"'There's the man that shot my paw!' cried the limping hound."
```

You can also use three single quotes (''') or three double quotes ("""):

```
>>> '''Boom!'''
'Boom'
>>> """Eek!"""
'Eek!'
```

Triple quotes aren't very useful for short strings like these. Their most common use is to create *multiline strings*, like this classic poem from Edward Lear:

```
>>> poem = '''There was a Young Lady of Norway,
... Who casually sat in a doorway;
... When the door squeezed her flat,
```

```
... She exclaimed, "What of that?"
... This courageous Young Lady of Norway.'''
>>>
```

(This was entered in the interactive interpreter, which prompted us with >>> for the first line and continuation prompts ... until we entered the final triple quotes and went to the next line.)

If you tried to create that poem without triple quotes, Python would make a fuss when you went to the second line:

```
>>> poem = 'There was a young lady of Norway,
  File "<stdin>", line 1
    poem = 'There was a young lady of Norway,
                                              ^
SyntaxError: EOL while scanning string literal
>>>
```

If you have multiple lines within triple quotes, the line ending characters will be preserved in the string. If you have leading or trailing spaces, they'll also be kept:

```
>>> poem2 = '''I do not like thee, Doctor Fell.
...     The reason why, I cannot tell.
...     But this I know, and know full well:
...     I do not like thee, Doctor Fell.
... '''
>>> print(poem2)
I do not like thee, Doctor Fell.
    The reason why, I cannot tell.
    But this I know, and know full well:
    I do not like thee, Doctor Fell.

>>>
```

By the way, there's a difference between the output of print() and the automatic echoing done by the interactive interpreter:

```
>>> poem2
'I do not like thee, Doctor Fell.\n    The reason why, I cannot tell.\n    But
this I know, and know full well:\n    I do not like thee, Doctor Fell.\n'
```

print() strips quotes from strings and prints their contents. It's meant for human output. It helpfully adds a space between each of the things it prints, and a newline at the end:

```
>>> print('Give', "us", '''some''', """space""")
Give us some space
```

If you don't want the space or newline, Chapter 14 explains how to avoid them.

The interactive interpreter prints the string with individual quotes and *escape characters* such as \n, which are explained in "Escape with \" on page 66.

```
>>> """'Guten Morgen, mein Herr!'
... said mad king Ludwig to his wig."""
"'Guten Morgen, mein Herr!'\nsaid mad king Ludwig to his wig."
```

Finally, there is the *empty string*, which has no characters at all but is perfectly valid. You can create an empty string with any of the aforementioned quotes:

```
>>> ''
''
>>> ""
''
>>> ''''''
''
>>> """"""
''
>>>
```

Create with str()

You can make a string from another data type by using the `str()` function:

```
>>> str(98.6)
'98.6'
>>> str(1.0e4)
'10000.0'
>>> str(True)
'True'
```

Python uses the `str()` function internally when you call `print()` with objects that are not strings and when doing *string formatting*, which you'll see later in this chapter.

Escape with \

Python lets you *escape* the meaning of some characters within strings to achieve effects that would otherwise be difficult to express. By preceding a character with a backslash (\), you give it a special meaning. The most common escape sequence is \n, which means to begin a new line. With this you can create multiline strings from a one-line string:

```
>>> palindrome = 'A man,\nA plan,\nA canal:\nPanama.'
>>> print(palindrome)
A man,
A plan,
A canal:
Panama.
```

You will see the escape sequence \t (tab) used to align text:

```
>>> print('\tabc')
	abc
>>> print('a\tbc')
```

```
a       bc
>>> print('ab\tc')
ab        c
>>> print('abc\t')
abc
```

(The final string has a terminating tab which, of course, you can't see.)

You might also need \' or \" to specify a literal single or double quote inside a string that's quoted by the same character:

```
>>> testimony = "\"I did nothing!\" he said. \"Or that other thing.\""
>>> testimony
'"I did nothing!" he said. "Or that other thing."'
>>> print(testimony)
"I did nothing!" he said. "Or that other thing."

>>> fact = "The world's largest rubber duck was 54'2\" by 65'7\" by 105'"
>>> print(fact)
The world's largest rubber duck was 54'2" by 65'7" by 105'
```

And if you need a literal backslash, type two of them (the first escapes the second):

```
>>> speech = 'The backslash (\\) bends over backwards to please you.'
>>> print(speech)
The backslash (\) bends over backwards to please you.
>>>
```

As I mentioned early in this chapter, a *raw string* negates these escapes:

```
>>> info = r'Type a \n to get a new line in a normal string'
>>> info
'Type a \\n to get a new line in a normal string'
>>> print(info)
Type a \n to get a new line in a normal string
```

(The extra backslash in the first info output was added by the interactive interpreter.)

A raw string does not undo any real (not '\n') newlines:

```
>>> poem = r'''Boys and girls, come out to play.
... The moon doth shine as bright as day.'''
>>> poem
'Boys and girls, come out to play.\nThe moon doth shine as bright as day.'
>>> print(poem)
Boys and girls, come out to play.
The moon doth shine as bright as day.
```

Combine by Using +

You can combine literal strings or string variables in Python by using the + operator:

```
>>> 'Release the kraken! ' + 'No, wait!'
'Release the kraken! No, wait!'
```

You can also combine *literal strings* (not string variables) just by having one after the other:

```
>>> "My word! " "A gentleman caller!"
'My word! A gentleman caller!'
>>> "Alas! ""The kraken!"
'Alas! The kraken!'
```

If you have a lot of these, you can avoid escaping the line endings by surrounding them with parentheses:

```
>>> vowels = ( 'a'
... "e" '''i'''
... 'o' """u"""
... )
>>> vowels
'aeiou'
```

Python does *not* add spaces for you when concatenating strings, so in some earlier examples, we needed to include spaces explicitly. Python *does* add a space between each argument to a `print()` statement and a newline at the end.

```
>>> a = 'Duck.'
>>> b = a
>>> c = 'Grey Duck!'
>>> a + b + c
'Duck.Duck.Grey Duck!'
>>> print(a, b, c)
Duck. Duck. Grey Duck!
```

Duplicate with *

You use the * operator to duplicate a string. Try typing these lines into your interactive interpreter and see what they print:

```
>>> start = 'Na ' * 4 + '\n'
>>> middle = 'Hey ' * 3 + '\n'
>>> end = 'Goodbye.'
>>> print(start + start + middle + end)
```

Notice that the * has higher precedence than +, so the string is duplicated before the line feed is tacked on.

Get a Character with []

To get a single character from a string, specify its *offset* inside square brackets after the string's name. The first (leftmost) offset is 0, the next is 1, and so on. The last (rightmost) offset can be specified with –1, so you don't have to count; going to the left are –2, –3, and so on:

```
>>> letters = 'abcdefghijklmnopqrstuvwxyz'
>>> letters[0]
'a'
>>> letters[1]
'b'
>>> letters[-1]
'z'
>>> letters[-2]
'y'
>>> letters[25]
'z'
>>> letters[5]
'f'
```

If you specify an offset that is the length of the string or longer (remember, offsets go from 0 to length–1), you'll get an exception:

```
>>> letters[100]
Traceback (most recent call last):
  File "<stdin>", line 1, in <module>
IndexError: string index out of range
```

Indexing works the same with the other sequence types (lists and tuples), which I cover in Chapter 7.

Because strings are immutable, you can't insert a character directly into one or change the character at a specific index. Let's try to change 'Henny' to 'Penny' and see what happens:

```
>>> name = 'Henny'
>>> name[0] = 'P'
Traceback (most recent call last):
  File "<stdin>", line 1, in <module>
TypeError: 'str' object does not support item assignment
```

Instead you need to use some combination of string functions such as replace() or a *slice* (which we look at in a moment):

```
>>> name = 'Henny'
>>> name.replace('H', 'P')
'Penny'
>>> 'P' + name[1:]
'Penny'
```

We didn't change the value of name. The interactive interpreter just printed the result of the replacement.

Get a Substring with a Slice

You can extract a *substring* (a part of a string) from a string by using a *slice*. You define a slice by using square brackets, a *start* offset, an *end* offset, and an optional *step* count between them. You can omit some of these. The slice will include characters from offset *start* to one before *end*:

- [:] extracts the entire sequence from start to end.
- [*start* :] specifies from the *start* offset to the end.
- [: *end*] specifies from the beginning to the *end* offset minus 1.
- [*start* : *end*] indicates from the *start* offset to the *end* offset minus 1.
- [*start* : *end* : *step*] extracts from the *start* offset to the *end* offset minus 1, skipping characters by *step*.

As before, offsets go 0, 1, and so on from the start to the right, and –1,–2, and so forth from the end to the left. If you don't specify *start*, the slice uses 0 (the beginning). If you don't specify *end*, it uses the end of the string.

Let's make a string of the lowercase English letters:

```
>>> letters = 'abcdefghijklmnopqrstuvwxyz'
```

Using a plain : is the same as 0: (the entire string):

```
>>> letters[:]
'abcdefghijklmnopqrstuvwxyz'
```

Here's an example from offset 20 to the end:

```
>>> letters[20:]
'uvwxyz'
```

Now, from offset 10 to the end:

```
>>> letters[10:]
'klmnopqrstuvwxyz'
```

And another, offset 12 through 14. Python does not include the end offset in the slice. The start offset is *inclusive*, and the end offset is *exclusive*:

```
>>> letters[12:15]
'mno'
```

The three last characters:

```
>>> letters[-3:]
'xyz'
```

In this next example, we go from offset 18 to the fourth before the end; notice the difference from the previous example, in which starting at −3 gets the x, but ending at −3 actually stops at −4, the w:

```
>>> letters[18:-3]
'stuvw'
```

In the following, we extract from 6 before the end to 3 before the end:

```
>>> letters[-6:-2]
'uvwx'
```

If you want a step size other than 1, specify it after a second colon, as shown in the next series of examples.

From the start to the end, in steps of 7 characters:

```
>>> letters[::7]
'ahov'
```

From offset 4 to 19, by 3:

```
>>> letters[4:20:3]
'ehknqt'
```

From offset 19 to the end, by 4:

```
>>> letters[19::4]
'tx'
```

From the start to offset 20 by 5:

```
>>> letters[:21:5]
'afkpu'
```

(Again, the *end* needs to be one more than the actual offset.)

And that's not all! Given a negative step size, this handy Python slicer can also step backward. This starts at the end and ends at the start, skipping nothing:

```
>>> letters[-1::-1]
'zyxwvutsrqponmlkjihgfedcba'
```

It turns out that you can get the same result by using this:

```
>>> letters[::-1]
'zyxwvutsrqponmlkjihgfedcba'
```

Slices are more forgiving of bad offsets than are single-index lookups with [ ]. A slice offset earlier than the beginning of a string is treated as 0, and one after the end is treated as -1, as is demonstrated in this next series of examples.

From 50 before the end to the end:

```
>>> letters[-50:]
'abcdefghijklmnopqrstuvwxyz'
```

From 51 before the end to 50 before the end:

```
>>> letters[-51:-50]
''
```

From the start to 69 after the start:

```
>>> letters[:70]
'abcdefghijklmnopqrstuvwxyz'
```

From 70 after the start to 70 after the start:

```
>>> letters[70:71]
''
```

Get Length with len()

So far, we've used special punctuation characters such as + to manipulate strings. But there are only so many of these. Now let's begin to use some of Python's built-in *functions*: named pieces of code that perform certain operations.

The len() function counts characters in a string:

```
>>> len(letters)
26
>>> empty = ""
>>> len(empty)
0
```

You can use len() with other sequence types, too, as you'll see in Chapter 7.

Split with split()

Unlike len(), some functions are specific to strings. To use a string function, type the name of the string, a dot, the name of the function, and any *arguments* that the function needs: *string.function(arguments)*. There's a longer discussion of functions in Chapter 9.

You can use the built-in string split() function to break a string into a *list* of smaller strings based on some *separator*. We look at lists in Chapter 7. A list is a sequence of values, separated by commas and surrounded by square brackets:

```
>>> tasks = 'get gloves,get mask,give cat vitamins,call ambulance'
>>> tasks.split(',')
['get gloves', 'get mask', 'give cat vitamins', 'call ambulance']
```

In the preceding example, the string was called `tasks` and the string function was called `split()`, with the single separator argument `','`. If you don't specify a separator, `split()` uses any sequence of white space characters—newlines, spaces, and tabs:

```
>>> tasks.split()
['get', 'gloves,get', 'mask,give', 'cat', 'vitamins,call', 'ambulance']
```

You still need the parentheses when calling `split` with no arguments—that's how Python knows you're calling a function.

Combine by Using join()

Not too surprisingly, the `join()` function is the opposite of `split()`: it collapses a list of strings into a single string. It looks a bit backward because you specify the string that glues everything together first, and then the list of strings to glue: *string* `.join(` *list* `)`. So, to join the list `lines` with separating newlines, you would say `'\n'.join(lines)`. In the following example, let's join some names in a list with a comma and a space:

```
>>> crypto_list = ['Yeti', 'Bigfoot', 'Loch Ness Monster']
>>> crypto_string = ', '.join(crypto_list)
>>> print('Found and signing book deals:', crypto_string)
Found and signing book deals: Yeti, Bigfoot, Loch Ness Monster
```

Substitute by Using replace()

You use `replace()` for simple substring substitution. Give it the old substring, the new one, and how many instances of the old substring to replace. It returns the changed string but does not modify the original string. If you omit this final count argument, it replaces all instances. In this example, only one string (`'duck'`) is matched and replaced in the returned string:

```
>>> setup = "a duck goes into a bar..."
>>> setup.replace('duck', 'marmoset')
'a marmoset goes into a bar...'
>>> setup
'a duck goes into a bar...'
```

Change up to 100 of them:

```
>>> setup.replace('a ', 'a famous ', 100)
'a famous duck goes into a famous bar...'
```

When you know the exact substring(s) you want to change, `replace()` is a good choice. But watch out. In the second example, if we had substituted for the single character string `'a'` rather than the two character string `'a '` (a followed by a space), we would have also changed a in the middle of other words:

```
>>> setup.replace('a', 'a famous', 100)
'a famous duck goes into a famous ba famousr...'
```

Sometimes, you want to ensure that the substring is a whole word, or the beginning of a word, and so on. In those cases, you need *regular expressions*, which are described in numbing detail in Chapter 12.

Strip with strip()

It's very common to strip leading or trailing "padding" characters from a string, especially spaces. The `strip()` functions shown here assume that you want to get rid of whitespace characters (`' '`, `'\t'`, `'\n'`) if you don't give them an argument. `strip()` strips both ends, `lstrip()` only from the left, and `rstrip()` only from the right. Let's say the string variable `world` contains the string `"earth"` floating in spaces:

```
>>> world = "    earth    "
>>> world.strip()
'earth'
>>> world.strip(' ')
'earth'
>>> world.lstrip()
'earth    '
>>> world.rstrip()
'    earth'
```

If the character were not there, nothing happens:

```
>>> world.strip('!')
'    earth    '
```

Besides no argument (meaning whitespace characters) or a single character, you can also tell `strip()` to remove any character in a multicharacter string:

```
>>> blurt = "What the...!!?"
>>> blurt.strip('.?!')
'What the'
```

Appendix E shows some definitions of character groups that are useful with `strip()`:

```
>>> import string
>>> string.whitespace
' \t\n\r\x0b\x0c'
>>> string.punctuation
'!"#$%&\'()*+,-./:;<=>?@[\\]^_`{|}~'
>>> blurt = "What the...!!?"
>>> blurt.strip(string.punctuation)
'What the'
>>> prospector = "What in tarnation ...??!!"
```

```
>>> prospector.strip(string.whitespace + string.punctuation)
'What in tarnation'
```

Search and Select

Python has a large set of string functions. Let's explore how the most common of them work. Our test subject is the following string containing the text of the immortal poem "What Is Liquid?" by Margaret Cavendish, Duchess of Newcastle:

```
>>> poem = '''All that doth flow we cannot liquid name
... Or else would fire and water be the same;
... But that is liquid which is moist and wet
... Fire that property can never get.
... Then 'tis not cold that doth the fire put out
... But 'tis the wet that makes it die, no doubt.'''
```

Inspiring!

To begin, get the first 13 characters (offsets 0 to 12):

```
>>> poem[:13]
'All that doth'
```

How many characters are in this poem? (Spaces and newlines are included in the count.)

```
>>> len(poem)
250
```

Does it start with the letters All?

```
>>> poem.startswith('All')
True
```

Does it end with That's all, folks!?

```
>>> poem.endswith('That\'s all, folks!')
False
```

Python has two methods (find() and index()) for finding the offset of a substring, and has two versions of each (starting from the beginning or the end). They work the same if the substring is found. If it isn't, find() returns -1, and index() raises an exception.

Let's find the offset of the first occurrence of the word the in the poem:

```
>>> word = 'the'
>>> poem.find(word)
73
>>> poem.index(word)
73
```

And the offset of the last the:

```
>>> word = 'the'
>>> poem.rfind(word)
214
>>> poem.rindex(word)
214
```

But if the substring isn't in there:

```
>>> word = "duck"
>>> poem.find(word)
-1
>>> poem.rfind(word)
-1
>>> poem.index(word)
Traceback (most recent call last):
  File "<stdin>", line 1, in <module>
ValueError: substring not found
>>> poem.rfind(word)
-1
>>> poem.rindex(word)
Traceback (most recent call last):
  File "<stdin>", line 1, in <module>
ValueError: substring not found
```

How many times does the three-letter sequence the occur?

```
>>> word = 'the'
>>> poem.count(word)
3
```

Are all of the characters in the poem either letters or numbers?

```
>>> poem.isalnum()
False
```

Nope, there were some punctuation characters.

Case

In this section, we look at some more uses of the built-in string functions. Our test string is again the following:

```
>>> setup = 'a duck goes into a bar...'
```

Remove . sequences from both ends:

```
>>> setup.strip('.')
'a duck goes into a bar'
```

Because strings are immutable, none of these examples actually changes the setup string. Each example just takes the value of setup, does something to it, and returns the result as a new string.

Capitalize the first word:

```
>>> setup.capitalize()
'A duck goes into a bar...'
```

Capitalize all the words:

```
>>> setup.title()
'A Duck Goes Into A Bar...'
```

Convert all characters to uppercase:

```
>>> setup.upper()
'A DUCK GOES INTO A BAR...'
```

Convert all characters to lowercase:

```
>>> setup.lower()
'a duck goes into a bar...'
```

Swap uppercase and lowercase:

```
>>> setup.swapcase()
'A DUCK GOES INTO A BAR...'
```

Alignment

Now, let's work with some layout alignment functions. The string is aligned within the specified total number of spaces (30 here).

Center the string within 30 spaces:

```
>>> setup.center(30)
'   a duck goes into a bar...   '
```

Left justify:

```
>>> setup.ljust(30)
'a duck goes into a bar...      '
```

Right justify:

```
>>> setup.rjust(30)
'      a duck goes into a bar...'
```

Next, we look at more ways to align a string.

Formatting

You've seen that you can *concatenate* strings by using +. Let's look at how to *interpolate* data values into strings using various formats. You can use this to produce reports, forms, and other outputs where appearances need to be just so.

Besides the functions in the previous section, Python has three ways of formatting strings:

- *old style* (supported in Python 2 and 3)
- *new style* (Python 2.6 and up)
- *f-strings* (Python 3.6 and up)

Old style: %

The old style of string formatting has the form *format_string % data*. Inside the format string are interpolation sequences. Table 5-1 illustrates that the very simplest sequence is a % followed by a letter indicating the data type to be formatted.

Table 5-1. Conversion types

%s	string
%d	decimal integer
%x	hex integer
%o	octal integer
%f	decimal float
%e	exponential float
%g	decimal or exponential float
%%	a literal %

You can use a %s for any data type, and Python will format it as a string with no extra spaces.

Following are some simple examples. First, an integer:

```
>>> '%s' % 42
'42'
>>> '%d' % 42
'42'
>>> '%x' % 42
'2a'
>>> '%o' % 42
'52'
```

A float:

```
>>> '%s' % 7.03
'7.03'
>>> '%f' % 7.03
'7.030000'
>>> '%e' % 7.03
'7.030000e+00'
>>> '%g' % 7.03
'7.03'
```

An integer and a literal %:

```
>>> '%d%%' % 100
'100%'
```

Let's try some string and integer interpolation:

```
>>> actor = 'Richard Gere'
>>> cat = 'Chester'
>>> weight = 28

>>> "My wife's favorite actor is %s" % actor
"My wife's favorite actor is Richard Gere"

>>> "Our cat %s weighs %s pounds" % (cat, weight)
'Our cat Chester weighs 28 pounds'
```

That %s inside the string means to interpolate a string. The number of % appearances in the string needs to match the number of data items after the % that follows the string. A single data item such as actor goes right after that final %. Multiple data must be grouped into a *tuple* (details in Chapter 7; it's bounded by parentheses, separated by commas) such as (cat, weight).

Even though weight is an integer, the %s inside the string converted it to a string.

You can add other values in the format string between the % and the type specifier to designate minimum and maximum widths, alignment, and character filling. This is a little language in its own right, and more limited than the one in the next two sections. Let's take a quick look at these values:

- An initial '%' character.
- An optional *alignment* character: nothing or '+' means right-align, and '-' means left-align.
- An optional *minwidth* field width to use.
- An optional '.' character to separate *minwidth* and *maxchars*.

- An optional *maxchars* (if conversion type is s) saying how many characters to print from the data value. If the conversion type is f, this specifies *precision* (how many digits to print after the decimal point).

- The *conversion type* character from the earlier table.

This is confusing, so here are some examples for a string:

```
>>> thing = 'woodchuck'
>>> '%s' % thing
'woodchuck'
>>> '%12s' % thing
'   woodchuck'
>>> '%+12s' % thing
'   woodchuck'
>>> '%-12s' % thing
'woodchuck   '
>>> '%.3s' % thing
'woo'
>>> '%12.3s' % thing
'         woo'
>>> '%-12.3s' % thing
'woo         '
```

Once more with feeling, and a float with %f variants:

```
>>> thing = 98.6
>>> '%f' % thing
'98.600000'
>>> '%12f' % thing
'   98.600000'
>>> '%+12f' % thing
'  +98.600000'
>>> '%-12f' % thing
'98.600000   '
>>> '%.3f' % thing
'98.600'
>>> '%12.3f' % thing
'      98.600'
>>> '%-12.3f' % thing
'98.600      '
```

And an integer with %d:

```
>>> thing = 9876
>>> '%d' % thing
'9876'
>>> '%12d' % thing
'        9876'
>>> '%+12d' % thing
'       +9876'
>>> '%-12d' % thing
'9876        '
```

```
>>> '%.3d' % thing
'9876'
>>> '%12.3d' % thing
'        9876'
>>> '%-12.3d' % thing
'9876        '
```

For an integer, the %+12d just forces the sign to be printed, and the format strings with .3 in them have no effect as they do for a float.

New style: {} and format()

Old style formatting is still supported. In Python 2, which will freeze at version 2.7, it will be supported forever. For Python 3, use the "new style" formatting described in this section. If you have Python 3.6 or newer, *f-strings* ("Newest Style: f-strings" on page 82) are even better.

"New style" formatting has the form *format_string*.format(*data*).

The format string is not exactly the same as the one in the previous section. The simplest usage is demonstrated here:

```
>>> thing = 'woodchuck'
>>> '{}'.format(thing)
'woodchuck'
```

The arguments to the format() function need to be in the order as the {} placeholders in the format string:

```
>>> thing = 'woodchuck'
>>> place = 'lake'
>>> 'The {} is in the {}.'.format(thing, place)
'The woodchuck is in the lake.'
```

With new-style formatting, you can also specify the arguments by position like this:

```
>>> 'The {1} is in the {0}.'.format(place, thing)
'The woodchuck is in the lake.'
```

The value 0 referred to the first argument, place, and 1 referred to thing.

The arguments to format() can also be named arguments

```
>>> 'The {thing} is in the {place}'.format(thing='duck', place='bathtub')
'The duck is in the bathtub'
```

or a dictionary:

```
>>> d = {'thing': 'duck', 'place': 'bathtub'}
```

In the following example, {0} is the first argument to `format()` (the dictionary d):

```
>>> 'The {0[thing]} is in the {0[place]}.'.format(d)
'The duck is in the bathtub.'
```

These examples all printed their arguments with default formats. New-style formatting has a slightly different format string definition from the old-style one (examples follow):

- An initial colon (`':'`).
- An optional *fill* character (default `' '`) to pad the value string if it's shorter than *minwidth*.
- An optional *alignment* character. This time, left alignment is the default. `'<'` also means left, `'>'` means right, and `'^'` means center.
- An optional *sign* for numbers. Nothing means only prepend a minus sign (`'-'`) for negative numbers. `' '` means prepend a minus sign for negative numbers, and a space (`' '`) for positive ones.
- An optional *minwidth*. An optional period (`'.'`) to separate *minwidth* and *maxchars*.
- An optional *maxchars*.
- The *conversion type*.

```
>>> thing = 'wraith'
>>> place = 'window'
>>> 'The {} is at the {}'.format(thing, place)
'The wraith is at the window'
>>> 'The {:10s} is at the {:10s}'.format(thing, place)
'The wraith     is at the window    '
>>> 'The {:<10s} is at the {:<10s}'.format(thing, place)
'The wraith     is at the window    '
>>> 'The {:^10s} is at the {:^10s}'.format(thing, place)
'The   wraith   is at the   window   '
>>> 'The {:>10s} is at the {:>10s}'.format(thing, place)
'The     wraith is at the     window'
>>> 'The {:!^10s} is at the {:!^10s}'.format(thing, place)
'The !!wraith!! is at the !!window!!'
```

Newest Style: f-strings

f-strings appeared in Python 3.6, and are now the recommended way of formatting strings.

To make an f-string:

- Type the letter `f` or `F` directly before the initial quote.

- Include variable names or expressions within curly brackets ({}) to get their values into the string.

It's like the previous section's "new-style" formatting, but without the `format()` function, and without empty brackets ({}) or positional ones ({1}) in the format string.

```
>>> thing = 'wereduck'
>>> place = 'werepond'
>>> f'The {thing} is in the {place}'
'The wereduck is in the werepond'
```

As I already mentioned, expressions are also allowed inside the curly brackets:

```
>>> f'The {thing.capitalize()} is in the {place.rjust(20)}'
'The Wereduck is in the             werepond'
```

This means that the things that you could do inside `format()` in the previous section, you can now do inside a {} in your main string. This seems easier to read.

f-strings use the same formatting language (width, padding, alignment) as new-style formatting, after a `':'`.

```
>>> f'The {thing:>20} is in the {place:.^20}'
'The             wereduck is in the ......werepond......'
```

Starting in Python 3.8, f-strings gain a new shortcut that's helpful when you want to print variable names as well as their values. This is handy when debugging. The trick is to have a single = after the name in the {}-enclosed part of the f-string:

```
>>> f'{thing =}, {place =}'
thing = 'wereduck', place = 'werepond'
```

The name can actually be an expression, and it will be printed literally:

```
>>> f'{thing[-4:] =}, {place.title() =}'
thing[-4:] = 'duck', place.title() = 'Werepond'
```

Finally, the = can be followed by a : and the formatting arguments like width and alignment:

```
>>> f'{thing = :>4.4}'
thing = 'were'
```

More String Things

Python has many more string functions than I've shown here. Some will turn up in later chapters (especially Chapter 12), but you can find all the details at the standard documentation link (*http://bit.ly/py-docs-strings*).

Coming Up

You'll find Froot Loops at the grocery store, but Python loops are at the first counter in the next chapter.

Things to Do

5.1 Capitalize the word starting with m:

```
>>> song = """When an eel grabs your arm,
... And it causes great harm,
... That's - a moray!"""
```

5.2 Print each list question with its correctly matching answer, in the form:

Q: *question*
A: *answer*

```
>>> questions = [
...     "We don't serve strings around here. Are you a string?",
...     "What is said on Father's Day in the forest?",
...     "What makes the sound 'Sis! Boom! Bah!'?"
...     ]
>>> answers = [
...     "An exploding sheep.",
...     "No, I'm a frayed knot.",
...     "'Pop!' goes the weasel."
...     ]
```

5.3 Write the following poem by using old-style formatting. Substitute the strings 'roast beef', 'ham', 'head', and 'clam' into this string:

```
My kitty cat likes %s,
My kitty cat likes %s,
My kitty cat fell on his %s
And now thinks he's a %s.
```

5.4 Write a form letter by using new-style formatting. Save the following string as letter (you'll use it in the next exercise):

```
Dear {salutation} {name},

Thank you for your letter. We are sorry that our {product}
{verbed} in your {room}. Please note that it should never
be used in a {room}, especially near any {animals}.

Send us your receipt and {amount} for shipping and handling.
We will send you another {product} that, in our tests,
is {percent}% less likely to have {verbed}.

Thank you for your support.
```

```
Sincerely,
{spokesman}
{job_title}
```

5.5 Assign values to variable strings named `'salutation'`, `'name'`, `'product'`, `'verbed'` (past tense verb), `'room'`, `'animals'`, `'percent'`, `'spokesman'`, and `'job_title'`. Print `letter` with these values, using `letter.format()`.

5.6 After public polls to name things, a pattern emerged: an English submarine (Boaty McBoatface), an Australian racehorse (Horsey McHorseface), and a Swedish train (Trainy McTrainface). Use `%` formatting to print the winning name at the state fair for a prize duck, gourd, and spitz.

5.7 Do the same, with `format()` formatting.

5.8 Once more, with feeling, and *f strings*.

CHAPTER 6

Loop with while and for

For a' that, an' a' that, Our toils obscure, an' a' that …

—Robert Burns, *For a' That and a' That*

Testing with `if`, `elif`, and `else` runs from top to bottom. Sometimes, we need to do something more than once. We need a *loop*, and Python gives us two choices: `while` and `for`.

Repeat with while

The simplest looping mechanism in Python is `while`. Using the interactive interpreter, try this example, which is a simple loop that prints the numbers from 1 to 5:

```
>>> count = 1
>>> while count <= 5:
...     print(count)
...     count += 1
...
1
2
3
4
5
>>>
```

We first assigned the value 1 to `count`. The `while` loop compared the value of `count` to 5 and continued if `count` was less than or equal to 5. Inside the loop, we printed the value of `count` and then *incremented* its value by one with the statement `count += 1`. Python goes back to the top of the loop, and again compares `count` with 5. The value of count is now 2, so the contents of the while loop are again executed, and count is incremented to 3.

This continues until count is incremented from 5 to 6 at the bottom of the loop. On the next trip to the top, count <= 5 is now False, and the while loop ends. Python moves on to the next lines.

Cancel with break

If you want to loop until something occurs, but you're not sure when that might happen, you can use an *infinite loop* with a break statement. This time, let's read a line of input from the keyboard via Python's input() function and then print it with the first letter capitalized. We break out of the loop when a line containing only the letter q is typed:

```
>>> while True:
...     stuff = input("String to capitalize [type q to quit]: ")
...     if stuff == "q":
...         break
...     print(stuff.capitalize())
...
String to capitalize [type q to quit]: test
Test
String to capitalize [type q to quit]: hey, it works
Hey, it works
String to capitalize [type q to quit]: q
>>>
```

Skip Ahead with continue

Sometimes, you don't want to break out of a loop but just want to skip ahead to the next iteration for some reason. Here's a contrived example: let's read an integer, print its square if it's odd, and skip it if it's even. We even added a few comments. Again, we use q to stop the loop:

```
>>> while True:
...     value = input("Integer, please [q to quit]: ")
...     if value == 'q':      # quit
...         break
...     number = int(value)
...     if number % 2 == 0:   # an even number
...         continue
...     print(number, "squared is", number*number)
...
Integer, please [q to quit]: 1
1 squared is 1
Integer, please [q to quit]: 2
Integer, please [q to quit]: 3
3 squared is 9
```

```
Integer, please [q to quit]: 4
Integer, please [q to quit]: 5
5 squared is 25
Integer, please [q to quit]: q
>>>
```

Check break Use with else

If the while loop ended normally (no break call), control passes to an optional else. You use this when you've coded a while loop to check for something, and breaking as soon as it's found. The else would be run if the while loop completed but the object was not found:

```
>>> numbers = [1, 3, 5]
>>> position = 0
>>> while position < len(numbers):
...     number = numbers[position]
...     if number % 2 == 0:
...         print('Found even number', number)
...         break
...     position += 1
... else:  # break not called
...     print('No even number found')
...
No even number found
```

This use of else might seem nonintuitive. Consider it a *break checker*.

Iterate with for and in

Python makes frequent use of *iterators*, for good reason. They make it possible for you to traverse data structures without knowing how large they are or how they are implemented. You can even iterate over data that is created on the fly, allowing processing of data *streams* that would otherwise not fit in the computer's memory all at once.

To show iteration, we need something to iterate over. You've already seen strings in Chapter 5, but have not yet read the details on other *iterables* like lists and tuples (Chapter 7) or dictionaries (Chapter 8). I'll show two ways to walk through a string here, and show iteration for the other types in their own chapters.

It's legal Python to step through a string like this:

```
>>> word = 'thud'
>>> offset = 0
>>> while offset < len(word):
...     print(word[offset])
...     offset += 1
...
t
h
u
d
```

But there's a better, more Pythonic way:

```
>>> for letter in word:
...     print(letter)
...
t
h
u
d
```

String iteration produces one character at a time.

Cancel with break

A break in a for loop breaks out of the loop, as it does for a `while` loop:

```
>>> word = 'thud'
>>> for letter in word:
...     if letter == 'u':
...         break
...     print(letter)
...
t
h
```

Skip with continue

Inserting a `continue` in a for loop jumps to the next iteration of the loop, as it does for a `while` loop.

Check break Use with else

Similar to `while`, `for` has an optional `else` that checks whether the `for` completed normally. If `break` was *not* called, the `else` statement is run.

This is useful when you want to verify that the previous for loop ran to completion instead of being stopped early with a break:

```
>>> word = 'thud'
>>> for letter in word:
...     if letter == 'x':
...         print("Eek! An 'x'!")
...         break
...     print(letter)
... else:
...     print("No 'x' in there.")
...
t
h
u
d
No 'x' in there.
```

 As with while, the use of else with for might seem nonintuitive. It makes more sense if you think of the for as looking for something, and else being called if you didn't find it. To get the same effect without else, use some variable to indicate whether you found what you wanted in the for loop.

Generate Number Sequences with range()

The range() function returns a stream of numbers within a specified range. without first having to create and store a large data structure such as a list or tuple. This lets you create huge ranges without using all the memory in your computer and crashing your program.

You use range() similar to how to you use slices: range(*start, stop, step*). If you omit *start*, the range begins at 0. The only required value is *stop*; as with slices, the last value created will be just before *stop*. The default value of *step* is 1, but you can go backward with -1.

Like zip(), range() returns an *iterable* object, so you need to step through the values with for ... in, or convert the object to a sequence like a list. Let's make the range 0, 1, 2:

```
>>> for x in range(0,3):
...     print(x)
...
0
1
2
```

```
>>> list( range(0, 3) )
[0, 1, 2]
```

Here's how to make a range from 2 down to 0:

```
>>> for x in range(2, -1, -1):
...     print(x)
...
2
1
0
>>> list( range(2, -1, -1) )
[2, 1, 0]
```

The following snippet uses a step size of 2 to get the even numbers from 0 to 10:

```
>>> list( range(0, 11, 2) )
[0, 2, 4, 6, 8, 10]
```

Other Iterators

Chapter 14 shows iteration over files. In Chapter 10, you can see how to enable iteration over objects that you've defined yourself. Also, Chapter 11 talks about `itertools` —a standard Python module with many useful shortcuts.

Coming Up

Chain individual data into *lists* and *tuples*.

Things to Do

6.1 Use a for loop to print the values of the list [3, 2, 1, 0].

6.2 Assign the value 7 to the variable guess_me, and the value 1 to the variable num ber. Write a while loop that compares number with guess_me. Print 'too low' if num ber is less than guess me. If number equals guess_me, print 'found it!' and then exit the loop. If number is greater than guess_me, print 'oops' and then exit the loop. Increment number at the end of the loop.

6.3 Assign the value 5 to the variable guess_me. Use a for loop to iterate a variable called number over range(10). If number is less than guess_me, print 'too low'. If it equals guess_me, print found it! and then break out of the for loop. If number is greater than guess_me, print 'oops' and then exit the loop.

CHAPTER 7

Tuples and Lists

> The human animal differs from the lesser primates in his passion for lists.
>
> —H. Allen Smith

In the previous chapters, we started with some of Python's basic data types: booleans, integers, floats, and strings. If you think of those as atoms, the data structures in this chapter are like molecules. That is, we combine those basic types in more complex ways. You will use these every day. Much of programming consists of chopping and gluing data into specific forms, and these are your hacksaws and glue guns.

Most computer languages can represent a sequence of items indexed by their integer position: first, second, and so on down to the last. You've already seen Python *strings*, which are sequences of characters.

Python has two other sequence structures: *tuples* and *lists*. These contain zero or more elements. Unlike strings, the elements can be of different types. In fact, each element can be *any* Python object. This lets you create structures as deep and complex as you like.

Why does Python contain both lists and tuples? Tuples are *immutable*; when you assign elements (only once) to a tuple, they're baked in the cake and can't be changed. Lists are *mutable*, meaning you can insert and delete elements with great enthusiasm. I'll show many examples of each, with an emphasis on lists.

Tuples

Let's get one thing out of the way first. You may hear two different pronunciations for *tuple*. Which is right? If you guess wrong, do you risk being considered a Python poseur? No worries. Guido van Rossum, the creator of Python, said via Twitter (*http://bit.ly/tupletweet*):

> I pronounce tuple too-pull on Mon/Wed/Fri and tub-pull on Tue/Thu/Sat. On Sunday I don't talk about them. :)

Create with Commas and ()

The syntax to make tuples is a little inconsistent, as the following examples demonstrate. Let's begin by making an empty tuple using ():

```
>>> empty_tuple = ()
>>> empty_tuple
()
```

To make a tuple with one or more elements, follow each element with a comma. This works for one-element tuples:

```
>>> one_marx = 'Groucho',
>>> one_marx
('Groucho',)
```

You could enclose them in parentheses and still get the same tuple:

```
>>> one_marx = ('Groucho',)
>>> one_marx
('Groucho',)
```

Here's a little gotcha: if you have a single thing in parentheses and omit that comma, you would not get a tuple, but just the thing (in this example, the string 'Groucho'):

```
>>> one_marx = ('Groucho')
>>> one_marx
'Groucho'
>>> type(one_marx)
<class 'str'>
```

If you have more than one element, follow all but the last one with a comma:

```
>>> marx_tuple = 'Groucho', 'Chico', 'Harpo'
>>> marx_tuple
('Groucho', 'Chico', 'Harpo')
```

Python includes parentheses when echoing a tuple. You often don't need them when you define a tuple, but using parentheses is a little safer, and it helps to make the tuple more visible:

```
>>> marx_tuple = ('Groucho', 'Chico', 'Harpo')
>>> marx_tuple
('Groucho', 'Chico', 'Harpo')
```

You do need the parentheses for cases in which commas might also have another use. In this example, you can create and assign a single-element tuple with just a trailing comma, but you can't pass it as an argument to a function:

```
>>> one_marx = 'Groucho',
>>> type(one_marx)
<class 'tuple'>
>>> type('Groucho',)
<class 'str'>
>>> type(('Groucho',))
<class 'tuple'>
```

Tuples let you assign multiple variables at once:

```
>>> marx_tuple = ('Groucho', 'Chico', 'Harpo')
>>> a, b, c = marx_tuple
>>> a
'Groucho'
>>> b
'Chico'
>>> c
'Harpo'
```

This is sometimes called *tuple unpacking*.

You can use tuples to exchange values in one statement without using a temporary variable:

```
>>> password = 'swordfish'
>>> icecream = 'tuttifrutti'
>>> password, icecream = icecream, password
>>> password
'tuttifrutti'
>>> icecream
'swordfish'
>>>
```

Create with tuple()

The tuple() conversion function makes tuples from other things:

```
>>> marx_list = ['Groucho', 'Chico', 'Harpo']
>>> tuple(marx_list)
('Groucho', 'Chico', 'Harpo')
```

Combine Tuples by Using +

This is similar to combining strings:

```
>>> ('Groucho',) + ('Chico', 'Harpo')
('Groucho', 'Chico', 'Harpo')
```

Duplicate Items with *

This is like repeated use of +:

```
>>> ('yada',) * 3
('yada', 'yada', 'yada')
```

Compare Tuples

This works much like list comparisons:

```
>>> a = (7, 2)
>>> b = (7, 2, 9)
>>> a == b
False
>>> a <= b
True
>>> a < b
True
```

Iterate with for and in

Tuple iteration is like iteration of other types:

```
>>> words = ('fresh','out', 'of', 'ideas')
>>> for word in words:
...     print(word)
...
fresh
out
of
ideas
```

Modify a Tuple

You can't! Like strings, tuples are immutable, so you can't change an existing one. As you saw just before, you can *concatenate* (combine) tuples to make a new one, as you can with strings:

```
>>> t1 = ('Fee', 'Fie', 'Foe')
>>> t2 = ('Flop,')
>>> t1 + t2
('Fee', 'Fie', 'Foe', 'Flop')
```

This means that you can appear to modify a tuple like this:

```
>>> t1 = ('Fee', 'Fie', 'Foe')
>>> t2 = ('Flop,')
>>> t1 += t2
```

```
>>> t1
('Fee', 'Fie', 'Foe', 'Flop')
```

But it isn't the same t1. Python made a new tuple from the original tuples pointed to by t1 and t2, and assigned the name t1 to this new tuple. You can see with id() when a variable name is pointing to a new value:

```
>>> t1 = ('Fee', 'Fie', 'Foe')
>>> t2 = ('Flop',)
>>> id(t1)
4365405712
>>> t1 += t2
>>> id(t1)
4364770744
```

Lists

Lists are good for keeping track of things by their order, especially when the order and contents might change. Unlike strings, lists are mutable. You can change a list in place, add new elements, and delete or replace existing elements. The same value can occur more than once in a list.

Create with []

A list is made from zero or more elements, separated by commas and surrounded by square brackets:

```
>>> empty_list = [ ]
>>> weekdays = ['Monday', 'Tuesday', 'Wednesday', 'Thursday', 'Friday']
>>> big_birds = ['emu', 'ostrich', 'cassowary']
>>> first_names = ['Graham', 'John', 'Terry', 'Terry', 'Michael']
>>> leap_years = [2000, 2004, 2008]
>>> randomness = ['Punxsatawney', {"groundhog": "Phil"}, "Feb. 2"}
```

The first_names list shows that values do not need to be unique.

 If you want to keep track of only unique values and don't care about order, a Python *set* might be a better choice than a list. In the previous example, big_birds could have been a set. We explore sets in Chapter 8.

Create or Convert with list()

You can also make an empty list with the list() function:

```
>>> another_empty_list = list()
>>> another_empty_list
[]
```

Python's list() function also converts other *iterable* data types (such as tuples, strings, sets, and dictionaries) to lists. The following example converts a string to a list of one-character strings:

```
>>> list('cat')
['c', 'a', 't']
```

This example converts a tuple to a list:

```
>>> a_tuple = ('ready', 'fire', 'aim')
>>> list(a_tuple)
['ready', 'fire', 'aim']
```

Create from a String with split()

As I mentioned earlier in "Split with split()" on page 72, use split() to chop a string into a list by some separator:

```
>>> talk_like_a_pirate_day = '9/19/2019'
>>> talk_like_a_pirate_day.split('/')
['9', '19', '2019']
```

What if you have more than one separator string in a row in your original string? Well, you get an empty string as a list item:

```
>>> splitme = 'a/b//c/d///e'
>>> splitme.split('/')
['a', 'b', '', 'c', 'd', '', '', 'e']
```

If you had used the two-character separator string //, instead, you would get this:

```
>>> splitme = 'a/b//c/d///e'
>>> splitme.split('//')
>>>
['a/b', 'c/d', '/e']
```

Get an Item by [*offset*]

As with strings, you can extract a single value from a list by specifying its offset:

```
>>> marxes = ['Groucho', 'Chico', 'Harpo']
>>> marxes[0]
'Groucho'
>>> marxes[1]
'Chico'
>>> marxes[2]
'Harpo'
```

Again, as with strings, negative indexes count backward from the end:

```
>>> marxes[-1]
'Harpo'
>>> marxes[-2]
'Chico'
>>> marxes[-3]
'Groucho'
>>>
```

 The offset has to be a valid one for this list—a position you have assigned a value previously. If you specify an offset before the beginning or after the end, you'll get an exception (error). Here's what happens if we try to get the sixth Marx brother (offset 5 counting from 0), or the fifth before the end:

```
>>> marxes = ['Groucho', 'Chico', 'Harpo']
>>> marxes[5]
Traceback (most recent call last):
  File "<stdin>", line 1, in <module>
IndexError: list index out of range
>>> marxes[-5]
Traceback (most recent call last):
  File "<stdin>", line 1, in <module>
IndexError: list index out of range
```

Get Items with a Slice

You can extract a subsequence of a list by using a *slice*:

```
>>> marxes = ['Groucho', 'Chico', 'Harpo']
>>> marxes[0:2]
['Groucho', 'Chico']
```

A slice of a list is also a list.

As with strings, slices can step by values other than one. The next example starts at the beginning and goes right by 2:

```
>>> marxes[::2]
['Groucho', 'Harpo']
```

Here, we start at the end and go left by 2:

```
>>> marxes[::-2]
['Harpo', 'Groucho']
```

And finally, the trick to reverse a list:

```
>>> marxes[::-1]
['Harpo', 'Chico', 'Groucho']
```

None of these slices changed the marxes list itself, because we didn't assign them to marxes. To reverse a list in place, use *list*.reverse():

```
>>> marxes = ['Groucho', 'Chico', 'Harpo']
>>> marxes.reverse()
>>> marxes
['Harpo', 'Chico', 'Groucho']
```

 The reverse() function changes the list but doesn't return its value.

As you saw with strings, a slice can specify an invalid index, but will not cause an exception. It will "snap" to the closest valid index or return nothing:

```
>>> marxes = ['Groucho', 'Chico', 'Harpo']
>>> marxes[4:]
[]
>>> marxes[-6:]
['Groucho', 'Chico', 'Harpo']
>>> marxes[-6:-2]
['Groucho']
>>> marxes[-6:-4]
[]
```

Add an Item to the End with append()

The traditional way of adding items to a list is to append() them one by one to the end. In the previous examples, we forgot Zeppo, but that's alright because the list is mutable, so we can add him now:

```
>>> marxes = ['Groucho', 'Chico', 'Harpo']
>>> marxes.append('Zeppo')
>>> marxes
['Groucho', 'Chico', 'Harpo', 'Zeppo']
```

Add an Item by Offset with insert()

The append() function adds items only to the end of the list. When you want to add an item before any offset in the list, use insert(). Offset 0 inserts at the beginning. An offset beyond the end of the list inserts at the end, like append(), so you don't need to worry about Python throwing an exception:

```
>>> marxes = ['Groucho', 'Chico', 'Harpo']
>>> marxes.insert(2, 'Gummo')
>>> marxes
['Groucho', 'Chico', 'Gummo', 'Harpo']
>>> marxes.insert(10, 'Zeppo')
```

```
>>> marxes
['Groucho', 'Chico', 'Gummo', 'Harpo', 'Zeppo']
```

Duplicate All Items with *

In Chapter 5, you saw that you can duplicate a string's characters with *. The same
works for a list:

```
>>> ["blah"] * 3
['blah', 'blah', 'blah']
```

Combine Lists by Using extend() or +

You can merge one list into another by using extend(). Suppose that a well-meaning
person gave us a new list of Marxes called others, and we'd like to merge them into
the main marxes list:

```
>>> marxes = ['Groucho', 'Chico', 'Harpo', 'Zeppo']
>>> others = ['Gummo', 'Karl']
>>> marxes.extend(others)
>>> marxes
['Groucho', 'Chico', 'Harpo', 'Zeppo', 'Gummo', 'Karl']
```

Alternatively, you can use + or +=:

```
>>> marxes = ['Groucho', 'Chico', 'Harpo', 'Zeppo']
>>> others = ['Gummo', 'Karl']
>>> marxes += others
>>> marxes
['Groucho', 'Chico', 'Harpo', 'Zeppo', 'Gummo', 'Karl']
```

If we had used append(), others would have been added as a *single* list item rather
than merging its items:

```
>>> marxes = ['Groucho', 'Chico', 'Harpo', 'Zeppo']
>>> others = ['Gummo', 'Karl']
>>> marxes.append(others)
>>> marxes
['Groucho', 'Chico', 'Harpo', 'Zeppo', ['Gummo', 'Karl']]
```

This again demonstrates that a list can contain elements of different types. In this
case, four strings, and a list of two strings.

Change an Item by [*offset*]

Just as you can get the value of a list item by its offset, you can change it:

```
>>> marxes = ['Groucho', 'Chico', 'Harpo']
>>> marxes[2] = 'Wanda'
>>> marxes
['Groucho', 'Chico', 'Wanda']
```

Again, the list offset needs to be a valid one for this list.

You can't change a character in a string in this way, because strings are immutable. Lists are mutable. You can change how many items a list contains as well as the items themselves.

Change Items with a Slice

The previous section showed how to get a sublist with a slice. You can also assign values to a sublist with a slice:

```
>>> numbers = [1, 2, 3, 4]
>>> numbers[1:3] = [8, 9]
>>> numbers
[1, 8, 9, 4]
```

The righthand thing that you're assigning to the list doesn't even need to have the same number of elements as the slice on the left:

```
>>> numbers = [1, 2, 3, 4]
>>> numbers[1:3] = [7, 8, 9]
>>> numbers
[1, 7, 8, 9, 4]
>>> numbers = [1, 2, 3, 4]
>>> numbers[1:3] = []
>>> numbers
[1, 4]
```

Actually, the righthand thing doesn't even need to be a list. Any Python *iterable* will do, separating its items and assigning them to list elements:

```
>>> numbers = [1, 2, 3, 4]
>>> numbers[1:3] = (98, 99, 100)
>>> numbers
[1, 98, 99, 100, 4]
>>> numbers = [1, 2, 3, 4]
>>> numbers[1:3] = 'wat?'
>>> numbers
[1, 'w', 'a', 't', '?', 4]
```

Delete an Item by Offset with del

Our fact checkers have just informed us that Gummo was indeed one of the Marx Brothers, but Karl wasn't, and that whoever inserted him earlier was very rude. Let's fix that:

```
>>> marxes = ['Groucho', 'Chico', 'Harpo', 'Gummo', 'Karl']
>>> marxes[-1]
'Karl'
>>> del marxes[-1]
```

```
>>> marxes
['Groucho', 'Chico', 'Harpo', 'Gummo']
```

When you delete an item by its position in the list, the items that follow it move back to take the deleted item's space, and the list's length decreases by one. If we deleted 'Chico' from the last version of the marxes list, we get this as a result:

```
>>> marxes = ['Groucho', 'Chico', 'Harpo', 'Gummo']
>>> del marxes[1]
>>> marxes
['Groucho', 'Harpo', 'Gummo']
```

 del is a Python *statement*, not a list method—you don't say marxes[-1].del(). It's sort of the reverse of assignment (=): it detaches a name from a Python object and can free up the object's memory if that name were the last reference to it.

Delete an Item by Value with remove()

If you're not sure or don't care where the item is in the list, use remove() to delete it by value. Goodbye, Groucho:

```
>>> marxes = ['Groucho', 'Chico', 'Harpo']
>>> marxes.remove('Groucho')
>>> marxes
['Chico', 'Harpo']
```

If you had duplicate list items with the same value, remove() deletes only the first one it finds.

Get an Item by Offset and Delete It with pop()

You can get an item from a list and delete it from the list at the same time by using pop(). If you call pop() with an offset, it will return the item at that offset; with no argument, it uses -1. So, pop(0) returns the head (start) of the list, and pop() or pop(-1) returns the tail (end), as shown here:

```
>>> marxes = ['Groucho', 'Chico', 'Harpo', 'Zeppo']
>>> marxes.pop()
'Zeppo'
>>> marxes
['Groucho', 'Chico', 'Harpo']
>>> marxes.pop(1)
'Chico'
>>> marxes
['Groucho', 'Harpo']
```

It's computing jargon time! Don't worry, these won't be on the final exam. If you use append() to add new items to the end and pop() to remove them from the same end, you've implemented a data structure known as a *LIFO* (last in, first out) queue. This is more commonly known as a *stack*. pop(0) would create a *FIFO* (first in, first out) queue. These are useful when you want to collect data as they arrive and work with either the oldest first (FIFO) or the newest first (LIFO).

Delete All Items with clear()

Python 3.3 introduced a method to clear a list of all its elements:

```
>>> work_quotes = ['Working hard?', 'Quick question!', 'Number one priorities!']
>>> work_quotes
['Working hard?', 'Quick question!', 'Number one priorities!']
>>> work_quotes.clear()
>>> work_quotes
[]
```

Find an Item's Offset by Value with index()

If you want to know the offset of an item in a list by its value, use index():

```
>>> marxes = ['Groucho', 'Chico', 'Harpo', 'Zeppo']
>>> marxes.index('Chico')
1
```

If the value is in the list more than once, only the offset of the first one is returned:

```
>>> simpsons = ['Lisa', 'Bart', 'Marge', 'Homer', 'Bart']
>>> simpsons.index('Bart')
1
```

Test for a Value with in

The Pythonic way to check for the existence of a value in a list is using in:

```
>>> marxes = ['Groucho', 'Chico', 'Harpo', 'Zeppo']
>>> 'Groucho' in marxes
True
>>> 'Bob' in marxes
False
```

The same value may be in more than one position in the list. As long as it's in there at least once, in will return True:

```
>>> words = ['a', 'deer', 'a' 'female', 'deer']
>>> 'deer' in words
True
```

If you check for the existence of some value in a list often and don't care about the order of items, a Python *set* is a more appropriate way to store and look up unique values. We talk about sets in Chapter 8.

Count Occurrences of a Value with count()

To count how many times a particular value occurs in a list, use count():

```
>>> marxes = ['Groucho', 'Chico', 'Harpo']
>>> marxes.count('Harpo')
1
>>> marxes.count('Bob')
0
>>> snl_skit = ['cheeseburger', 'cheeseburger', 'cheeseburger']
>>> snl_skit.count('cheeseburger')
3
```

Convert a List to a String with join()

"Combine by Using join()" on page 73 discussed join() in greater detail, but here's another example of what you can do with it:

```
>>> marxes = ['Groucho', 'Chico', 'Harpo']
>>> ', '.join(marxes)
'Groucho, Chico, Harpo'
```

You might be thinking that this seems a little backward. join() is a string method, not a list method. You can't say marxes.join(', '), even though it seems more intuitive. The argument to join() is a string or any iterable sequence of strings (including a list), and its output is a string. If join() were just a list method, you couldn't use it with other iterable objects such as tuples or strings. If you did want it to work with any iterable type, you'd need special code for each type to handle the actual joining. It might help to remember—join() *is the opposite of* split(), as shown here:

```
>>> friends = ['Harry', 'Hermione', 'Ron']
>>> separator = ' * '
>>> joined = separator.join(friends)
>>> joined
'Harry * Hermione * Ron'
>>> separated = joined.split(separator)
>>> separated
['Harry', 'Hermione', 'Ron']
>>> separated == friends
True
```

Reorder Items with sort() or sorted()

You'll often need to sort the items in a list by their values rather than their offsets. Python provides two functions:

- The list method sort() sorts the list itself, *in place*.
- The general function sorted() returns a sorted *copy* of the list.

If the items in the list are numeric, they're sorted by default in ascending numeric order. If they're strings, they're sorted in alphabetical order:

```
>>> marxes = ['Groucho', 'Chico', 'Harpo']
>>> sorted_marxes = sorted(marxes)
>>> sorted_marxes
['Chico', 'Groucho', 'Harpo']
```

sorted_marxes is a new list, and creating it did not change the original list:

```
>>> marxes
['Groucho', 'Chico', 'Harpo']
```

But calling the list function sort() on the marxes list does change marxes:

```
>>> marxes.sort()
>>> marxes
['Chico', 'Groucho', 'Harpo']
```

If the elements of your list are all of the same type (such as strings in marxes), sort() will work correctly. You can sometimes even mix types—for example, integers and floats—because they are automatically converted to one another by Python in expressions:

```
>>> numbers = [2, 1, 4.0, 3]
>>> numbers.sort()
>>> numbers
[1, 2, 3, 4.0]
```

The default sort order is ascending, but you can add the argument reverse=True to set it to descending:

```
>>> numbers = [2, 1, 4.0, 3]
>>> numbers.sort(reverse=True)
>>> numbers
[4.0, 3, 2, 1]
```

Get Length with len()

len() returns the number of items in a list:

```
>>> marxes = ['Groucho', 'Chico', 'Harpo']
>>> len(marxes)
3
```

Assign with =

When you assign one list to more than one variable, changing the list in one place also changes it in the other, as illustrated here:

```
>>> a = [1, 2, 3]
>>> a
[1, 2, 3]
>>> b = a
>>> b
[1, 2, 3]
>>> a[0] = 'surprise'
>>> a
['surprise', 2, 3]
```

So what's in b now? Is it still [1, 2, 3], or ['surprise', 2, 3]? Let's see:

```
>>> b
['surprise', 2, 3]
```

Remember the box (object) and string with note (variable name) analogy in Chapter 2? b just refers to the same list object as a (both name strings lead to the same object box). Whether we change the list contents by using the name a or b, it's reflected in both:

```
>>> b
['surprise', 2, 3]
>>> b[0] = 'I hate surprises'
>>> b
['I hate surprises', 2, 3]
>>> a
['I hate surprises', 2, 3]
```

Copy with copy(), list(), or a Slice

You can *copy* the values of a list to an independent, fresh list by using any of these methods:

- The list copy() method
- The list() conversion function
- The list slice [:]

Our original list will be a again. We make b with the list copy() function, c with the list() conversion function, and d with a list slice:

```
>>> a = [1, 2, 3]
>>> b = a.copy()
>>> c = list(a)
>>> d = a[:]
```

Again, b, c, and d are *copies* of a: they are new objects with their own values and no connection to the original list object [1, 2, 3] to which a refers. Changing a does *not* affect the copies b, c, and d:

```
>>> a[0] = 'integer lists are boring'
>>> a
['integer lists are boring', 2, 3]
>>> b
[1, 2, 3]
>>> c
[1, 2, 3]
>>> d
[1, 2, 3]
```

Copy Everything with deepcopy()

The copy() function works well if the list values are all immutable. As you've seen before, mutable values (like lists, tuples, or dicts) are references. A change in the original or the copy would be reflected in both.

Let's use the previous example but make the last element in list a the list [8, 9] instead of the integer 3:

```
>>> a = [1, 2, [8, 9]]
>>> b = a.copy()
>>> c = list(a)
>>> d = a[:]
>>> a
[1, 2, [8, 9]]
>>> b
[1, 2, [8, 9]]
>>> c
[1, 2, [8, 9]]
>>> d
[1, 2, [8, 9]]
```

So far, so good. Now change an element in that sublist in a:

```
>>> a[2][1] = 10
>>> a
[1, 2, [8, 10]]
>>> b
[1, 2, [8, 10]]
>>> c
[1, 2, [8, 10]]
```

```
>>> d
[1, 2, [8, 10]]
```

The value of a[2] is now a list, and its elements can be changed. All the list-copying methods we used were *shallow* (not a value judgment, just a depth one).

To fix this, we need to use the deepcopy() function:

```
>>> import copy
>>> a = [1, 2, [8, 9]]
>>> b = copy.deepcopy(a)
>>> a
[1, 2, [8, 9]]
>>> b
[1, 2, [8, 9]]
>>> a[2][1] = 10
>>> a
[1, 2, [8, 10]]
>>> b
[1, 2, [8, 9]]
```

deepcopy() can handle deeply nested lists, dictionaries, and other objects.

You'll read more about import in Chapter 9.

Compare Lists

You can directly compare lists with the comparison operators like ==, <, and so on. The operators walk through both lists, comparing elements at the same offsets. If list a is shorter than list b, and all of its elements are equal, a is less than b:

```
>>> a = [7, 2]
>>> b = [7, 2, 9]
>>> a == b
False
>>> a <= b
True
>>> a < b
True
```

Iterate with for and in

In Chapter 6, you saw how to iterate over a string with for, but it's much more common to iterate over lists:

```
>>> cheeses = ['brie', 'gjetost', 'havarti']
>>> for cheese in cheeses:
...     print(cheese)
...
brie
```

```
gjetost
havarti
```

As before, break ends the for loop and continue steps to the next iteration:

```
>>> cheeses = ['brie', 'gjetost', 'havarti']
>>> for cheese in cheeses:
...     if cheese.startswith('g'):
...         print("I won't eat anything that starts with 'g'")
...         break
...     else:
...         print(cheese)
...
brie
I won't eat anything that starts with 'g'
```

You can still use the optional else if the for completed without a break:

```
>>> cheeses = ['brie', 'gjetost', 'havarti']
>>> for cheese in cheeses:
...     if cheese.startswith('x'):
...         print("I won't eat anything that starts with 'x'")
...         break
...     else:
...         print(cheese)
... else:
...     print("Didn't find anything that started with 'x'")
...
brie
gjetost
havarti
Didn't find anything that started with 'x'
```

If the initial for never ran, control goes to the else also:

```
>>> cheeses = []
>>> for cheese in cheeses:
...     print('This shop has some lovely', cheese)
...     break
... else:  # no break means no cheese
...     print('This is not much of a cheese shop, is it?')
...
This is not much of a cheese shop, is it?
```

Because the cheeses list was empty in this example, for cheese in cheeses never completed a single loop and its break statement was never executed.

Iterate Multiple Sequences with zip()

There's one more nice iteration trick: iterating over multiple sequences in parallel by using the zip() function:

```
>>> days = ['Monday', 'Tuesday', 'Wednesday']
>>> fruits = ['banana', 'orange', 'peach']
>>> drinks = ['coffee', 'tea', 'beer']
>>> desserts = ['tiramisu', 'ice cream', 'pie', 'pudding']
>>> for day, fruit, drink, dessert in zip(days, fruits, drinks, desserts):
...     print(day, ": drink", drink, "- eat", fruit, "- enjoy", dessert)
...
Monday : drink coffee - eat banana - enjoy tiramisu
Tuesday : drink tea - eat orange - enjoy ice cream
Wednesday : drink beer - eat peach - enjoy pie
```

zip() stops when the shortest sequence is done. One of the lists (desserts) was longer than the others, so no one gets any pudding unless we extend the other lists.

Chapter 8 shows you how the dict() function can create dictionaries from two-item sequences like tuples, lists, or strings. You can use zip() to walk through multiple sequences and make tuples from items at the same offsets. Let's make two tuples of corresponding English and French words:

```
>>> english = 'Monday', 'Tuesday', 'Wednesday'
>>> french = 'Lundi', 'Mardi', 'Mercredi'
```

Now, use zip() to pair these tuples. The value returned by zip() is itself not a tuple or list, but an iterable value that can be turned into one:

```
>>> list( zip(english, french) )
[('Monday', 'Lundi'), ('Tuesday', 'Mardi'), ('Wednesday', 'Mercredi')]
```

Feed the result of zip() directly to dict() and voilà: a tiny English-French dictionary!

```
>>> dict( zip(english, french) )
{'Monday': 'Lundi', 'Tuesday': 'Mardi', 'Wednesday': 'Mercredi'}
```

Create a List with a Comprehension

You saw how to create a list with square brackets or the list() function. Here, we look at how to create a list with a *list comprehension*, which incorporates the for/in iteration that you just saw.

You could build a list of integers from 1 to 5, one item at a time, like this:

```
>>> number_list = []
>>> number_list.append(1)
>>> number_list.append(2)
>>> number_list.append(3)
>>> number_list.append(4)
>>> number_list.append(5)
>>> number_list
[1, 2, 3, 4, 5]
```

Or, you could also use an iterator and the `range()` function:

```
>>> number_list = []
>>> for number in range(1, 6):
...     number_list.append(number)
...
>>> number_list
[1, 2, 3, 4, 5]
```

Or, you could just turn the output of `range()` into a list directly:

```
>>> number_list = list(range(1, 6))
>>> number_list
[1, 2, 3, 4, 5]
```

All of these approaches are valid Python code and will produce the same result. However, a more Pythonic (and often faster) way to build a list is by using a *list comprehension*. The simplest form of list comprehension looks like this:

```
[expression for item in iterable]
```

Here's how a list comprehension would build the integer list:

```
>>> number_list = [number for number in range(1,6)]
>>> number_list
[1, 2, 3, 4, 5]
```

In the first line, you need the first `number` variable to produce values for the list: that is, to put a result of the loop into `number_list`. The second `number` is part of the `for` loop. To show that the first `number` is an expression, try this variant:

```
>>> number_list = [number-1 for number in range(1,6)]
>>> number_list
[0, 1, 2, 3, 4]
```

The list comprehension moves the loop inside the square brackets. This comprehension example really wasn't simpler than the previous example, but there's more that you can do. A list comprehension can include a conditional expression, looking something like this:

```
[expression for item
in iterable if condition]
```

Let's make a new comprehension that builds a list of only the odd numbers between 1 and 5 (remember that `number % 2` is `True` for odd numbers and `False` for even numbers):

```
>>> a_list = [number for number in range(1,6) if number % 2 == 1]
>>> a_list
[1, 3, 5]
```

Now, the comprehension is a little more compact than its traditional counterpart:

```
>>> a_list = []
>>> for number in range(1,6):
...     if number % 2 == 1:
...         a_list.append(number)
...
>>>  a_list
[1, 3, 5]
```

Finally, just as there can be nested loops, there can be more than one set of for ... clauses in the corresponding comprehension. To show this, let's first try a plain old nested loop and print the results:

```
>>> rows = range(1,4)
>>> cols = range(1,3)
>>> for row in rows:
...     for col in cols:
...         print(row, col)
...
1 1
1 2
2 1
2 2
3 1
3 2
```

Now, let's use a comprehension and assign it to the variable cells, making it a list of (row, col) tuples:

```
>>> rows = range(1,4)
>>> cols = range(1,3)
>>> cells = [(row, col) for row in rows for col in cols]
>>> for cell in cells:
...     print(cell)
...
(1, 1)
(1, 2)
(2, 1)
(2, 2)
(3, 1)
(3, 2)
```

By the way, you can also use *tuple unpacking* to get the row and col values from each tuple as you iterate over the cells list:

```
>>> for row, col in cells:
...     print(row, col)
...
1 1
1 2
2 1
2 2
```

```
3 1
3 2
```

The for row ... and for col ... fragments in the list comprehension could also have had their own if tests.

Lists of Lists

Lists can contain elements of different types, including other lists, as illustrated here:

```
>>> small_birds = ['hummingbird', 'finch']
>>> extinct_birds = ['dodo', 'passenger pigeon', 'Norwegian Blue']
>>> carol_birds = [3, 'French hens', 2, 'turtledoves']
>>> all_birds = [small_birds, extinct_birds, 'macaw', carol_birds]
```

So what does all_birds, a list of lists, look like?

```
>>> all_birds
[['hummingbird', 'finch'], ['dodo', 'passenger pigeon', 'Norwegian Blue'], 'macaw',
[3, 'French hens', 2, 'turtledoves']]
```

Let's look at the first item in it:

```
>>> all_birds[0]
['hummingbird', 'finch']
```

The first item is a list: in fact, it's small_birds, the first item we specified when creating all_birds. You should be able to guess what the second item is:

```
>>> all_birds[1]
['dodo', 'passenger pigeon', 'Norwegian Blue']
```

It's the second item we specified, extinct_birds. If we want the first item of extinct_birds, we can extract it from all_birds by specifying two indexes:

```
>>> all_birds[1][0]
'dodo'
```

The [1] refers to the list that's the second item in all_birds, and the [0] refers to the first item in that inner list.

Tuples Versus Lists

You can often use tuples in place of lists, but they have many fewer functions—there is no append(), insert(), and so on—because they can't be modified after creation. Why not just use lists instead of tuples everywhere?

- Tuples use less space.
- You can't clobber tuple items by mistake.
- You can use tuples as dictionary keys (see Chapter 8).

- *Named tuples* (see "Named Tuples" on page 195) can be a simple alternative to objects.

I won't go into much more detail about tuples here. In everyday programming, you'll use lists and dictionaries more.

There Are No Tuple Comprehensions

Mutable types (lists, dictionaries, and sets) have comprehensions. Immutable types like strings and tuples need to be created with the other methods listed in their sections.

You might have thought that changing the square brackets of a list comprehension to parentheses would create a tuple comprehension. And it would appear to work because there's no exception if you type this:

```
>>> number_thing = (number for number in range(1, 6))
```

The thing between the parentheses is something else entirely: a *generator comprehension*, and it returns a *generator object*:

```
>>> type(number_thing)
<class 'generator'>
```

I'll get into generators in more detail in "Generators" on page 157. A generator is one way to provide data to an iterator.

Coming Up

They're so swell, they get their own chapter: *dictionaries* and *sets*.

Things to Do

Use lists and tuples with numbers (Chapter 3) and strings (Chapter 5) to represent elements in the real world with great variety.

7.1 Create a list called years_list, starting with the year of your birth, and each year thereafter until the year of your fifth birthday. For example, if you were born in 1980, the list would be years_list = [1980, 1981, 1982, 1983, 1984, 1985]. If you're less than five years old and reading this book, I don't know what to tell you.

7.2 In which year in years_list was your third birthday? Remember, you were 0 years of age for your first year.

7.3 In which year in years_list were you the oldest?

7.4 Make a list called `things` with these three strings as elements: `"mozzarella"`, `"cinderella"`, `"salmonella"`.

7.5 Capitalize the element in `things` that refers to a person and then print the list. Did it change the element in the list?

7.6 Make the cheesy element of `things` all uppercase and then print the list.

7.7 Delete the disease element from `things`, collect your Nobel Prize, and print the list.

7.8 Create a list called `surprise` with the elements `"Groucho"`, `"Chico"`, and `"Harpo"`.

7.9 Lowercase the last element of the `surprise` list, reverse it, and then capitalize it.

7.10 Use a list comprehension to make a list called `even` of the even numbers in `range(10)`.

7.11 Let's create a jump rope rhyme maker. You'll print a series of two-line rhymes. Start with this program fragment:

```
start1 = ["fee", "fie", "foe"]
rhymes = [
    ("flop", "get a mop"),
    ("fope", "turn the rope"),
    ("fa", "get your ma"),
    ("fudge", "call the judge"),
    ("fat", "pet the cat"),
    ("fog", "walk the dog"),
    ("fun", "say we're done"),
    ]
start2 = "Someone better"
```

For each tuple (`first`, `second`) in `rhymes`:

For the first line:

- Print each string in `start1`, capitalized and followed by an exclamation point and a space.
- Print `first`, also capitalized and followed by an exclamation point.

For the second line:

- Print `start2` and a space.
- Print `second` and a period.

Dictionaries and Sets

If a word in the dictionary were misspelled, how would we know?

—Steven Wright

Dictionaries

A *dictionary* is similar to a list, but the order of items doesn't matter, and they aren't selected by an offset such as 0 or 1. Instead, you specify a unique *key* to associate with each *value*. This key is often a string, but it can actually be any of Python's immutable types: boolean, integer, float, tuple, string, and others that you'll see in later chapters. Dictionaries are mutable, so you can add, delete, and change their key-value elements. If you've worked with languages that support only arrays or lists, you'll love dictionaries.

 In other languages, dictionaries might be called *associative arrays*, *hashes*, or *hashmaps*. In Python, a dictionary is also called a *dict* to save syllables and make teenage boys snicker.

Create with {}

To create a dictionary, you place curly brackets ({}) around comma-separated *key* : *value* pairs. The simplest dictionary is an empty one, containing no keys or values at all:

```
>>> empty_dict = {}
>>> empty_dict
{}
```

Let's make a small dictionary with quotes from Ambrose Bierce's *The Devil's Dictionary*:

```
>>> bierce = {
...     "day": "A period of twenty-four hours, mostly misspent",
...     "positive": "Mistaken at the top of one's voice",
...     "misfortune": "The kind of fortune that never misses",
...     }
>>>
```

Typing the dictionary's name in the interactive interpreter will print its keys and values:

```
>>> bierce
{'day': 'A period of twenty-four hours, mostly misspent',
 'positive': "Mistaken at the top of one's voice",
 'misfortune': 'The kind of fortune that never misses'}
```

 In Python, it's okay to leave a comma after the last item of a list, tuple, or dictionary. Also, you don't need to indent, as I did in the preceding example, when you're typing keys and values within the curly braces. It just helps readability.

Create with dict()

Some people don't like typing so many curly brackets and quotes. You can also create a dictionary by passing named arguments and values to the dict() function.

The traditional way:

```
>>> acme_customer = {'first': 'Wile', 'middle': 'E', 'last': 'Coyote'}
>>> acme_customer
{'first': 'Wile', 'middle': 'E', 'last': 'Coyote'}
```

Using dict():

```
>>> acme_customer = dict(first="Wile", middle="E", last="Coyote")
>>> acme_customer
{'first': 'Wile', 'middle': 'E', 'last': 'Coyote'}
```

One limitation of the second way is that the argument names need to be legal variable names (no spaces, no reserved words):

```
>>> x = dict(name="Elmer", def="hunter")
  File "<stdin>", line 1
    x = dict(name="Elmer", def="hunter")
                             ^
SyntaxError: invalid syntax
```

Convert with dict()

You can also use the dict() function to convert two-value sequences into a dictionary. You might run into such key-value sequences at times, such as "Strontium, 90, Carbon, 14."[1] The first item in each sequence is used as the key and the second as the value.

First, here's a small example using lol (a list of two-item lists):

```
>>> lol = [ ['a', 'b'], ['c', 'd'], ['e', 'f'] ]
>>> dict(lol)
{'a': 'b', 'c': 'd', 'e': 'f'}
```

We could have used any sequence containing two-item sequences. Here are other examples.

A list of two-item tuples:

```
>>> lot = [ ('a', 'b'), ('c', 'd'), ('e', 'f') ]
>>> dict(lot)
{'a': 'b', 'c': 'd', 'e': 'f'}
```

A tuple of two-item lists:

```
>>> tol = ( ['a', 'b'], ['c', 'd'], ['e', 'f'] )
>>> dict(tol)
{'a': 'b', 'c': 'd', 'e': 'f'}
```

A list of two-character strings:

```
>>> los = [ 'ab', 'cd', 'ef' ]
>>> dict(los)
{'a': 'b', 'c': 'd', 'e': 'f'}
```

A tuple of two-character strings:

```
>>> tos = ( 'ab', 'cd', 'ef' )
>>> dict(tos)
{'a': 'b', 'c': 'd', 'e': 'f'}
```

The section "Iterate Multiple Sequences with zip()" on page 110 introduces you to the zip() function, which makes it easy to create these two-item sequences.

Add or Change an Item by [key]

Adding an item to a dictionary is easy. Just refer to the item by its key and assign a value. If the key was already present in the dictionary, the existing value is replaced by the new one. If the key is new, it's added to the dictionary with its value. Unlike lists,

---

1 Also, the final score in the Strontium-Carbon game.

you don't need to worry about Python throwing an exception during assignment by specifying an index that's out of range.

Let's make a dictionary of most of the members of Monty Python, using their last names as keys, and first names as values:

```
>>> pythons = {
...     'Chapman': 'Graham',
...     'Cleese': 'John',
...     'Idle': 'Eric',
...     'Jones': 'Terry',
...     'Palin': 'Michael',
...     }
>>> pythons
{'Chapman': 'Graham', 'Cleese': 'John', 'Idle': 'Eric',
'Jones': 'Terry', 'Palin': 'Michael'}
```

We're missing one member: the one born in America, Terry Gilliam. Here's an attempt by an anonymous programmer to add him, but he's botched the first name:

```
>>> pythons['Gilliam'] = 'Gerry'
>>> pythons
{'Chapman': 'Graham', 'Cleese': 'John', 'Idle': 'Eric',
'Jones': 'Terry', 'Palin': 'Michael', 'Gilliam': 'Gerry'}
```

And here's some repair code by another programmer who is Pythonic in more than one way:

```
>>> pythons['Gilliam'] = 'Terry'
>>> pythons
{'Chapman': 'Graham', 'Cleese': 'John', 'Idle': 'Eric',
'Jones': 'Terry', 'Palin': 'Michael', 'Gilliam': 'Terry'}
```

By using the same key ('Gilliam'), we replaced the original value 'Gerry' with 'Terry'.

Remember that dictionary keys must be *unique*. That's why we used last names for keys instead of first names here—two members of Monty Python have the first name 'Terry'! If you use a key more than once, the last value wins:

```
>>> some_pythons = {
...     'Graham': 'Chapman',
...     'John': 'Cleese',
...     'Eric': 'Idle',
...     'Terry': 'Gilliam',
...     'Michael': 'Palin',
...     'Terry': 'Jones',
...     }
>>> some_pythons
{'Graham': 'Chapman', 'John': 'Cleese', 'Eric': 'Idle',
'Terry': 'Jones', 'Michael': 'Palin'}
```

We first assigned the value 'Gilliam' to the key 'Terry' and then replaced it with the value 'Jones'.

Get an Item by [key] or with get()

This is the most common use of a dictionary. You specify the dictionary and key to get the corresponding value: Using some_pythons from the previous section:

```
>>> some_pythons['John']
'Cleese'
```

If the key is not present in the dictionary, you'll get an exception:

```
>>> some_pythons['Groucho']
Traceback (most recent call last):
  File "<stdin>", line 1, in <module>
KeyError: 'Groucho'
```

There are two good ways to avoid this. The first is to test for the key at the outset by using in, as you saw in the previous section:

```
>>> 'Groucho' in some_pythons
False
```

The second is to use the special dictionary get() function. You provide the dictionary, key, and an optional value. If the key exists, you get its value:

```
>>> some_pythons.get('John')
'Cleese'
```

If not, you get the optional value, if you specified one:

```
>>> some_pythons.get('Groucho', 'Not a Python')
'Not a Python'
```

Otherwise, you get None (which displays nothing in the interactive interpreter):

```
>>> some_pythons.get('Groucho')
>>>
```

Get All Keys with keys()

You can use keys() to get all of the keys in a dictionary. We'll use a different sample dictionary for the next few examples:

```
>>> signals = {'green': 'go', 'yellow': 'go faster', 'red': 'smile for the camera'}
>>> signals.keys()
dict_keys(['green', 'yellow', 'red'])
```

In Python 2, keys() just returns a list. Python 3 returns dict_keys(), which is an iterable view of the keys. This is handy with large dictionaries because it doesn't use the time and memory to create and store a list that you might not use. But often you actually *do* want a list. In Python 3, you need to call list() to convert a dict_keys object to a list.

```
>>> list( signals.keys() )
['green', 'yellow', 'red']
```

In Python 3, you also need to use the list() function to turn the results of values() and items() into normal Python lists. I use that in these examples.

Get All Values with values()

To obtain all the values in a dictionary, use values():

```
>>> list( signals.values() )
['go', 'go faster', 'smile for the camera']
```

Get All Key-Value Pairs with items()

When you want to get all the key-value pairs from a dictionary, use the items() function:

```
>>> list( signals.items() )
[('green', 'go'), ('yellow', 'go faster'), ('red', 'smile for the camera')]
```

Each key and value is returned as a tuple, such as ('green', 'go').

Get Length with len()

Count your key-value pairs:

```
>>> len(signals)
3
```

Combine Dictionaries with {**a, **b}

Starting with Python 3.5, there's a new way to merge dictionaries, using the ** unicorn glitter, which has a very different use in Chapter 9:

```
>>> first = {'a': 'agony', 'b': 'bliss'}
>>> second = {'b': 'bagels', 'c': 'candy'}
>>> {**first, **second}
{'a': 'agony', 'b': 'bagels', 'c': 'candy'}
```

Actually, you can pass more than two dictionaries:

```
>>> third = {'d': 'donuts'}
>>> {**first, **third, **second}
{'a': 'agony', 'b': 'bagels', 'd': 'donuts', 'c': 'candy'}
```

These are *shallow* copies. See the discussion of deepcopy() ("Copy Everything with deepcopy()" on page 126) if you want full copies of the keys and values, with no connection to their origin dictionaries.

Combine Dictionaries with update()

You can use the update() function to copy the keys and values of one dictionary into another.

Let's define the pythons dictionary, with all members:

```
>>> pythons = {
...     'Chapman': 'Graham',
...     'Cleese': 'John',
...     'Gilliam': 'Terry',
...     'Idle': 'Eric',
...     'Jones': 'Terry',
...     'Palin': 'Michael',
...     }
>>> pythons
{'Chapman': 'Graham', 'Cleese': 'John', 'Gilliam': 'Terry',
'Idle': 'Eric', 'Jones': 'Terry', 'Palin': 'Michael'}
```

We also have a dictionary of other humorous persons called others:

```
>>> others = { 'Marx': 'Groucho', 'Howard': 'Moe' }
```

Now, along comes another anonymous programmer who decides that the members of others should be members of Monty Python:

```
>>> pythons.update(others)
>>> pythons
{'Chapman': 'Graham', 'Cleese': 'John', 'Gilliam': 'Terry',
'Idle': 'Eric', 'Jones': 'Terry', 'Palin': 'Michael',
'Marx': 'Groucho', 'Howard': 'Moe'}
```

What happens if the second dictionary has the same key as the dictionary into which it's being merged? The value from the second dictionary wins:

```
>>> first = {'a': 1, 'b': 2}
>>> second = {'b': 'platypus'}
>>> first.update(second)
>>> first
{'a': 1, 'b': 'platypus'}
```

Delete an Item by Key with del

The previous `pythons.update(others)` code from our anonymous programmer was technically correct, but factually wrong. The members of `others`, although funny and famous, were not in Monty Python. Let's undo those last two additions:

```
>>> del pythons['Marx']
>>> pythons
{'Chapman': 'Graham', 'Cleese': 'John', 'Gilliam': 'Terry',
 'Idle': 'Eric', 'Jones': 'Terry', 'Palin': 'Michael',
 'Howard': 'Moe'}
>>> del pythons['Howard']
>>> pythons
{'Chapman': 'Graham', 'Cleese': 'John', 'Gilliam': 'Terry',
 'Idle': 'Eric', 'Jones': 'Terry', 'Palin': 'Michael'}
```

Get an Item by Key and Delete It with pop()

This combines `get()` and `del`. If you give `pop()` a key and it exists in the dictionary, it returns the matching value and deletes the key-value pair. If it doesn't exist, it raises an exception:

```
>>> len(pythons)
6
>>> pythons.pop('Palin')
'Michael'
>>> len(pythons)
5
>>> pythons.pop('Palin')
Traceback (most recent call last):
  File "<stdin>", line 1, in <module>
KeyError: 'Palin'
```

But if you give `pop()` a second default argument (as with `get()`), all is well and the dictionary is not changed:

```
>>> pythons.pop('First', 'Hugo')
'Hugo'
>>> len(pythons)
5
```

Delete All Items with clear()

To delete all keys and values from a dictionary, use `clear()` or just reassign an empty dictionary (`{}`) to the name:

```
>>> pythons.clear()
>>> pythons
{}
>>> pythons = {}
```

```
>>> pythons
{}
```

Test for a Key with in

If you want to know whether a key exists in a dictionary, use in. Let's redefine the pythons dictionary again, this time omitting a name or two:

```
>>> pythons = {'Chapman': 'Graham', 'Cleese': 'John',
... 'Jones': 'Terry', 'Palin': 'Michael', 'Idle': 'Eric'}
```

Now let's see who's in there:

```
>>> 'Chapman' in pythons
True
>>> 'Palin' in pythons
True
```

Did we remember to add Terry Gilliam this time?

```
>>> 'Gilliam' in pythons
False
```

Drat.

Assign with =

As with lists, if you make a change to a dictionary, it will be reflected in all the names that refer to it:

```
>>> signals = {'green': 'go',
... 'yellow': 'go faster',
... 'red': 'smile for the camera'}
>>> save_signals = signals
>>> signals['blue'] = 'confuse everyone'
>>> save_signals
{'green': 'go',
'yellow': 'go faster',
'red': 'smile for the camera',
'blue': 'confuse everyone'}
```

Copy with copy()

To actually copy keys and values from a dictionary to another dictionary and avoid this, you can use copy():

```
>>> signals = {'green': 'go',
... 'yellow': 'go faster',
... 'red': 'smile for the camera'}
>>> original_signals = signals.copy()
>>> signals['blue'] = 'confuse everyone'
>>> signals
{'green': 'go',
```

```
'yellow': 'go faster',
'red': 'smile for the camera',
'blue': 'confuse everyone'}
>>> original_signals
{'green': 'go',
'yellow': 'go faster',
'red': 'smile for the camera'}
>>>
```

This is a *shallow* copy, and works if the dictionary values are immutable (as they are in this case). If they aren't, you need deepcopy().

Copy Everything with deepcopy()

Suppose that the value for red in the previous example was a list instead of a single string:

```
>>> signals = {'green': 'go',
... 'yellow': 'go faster',
... 'red': ['stop', 'smile']}
>>> signals_copy = signals.copy()
>>> signals
{'green': 'go',
'yellow': 'go faster',
'red': ['stop', 'smile']}
>>> signals_copy
{'green': 'go',
'yellow': 'go faster',
'red': ['stop', 'smile']}
>>>
```

Let's change one of the values in the red list:

```
>>> signals['red'][1] = 'sweat'
>>> signals
{'green': 'go',
'yellow': 'go faster',
'red': ['stop', 'sweat']}
>>> signals_copy
{'green': 'go',
'yellow': 'go faster',
'red': ['stop', 'sweat']}
```

You get the usual change-by-either-name behavior. The copy() method copied the values as-is, meaning signal_copy got the same list value for 'red' that signals had.

The solution is deepcopy():

```
>>> import copy
>>> signals = {'green': 'go',
... 'yellow': 'go faster',
... 'red': ['stop', 'smile']}
>>> signals_copy = copy.deepcopy(signals)
```

```
>>> signals
{'green': 'go',
 'yellow': 'go faster',
 'red': ['stop', 'smile']}
>>> signals_copy
{'green': 'go',
 'yellow':'go faster',
 'red': ['stop', 'smile']}
>>> signals['red'][1] = 'sweat'
>>> signals
{'green': 'go',
 'yellow': 'go faster',
 red': ['stop', 'sweat']}
>>> signals_copy
{'green': 'go',
 'yellow': 'go faster',
 red': ['stop', 'smile']}
```

Compare Dictionaries

Much like lists and tuples in the previous chapter, dictionaries can be compared with the simple comparison operators == and !=:

```
>>> a = {1:1, 2:2, 3:3}
>>> b = {3:3, 1:1, 2:2}
>>> a == b
True
```

Other operators won't work:

```
>>> a = {1:1, 2:2, 3:3}
>>> b = {3:3, 1:1, 2:2}
>>> a <= b
Traceback (most recent call last):
  File "<stdin>", line 1, in <module>
TypeError: '<=' not supported between instances of 'dict' and 'dict'
```

Python compares the keys and values one by one. The order in which they were originally created doesn't matter. In this example, a and b are equal, except key 1 has the list value [1, 2] in a and the list value [1, 1] in b:

```
>>> a = {1: [1, 2], 2: [1], 3:[1]}
>>> b = {1: [1, 1], 2: [1], 3:[1]}
>>> a == b
False
```

Iterate with for and in

Iterating over a dictionary (or its keys() function) returns the keys. In this example, the keys are the types of cards in the board game Clue (Cluedo outside of North America):

```
>>> accusation = {'room': 'ballroom', 'weapon': 'lead pipe',
...               'person': 'Col. Mustard'}
>>> for card in accusation:  # or, for card in accusation.keys():
...     print(card)
...
room
weapon
person
```

To iterate over the values rather than the keys, you use the dictionary's values()
function:

```
>>> for value in accusation.values():
...     print(value)
...
ballroom
lead pipe
Col. Mustard
```

To return both the key and value as a tuple, you can use the items() function:

```
>>> for item in accusation.items():
...     print(item)
...
('room', 'ballroom')
('weapon', 'lead pipe')
('person', 'Col. Mustard')
```

You can assign to a tuple in one step. For each tuple returned by items(), assign the
first value (the key) to card, and the second (the value) to contents:

```
>>> for card, contents in accusation.items():
...     print('Card', card, 'has the contents', contents)
...
Card weapon has the contents lead pipe
Card person has the contents Col. Mustard
Card room has the contents ballroom
```

Dictionary Comprehensions

Not to be outdone by those bourgeois lists, dictionaries also have comprehensions.
The simplest form looks familiar:

```
{key_expression : value_expression for expression in iterable}
>>> word = 'letters'
>>> letter_counts = {letter: word.count(letter) for letter in word}
>>> letter_counts
{'l': 1, 'e': 2, 't': 2, 'r': 1, 's': 1}
```

We're running a loop over each of the seven letters in the string 'letters' and
counting how many times that letter appears. Two uses of word.count(letter) are a
waste of time because we have to count all the e's twice and all the t's twice. But when

we count the e's the second time, we do no harm because we just replace the entry in the dictionary that was already there; the same goes for counting the t's. So, the following would have been a teeny bit more Pythonic:

```
>>> word = 'letters'
>>> letter_counts = {letter: word.count(letter) for letter in set(word)}
>>> letter_counts
{'t': 2, 'l': 1, 'e': 2, 'r': 1, 's': 1}
```

The dictionary's keys are in a different order than the previous example because iterating set(word) returns letters in a different order than iterating the string word.

Similar to list comprehensions, dictionary comprehensions can also have if tests and multiple for clauses:

```
{key_expression : value_expression for expression in iterable if condition}
>>> vowels = 'aeiou'
>>> word = 'onomatopoeia'
>>> vowel_counts = {letter: word.count(letter) for letter in set(word)
        if letter in vowels}
>>> vowel_counts
{'e': 1, 'i': 1, 'o': 4, 'a': 2}
```

See PEP-274 (*https://oreil.ly/6udkb*) for more examples of dictionary comprehensions.

Sets

A *set* is like a dictionary with its values thrown away, leaving only the keys. As with a dictionary, each key must be unique. You use a set when you only want to know that something exists, and nothing else about it. It's a bag of keys. Use a dictionary if you want to attach some information to the key as a value.

At some bygone time, in some places, set theory was taught in elementary school along with basic mathematics. If your school skipped it (or you were staring out the window), Figure 8-1 shows the ideas of set union and intersection.

Suppose that you take the union of two sets that have some keys in common. Because a set must contain only one of each item, the union of two sets will contain only one of each key. The *null* or *empty* set is a set with zero elements. In Figure 8-1, an example of a null set would be female names beginning with X.

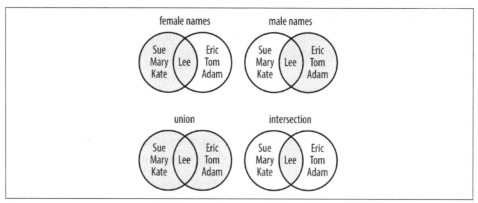

Figure 8-1. Common things to do with sets

Create with set()

To create a set, you use the `set()` function or enclose one or more comma-separated values in curly brackets, as shown here:

```
>>> empty_set = set()
>>> empty_set
set()
>>> even_numbers = {0, 2, 4, 6, 8}
>>> even_numbers
{0, 2, 4, 6, 8}
>>> odd_numbers = {1, 3, 5, 7, 9}
>>> odd_numbers
{1, 3, 5, 7, 9}
```

Sets are unordered.

 Because [] creates an empty list, you might expect {} to create an empty set. Instead, {} creates an empty dictionary. That's also why the interpreter prints an empty set as `set()` instead of {}. Why? Dictionaries were in Python first and took possession of the curly brackets. And possession is nine-tenths of the law.[2]

Convert with set()

You can create a set from a list, string, tuple, or dictionary, discarding any duplicate values.

First, let's take a look at a string with more than one occurrence of some letters:

---

2 According to lawyers and exorcists.

```
>>> set( 'letters' )
{'l', 'r', 's', 't', 'e'}
```

Notice that the set contains only one `'e'` or `'t'`, even though `'letters'` contained two of each.

Now, let's make a set from a list:

```
>>> set( ['Dasher', 'Dancer', 'Prancer', 'Mason-Dixon'] )
{'Dancer', 'Dasher', 'Mason-Dixon', 'Prancer'}
```

This time, a set from a tuple:

```
>>> set( ('Ummagumma', 'Echoes', 'Atom Heart Mother') )
{'Ummagumma', 'Atom Heart Mother', 'Echoes'}
```

When you give `set()` a dictionary, it uses only the keys:

```
>>> set( {'apple': 'red', 'orange': 'orange', 'cherry': 'red'} )
{'cherry', 'orange', 'apple'}
```

Get Length with len()

Let's count our reindeer:

```
>>> reindeer = set( ['Dasher', 'Dancer', 'Prancer', 'Mason-Dixon'] )
>>> len(reindeer)
4
```

Add an Item with add()

Throw another item into a set with the set `add()` method:

```
>>> s = set((1,2,3))
>>> s
{1, 2, 3}
>>> s.add(4)
>>> s
{1, 2, 3, 4}
```

Delete an Item with remove()

You can delete a value from a set by value:

```
>>> s = set((1,2,3))
>>> s.remove(3)
>>> s
{1, 2}
```

Iterate with for and in

Like dictionaries, you can iterate over all items in a set:

```
>>> furniture = set(('sofa', 'ottoman', 'table'))
>>> for piece in furniture:
...     print(piece)
...
ottoman
table
sofa
```

Test for a Value with in

This is the most common use of a set. We'll make a dictionary called drinks. Each key is the name of a mixed drink, and the corresponding value is a set of that drink's ingredients:

```
>>> drinks = {
...     'martini': {'vodka', 'vermouth'},
...     'black russian': {'vodka', 'kahlua'},
...     'white russian': {'cream', 'kahlua', 'vodka'},
...     'manhattan': {'rye', 'vermouth', 'bitters'},
...     'screwdriver': {'orange juice', 'vodka'}
...     }
```

Even though both are enclosed by curly braces ({ and }), a set is just a bunch of values, and a dictionary contains *key : value* pairs.

Which drinks contain vodka?

```
>>> for name, contents in drinks.items():
...     if 'vodka' in contents:
...         print(name)
...
screwdriver
martini
black russian
white russian
```

We want something with vodka but are lactose intolerant, and think vermouth tastes like kerosene:

```
>>> for name, contents in drinks.items():
...     if 'vodka' in contents and not ('vermouth' in contents or
...         'cream' in contents):
...         print(name)
...
screwdriver
black russian
```

We'll rewrite this a bit more succinctly in the next section.

Combinations and Operators

What if you want to check for combinations of set values? Suppose that you want to find any drink that has orange juice or vermouth? Let's use the *set intersection operator*, which is an ampersand (&):

```
>>> for name, contents in drinks.items():
...     if contents & {'vermouth', 'orange juice'}:
...         print(name)
...
screwdriver
martini
manhattan
```

The result of the & operator is a set that contains all of the items that appear in both lists that you compare. If neither of those ingredients were in contents, the & returns an empty set, which is considered False.

Now, let's rewrite the example from the previous section, in which we wanted vodka but neither cream nor vermouth:

```
>>> for name, contents in drinks.items():
...     if 'vodka' in contents and not contents & {'vermouth', 'cream'}:
...         print(name)
...
screwdriver
black russian
```

Let's save the ingredient sets for these two drinks in variables, just to save our delicate fingers some typing in the coming examples:

```
>>> bruss = drinks['black russian']
>>> wruss = drinks['white russian']
```

The following are examples of all the set operators. Some have special punctuation, some have special functions, and some have both. Let's use test sets a (contains 1 and 2) and b (contains 2 and 3):

```
>>> a = {1, 2}
>>> b = {2, 3}
```

As you saw earlier, you get the *intersection* (members common to both sets) with the special punctuation symbol &. The set intersection() function does the same:

```
>>> a & b
{2}
>>> a.intersection(b)
{2}
```

This snippet uses our saved drink variables:

```
>>> bruss & wruss
{'kahlua', 'vodka'}
```

In this example, get the *union* (members of either set) by using | or the set union() function:

```
>>> a | b
{1, 2, 3}
>>> a.union(b)
{1, 2, 3}
```

And here's the alcoholic version:

```
>>> bruss | wruss
{'cream', 'kahlua', 'vodka'}
```

The *difference* (members of the first set but not the second) is obtained by using the character - or the difference() function:

```
>>> a - b
{1}
>>> a.difference(b)
{1}

>>> bruss - wruss
set()
>>> wruss - bruss
{'cream'}
```

By far, the most common set operations are union, intersection, and difference. I've included the others for completeness in the examples that follow, but you might never use them.

The *exclusive or* (items in one set or the other, but not both) uses ^ or symmetric_difference():

```
>>> a ^ b
{1, 3}
>>> a.symmetric_difference(b)
{1, 3}
```

This finds the exclusive ingredient in our two russian drinks:

```
>>> bruss ^ wruss
{'cream'}
```

You can check whether one set is a *subset* of another (all members of the first set are also in the second set) by using <= or issubset():

```
>>> a <= b
False
>>> a.issubset(b)
False
```

Adding cream to a black russian makes a white russian, so wruss is a superset of bruss:

```
>>> bruss <= wruss
True
```

Is any set a subset of itself? Yup.[3]

```
>>> a <= a
True
>>> a.issubset(a)
True
```

To be a *proper subset*, the second set needs to have all the members of the first and more. Calculate it by using <, as in this example:

```
>>> a < b
False
>>> a < a
False

>>> bruss < wruss
True
```

A *superset* is the opposite of a subset (all members of the second set are also members of the first). This uses >= or issuperset():

```
>>> a >= b
False
>>> a.issuperset(b)
False

>>> wruss >= bruss
True
```

Any set is a superset of itself:

```
>>> a >= a
True
>>> a.issuperset(a)
True
```

And finally, you can find a *proper superset* (the first set has all members of the second, and more) by using >, as shown here:

```
>>> a > b
False

>>> wruss > bruss
True
```

You can't be a proper superset of yourself:

```
>>> a > a
False
```

---

3 Although, paraphrasing Groucho Marx, "I wouldn't want to belong to a club that would have someone like me as a member."

Set Comprehensions

No one wants to be left out, so even sets have comprehensions. The simplest version looks like the list and dictionary comprehensions that you've just seen:

{ *expression* for *expression* in *iterable* }

And it can have the optional condition tests:

{ *expression* for *expression* in *iterable* if *condition* }

```
>>> a_set = {number for number in range(1,6) if number % 3 == 1}
>>> a_set
{1, 4}
```

Create an Immutable Set with frozenset()

If you want to create a set that can't be changed, call the `frozenset()` function with any iterable argument:

```
>>> frozenset([3, 2, 1])
frozenset({1, 2, 3})
>>> frozenset(set([2, 1, 3]))
frozenset({1, 2, 3})
>>> frozenset({3, 1, 2})
frozenset({1, 2, 3})
>>> frozenset( (2, 3, 1) )
frozenset({1, 2, 3})
```

Is it really frozen?

```
>>> fs = frozenset([3, 2, 1])
>>> fs
frozenset({1, 2, 3})
>>> fs.add(4)
Traceback (most recent call last):
  File "<stdin>", line 1, in <module>
AttributeError: 'frozenset' object has no attribute 'add'
```

Yes, pretty frosty.

Data Structures So Far

To review, you *make*:

- A list by using square brackets ([ ])
- A tuple by using commas and optional parentheses
- A dictionary or set by using curly brackets ({})

For all but sets, you *access* a single element with square brackets. For the list and tuple, the value between the square brackets is an integer offset. For the dictionary, it's a key. For all three, the result is a value. For the set, it's either there or it's not; there's no index or key:

```
>>> marx_list = ['Groucho', 'Chico', 'Harpo']
>>> marx_tuple = ('Groucho', 'Chico', 'Harpo')
>>> marx_dict = {'Groucho': 'banjo', 'Chico': 'piano', 'Harpo': 'harp'}
>>> marx_set = {'Groucho', 'Chico', 'Harpo'}
>>> marx_list[2]
'Harpo'
>>> marx_tuple[2]
'Harpo'
>>> marx_dict['Harpo']
'harp'
>>> 'Harpo' in marx_list
True
>>> 'Harpo' in marx_tuple
True
>>> 'Harpo' in marx_dict
True
>>> 'Harpo' in marx_set
True
```

Make Bigger Data Structures

We worked up from simple booleans, numbers, and strings to lists, tuples, sets, and dictionaries. You can combine these built-in data structures into bigger, more complex structures of your own. Let's start with three different lists:

```
>>> marxes = ['Groucho', 'Chico', 'Harpo']
>>> pythons = ['Chapman', 'Cleese', 'Gilliam', 'Jones', 'Palin']
>>> stooges = ['Moe', 'Curly', 'Larry']
```

We can make a tuple that contains each list as an element:

```
>>> tuple_of_lists = marxes, pythons, stooges
>>> tuple_of_lists
(['Groucho', 'Chico', 'Harpo'],
['Chapman', 'Cleese', 'Gilliam', 'Jones', 'Palin'],
['Moe', 'Curly', 'Larry'])
```

And we can make a list that contains the three lists:

```
>>> list_of_lists = [marxes, pythons, stooges]
>>> list_of_lists
[['Groucho', 'Chico', 'Harpo'],
['Chapman', 'Cleese', 'Gilliam', 'Jones', 'Palin'],
['Moe', 'Curly', 'Larry']]
```

Finally, let's create a dictionary of lists. In this example, let's use the name of the comedy group as the key and the list of members as the value:

```
>>> dict_of_lists = {'Marxes': marxes, 'Pythons': pythons, 'Stooges': stooges}
>> dict_of_lists
{'Marxes': ['Groucho', 'Chico', 'Harpo'],
 'Pythons': ['Chapman', 'Cleese', 'Gilliam', 'Jones', 'Palin'],
 'Stooges': ['Moe', 'Curly', 'Larry']}
```

Your only limitations are those in the data types themselves. For example, dictionary keys need to be immutable, so a list, dictionary, or set can't be a key for another dictionary. But a tuple can be. For example, you could index sites of interest by GPS coordinates (latitude, longitude, and altitude; see Chapter 21 for more mapping examples):

```
>>> houses = {
        (44.79, -93.14, 285): 'My House',
        (38.89, -77.03, 13): 'The White House'
        }
```

Coming Up

Back to code structures. You'll learn how to wrap code in *functions*, and how to deal with *exceptions* when things go awry.

Things to Do

8.1 Make an English-to-French dictionary called e2f and print it. Here are your starter words: dog is chien, cat is chat, and walrus is morse.

8.2 Using your three-word dictionary e2f, print the French word for walrus.

8.3 Make a French-to-English dictionary called f2e from e2f. Use the items method.

8.4 Print the English equivalent of the French word chien.

8.5 Print the set of English words from e2f.

8.6 Make a multilevel dictionary called life. Use these strings for the topmost keys: 'animals', 'plants', and 'other'. Make the 'animals' key refer to another dictionary with the keys 'cats', 'octopi', and 'emus'. Make the 'cats' key refer to a list of strings with the values 'Henri', 'Grumpy', and 'Lucy'. Make all the other keys refer to empty dictionaries.

8.7 Print the top-level keys of life.

8.8 Print the keys for life['animals'].

8.9 Print the values for life['animals']['cats'].

8.10 Use a dictionary comprehension to create the dictionary squares. Use range(10) to return the keys, and use the square of each key as its value.

8.11 Use a set comprehension to create the set odd from the odd numbers in range(10).

8.12 Use a generator comprehension to return the string 'Got ' and a number for the numbers in range(10). Iterate through this by using a for loop.

8.13 Use zip() to make a dictionary from the key tuple ('optimist', 'pessimist', 'troll') and the values tuple ('The glass is half full', 'The glass is half empty', 'How did you get a glass?').

8.14 Use zip() to make a dictionary called movies that pairs these lists: titles = ['Creature of Habit', 'Crewel Fate', 'Sharks On a Plane'] and plots = ['A nun turns into a monster', 'A haunted yarn shop', 'Check your exits']

CHAPTER 9

Functions

The smaller the function, the greater the management.
—C. Northcote Parkinson

So far, all of our Python code examples have been little fragments. These are good for small tasks, but no one wants to retype fragments all the time. We need some way of organizing larger code into manageable pieces.

The first step to code reuse is the *function*: a named piece of code, separate from all others. A function can take any number and type of input *parameters* and return any number and type of output *results*.

You can do two things with a function:

- *Define* it, with zero or more parameters
- *Call* it, and get zero or more results

Define a Function with def

To define a Python function, you type def, the function name, parentheses enclosing any input *parameters* to the function, and then finally, a colon (:). Function names have the same rules as variable names (they must start with a letter or _ and contain only letters, numbers, or _).

Let's take things one step at a time, and first define and call a function that has no parameters. Here's the simplest Python function:

```
>>> def do_nothing():
...     pass
```

Even for a function with no parameters like this one, you still need the parentheses and the colon in its definition. The next line needs to be indented, just as you would indent code under an if statement. Python requires the pass statement to show that this function does nothing. It's the equivalent of *This page intentionally left blank* (even though it isn't anymore).

Call a Function with Parentheses

You call this function just by typing its name and parentheses. It works as advertised, doing nothing, but doing it very well:

```
>>> do_nothing()
>>>
```

Now let's define and call another function that has no parameters but prints a single word:

```
>>> def make_a_sound():
...     print('quack')
...
>>> make_a_sound()
quack
```

When you called the make_a_sound() function, Python ran the code inside its definition. In this case, it printed a single word and returned to the main program.

Let's try a function that has no parameters but *returns* a value:

```
>>> def agree():
...     return True
...
```

You can call this function and test its returned value by using if:

```
>>> if agree():
...     print('Splendid!')
... else:
...     print('That was unexpected.')
...
Splendid!
```

You've just made a big step. The combination of functions with tests such as if and loops such as while make it possible for you to do things that you could not do before.

Arguments and Parameters

At this point, it's time to put something between those parentheses. Let's define the function echo() with one parameter called anything. It uses the return statement to send the value of anything back to its caller twice, with a space between:

```
>>> def echo(anything):
...     return anything + ' ' + anything
...
>>>
```

Now let's call echo() with the string 'Rumplestiltskin':

```
>>> echo('Rumplestiltskin')
'Rumplestiltskin Rumplestiltskin'
```

The values you pass into the function when you call it are known as *arguments*. When you call a function with arguments, the values of those arguments are copied to their corresponding *parameters* inside the function.

 Saying it another way: they're called *arguments* outside of the function, but *parameters* inside.

In the previous example, the function echo() was called with the argument string 'Rumplestiltskin'. This value was copied within echo() to the parameter any thing, and then returned (in this case doubled, with a space) to the caller.

These function examples were pretty basic. Let's write a function that takes an input argument and actually does something with it. We'll adapt the earlier code fragment that comments on a color. Call it commentary and have it take an input string parameter called color. Make it return the string description to its caller, which can decide what to do with it:

```
>>> def commentary(color):
...     if color == 'red':
...         return "It's a tomato."
...     elif color == "green":
...         return "It's a green pepper."
...     elif color == 'bee purple':
...         return "I don't know what it is, but only bees can see it."
...     else:
...         return "I've never heard of the color "  + color +  "."
...
>>>
```

Call the function commentary() with the string argument 'blue'.

```
>>> comment = commentary('blue')
```

The function does the following:

- Assigns the value 'blue' to the function's internal color parameter
- Runs through the if-elif-else logic chain

- Returns a string

The caller then assigns the string to the variable comment.

What did we get back?

```
>>> print(comment)
I've never heard of the color blue.
```

A function can take any number of input arguments (including zero) of any type. It can return any number of output results (also including zero) of any type. If a function doesn't call return explicitly, the caller gets the result None.

```
>>> print(do_nothing())
None
```

None Is Useful

None is a special Python value that holds a place when there is nothing to say. It is not the same as the boolean value False, although it looks false when evaluated as a boolean. Here's an example:

```
>>> thing = None
>>> if thing:
...     print("It's some thing")
... else:
...     print("It's no thing")
...
It's no thing
```

To distinguish None from a boolean False value, use Python's is operator:

```
>>> thing = None
>>> if thing is None:
...     print("It's nothing")
... else:
...     print("It's something")
...
It's nothing
```

This seems like a subtle distinction, but it's important in Python. You'll need None to distinguish a missing value from an empty value. Remember that zero-valued integers or floats, empty strings (''), lists ([]), tuples ((,)), dictionaries ({}), and sets (set()) are all False, but are not the same as None.

Let's write a quick function that prints whether its argument is None, True, or False:

```
>>> def whatis(thing):
...     if thing is None:
...         print(thing, "is None")
...     elif thing:
...         print(thing, "is True")
```

```
...      else:
...          print(thing, "is False")
...
```

Let's run some sanity tests:

```
>>> whatis(None)
None is None
>>> whatis(True)
True is True
>>> whatis(False)
False is False
```

How about some real values?

```
>>> whatis(0)
0 is False
>>> whatis(0.0)
0.0 is False
>>> whatis('')
 is False
>>> whatis("")
 is False
>>> whatis('''''')
 is False
>>> whatis(())
() is False
>>> whatis([])
[] is False
>>> whatis({})
{} is False
>>> whatis(set())
set() is False

>>> whatis(0.00001)
1e-05 is True
>>> whatis([0])
[0] is True
>>> whatis([''])
[''] is True
>>> whatis(' ')
  is True
```

Positional Arguments

Python handles function arguments in a manner that's very flexible, when compared to many languages. The most familiar types of arguments are *positional arguments*, whose values are copied to their corresponding parameters in order.

This function builds a dictionary from its positional input arguments and returns it:

```
>>> def menu(wine, entree, dessert):
...      return {'wine': wine, 'entree': entree, 'dessert': dessert}
...
```

```
>>> menu('chardonnay', 'chicken', 'cake')
{'wine': 'chardonnay', 'entree': 'chicken', 'dessert': 'cake'}
```

Although very common, a downside of positional arguments is that you need to remember the meaning of each position. If we forgot and called menu() with wine as the last argument instead of the first, the meal would be very different:

```
>>> menu('beef', 'bagel', 'bordeaux')
{'wine': 'beef', 'entree': 'bagel', 'dessert': 'bordeaux'}
```

Keyword Arguments

To avoid positional argument confusion, you can specify arguments by the names of their corresponding parameters, even in a different order from their definition in the function:

```
>>> menu(entree='beef', dessert='bagel', wine='bordeaux')
{'wine': 'bordeaux', 'entree': 'beef', 'dessert': 'bagel'}
```

You can mix positional and keyword arguments. Let's specify the wine first, but use keyword arguments for the entree and dessert:

```
>>> menu('frontenac', dessert='flan', entree='fish')
{'wine': 'frontenac', 'entree': 'fish', 'dessert': 'flan'}
```

If you call a function with both positional and keyword arguments, the positional arguments need to come first.

Specify Default Parameter Values

You can specify default values for parameters. The default is used if the caller does not provide a corresponding argument. This bland-sounding feature can actually be quite useful. Using the previous example:

```
>>> def menu(wine, entree, dessert='pudding'):
...     return {'wine': wine, 'entree': entree, 'dessert': dessert}
```

This time, try calling menu() without the dessert argument:

```
>>> menu('chardonnay', 'chicken')
{'wine': 'chardonnay', 'entree': 'chicken', 'dessert': 'pudding'}
```

If you do provide an argument, it's used instead of the default:

```
>>> menu('dunkelfelder', 'duck', 'doughnut')
{'wine': 'dunkelfelder', 'entree': 'duck', 'dessert': 'doughnut'}
```

 Default parameter values are calculated when the function is *defined*, not when it is run. A common error with new (and sometimes not-so-new) Python programmers is to use a mutable data type such as a list or dictionary as a default parameter.

In the following test, the buggy() function is expected to run each time with a fresh empty result list, add the arg argument to it, and then print a single-item list. However, there's a bug: it's empty only the first time it's called. The second time, result still has one item from the previous call:

```
>>> def buggy(arg, result=[]):
...     result.append(arg)
...     print(result)
...
>>> buggy('a')
['a']
>>> buggy('b')    # expect ['b']
['a', 'b']
```

It would have worked if it had been written like this:

```
>>> def works(arg):
...     result = []
...     result.append(arg)
...     return result
...
>>> works('a')
['a']
>>> works('b')
['b']
```

The fix is to pass in something else to indicate the first call:

```
>>> def nonbuggy(arg, result=None):
...     if result is None:
...         result = []
...     result.append(arg)
...     print(result)
...
>>> nonbuggy('a')
['a']
>>> nonbuggy('b')
['b']
```

This is sometimes a Python job interview question. You've been warned.

Explode/Gather Positional Arguments with *

If you've programmed in C or C++, you might assume that an asterisk (*) in a Python program has something to do with a *pointer*. Nope, Python doesn't have pointers.

When used inside the function with a parameter, an asterisk groups a variable number of positional arguments into a single tuple of parameter values. In the following example, args is the parameter tuple that resulted from zero or more arguments that were passed to the function print_args():

```
>>> def print_args(*args):
...     print('Positional tuple:', args)
...
```

If you call the function with no arguments, you get nothing in *args:

```
>>> print_args()
Positional tuple: ()
```

Whatever you give it will be printed as the args tuple:

```
>>> print_args(3, 2, 1, 'wait!', 'uh...')
Positional tuple: (3, 2, 1, 'wait!', 'uh...')
```

This is useful for writing functions such as print() that accept a variable number of arguments. If your function has *required* positional arguments, as well, put them first; *args goes at the end and grabs all the rest:

```
>>> def print_more(required1, required2, *args):
...     print('Need this one:', required1)
...     print('Need this one too:', required2)
...     print('All the rest:', args)
...
>>> print_more('cap', 'gloves', 'scarf', 'monocle', 'mustache wax')
Need this one: cap
Need this one too: gloves
All the rest: ('scarf', 'monocle', 'mustache wax')
```

 When using *, you don't need to call the tuple argument *args, but it's a common idiom in Python. It's also common to use *args inside the function, as in the preceding example, although technically it's called a parameter and could be referred to as *params.

Summarizing:

- You can pass positional argument to a function, which will match them inside to positional parameters. This is what you've seen so far in this book.
- You can pass a tuple argument to a function, and inside it will be a tuple parameter. This is a simple case of the preceding one.
- You can pass positional arguments to a function, and gather them inside as the parameter *args, which resolves to the tuple args. This was described in this section.
- You can also "explode" a tuple argument called args to positional parameters *args inside the function, which will be regathered inside into the tuple parameter args:

```
>>> print_args(2, 5, 7, 'x')
Positional tuple: (2, 5, 7, 'x')
```

```
>>> args = (2,5,7,'x')
>>> print_args(args)
Positional tuple: ((2, 5, 7, 'x'),)
>>> print_args(*args)
Positional tuple: (2, 5, 7, 'x')
```

You can only use the * syntax in a function call or definition:

```
>>> *args
  File "<stdin>", line 1
SyntaxError: can't use starred expression here
```

So:

- Outside the function, *args explodes the tuple args into comma-separated positional parameters.

- Inside the function, *args gathers all of the positional arguments into a single args tuple. You could use the names *params and params, but it's common practice to use *args for both the outside argument and inside parameter.

Readers with synesthesia might also faintly hear *args as *puff-args* on the outside and *inhale-args* on the inside, as values are either exploded or gathered.

Explode/Gather Keyword Arguments with **

You can use two asterisks (**) to group keyword arguments into a dictionary, where the argument names are the keys, and their values are the corresponding dictionary values. The following example defines the function print_kwargs() to print its keyword arguments:

```
>>> def print_kwargs(**kwargs):
...     print('Keyword arguments:', kwargs)
...
```

Now try calling it with some keyword arguments:

```
>>> print_kwargs()
Keyword arguments: {}
>>> print_kwargs(wine='merlot', entree='mutton', dessert='macaroon')
Keyword arguments: {'dessert': 'macaroon', 'wine': 'merlot',
'entree': 'mutton'}
```

Inside the function, kwargs is a dictionary parameter.

Argument order is:

- Required positional arguments
- Optional positional arguments (*args)

- Optional keyword arguments (`**kwargs`)

As with `args`, you don't need to call this keyword argument `kwargs`, but it's common usage.[1]

The `**` syntax is valid only in a function call or definition:[2]

```
>>> **kwparams
  File "<stdin>", line 1
    **kwparams
    ^
SyntaxError: invalid syntax
```

Summarizing:

- You can pass keyword arguments to a function, which will match them inside to keyword parameters. This is what you've seen so far.
- You can pass a dictionary argument to a function, and inside it will be dictionary parameters. This is a simple case of the preceding one.
- You can pass one or more keyword arguments (*name=value*) to a function, and gather them inside as `**kwargs`, which resolves to the dictionary parameter called `kwargs`. This was described in this section.
- Outside a function, `**kwargs` *explodes* a dictionary `kwargs` into *name=value* arguments.
- Inside a function, `**kwargs` *gathers* `name=value` arguments into the single dictionary parameter `kwargs`.

If auditory hallucinations help, imagine a puff for each asterisk exploding outside the function, and a little inhaling sound for each one gathering inside.

Keyword-Only Arguments

It's possible to pass in a keyword argument that has the same name as a positional parameter, probably not resulting in what you want. Python 3 lets you specify *keyword-only arguments*. As the name says, they must be provided as *name=value*, not positionally as *value*. The single `*` in the function definition means that the following parameters `start` and end must be provided as named arguments if we don't want their default values:

```
>>> def print_data(data, *, start=0, end=100):
...     for value in (data[start:end]):
```

---

1 Although *Args* and *Kwargs* sound like the names of pirate parrots.

2 Or, as of Python 3.5, a dictionary merge of the form {`**a`, `**b`}, as you saw in Chapter 8.

```
...         print(value)
...
>>> data = ['a', 'b', 'c', 'd', 'e', 'f']
>>> print_data(data)
a
b
c
d
e
f
>>> print_data(data, start=4)
e
f
>>> print_data(data, end=2)
a
b
```

Mutable and Immutable Arguments

Remember that if you assigned the same list to two variables, you could change it by using either one? And that you could not if the variables both referred to something like an integer or a string? That was because the list was mutable and the integer and string were immutable.

You need to watch for the same behavior when passing arguments to functions. If an argument is mutable, its value can be changed *from inside the function* via its corresponding parameter:[3]

```
>>> outside = ['one', 'fine', 'day']
>>> def mangle(arg):
...     arg[1] = 'terrible!'
...
>>> outside
['one', 'fine', 'day']
>>> mangle(outside)
>>> outside
['one', 'terrible!', 'day']
```

It's good practice to, uh, not do this.[4] Either document that an argument may be changed, or return the new value.

---

3 Like the teens-in-peril movies where they learn "The call's coming from inside the house!"

4 Like the old doctor joke: "It hurts when I do this." "Well, then don't do that."

Docstrings

Readability counts, the Zen of Python verily saith. You can attach documentation to a function definition by including a string at the beginning of the function body. This is the function's *docstring*:

```
>>> def echo(anything):
...     'echo returns its input argument'
...     return anything
```

You can make a docstring quite long, and even add rich formatting if you want:

```
def print_if_true(thing, check):
    '''
    Prints the first argument if a second argument is true.
    The operation is:
        1. Check whether the *second* argument is true.
        2. If it is, print the *first* argument.
    '''
    if check:
        print(thing)
```

To print a function's docstring, call the Python help() function. Pass the function's name to get a listing of arguments along with the nicely formatted docstring:

```
>>> help(echo)
Help on function echo in module __main__:

echo(anything)
    echo returns its input argument
```

If you want to see just the raw docstring, without the formatting:

```
>>> print(echo.__doc__)
echo returns its input argument
```

That odd-looking __doc__ is the internal name of the docstring as a variable within the function. Double underscores (aka *dunder* in Python-speak) are used in many places to name Python internal variables, because programmers are unlikely to use them in their own variable names.

Functions Are First-Class Citizens

I've mentioned the Python mantra, *everything is an object*. This includes numbers, strings, tuples, lists, dictionaries—and functions, as well. Functions are first-class citizens in Python. You can assign them to variables, use them as arguments to other functions, and return them from functions. This gives you the capability to do some things in Python that are difficult-to-impossible to carry out in many other languages.

To test this, let's define a simple function called answer() that doesn't have any arguments; it just prints the number 42:

```
>>> def answer():
...     print(42)
```

If you run this function, you know what you'll get:

```
>>> answer()
42
```

Now let's define another function named run_something. It has one argument called func, a function to run. Once inside, it just calls the function:

```
>>> def run_something(func):
...     func()
```

If we pass answer to run_something(), we're using a function as data, just as with anything else:

```
>>> run_something(answer)
42
```

Notice that you passed answer, not answer(). In Python, those parentheses mean *call this function*. With no parentheses, Python just treats the function like any other object. That's because, like everything else in Python, it *is* an object:

```
>>> type(run_something)
<class 'function'>
```

Let's try running a function with arguments. Define a function add_args() that prints the sum of its two numeric arguments, arg1 and arg2:

```
>>> def add_args(arg1, arg2):
...     print(arg1 + arg2)
```

And what is add_args()?

```
>>> type(add_args)
<class 'function'>
```

At this point, let's define a function called run_something_with_args() that takes three arguments:

func
> The function to run

arg1
> The first argument for func

arg2
> The second argument for func

```
>>> def run_something_with_args(func, arg1, arg2):
...     func(arg1, arg2)
```

When you call `run_something_with_args()`, the function passed by the caller is assigned to the `func` parameter, whereas `arg1` and `arg2` get the values that follow in the argument list. Then, running `func(arg1, arg2)` executes that function with those arguments because the parentheses told Python to do so.

Let's test it by passing the function name `add_args` and the arguments 5 and 9 to `run_something_with_args()`:

```
>>> run_something_with_args(add_args, 5, 9)
14
```

Within the function `run_something_with_args()`, the function name argument `add_args` was assigned to the parameter `func`, 5 to `arg1`, and 9 to `arg2`. This ended up running:

```
add_args(5, 9)
```

You can combine this with the `*args` and `**kwargs` techniques.

Let's define a test function that takes any number of positional arguments, calculates their sum by using the `sum()` function, and then returns that sum:

```
>>> def sum_args(*args):
...     return sum(args)
```

I haven't mentioned `sum()` before. It's a built-in Python function that calculates the sum of the values in its iterable numeric (int or float) argument.

Let's define the new function `run_with_positional_args()`, which takes a function and any number of positional arguments to pass to it:

```
>>> def run_with_positional_args(func, *args):
...     return func(*args)
```

Now go ahead and call it:

```
>>> run_with_positional_args(sum_args, 1, 2, 3, 4)
10
```

You can use functions as elements of lists, tuples, sets, and dictionaries. Functions are immutable, so you can also use them as dictionary keys.

Inner Functions

You can define a function within another function:

```
>>> def outer(a, b):
...     def inner(c, d):
...         return c + d
```

```
...        return inner(a, b)
...
>>>
>>> outer(4, 7)
11
```

An inner function can be useful when performing some complex task more than once within another function, to avoid loops or code duplication. For a string example, this inner function adds some text to its argument:

```
>>> def knights(saying):
...     def inner(quote):
...         return "We are the knights who say: '%s'" % quote
...     return inner(saying)
...
>>> knights('Ni!')
"We are the knights who say: 'Ni!'"
```

Closures

An inner function can act as a *closure*. This is a function that is dynamically generated by another function and can both change and remember the values of variables that were created outside the function.

The following example builds on the previous knights() example. Let's call the new one knights2(), because we have no imagination, and turn the inner() function into a closure called inner2(). Here are the differences:

- inner2() uses the outer saying parameter directly instead of getting it as an argument.

- knights2() returns the inner2 function name instead of calling it:

  ```
  >>> def knights2(saying):
  ...     def inner2():
  ...         return "We are the knights who say: '%s'" % saying
  ...     return inner2
  ...
  ```

The inner2() function knows the value of saying that was passed in and remembers it. The line return inner2 returns this specialized copy of the inner2 function (but doesn't call it). That's a kind of closure: a dynamically created function that remembers where it came from.

Let's call knights2() twice, with different arguments:

```
>>> a = knights2('Duck')
>>> b = knights2('Hasenpfeffer')
```

Okay, so what are a and b?

```
>>> type(a)
<class 'function'>
>>> type(b)
<class 'function'>
```

They're functions, but they're also closures:

```
>>> a
<function knights2.<locals>.inner2 at 0x10193e158>
>>> b
<function knights2.<locals>.inner2 at 0x10193e1e0>
```

If we call them, they remember the saying that was used when they were created by knights2:

```
>>> a()
"We are the knights who say: 'Duck'"
>>> b()
"We are the knights who say: 'Hasenpfeffer'"
```

Anonymous Functions: lambda

A Python *lambda function* is an anonymous function expressed as a single statement. You can use it instead of a normal tiny function.

To illustrate it, let's first make an example that uses normal functions. To begin, let's define the function edit_story(). Its arguments are the following:

- words—a list of words
- func—a function to apply to each word in words

```
>>> def edit_story(words, func):
...     for word in words:
...         print(func(word))
```

Now we need a list of words and a function to apply to each word. For the words, here's a list of (hypothetical) sounds made by my cat if he (hypothetically) missed one of the stairs:

```
>>> stairs = ['thud', 'meow', 'thud', 'hiss']
```

And for the function, this will capitalize each word and append an exclamation point, perfect for feline tabloid newspaper headlines:

```
>>> def enliven(word):    # give that prose more punch
...     return word.capitalize() + '!'
```

Mixing our ingredients:

```
>>> edit_story(stairs, enliven)
Thud!
Meow!
```

```
Thud!
Hiss!
```

Finally, we get to the lambda. The `enliven()` function was so brief that we could replace it with a lambda:

```
>>> edit_story(stairs, lambda word: word.capitalize() + '!')
Thud!
Meow!
Thud!
Hiss!
```

A lambda has zero or more comma-separated arguments, followed by a colon (:), and then the definition of the function. We're giving this lambda one argument, word. You don't use parentheses with `lambda` as you would when calling a function created with `def`.

Often, using real functions such as `enliven()` is much clearer than using lambdas. Lambdas are mostly useful for cases in which you would otherwise need to define many tiny functions and remember what you called them all. In particular, you can use lambdas in graphical user interfaces to define *callback functions*; see Chapter 20 for examples.

Generators

A *generator* is a Python sequence creation object. With it, you can iterate through potentially huge sequences without creating and storing the entire sequence in memory at once. Generators are often the source of data for iterators. If you recall, we already used one of them, `range()`, in earlier code examples to generate a series of integers. In Python 2, `range()` returns a list, which limits it to fit in memory. Python 2 also has the generator `xrange()`, which became the normal `range()` in Python 3. This example adds all the integers from 1 to 100:

```
>>> sum(range(1, 101))
5050
```

Every time you iterate through a generator, it keeps track of where it was the last time it was called and returns the next value. This is different from a normal function, which has no memory of previous calls and always starts at its first line with the same state.

Generator Functions

If you want to create a potentially large sequence, you can write a *generator function*. It's a normal function, but it returns its value with a `yield` statement rather than `return`. Let's write our own version of `range()`:

```
>>> def my_range(first=0, last=10, step=1):
...     number = first
...     while number < last:
...         yield number
...         number += step
...
```

It's a normal function:

```
>>> my_range
<function my_range at 0x10193e268>
```

And it returns a generator object:

```
>>> ranger = my_range(1, 5)
>>> ranger
<generator object my_range at 0x101a0a168>
```

We can iterate over this generator object:

```
>>> for x in ranger:
...     print(x)
...
1
2
3
4
```

 A generator can be run only once. Lists, sets, strings, and dictionaries exist in memory, but a generator creates its values on the fly and hands them out one at a time through an iterator. It doesn't remember them, so you can't restart or back up a generator.

If you try to iterate this generator again, you'll find that it's tapped out:

```
>>> for try_again in ranger:
...     print(try_again)
...
>>>
```

Generator Comprehensions

You've seen comprehensions for lists, dictionaries, and sets. A *generator comprehension* looks like those, but is surrounded by parentheses instead of square or curly brackets. It's like a shorthand version of a generator function, doing the yield invisibly, and also returns a generator object:

```
>>> genobj = (pair for pair in zip(['a', 'b'], ['1', '2']))
>>> genobj
<generator object <genexpr> at 0x10308fde0>
>>> for thing in genobj:
...     print(thing)
```

```
...
('a', '1')
('b', '2')
```

Decorators

Sometimes, you want to modify an existing function without changing its source code. A common example is adding a debugging statement to see what arguments were passed in.

A *decorator* is a function that takes one function as input and returns another function. Let's dig into our bag of Python tricks and use the following:

- *args and **kwargs
- Inner functions
- Functions as arguments

The function document_it() defines a decorator that will do the following:

- Print the function's name and the values of its arguments
- Run the function with the arguments
- Print the result
- Return the modified function for use

Here's what the code looks like:

```
>>> def document_it(func):
...     def new_function(*args, **kwargs):
...         print('Running function:', func.__name__)
...         print('Positional arguments:', args)
...         print('Keyword arguments:', kwargs)
...         result = func(*args, **kwargs)
...         print('Result:', result)
...         return result
...     return new_function
```

Whatever func you pass to document_it(), you get a new function that includes the extra statements that document_it() adds. A decorator doesn't actually have to run any code from func, but document_it() calls func partway through so that you get the results of func as well as all the extras.

So, how do you use this? You can apply the decorator manually:

```
>>> def add_ints(a, b):
...     return a + b
...
>>> add_ints(3, 5)
```

```
8
>>> cooler_add_ints = document_it(add_ints)  # manual decorator assignment
>>> cooler_add_ints(3, 5)
Running function: add_ints
Positional arguments: (3, 5)
Keyword arguments: {}
Result: 8
8
```

As an alternative to the manual decorator assignment we just looked at, you can add
@*decorator_name* before the function that you want to decorate:

```
>>> @document_it
... def add_ints(a, b):
...     return a + b
...
>>> add_ints(3, 5)
Start function add_ints
Positional arguments: (3, 5)
Keyword arguments: {}
Result: 8
8
```

You can have more than one decorator for a function. Let's write another decorator
called square_it() that squares the result:

```
>>> def square_it(func):
...     def new_function(*args, **kwargs):
...         result = func(*args, **kwargs)
...         return result * result
...     return new_function
...
```

The decorator that's used closest to the function (just above the def) runs first and
then the one above it. Either order gives the same end result, but you can see how the
intermediate steps change:

```
>>> @document_it
... @square_it
... def add_ints(a, b):
...     return a + b
...
>>> add_ints(3, 5)
Running function: new_function
Positional arguments: (3, 5)
Keyword arguments: {}
Result: 64
64
```

Let's try reversing the decorator order:

```
>>> @square_it
... @document_it
... def add_ints(a, b):
```

```
...        return a + b
...
>>> add_ints(3, 5)
Running function: add_ints
Positional arguments: (3, 5)
Keyword arguments: {}
Result: 8
64
```

Namespaces and Scope

Desiring this man's art and that man's scope

—William Shakespeare

A name can refer to different things, depending on where it's used. Python programs have various *namespaces*—sections within which a particular name is unique and unrelated to the same name in other namespaces.

Each function defines its own namespace. If you define a variable called x in a main program and another variable called x in a function, they refer to different things. But the walls can be breached: if you need to, you can access names in other namespaces in various ways.

The main part of a program defines the *global* namespace; thus, the variables in that namespace are *global variables*.

You can get the value of a global variable from within a function:

```
>>> animal = 'fruitbat'
>>> def print_global():
...        print('inside print_global:', animal)
...
>>> print('at the top level:', animal)
at the top level: fruitbat
>>> print_global()
inside print_global: fruitbat
```

But if you try to get the value of the global variable *and* change it within the function, you get an error:

```
>>> def change_and_print_global():
...        print('inside change_and_print_global:', animal)
...        animal = 'wombat'
...        print('after the change:', animal)
...
>>> change_and_print_global()
Traceback (most recent call last):
  File "<stdin>", line 1, in <module>
  File "<stdin>", line 2, in change_and_print_global
UnboundLocalError: local variable 'animal' referenced before assignment
```

If you just change it, it changes a different variable also named `animal`, but this variable is inside the function:

```
>>> def change_local():
...     animal = 'wombat'
...     print('inside change_local:', animal, id(animal))
...
>>> change_local()
inside change_local: wombat 4330406160
>>> animal
'fruitbat'
>>> id(animal)
4330390832
```

What happened here? The first line assigned the string `'fruitbat'` to a global variable named `animal`. The `change_local()` function also has a variable named `animal`, but that's in its local namespace.

I used the Python function `id()` here to print the unique value for each object and prove that the variable `animal` inside `change_local()` is not the same as `animal` at the main level of the program.

To access the global variable rather than the local one within a function, you need to be explicit and use the `global` keyword (you knew this was coming: *explicit is better than implicit*):

```
>>> animal = 'fruitbat'
>>> def change_and_print_global():
...     global animal
...     animal = 'wombat'
...     print('inside change_and_print_global:', animal)
...
>>> animal
'fruitbat'
>>> change_and_print_global()
inside change_and_print_global: wombat
>>> animal
'wombat'
```

If you don't say `global` within a function, Python uses the local namespace and the variable is local. It goes away after the function completes.

Python provides two functions to access the contents of your namespaces:

- `locals()` returns a dictionary of the contents of the local namespace.
- `globals()` returns a dictionary of the contents of the global namespace.

And here they are in use:

```
>>> animal = 'fruitbat'
>>> def change_local():
...     animal = 'wombat'  # local variable
...     print('locals:', locals())
...
>>> animal
'fruitbat'
>>> change_local()
locals: {'animal': 'wombat'}
>>> print('globals:', globals()) # reformatted a little for presentation
globals: {'animal': 'fruitbat',
'__doc__': None,
'change_local': <function change_local at 0x1006c0170>,
'__package__': None,
'__name__': '__main__',
'__loader__': <class '_frozen_importlib.BuiltinImporter'>,
'__builtins__': <module 'builtins'>}
>>> animal
'fruitbat'
```

The local namespace within change_local() contained only the local variable animal. The global namespace contained the separate global variable animal and a number of other things.

Uses of _ and __ in Names

Names that begin and end with two underscores (__) are reserved for use within Python, so you should not use them with your own variables. This naming pattern was chosen because it seemed unlikely to be selected by application developers for their own variables.

For instance, the name of a function is in the system variable *function.__name__*, and its documentation string is *function.__doc__*:

```
>>> def amazing():
...     '''This is the amazing function.
...     Want to see it again?'''
...     print('This function is named:', amazing.__name__)
...     print('And its docstring is:', amazing.__doc__)
...
>>> amazing()
This function is named: amazing
And its docstring is: This is the amazing function.
    Want to see it again?
```

As you saw in the earlier globals printout, the main program is assigned the special name __main__.

Recursion

So far, we've called functions that do some things directly, and maybe call other functions. But what if a function calls itself?[5] This is called *recursion*. Like an unbroken infinite loop with while or for, you don't want infinite recursion. Do we still need to worry about cracks in the space-time continuum?

Python saves the universe again by raising an exception if you get too deep:

```
>>> def dive():
...     return dive()
...
>>> dive()
Traceback (most recent call last):
  File "<stdin>", line 1, in <module>
  File "<stdin>", line 2, in dive
  File "<stdin>", line 2, in dive
  File "<stdin>", line 2, in dive
  [Previous line repeated 996 more times]
RecursionError: maximum recursion depth exceeded
```

Recursion is useful when you're dealing with "uneven" data, like lists of lists of lists. Suppose that you want to "flatten" all sublists of a list,[6] no matter how deeply nested. A generator function is just the thing:

```
>>> def flatten(lol):
...     for item in lol:
...         if isinstance(item, list):
...             for subitem in flatten(item):
...                 yield subitem
...         else:
...             yield item
...
>>> lol = [1, 2, [3,4,5], [6,[7,8,9], []]]
>>> flatten(lol)
<generator object flatten at 0x10509a750>
>>> list(flatten(lol))
[1, 2, 3, 4, 5, 6, 7, 8, 9]
```

Python 3.3 added the yield from expression, which lets a generator hand off some work to another generator. We can use it to simplify flatten():

```
>>> def flatten(lol):
...     for item in lol:
...         if isinstance(item, list):
...             yield from flatten(item)
...         else:
```

---

5 It's like saying, "I wish I had a dollar for every time I wished I had a dollar."

6 Another Python interview question. Collect the whole set!

```
...            yield item
...
>>> lol = [1, 2, [3,4,5], [6,[7,8,9], []]]
>>> list(flatten(lol))
[1, 2, 3, 4, 5, 6, 7, 8, 9]
```

Async Functions

The keywords `async` and `await` were added to Python 3.5 to define and run *asynchronous functions*. They're:

- Relatively new
- Different enough to be harder to understand
- Will become more important and better known over time

For these reasons, I've moved discussion of these and other async topics to Appendix C.

For now, you need to know that if you see `async` before the `def` line for a function, it's an asynchronous function. Likewise, if you see `await` before a function call, that function is asynchronous.

The main difference between asynchronous and normal functions is that async ones can "give up control" rather than running to completion.

Exceptions

In some languages, errors are indicated by special function return values. When things go south,[7] Python uses *exceptions*: code that is executed when an associated error occurs.

You've seen some of these already, such as accessing a list or tuple with an out-of-range position, or a dictionary with a nonexistent key. When you run code that might fail under some circumstances, you also need appropriate *exception handlers* to intercept any potential errors.

It's good practice to add exception handling anywhere an exception might occur to let the user know what is happening. You might not be able to fix the problem, but at least you can note the circumstances and shut your program down gracefully. If an exception occurs in some function and is not caught there, it *bubbles up* until it is caught by a matching handler in some calling function. If you don't provide your own exception handler, Python prints an error message and some information about

---

7 Is this northern hemispherism? Do Aussies and Kiwis say that things go "north" when they mess up?

where the error occurred and then terminates the program, as demonstrated in the following snippet:

```
>>> short_list = [1, 2, 3]
>>> position = 5
>>> short_list[position]
Traceback (most recent call last):
  File "<stdin>", line 1, in <module>
IndexError: list index out of range
```

Handle Errors with try and except

Do, or do not. There is no try.

—Yoda

Rather than leaving things to chance, use try to wrap your code, and except to provide the error handling:

```
>>> short_list = [1, 2, 3]
>>> position = 5
>>> try:
...     short_list[position]
... except:
...     print('Need a position between 0 and', len(short_list)-1, ' but got',
...             position)
...
Need a position between 0 and 2 but got 5
```

The code inside the try block is run. If there is an error, an exception is raised and the code inside the except block runs. If there are no errors, the except block is skipped.

Specifying a plain except with no arguments, as we did here, is a catchall for any exception type. If more than one type of exception could occur, it's best to provide a separate exception handler for each. No one forces you to do this; you can use a bare except to catch all exceptions, but your treatment of them would probably be generic (something akin to printing *Some error occurred*). You can use any number of specific exception handlers.

Sometimes, you want exception details beyond the type. You get the full exception object in the variable *name* if you use the form:

```
except exceptiontype as name
```

The example that follows looks for an IndexError first, because that's the exception type raised when you provide an illegal position to a sequence. It saves an IndexError exception in the variable err, and any other exception in the variable other. The example prints everything stored in other to show what you get in that object:

```
>>> short_list = [1, 2, 3]
>>> while True:
...     value = input('Position [q to quit]? ')
...     if value == 'q':
...         break
...     try:
...         position = int(value)
...         print(short_list[position])
...     except IndexError as err:
...         print('Bad index:', position)
...     except Exception as other:
...         print('Something else broke:', other)
...
Position [q to quit]? 1
2
Position [q to quit]? 0
1
Position [q to quit]? 2
3
Position [q to quit]? 3
Bad index: 3
Position [q to quit]? 2
3
Position [q to quit]? two
Something else broke: invalid literal for int() with base 10: 'two'
Position [q to quit]? q
```

Inputting position 3 raised an `IndexError` as expected. Entering `two` annoyed the `int()` function, which we handled in our second, catchall `except` code.

Make Your Own Exceptions

The previous section discussed handling exceptions, but all of the exceptions (such as `IndexError`) were predefined in Python or its standard library. You can use any of these for your own purposes. You can also define your own exception types to handle special situations that might arise in your own programs.

This requires defining a new object type with a *class*—something we don't get into until Chapter 10. So, if you're unfamiliar with classes, you might want to return to this section later.

An exception is a class. It is a child of the class `Exception`. Let's make an exception called `UppercaseException` and raise it when we encounter an uppercase word in a string:

```
>>> class UppercaseException(Exception):
...     pass
...
```

```
>>> words = ['eenie', 'meenie', 'miny', 'MO']
>>> for word in words:
...     if word.isupper():
...         raise UppercaseException(word)
...
Traceback (most recent call last):
  File "<stdin>", line 3, in <module>
__main__.UppercaseException: MO
```

We didn't even define any behavior for UppercaseException (notice we just used pass), letting its parent class Exception figure out what to print when the exception was raised.

You can access the exception object itself and print it:

```
>>> try:
...     raise OopsException('panic')
... except OopsException as exc:
...     print(exc)
...
panic
```

Coming Up

Objects! We had to get to them sometime in a book about an object-oriented language.

Things to Do

9.1 Define a function called good() that returns the following list: ['Harry', 'Ron', 'Hermione'].

9.2 Define a generator function called get_odds() that returns the odd numbers from range(10). Use a for loop to find and print the third value returned.

9.3 Define a decorator called test that prints 'start' when a function is called, and 'end' when it finishes.

9.4 Define an exception called OopsException. Raise this exception to see what happens. Then, write the code to catch this exception and print 'Caught an oops'.

CHAPTER 10

Oh Oh: Objects and Classes

No object is mysterious. The mystery is your eye.

—Elizabeth Bowen

Take an object. Do something to it. Do something else to it.

—Jasper Johns

As I've mentioned on various pages, everything in Python, from numbers to functions, is an object. However, Python hides most of the object machinery by means of special syntax. You can type num = 7 to create an object of type integer with the value 7, and assign an object reference to the name num. The only time you need to look inside objects is when you want to make your own or modify the behavior of existing objects. You'll see how to do both in this chapter.

What Are Objects?

An *object* is a custom data structure containing both data (variables, called *attributes*) and code (functions, called *methods*). It represents a unique instance of some concrete thing. Think of objects as nouns and their methods as verbs. An object represents an individual thing, and its methods define how it interacts with other things.

For example, the integer object with the value 7 is an object that facilitates methods such as addition and multiplication, as you saw in Chapter 3. 8 is a different object. This means there's an integer class built in somewhere in Python, to which both 7 and 8 belong. The strings 'cat' and 'duck' are also objects in Python, and have string methods that you've seen in Chapter 5, such as capitalize() and replace().

Unlike modules, you can have multiple objects (often referred to as *instances*) at the same time, each with potentially different attributes. They're like super data structures, with code thrown in.

Simple Objects

Let's start with basic object classes; we'll save the discussion of inheritance for a few pages.

Define a Class with class

To create a new object that no one has ever created before, you first define a *class* that indicates what it contains.

In Chapter 2, I compared an object to a plastic box. A *class* is like the mold that makes that box. For instance, Python has a built-in class that makes string objects such as 'cat' and 'duck', and the other standard data types—lists, dictionaries, and so on. To create your own custom object in Python, you first need to define a class by using the class keyword. Let's walk through some simple examples.

Suppose that you want to define objects to represent information about cats.[1] Each object will represent one feline. You'll first want to define a class called Cat as the mold. In the examples that follow, we try more than one version of this class as we build up from the simplest class to ones that actually do something useful.

 We're following the naming conventions of Python's PEP-8 (*https://oreil.ly/gAJOF*).

Our first try is the simplest possible class, an empty one:

```
>>> class Cat():
...     pass
```

You can also say:

```
>>> class Cat:
...     pass
```

Just as with functions, we needed to say pass to indicate that this class was empty. This definition is the bare minimum to create an object.

You create an object from a class by calling the class name as though it were a function:

```
>>> a_cat = Cat()
>>> another_cat = Cat()
```

---

1 Or even if you don't want to.

In this case, calling Cat() creates two individual objects from the Cat class, and we assigned them to the names a_cat and another_cat. But our Cat class had no other code, so the objects that we created from it just sit there and can't do much else.

Well, they can do a little.

Attributes

An *attribute* is a variable inside a class or object. During and after an object or class is created, you can assign attributes to it. An attribute can be any other object. Let's make two cat objects again:

```
>>> class Cat:
...     pass
...
>>> a_cat = Cat()
>>> a_cat
<__main__.Cat object at 0x100cd1da0>
>>> another_cat = Cat()
>>> another_cat
<__main__.Cat object at 0x100cd1e48>
```

When we defined the Cat class, we didn't specify how to print an object from that class. Python jumps in and prints something like <__main__.Cat object at 0x100cd1da0>. In "Magic Methods" on page 190, you'll see how to change this default behavior.

Now assign a few attributes to our first object:

```
>>> a_cat.age = 3
>>> a_cat.name = "Mr. Fuzzybuttons"
>>> a_cat.nemesis = another_cat
```

Can we access these? We sure hope so:

```
>>> a_cat.age
3
>>> a_cat.name
'Mr. Fuzzybuttons'
>>> a_cat.nemesis
<__main__.Cat object at 0x100cd1e48>
```

Because nemesis was an attribute referring to another Cat object, we can use a_cat.nemesis to access it, but this other object doesn't have a name attribute yet:

```
>>> a_cat.nemesis.name
Traceback (most recent call last):
  File "<stdin>", line 1, in <module>
AttributeError: 'Cat' object has no attribute 'name'
```

Let's name our archfeline:

```
>>> a_cat.nemesis.name = "Mr. Bigglesworth"
>>> a_cat.nemesis.name
'Mr. Bigglesworth'
```

Even the simplest object like this one can be used to store multiple attributes. So, you can use multiple objects to store different values, instead of using something like a list or dictionary.

When you hear *attributes*, it usually means object attributes. There are also *class attributes*, and you'll see the differences later in "Class and Object Attributes" on page 185.

Methods

A *method* is a function in a class or object. A method looks like any other function, but can be used in special ways that you'll see in "Properties for Attribute Access" on page 182 and "Method Types" on page 186.

Initialization

If you want to assign object attributes at creation time, you need the special Python object initialization method __init__():

```
>>> class Cat:
...     def __init__(self):
...         pass
```

This is what you'll see in real Python class definitions. I admit that the __init__() and self look strange. __init__() is the special Python name for a method that initializes an individual object from its class definition.[2] The self argument specifies that it refers to the individual object itself.

When you define __init__() in a class definition, its first parameter should be named self. Although self is not a reserved word in Python, it's common usage. No one reading your code later (including you!) will need to guess what you meant if you use self.

But even this second Cat class definition didn't create an object that really did anything. The third try is the charm that really shows how to create a simple object in Python and assign one of its attributes. This time, we add the parameter name to the initialization method:

---

[2] You'll see many examples of double underscores in Python names; to save syllables, some people pronounce them as *dunder*.

```
>>> class Cat():
...     def __init__(self, name):
...         self.name = name
...
>>>
```

Now we can create an object from the Cat class by passing a string for the name parameter:

```
>>> furball = Cat('Grumpy')
```

Here's what this line of code does:

- Looks up the definition of the Cat class
- *Instantiates* (creates) a new object in memory
- Calls the object's __init__() method, passing this newly created object as self and the other argument ('Grumpy') as name
- Stores the value of name in the object
- Returns the new object
- Attaches the variable furball to the object

This new object is like any other object in Python. You can use it as an element of a list, tuple, dictionary, or set. You can pass it to a function as an argument, or return it as a result.

What about the name value that we passed in? It was saved with the object as an attribute. You can read and write it directly:

```
>>> print('Our latest addition: ', furball.name)
Our latest addition: Grumpy
```

Remember, *inside* the Cat class definition, you access the name attribute as self.name. When you create an actual object and assign it to a variable like furball, you refer to it as furball.name.

It is *not* necessary to have an __init__() method in every class definition; it's used to do anything that's needed to distinguish this object from others created from the same class. It's not what some other languages would call a "constructor." Python already constructed the object for you. Think of __init__() as an *initializer*.

You can make many individual objects from a single class. But remember that Python implements data as objects, so the class itself is an object. However, there's only one class object in your program. If you defined class Cat as we did here, it's like the Highlander—there can be only one.

Inheritance

When you're trying to solve some coding problem, often you'll find an existing class that creates objects that do almost what you need. What can you do?

You could modify this old class, but you'll make it more complicated, and you might break something that used to work.

Or you could write a new class, cutting and pasting from the old one and merging your new code. But this means that you have more code to maintain, and the parts of the old and new classes that used to work the same might drift apart because they're now in separate places.

One solution is *inheritance*: creating a new class *from* an existing class, but with some additions or changes. It's a good way to reuse code. When you use inheritance, the new class can automatically use all the code from the old class but without you needing to copy any of it.

Inherit from a Parent Class

You define only what you need to add or change in the new class, and this overrides the behavior of the old class. The original class is called a *parent*, *superclass*, or *base class*; the new class is called a *child*, *subclass*, or *derived class*. These terms are interchangeable in object-oriented programming.

So, let's inherit something. In the next example, we define an empty class called Car. Next, we define a subclass of Car called Yugo.[3] You define a subclass by using the same class keyword but with the parent class name inside the parentheses (class Yugo(Car) here):

```
>>> class Car():
...     pass
...
>>> class Yugo(Car):
...     pass
...
```

You can check whether a class is derived from another class by using issubclass():

```
>>> issubclass(Yugo, Car)
True
```

Next, create an object from each class:

```
>>> give_me_a_car = Car()
>>> give_me_a_yugo = Yugo()
```

---

3 An inexpensive but not-so-good car from the '80s.

A child class is a specialization of a parent class; in object-oriented lingo, Yugo *is-a* Car. The object named give_me_a_yugo is an instance of class Yugo, but it also inherits whatever a Car can do. In this case, Car and Yugo are as useful as deckhands on a submarine, so let's try new class definitions that actually do something:

```
>>> class Car():
...     def exclaim(self):
...         print("I'm a Car!")
...
>>> class Yugo(Car):
...     pass
...
```

Finally, make one object from each class and call the exclaim method:

```
>>> give_me_a_car = Car()
>>> give_me_a_yugo = Yugo()
>>> give_me_a_car.exclaim()
I'm a Car!
>>> give_me_a_yugo.exclaim()
I'm a Car!
```

Without doing anything special, Yugo inherited the exclaim() method from Car. In fact, Yugo says that it *is* a Car, which might lead to an identity crisis. Let's see what we can do about that.

 Inheritance is appealing, but can be overused. Years of object-oriented programming experience have shown that too much use of inheritance can make programs hard to manage. Instead, it's often recommended to emphasize other techniques like aggregation and composition. We get to these alternatives in this chapter.

Override a Method

As you just saw, a new class initially inherits everything from its parent class. Moving forward, you'll see how to replace or override a parent method. Yugo should probably be different from Car in some way; otherwise, what's the point of defining a new class? Let's change how the exclaim() method works for a Yugo:

```
>>> class Car():
...     def exclaim(self):
...         print("I'm a Car!")
...
>>> class Yugo(Car):
...     def exclaim(self):
...         print("I'm a Yugo! Much like a Car, but more Yugo-ish.")
...
```

Now make two objects from these classes:

```
>>> give_me_a_car = Car()
>>> give_me_a_yugo = Yugo()
```

What do they say?

```
>>> give_me_a_car.exclaim()
I'm a Car!
>>> give_me_a_yugo.exclaim()
I'm a Yugo! Much like a Car, but more Yugo-ish.
```

In these examples, we overrode the exclaim() method. We can override any methods, including __init__(). Here's another example that uses a Person class. Let's make subclasses that represent doctors (MDPerson) and lawyers (JDPerson):

```
>>> class Person():
...     def __init__(self, name):
...         self.name = name
...
>>> class MDPerson(Person):
...     def __init__(self, name):
...         self.name = "Doctor " + name
...
>>> class JDPerson(Person):
...     def __init__(self, name):
...         self.name = name + ", Esquire"
...
```

In these cases, the initialization method __init__() takes the same arguments as the parent Person class but stores the value of name differently inside the object instance:

```
>>> person = Person('Fudd')
>>> doctor = MDPerson('Fudd')
>>> lawyer = JDPerson('Fudd')
>>> print(person.name)
Fudd
>>> print(doctor.name)
Doctor Fudd
>>> print(lawyer.name)
Fudd, Esquire
```

Add a Method

The child class can also *add* a method that was not present in its parent class. Going back to classes Car and Yugo, we'll define the new method need_a_push() for class Yugo only:

```
>>> class Car():
...     def exclaim(self):
...         print("I'm a Car!")
...
>>> class Yugo(Car):
```

```
...        def exclaim(self):
...            print("I'm a Yugo! Much like a Car, but more Yugo-ish.")
...        def need_a_push(self):
...            print("A little help here?")
...
```

Next, make a Car and a Yugo:

```
>>> give_me_a_car = Car()
>>> give_me_a_yugo = Yugo()
```

A Yugo object can react to a need_a_push() method call:

```
>>> give_me_a_yugo.need_a_push()
A little help here?
```

But a generic Car object cannot:

```
>>> give_me_a_car.need_a_push()
Traceback (most recent call last):
  File "<stdin>", line 1, in <module>
AttributeError: 'Car' object has no attribute 'need_a_push'
```

At this point, a Yugo can do something that a Car cannot, and the distinct personality of a Yugo can emerge.

Get Help from Your Parent with super()

We saw how the child class could add or override a method from the parent. What if it wanted to call that parent method? "I'm glad you asked," says super(). Here, we define a new class called EmailPerson that represents a Person with an email address. First, our familiar Person definition:

```
>>> class Person():
...        def __init__(self, name):
...            self.name = name
...
```

Notice that the __init__() call in the following subclass has an additional email parameter:

```
>>> class EmailPerson(Person):
...        def __init__(self, name, email):
...            super().__init__(name)
...            self.email = email
```

When you define an __init__() method for your class, you're replacing the __init__() method of its parent class, and the latter is not called automatically anymore. As a result, we need to call it explicitly. Here's what's happening:

- The super() gets the definition of the parent class, Person.

- The __init__() method calls the Person.__init__() method. It takes care of passing the self argument to the superclass, so you just need to give it any optional arguments. In our case, the only other argument Person() accepts is name.
- The self.email = email line is the new code that makes this EmailPerson different from a Person.

Moving on, let's make one of these creatures:

```
>>> bob = EmailPerson('Bob Frapples', 'bob@frapples.com')
```

We should be able to access both the name and email attributes:

```
>>> bob.name
'Bob Frapples'
>>> bob.email
'bob@frapples.com'
```

Why didn't we just define our new class as follows?

```
>>> class EmailPerson(Person):
...     def __init__(self, name, email):
...         self.name = name
...         self.email = email
```

We could have done that, but it would have defeated our use of inheritance. We used super() to make Person do its work, the same as a plain Person object would. There's another benefit: if the definition of Person changes in the future, using super() will ensure that the attributes and methods that EmailPerson inherits from Person will reflect the change.

Use super() when the child is doing something its own way but still needs something from the parent (as in real life).

Multiple Inheritance

You've just seen some class examples with no parent class, and some with one. Actually, objects can inherit from multiple parent classes.

If your class refers to a method or attribute that it doesn't have, Python will look in all the parents. What if more than one of them has something with that name? Who wins?

Unlike inheritance in people, where a dominant gene wins no matter who it came from, inheritance in Python depends on *method resolution order*. Each Python class has a special method called mro() that returns a list of the classes that would be visited to find a method or attribute for an object of that class. A similar attribute, called __mro__, is a tuple of those classes. Like a sudden-death playoff, the first one wins.

Here, we define a top `Animal` class, two child classes (`Horse` and `Donkey`), and then two derived from these:[4]

```
>>> class Animal:
...     def says(self):
...         return 'I speak!'
...
>>> class Horse(Animal):
...     def says(self):
...         return 'Neigh!'
...
>>> class Donkey(Animal):
...     def says(self):
...         return 'Hee-haw!'
...
>>> class Mule(Donkey, Horse):
...     pass
...
>>> class Hinny(Horse, Donkey):
...     pass
...
```

If we look for a method or attribute of a `Mule`, Python will look at the following things, in this order:

1. The object itself (of type `Mule`)

2. The object's class (`Mule`)

3. The class's first parent class (`Donkey`)

4. The class's second parent class (`Horse`)

5. The grandparent class (`Animal`) class

It's much the same for a `Hinny`, but with `Horse` before `Donkey`:

```
>>> Mule.mro()
[<class '__main__.Mule'>, <class '__main__.Donkey'>,
<class '__main__.Horse'>, <class '__main__.Animal'>,
<class 'object'>]
>>> Hinny.mro()
[<class '__main__.Hinny'>, <class '__main__.Horse'>,
<class '__main__.Donkey'>, <class '__main__.Animal'>,
class 'object'>]
```

So what do these fine beasts say?

```
>>> mule = Mule()
>>> hinny = Hinny()
```

---

4 A mule has a father donkey and mother horse; a hinny has a father horse and mother donkey.

```
>>> mule.says()
'hee-haw'
>>> hinny.says()
'neigh'
```

We listed the parent classes in (father, mother) order, so they talk like their dads.

If the Horse and Donkey did not have a says() method, the mule or hinny would have used the grandparent Animal class's says() method, and returned 'I speak!'.

Mixins

You may include an extra parent class in your class definition, but as a helper only. That is, it doesn't share any methods with the other parent classes, and avoids the method resolution ambiguity that I mentioned in the previous section.

Such a parent class is sometimes called a *mixin* class. Uses might include "side" tasks like logging. Here's a mixin that pretty-prints an object's attributes:

```
>>> class PrettyMixin():
...     def dump(self):
...         import pprint
...         pprint.pprint(vars(self))
...
>>> class Thing(PrettyMixin):
...     pass
...
>>> t = Thing()
>>> t.name = "Nyarlathotep"
>>> t.feature = "ichor"
>>> t.age = "eldritch"
>>> t.dump()
{'age': 'eldritch', 'feature': 'ichor', 'name': 'Nyarlathotep'}
```

In self Defense

One criticism of Python (besides the use of whitespace) is the need to include self as the first argument to instance methods (the kind of method you've seen in the previous examples). Python uses the self argument to find the right object's attributes and methods. For an example, I'll show how you would call an object's method, and what Python actually does behind the scenes.

Remember class Car from earlier examples? Let's call its exclaim() method again:

```
>>> a_car = Car()
>>> a_car.exclaim()
I'm a Car!
```

Here's what Python actually does, under the hood:

- Look up the class (Car) of the object a_car
- Pass the object a_car to the exclaim() method of the Car class as the self parameter

Just for fun, you can even run it this way yourself and it will work the same as the normal (a_car.exclaim()) syntax:

```
>>> Car.exclaim(a_car)
I'm a Car!
```

However, there's never a reason to use that lengthier style.

Attribute Access

In Python, object attributes and methods are normally public, and you're expected to behave yourself (this is sometimes called a "consenting adults" policy). Let's compare the direct approach with some alternatives.

Direct Access

As you've seen, you can get and set attribute values directly:

```
>>> class Duck:
...     def __init__(self, input_name):
...         self.name = input_name
...
>>> fowl = Duck('Daffy')
>>> fowl.name
'Daffy'
```

But what if someone misbehaves?

```
>>> fowl.name = 'Daphne'
>>> fowl.name
'Daphne'
```

The next two sections show ways to get some privacy for attributes that you don't want anyone to stomp by accident.

Getters and Setters

Some object-oriented languages support private object attributes that can't be accessed directly from the outside. Programmers then may need to write *getter* and *setter* methods to read and write the values of such private attributes.

Python doesn't have private attributes, but you can write getters and setters with obfuscated attribute names to get a little privacy. (The best solution is to use *properties*, described in the next section.)

In the following example, we define a `Duck` class with a single instance attribute called hidden_name. We don't want people to access this directly, so we define two methods: a getter (`get_name()`) and a setter (`set_name()`). Each is accessed by a property called name. I've added a `print()` statement to each method to show when it's being called:

```
>>> class Duck():
...     def __init__(self, input_name):
...         self.hidden_name = input_name
...     def get_name(self):
...         print('inside the getter')
...         return self.hidden_name
...     def set_name(self, input_name):
...         print('inside the setter')
...         self.hidden_name = input_name

>>> don = Duck('Donald')
>>> don.get_name()
inside the getter
'Donald'
>>> don.set_name('Donna')
inside the setter
>>> don.get_name()
inside the getter
'Donna'
```

Properties for Attribute Access

The Pythonic solution for attribute privacy is to use *properties*.

There are two ways to do this. The first way is to add name = property(get_name, set_name) as the final line of our previous Duck class definition:

```
>>> class Duck():
>>>     def __init__(self, input_name):
>>>         self.hidden_name = input_name
>>>     def get_name(self):
>>>         print('inside the getter')
>>>         return self.hidden_name
>>>     def set_name(self, input_name):
>>>         print('inside the setter')
>>>         self.hidden_name = input_name
>>>     name = property(get_name, set_name)
```

The old getter and setter still work:

```
>>> don = Duck('Donald')
>>> don.get_name()
inside the getter
'Donald'
>>> don.set_name('Donna')
inside the setter
>>> don.get_name()
```

```
inside the getter
'Donna'
```

But now you can also use the property name to get and set the hidden name:

```
>>> don = Duck('Donald')
>>> don.name
inside the getter
'Donald'
>>> don.name = 'Donna'
inside the setter
>>> don.name
inside the getter
'Donna'
```

In the second method, you add some decorators and replace the method names get_name and set_name with name:

- @property, which goes before the getter method
- @*name*.setter, which goes before the setter method

Here's how they actually look in the code:

```
>>> class Duck():
...     def __init__(self, input_name):
...         self.hidden_name = input_name
...     @property
...     def name(self):
...         print('inside the getter')
...         return self.hidden_name
...     @name.setter
...     def name(self, input_name):
...         print('inside the setter')
...         self.hidden_name = input_name
```

You can still access name as though it were an attribute:

```
>>> fowl = Duck('Howard')
>>> fowl.name
inside the getter
'Howard'
>>> fowl.name = 'Donald'
inside the setter
>>> fowl.name
inside the getter
'Donald'
```

 If anyone guessed that we called our attribute hidden_name, they could still read and write it directly as fowl.hidden_name. In "Name Mangling for Privacy" on page 184, you'll see how Python provides a special way to hide attribute names.

Properties for Computed Values

In the previous examples, we used the `name` property to refer to a single attribute (`hidden_name`) stored within the object.

A property can also return a *computed value*. Let's define a `Circle` class that has a `radius` attribute and a computed `diameter` property:

```
>>> class Circle():
...     def __init__(self, radius):
...         self.radius = radius
...     @property
...     def diameter(self):
...         return 2 * self.radius
...
```

Create a `Circle` object with an initial value for its `radius`:

```
>>> c = Circle(5)
>>> c.radius
5
```

We can refer to `diameter` as if it were an attribute such as `radius`:

```
>>> c.diameter
10
```

Here's the fun part: we can change the `radius` attribute at any time, and the diameter property will be computed from the current value of `radius`:

```
>>> c.radius = 7
>>> c.diameter
14
```

If you don't specify a setter property for an attribute, you can't set it from the outside. This is handy for read-only attributes:

```
>>> c.diameter = 20
Traceback (most recent call last):
  File "<stdin>", line 1, in <module>
AttributeError: can't set attribute
```

There's one more advantage of using a property over direct attribute access: if you ever change the definition of the attribute, you need to fix only the code within the class definition, not in all the callers.

Name Mangling for Privacy

In the `Duck` class example a little earlier, we called our (not completely) hidden attribute `hidden_name`. Python has a naming convention for attributes that should not be visible outside of their class definition: begin with two underscores (__).

Let's rename hidden_name to __name, as demonstrated here:

```
>>> class Duck():
...     def __init__(self, input_name):
...         self.__name = input_name
...     @property
...     def name(self):
...         print('inside the getter')
...         return self.__name
...     @name.setter
...     def name(self, input_name):
...         print('inside the setter')
...         self.__name = input_name
...
```

Take a moment to see whether everything still works:

```
>>> fowl = Duck('Howard')
>>> fowl.name
inside the getter
'Howard'
>>> fowl.name = 'Donald'
inside the setter
>>> fowl.name
inside the getter
'Donald'
```

Looks good. And you can't access the __name attribute:

```
>>> fowl.__name
Traceback (most recent call last):
  File "<stdin>", line 1, in <module>
AttributeError: 'Duck' object has no attribute '__name'
```

This naming convention doesn't make it completely private, but Python does *mangle* the attribute name to make it unlikely for external code to stumble upon it. If you're curious and promise not to tell everyone,[5] here's what it becomes:

```
>>> fowl._Duck__name
'Donald'
```

Notice that it didn't print inside the getter. Although this isn't perfect protection, name mangling discourages accidental or intentional direct access to the attribute.

Class and Object Attributes

You can assign attributes to classes, and they'll be inherited by their child objects:

```
>>> class Fruit:
...     color = 'red'
```

---

5 Can you keep a secret? Apparently, I can't.

```
...
>>> blueberry = Fruit()
>>> Fruit.color
'red'
>>> blueberry.color
'red'
```

But if you change the value of the attribute in the child object, it doesn't affect the class attribute:

```
>>> blueberry.color = 'blue'
>>> blueberry.color
'blue'
>>> Fruit.color
'red'
```

If you change the class attribute later, it won't affect existing child objects:

```
>>> Fruit.color = 'orange'
>>> Fruit.color
'orange'
>>> blueberry.color
'blue'
```

But it will affect new ones:

```
>>> new_fruit = Fruit()
>>> new_fruit.color
'orange'
```

Method Types

Some methods are part of the class itself, some are part of the objects that are created from that class, and some are none of the above:

- If there's no preceding decorator, it's an *instance method*, and its first argument should be self to refer to the individual object itself.

- If there's a preceding @classmethod decorator, it's a *class method*, and its first argument should be cls (or anything, just not the reserved word class), referring to the class itself.

- If there's a preceding @staticmethod decorator, it's a *static method*, and its first argument isn't an object or class.

The following sections have some details.

Instance Methods

When you see an initial self argument in methods within a class definition, it's an *instance method*. These are the types of methods that you would normally write when creating your own classes. The first parameter of an instance method is self, and Python passes the object to the method when you call it. These are the ones that you've seen so far.

Class Methods

In contrast, a *class method* affects the class as a whole. Any change you make to the class affects all of its objects. Within a class definition, a preceding @classmethod decorator indicates that that following function is a class method. Also, the first parameter to the method is the class itself. The Python tradition is to call the parameter cls, because class is a reserved word and can't be used here. Let's define a class method for A that counts how many object instances have been made from it:

```
>>> class A():
...     count = 0
...     def __init__(self):
...         A.count += 1
...     def exclaim(self):
...         print("I'm an A!")
...     @classmethod
...     def kids(cls):
...         print("A has", cls.count, "little objects.")
...
>>>
>>> easy_a = A()
>>> breezy_a = A()
>>> wheezy_a = A()
>>> A.kids()
A has 3 little objects.
```

Notice that we referred to A.count (the class attribute) in __init__() rather than self.count (which would be an object instance attribute). In the kids() method, we used cls.count, but we could just as well have used A.count.

Static Methods

A third type of method in a class definition affects neither the class nor its objects; it's just in there for convenience instead of floating around on its own. It's a *static method*, preceded by a @staticmethod decorator, with no initial self or cls parameter. Here's an example that serves as a commercial for the class CoyoteWeapon:

```
>>> class CoyoteWeapon():
...     @staticmethod
...     def commercial():
...         print('This CoyoteWeapon has been brought to you by Acme')
...
>>>
>>> CoyoteWeapon.commercial()
This CoyoteWeapon has been brought to you by Acme
```

Notice that we didn't need to create an object from class `CoyoteWeapon` to access this method. Very class-y.

Duck Typing

Python has a loose implementation of *polymorphism*; it applies the same operation to different objects, based on the method's name and arguments, regardless of their class.

Let's use the same `__init__()` initializer for all three `Quote` classes now, but add two new functions:

- `who()` just returns the value of the saved `person` string
- `says()` returns the saved `words` string with the specific punctuation

And here they are in action:

```
>>> class Quote():
...     def __init__(self, person, words):
...         self.person = person
...         self.words = words
...     def who(self):
...         return self.person
...     def says(self):
...         return self.words + '.'
...
>>> class QuestionQuote(Quote):
...     def says(self):
...         return self.words + '?'
...
>>> class ExclamationQuote(Quote):
...     def says(self):
...         return self.words + '!'
...
>>>
```

We didn't change how `QuestionQuote` or `ExclamationQuote` were initialized, so we didn't override their `__init__()` methods. Python then automatically calls the `__init__()` method of the parent class `Quote` to store the instance variables `person` and `words`. That's why we can access `self.words` in objects created from the subclasses `QuestionQuote` and `ExclamationQuote`.

Next up, let's make some objects:

```
>>> hunter = Quote('Elmer Fudd', "I'm hunting wabbits")
>>> print(hunter.who(), 'says:', hunter.says())
Elmer Fudd says: I'm hunting wabbits.
```

```
>>> hunted1 = QuestionQuote('Bugs Bunny', "What's up, doc")
>>> print(hunted1.who(), 'says:', hunted1.says())
Bugs Bunny says: What's up, doc?

>>> hunted2 = ExclamationQuote('Daffy Duck', "It's rabbit season")
>>> print(hunted2.who(), 'says:', hunted2.says())
Daffy Duck says: It's rabbit season!
```

Three different versions of the says() method provide different behavior for the three classes. This is traditional polymorphism in object-oriented languages. Python goes a little further and lets you run the who() and says() methods of *any* objects that have them. Let's define a class called BabblingBrook that has no relation to our previous woodsy hunter and huntees (descendants of the Quote class):

```
>>> class BabblingBrook():
...     def who(self):
...         return 'Brook'
...     def says(self):
...         return 'Babble'
...
>>> brook = BabblingBrook()
```

Now run the who() and says() methods of various objects, one (brook) completely unrelated to the others:

```
>>> def who_says(obj):
...     print(obj.who(), 'says', obj.says())
...
>>> who_says(hunter)
Elmer Fudd says I'm hunting wabbits.
>>> who_says(hunted1)
Bugs Bunny says What's up, doc?
>>> who_says(hunted2)
Daffy Duck says It's rabbit season!
>>> who_says(brook)
Brook says Babble
```

This behavior is sometimes called *duck typing*, after the old saying:

> If it walks like a duck and quacks like a duck, it's a duck.
>
> —A Wise Person

Who are we to argue with a wise saying about ducks?

Figure 10-1. Duck typing is not hunt-and-peck

Magic Methods

You can now create and use basic objects. What you'll learn in this section might surprise you—in a good way.

When you type something such as a = 3 + 8, how do the integer objects with values 3 and 8 know how to implement +? Or, if you type name = "Daffy" + " " + "Duck", how does Python know that + now means to concatenate these strings? And how do a and name know how to use = to get the result? You can get at these operators by using Python's *special methods* (or, more dramatically, *magic methods*).

The names of these methods begin and end with double underscores (__). Why? They're very unlikely to have been chosen by programmers as variable names. You've already seen one: __init__() initializes a newly created object from its class definition and any arguments that were passed in. You've also seen ("Name Mangling for Privacy" on page 184) how "dunder" naming helps to mangle class attribute names as well as methods.

Suppose that you have a simple Word class, and you want an equals() method that compares two words but ignores case. That is, a Word containing the value 'ha' would be considered equal to one containing 'HA'.

The example that follows is a first attempt, with a normal method we're calling equals(). self.text is the text string that this Word object contains, and the equals() method compares it with the text string of word2 (another Word object):

```
>>> class Word():
...     def __init__(self, text):
...         self.text = text
...
...     def equals(self, word2):
...         return self.text.lower() == word2.text.lower()
...
```

Then, make three Word objects from three different text strings:

```
>>> first = Word('ha')
>>> second = Word('HA')
>>> third = Word('eh')
```

When strings 'ha' and 'HA' are compared to lowercase, they should be equal:

```
>>> first.equals(second)
True
```

But the string 'eh' will not match 'ha':

```
>>> first.equals(third)
False
```

We defined the method equals() to do this lowercase conversion and comparison. It would be nice to just say if first == second, just like Python's built-in types. So, let's do that. We change the equals() method to the special name __eq__() (you'll see why in a moment):

```
>>> class Word():
...     def __init__(self, text):
...         self.text = text
...     def __eq__(self, word2):
...         return self.text.lower() == word2.text.lower()
...
```

Let's see whether it works:

```
>>> first = Word('ha')
>>> second = Word('HA')
>>> third = Word('eh')
>>> first == second
True
>>> first == third
False
```

Magic! All we needed was the Python's special method name for testing equality, __eq__(). Tables 10-1 and 10-2 list the names of the most useful magic methods.

Table 10-1. Magic methods for comparison

Method	Description
__eq__(*self, other*)	*self == other*
__ne__(*self, other*)	*self != other*
__lt__(*self, other*)	*self < other*
__gt__(*self, other*)	*self > other*
__le__(*self, other*)	*self <= other*
__ge__(*self, other*)	*self >= other*

Table 10-2. Magic methods for math

Method	Description
__add__(*self, other*)	*self + other*
__sub__(*self, other*)	*self – other*
__mul__(*self, other*)	*self * other*
__floordiv__(*self, other*)	*self // other*
__truediv__(*self, other*)	*self / other*
__mod__(*self, other*)	*self % other*
__pow__(*self, other*)	*self ** other*

You aren't restricted to use the math operators such as + (magic method __add__())
and – (magic method __sub__()) with numbers. For instance, Python string objects
use + for concatenation and * for duplication. There are many more, documented
online at Special method names (*http://bit.ly/pydocs-smn*). The most common among
them are presented in Table 10-3.

Table 10-3. Other, miscellaneous magic methods

Method	Description
__str__(*self*)	str(*self*)
__repr__(*self*)	repr(*self*)
__len__(*self*)	len(*self*)

Besides __init__(), you might find yourself using __str__() the most in your own
methods. It's how you print your object. It's used by print(), str(), and the string
formatters, which you can read about in Chapter 5. The interactive interpreter uses
the __repr__() function to echo variables to output. If you fail to define either
__str__() or __repr__(), you get Python's default string version of your object:

```
>>> first = Word('ha')
>>> first
<__main__.Word object at 0x1006ba3d0>
```

```
>>> print(first)
<__main__.Word object at 0x1006ba3d0>
```

Let's add both __str__() and __repr__() methods to the Word class to make it prettier:

```
>>> class Word():
...     def __init__(self, text):
...         self.text = text
...     def __eq__(self, word2):
...         return self.text.lower() == word2.text.lower()
...     def __str__(self):
...         return self.text
...     def __repr__(self):
...         return 'Word("'  + self.text  + '")'
...
>>> first = Word('ha')
>>> first          # uses __repr__
Word("ha")
>>> print(first)   # uses __str__
ha
```

To explore even more special methods, check out the Python documentation (*http:// bit.ly/pydocs-smn*).

Aggregation and Composition

Inheritance is a good technique to use when you want a child class to act like its parent class most of the time (when child *is-a* parent). It's tempting to build elaborate inheritance hierarchies, but sometimes *composition* or *aggregation* make more sense. What's the difference? In composition, one thing is part of another. A duck *is-a* bird (inheritance), but *has-a* tail (composition). A tail is not a kind of duck, but part of a duck. In this next example, let's make bill and tail objects and provide them to a new duck object:

```
>>> class Bill():
...     def __init__(self, description):
...         self.description = description
...
>>> class Tail():
...     def __init__(self, length):
...         self.length = length
...
>>> class Duck():
...     def __init__(self, bill, tail):
...         self.bill = bill
...         self.tail = tail
...     def about(self):
...         print('This duck has a', self.bill.description,
...             'bill and a', self.tail.length, 'tail')
...
```

```
>>> a_tail = Tail('long')
>>> a_bill = Bill('wide orange')
>>> duck = Duck(a_bill, a_tail)
>>> duck.about()
This duck has a wide orange bill and a long tail
```

Aggregation expresses relationships, but is a little looser: one thing *uses* another, but both exist independently. A duck *uses* a lake, but one is not a part of the other.

When to Use Objects or Something Else

Here are some guidelines for deciding whether to put your code and data in a class, module (discussion coming in Chapter 11), or something entirely different:

- Objects are most useful when you need a number of individual instances that have similar behavior (methods), but differ in their internal states (attributes).

- Classes support inheritance, modules don't.

- If you want only one of something, a module might be best. No matter how many times a Python module is referenced in a program, only one copy is loaded. (Java and C++ programmers: you can use a Python module as a *singleton*.)

- If you have a number of variables that contain multiple values and can be passed as arguments to multiple functions, it might be better to define them as classes. For example, you might use a dictionary with keys such as `size` and `color` to represent a color image. You could create a different dictionary for each image in your program, and pass them as arguments to functions such as `scale()` or `transform()`. This can get messy as you add keys and functions. It's more coherent to define an `Image` class with attributes `size` or `color` and methods `scale()` and `transform()`. Then, all the data and methods for a color image are defined in one place.

- Use the simplest solution to the problem. A dictionary, list, or tuple is simpler, smaller, and faster than a module, which is usually simpler than a class.

  Guido's advice:

  > Avoid overengineering datastructures. Tuples are better than objects (try namedtuple, too, though). Prefer simple fields over getter/setter functions...Built-in datatypes are your friends. Use more numbers, strings, tuples, lists, sets, dicts. Also check out the collections library, especially deque.
  >
  > —Guido van Rossum

- A newer alternative is the *dataclass*, in "Dataclasses" on page 196.

Named Tuples

Because Guido just mentioned them and I haven't yet, this is a good place to talk about *named tuples*. A named tuple is a subclass of tuples with which you can access values by name (with `.name`) as well as by position (with [*offset*]).

Let's take the example from the previous section and convert the `Duck` class to a named tuple, with `bill` and `tail` as simple string attributes. We'll call the `namedtuple` function with two arguments:

- The name
- A string of the field names, separated by spaces

Named tuples are not automatically supplied with Python, so you need to load a module before using them. We do that in the first line of the following example:

```
>>> from collections import namedtuple
>>> Duck = namedtuple('Duck', 'bill tail')
>>> duck = Duck('wide orange', 'long')
>>> duck
Duck(bill='wide orange', tail='long')
>>> duck.bill
'wide orange'
>>> duck.tail
'long'
```

You can also make a named tuple from a dictionary:

```
>>> parts = {'bill': 'wide orange', 'tail': 'long'}
>>> duck2 = Duck(**parts)
>>> duck2
Duck(bill='wide orange', tail='long')
```

In the preceding code, take a look at `**parts`. This is a *keyword argument*. It extracts the keys and values from the `parts` dictionary and supplies them as arguments to `Duck()`. It has the same effect as:

```
>>> duck2 = Duck(bill = 'wide orange', tail = 'long')
```

Named tuples are immutable, but you can replace one or more fields and return another named tuple:

```
>>> duck3 = duck2._replace(tail='magnificent', bill='crushing')
>>> duck3
Duck(bill='crushing', tail='magnificent')
```

We could have defined duck as a dictionary:

```
>>> duck_dict = {'bill': 'wide orange', 'tail': 'long'}
>>> duck_dict
{'tail': 'long', 'bill': 'wide orange'}
```

You can add fields to a dictionary:

```
>>> duck_dict['color'] = 'green'
>>> duck_dict
{'color': 'green', 'tail': 'long', 'bill': 'wide orange'}
```

But not to a named tuple:

```
>>> duck.color = 'green'
Traceback (most recent call last):
  File "<stdin>", line 1, in <module>
AttributeError: 'Duck' object has no attribute 'color'
```

To recap, here are some of the pros of a named tuple:

- It looks and acts like an immutable object.
- It is more space and time efficient than objects.
- You can access attributes by using dot notation instead of dictionary-style square brackets.
- You can use it as a dictionary key.

Dataclasses

Many people like to create objects mainly to store data (as object attributes), not so much behavior (methods). You just saw how named tuples can be an alternative data store. Python 3.7 introduced *dataclasses*.

Here's a plain old object with a single name attribute:

```
>> class TeenyClass():
...     def __init__(self, name):
...         self.name = name
...
>>> teeny = TeenyClass('itsy')
>>> teeny.name
'itsy'
```

Doing the same with a dataclass looks a little different:

```
>>> from dataclasses import dataclass
>>> @dataclass
... class TeenyDataClass:
...     name: str
...
>>> teeny = TeenyDataClass('bitsy')
>>> teeny.name
'bitsy'
```

Besides needing a @dataclass decorator, you define the class's attributes using *variable annotations* (*https://oreil.ly/NyGfE*) of the form *name: type* or *name: type =*

val, like color: str or color: str = "red". The *type* can be any Python object type, including classes you've created, not just the built-in ones like str or int.

When you're creating the dataclass object, you provide the arguments in the order in which they were specified in the class, or use named arguments in any order:

```
>>> from dataclasses import dataclass
>>> @dataclass
... class AnimalClass:
...     name: str
...     habitat: str
...     teeth: int = 0
...
>>> snowman = AnimalClass('yeti', 'Himalayas', 46)
>>> duck = AnimalClass(habitat='lake', name='duck')
>>> snowman
AnimalClass(name='yeti', habitat='Himalayas', teeth=46)
>>> duck
AnimalClass(name='duck', habitat='lake', teeth=0)
```

AnimalClass defined a default value for its teeth attribute, so we didn't need to provide it when making a duck.

You can refer to the object attributes like any other object's:

```
>>> duck.habitat
'lake'
>>> snowman.teeth
46
```

There's a lot more to dataclasses. See this guide (*https://oreil.ly/czTf-*) or the official (heavy) docs (*https://oreil.ly/J19Yl*).

Attrs

You've seen how to create classes and add attributes, and how they can involve a lot of typing—things like defining __init__(), assigning its arguments to self counterparts, and creating all those dunder methods like __str__(). Named tuples and dataclasses are alternatives in the standard library that may be easier when you mainly want to create a data collection.

The One Python Library Everyone Needs (*https://oreil.ly/QbbI1*) compares plain classes, named tuples, and dataclasses. It recommends the third-party package attrs (*https://oreil.ly/Rdwlx*) for many reasons—less typing, data validation, and more. Take a look and see whether you prefer it to the built-in solutions.

Coming Up

In the next chapter, you'll step up a level in code structures to Python *modules* and *packages*.

Things to Do

10.1 Make a class called Thing with no contents and print it. Then, create an object called example from this class and also print it. Are the printed values the same or different?

10.2 Make a new class called Thing2 and assign the value 'abc' to a class attribute called letters. Print letters.

10.3 Make yet another class called, of course, Thing3. This time, assign the value 'xyz' to an instance (object) attribute called letters. Print letters. Do you need to make an object from the class to do this?

10.4 Make a class called Element, with instance attributes name, symbol, and number. Create an object of this class with the values 'Hydrogen', 'H', and 1.

10.5 Make a dictionary with these keys and values: 'name': 'Hydrogen', 'symbol': 'H', 'number': 1. Then, create an object called hydrogen from class Element using this dictionary.

10.6 For the Element class, define a method called dump() that prints the values of the object's attributes (name, symbol, and number). Create the hydrogen object from this new definition and use dump() to print its attributes.

10.7 Call print(hydrogen). In the definition of Element, change the name of the method dump to __str__, create a new hydrogen object, and call print(hydrogen) again.

10.8 Modify Element to make the attributes name, symbol, and number private. Define a getter property for each to return its value.

10.9 Define three classes: Bear, Rabbit, and Octothorpe. For each, define only one method: eats(). This should return 'berries' (Bear), 'clover' (Rabbit), or 'campers' (Octothorpe). Create one object from each and print what it eats.

10.10 Define these classes: Laser, Claw, and SmartPhone. Each has only one method: does(). This returns 'disintegrate' (Laser), 'crush' (Claw), or 'ring' (Smart Phone). Then, define the class Robot that has one instance (object) of each of these. Define a does() method for the Robot that prints what its component objects do.

CHAPTER 11

Modules, Packages, and Goodies

During your bottom-up climb, you've progressed from built-in data types to constructing ever-larger data and code structures. In this chapter, you finally learn how to write realistic whole programs in Python. You'll write your own *modules* and learn how to use others from Python's *standard library* and other sources.

The text of this book is organized in a hierarchy: words, sentences, paragraphs, and chapters. Otherwise, it would be unreadable pretty quickly.[1] Code has a roughly similar bottom-up organization: data types are like words; expressions and statements are like sentences; functions are like paragraphs; and modules are like chapters. To continue the analogy, in this book, when I say that something will be explained in Chapter 8, in programming that's like referring to code in another module.

Modules and the import Statement

We'll create and use Python code in more than one file. A *module* is just a file of any Python code. You don't need to do anything special—any Python code can be used as a module by others.

We refer to code of other modules by using the Python `import` statement. This makes the code and variables in the imported module available to your program.

Import a Module

The simplest use of the `import` statement is `import module`, where *module* is the name of another Python file, without the *.py* extension.

---

1 At least, a little less readable than it already is.

Let's say you and a few others want something fast for lunch, but don't want a long discussion, and you always end up picking what the loudest person wants anyhow. Let the computer decide! Let's write a module with a single function that returns a random fast-food choice, and a main program that calls it and prints the choice.

The module (*fast.py*) is shown in Example 11-1.

Example 11-1. fast.py

```
from random import choice

places = ['McDonalds", "KFC", "Burger King", "Taco Bell",
    "Wendys", "Arbys", "Pizza Hut"]

def pick():  # see the docstring below?
    """Return random fast food place"""
    return choice(places)
```

And Example 11-2 shows the main program that imports it (call it *lunch.py*).

Example 11-2. lunch.py

```
import fast

place = fast.pick()
print("Let's go to", place)
```

If you have these two files in the same directory and instruct Python to run *lunch.py* as the main program, it will access the `fast` module and run its `pick()` function. We wrote this version of `pick()` to return a random result from a list of strings, so that's what the main program will get back and print:

```
$ python lunch.py
Let's go to Burger King
$ python lunch.py
Let's go to Pizza Hut
$ python lunch.py
Let's go to Arbys
```

We used imports in two different places:

- The main program *lunch.py* imported our new module `fast`.
- The module file *fast.py* imported the `choice` function from Python's standard library module named `random`.

We also used imports in two different ways in our main program and our module:

- In the first case, we imported the entire fast module but needed to use fast as a prefix to pick(). After this import statement, everything in *fast.py* is available to the main program, as long as we tack fast. before its name. By *qualifying* the contents of a module with the module's name, we avoid any nasty naming conflicts. There could be a pick() function in some other module, and we would not call it by mistake.

- In the second case, we're within a module and know that nothing else named choice is here, so we imported the choice() function from the random module directly.

We could have written *fast.py*, as shown in Example 11-3, importing random within the pick() function instead of at the top of the file.

Example 11-3. fast2.py

```
places = ['McDonalds", "KFC", "Burger King", "Taco Bell",
    "Wendys", "Arbys", "Pizza Hut"]

def pick():
    import random
    return random.choice(places)
```

Like many aspects of programming, use the style that seems the most clear to you. The module-qualified name (random.choice) is safer but requires a little more typing.

Consider importing from outside the function if the imported code might be used in more than one place, and from inside if you know its use will be limited. Some people prefer to put all their imports at the top of the file, just to make all the dependencies of their code explicit. Either way works.

Import a Module with Another Name

In our main *lunch.py* program, we called import fast. But what if you:

- Have another module named fast somewhere?
- Want to use a name that is more mnemonic?
- Caught your fingers in a door and want to minimize typing?

In these cases, you can import using an *alias*, as shown in Example 11-4. Let's use the alias f.

Example 11-4. fast3.py

```
import fast as f
place = f.pick()
print("Let's go to", place)
```

Import Only What You Want from a Module

You can import a whole module or just parts of it. You just saw the latter: we only wanted the choice() function from the random module.

Like the module itself, you can use an alias for each thing that you import.

Let's redo *lunch.py* a few more times. First, import pick() from the fast module with its original name (Example 11-5).

Example 11-5. fast4.py

```
from fast import pick
place = pick()
print("Let's go to", place)
```

Now import it as who_cares(Example 11-6).

Example 11-6. fast5.py

```
from fast import pick as who_cares
place = who_cares()
print("Let's go to", place)
```

Packages

We went from single lines of code, to multiline functions, to standalone programs, to multiple modules in the same directory. If you don't have many modules, the same directory works fine.

To allow Python applications to scale even more, you can organize modules into file and module hierarchies called *packages*. A package is just a subdirectory that contains *.py* files. And you can go more than one level deep, with directories inside those.

We just wrote a module that chooses a fast-food place. Let's add a similar module to dispense life advice. We'll make one new main program called *questions.py* in our current directory. Now make a subdirectory named *choices* and put two modules in it —*fast.py* and *advice.py*. Each module has a function that returns a string.

The main program (*questions.py*) has an extra import and line (Example 11-7).

Example 11-7. questions.py

```
from sources import fast, advice

print("Let's go to", fast.pick())
print("Should we take out?", advice.give())
```

That `from sources` makes Python look for a directory named *sources*, starting under your current directory. Inside *sources* it looks for the files *fast.py* and *advice.py*.

The first module (*choices/fast.py*) is the same code as before, just moved into the *choices* directory (Example 11-8).

Example 11-8. choices/fast.py

```
from random import choice

places = ["McDonalds", "KFC", "Burger King", "Taco Bell",
    "Wendys", "Arbys", "Pizza Hut"]

def pick():
    """Return random fast food place"""
    return choice(places)
```

The second module (*choices/advice.py*) is new, but it works a lot like its fast-food relative (Example 11-9).

Example 11-9. choices/advice.py

```
from random import choice

answers = ["Yes!", "No!", "Reply hazy", "Sorry, what?"]

def give():
    """Return random advice"""
    return choice(answers)
```

 If your version of Python is earlier than 3.3, you'll need one more thing in the *sources* subdirectory to make it a Python package: a file named *__init__.py*. This can be an empty file, but pre-3.3 Python needs it to treat the directory containing it as a package. (This is another common Python interview question.)

Run the main *questions.py* program (from your current directory, not in *sources*) to see what happens:

```
$ python questions.py
Let's go to KFC
Should we take out? Yes!
$ python questions.py
Let's go to Wendys
Should we take out? Reply hazy
$ python questions.py
Let's go to McDonalds
Should we take out? Reply hazy
```

The Module Search Path

I just said that Python looks under your current directory for the subdirectory *choices* and its modules. Actually, it looks in other places, as well, and you can control this.

Earlier, we imported the function choice() from the standard library's random module. That wasn't in your current directory, so Python needed to look elsewhere also.

To see all the places that your Python interpreter looks, import the standard sys module and use its path list. This is a list of directory names and ZIP archive files that Python searches in order to find modules to import.

You can access and modify this list. Here's the value of sys.path for Python 3.7 on my Mac:

```
>>> import sys
>>> for place in sys.path:
...     print(place)
...

/Library/Frameworks/Python.framework/Versions/3.7/lib/python37.zip
/Library/Frameworks/Python.framework/Versions/3.7/lib/python3.7
/Library/Frameworks/Python.framework/Versions/3.7/lib/python3.7/lib-dynload
```

That initial blank output line is the empty string '', which stands for the current directory. If '' is first in sys.path, Python looks in the current directory first when you try to import something: import fast looks for *fast.py*. This is Python's usual setup. Also, when we made that subdirectory called *sources* and put Python files in it, they could be imported with import sources or from sources import fast.

The first match will be used. This means that if you define a module named random and it's in the search path before the standard library, you won't be able to access the standard library's random now.

You can modify the search path within your code. Let's say you want Python to look in the */my/modules* directory before any other:

```
>>> import sys
>>> sys.path.insert(0, "/my/modules")
```

Relative and Absolute Imports

In our examples so far, we imported our own modules from:

- The current directory
- The subdirectory *choices*
- The Python standard library

This works well until you have a local module with the same name as a standard one. Which do you want?

Python supports *absolute* or *relative* imports. The examples that you've seen so far are absolute imports. If you typed `import rougarou`, for each directory in the search path, Python will look for a file named *rougarou.py* (a module) or a directory named *rougarou* (a package).

- If *rougarou.py* is in the same directory as your calling problem, you can import it *relative* to your location with `from . import rougarou`.
- If it's in the directory above you: `from .. import rougarou`.
- If it's under a sibling directory called `creatures`: `from ..creatures import rougarou`.

The `.` and `..` notation was borrowed from Unix's shorthand for *current directory* and *parent directory*.

For a good discussion of Python import problems that you may run into, see Traps for the Unwary in Python's Import System (*https://oreil.ly/QMWHY*).

Namespace Packages

You've seen that you can package Python modules as:

- A single *module* (*.py* file)
- A *package* (directory containing modules, and possibly other packages)

You can also split a package across directories with *namespace packages*. Say you want a package called *critters* that will contain a Python module for each dangerous creature (real or imagined, supposedly with background info and protective hints). This might get large over time, and you'd like to subdivide these by geographic location. One option is to add location subpackages under *critters* and move the existing *.py* module files under them, but this would break things for other modules that import them. Instead, we can go *up* and do the following:

- Make new location directories above *critters*

- Make cousin *critters* directories under these new parents
- Move existing modules to their respective directories.

This needs some illustration. Say we started with this file layout:

```
critters
  └ rougarou.py
  └ wendigo.py
```

Normal imports of these modules would look like this:

```
from critters import wendigo, rougarou
```

Now if we decided on US locations *north* and *south*, the files and directories would look like this:

```
north
  └ critters
      └ wendigo.py
south
  └ critters
      └ rougarou.py
```

If both *north* and *south* are in your module search path, you can import the modules as though they were still cohabiting a single-directory package:

```
from critters import wendigo, rougarou
```

Modules Versus Objects

When should you put your code into a module, and when into an object?

They look similar in many ways. An object or module called `thing` with an internal data value called `stuff` would let you access the value as `thing.stuff`. `stuff` may have been defined when the module or class was created, or it may have been assigned later.

All the classes, functions, and global variables in a module are available to the outside. Objects can use properties and "dunder" (__ ...) naming to hide or control access to their data attributes.

This means you can do this:

```
>>> import math
>>> math.pi
3.141592653589793
>>> math.pi = 3.0
>>> math.pi
3.0
```

Did you just ruin calculations for everyone on this computer? Yes! No, I'm kidding.[2] This did not affect the Python math module. You only changed the value of pi for the copy of the math module code imported by your calling program, and all evidence of your crimes will disappear when it finishes.

There's only one copy of any module imported by your program, even if you import it more than once. You can use it to save global things, of interest to any code that imports it. This is similar to a class, which also has only one copy, although you can have many objects created from it.

Goodies in the Python Standard Library

One of Python's prominent claims is that it has "batteries included"—a large standard library of modules that perform many useful tasks. They are kept separate to avoid bloating the core language. When you're about to write some Python code, it's often worthwhile to first check whether there's a standard module that already does what you want. It's surprising how often you encounter little gems in the standard library. Python also provides authoritative documentation (*http://docs.python.org/3/library*) for the modules, along with a tutorial (*http://bit.ly/library-tour*). Doug Hellmann's website Python Module of the Week (*http://bit.ly/py-motw*) and book *The Python Standard Library by Example* (*http://bit.ly/py-libex*) (Addison-Wesley Professional) are also very useful guides.

Upcoming chapters in this book feature many of the standard modules that are specific to the web, systems, databases, and so on. In this section, I talk about some standard modules that have generic uses.

Handle Missing Keys with setdefault() and defaultdict()

You've seen that trying to access a dictionary with a nonexistent key raises an exception. Using the dictionary get() function to return a default value avoids an exception. The setdefault() function is like get(), but also assigns an item to the dictionary if the key is missing:

```
>>> periodic_table = {'Hydrogen': 1, 'Helium': 2}
>>> periodic_table
{'Hydrogen': 1, 'Helium': 2}
```

If the key was *not* already in the dictionary, the new value is used:

```
>>> carbon = periodic_table.setdefault('Carbon', 12)
>>> carbon
12
```

---

2 Or am I? Bwa ha ha.

```
>>> periodic_table
{'Hydrogen': 1, 'Helium': 2, 'Carbon': 12}
```

If we try to assign a different default value to an *existing* key, the original value is returned and nothing is changed:

```
>>> helium = periodic_table.setdefault('Helium', 947)
>>> helium
2
>>> periodic_table
{'Hydrogen': 1, 'Helium': 2, 'Carbon': 12}
```

defaultdict() is similar, but specifies the default value for any new key up front, when the dictionary is created. Its argument is a function. In this example, we pass the function int, which will be called as int() and return the integer 0:

```
>>> from collections import defaultdict
>>> periodic_table = defaultdict(int)
```

Now any missing value will be an integer (int), with the value 0:

```
>>> periodic_table['Hydrogen'] = 1
>>> periodic_table['Lead']
0
>>> periodic_table
defaultdict(<class 'int'>, {'Hydrogen': 1, 'Lead': 0})
```

The argument to defaultdict() is a function that returns the value to be assigned to a missing key. In the following example, no_idea() is executed to return a value when needed:

```
>>> from collections import defaultdict
>>>
>>> def no_idea():
...     return 'Huh?'
...
>>> bestiary = defaultdict(no_idea)
>>> bestiary['A'] = 'Abominable Snowman'
>>> bestiary['B'] = 'Basilisk'
>>> bestiary['A']
'Abominable Snowman'
>>> bestiary['B']
'Basilisk'
>>> bestiary['C']
'Huh?'
```

You can use the functions int(), list(), or dict() to return default empty values for those types: int() returns 0, list() returns an empty list ([]), and dict() returns an empty dictionary ({}). If you omit the argument, the initial value of a new key will be set to None.

By the way, you can use `lambda` to define your default-making function right inside the call:

```
>>> bestiary = defaultdict(lambda: 'Huh?')
>>> bestiary['E']
'Huh?'
```

Using `int` is one way to make your own counter:

```
>>> from collections import defaultdict
>>> food_counter = defaultdict(int)
>>> for food in ['spam', 'spam', 'eggs', 'spam']:
...     food_counter[food] += 1
...
>>> for food, count in food_counter.items():
...     print(food, count)
...
eggs 1
spam 3
```

In the preceding example, if `food_counter` had been a normal dictionary instead of a `defaultdict`, Python would have raised an exception every time we tried to increment the dictionary element `food_counter[food]` because it would not have been initialized. We would have needed to do some extra work, as shown here:

```
>>> dict_counter = {}
>>> for food in ['spam', 'spam', 'eggs', 'spam']:
...     if not food in dict_counter:
...         dict_counter[food] = 0
...     dict_counter[food] += 1
...
>>> for food, count in dict_counter.items():
...     print(food, count)
...
spam 3
eggs 1
```

Count Items with Counter()

Speaking of counters, the standard library has one that does the work of the previous example and more:

```
>>> from collections import Counter
>>> breakfast = ['spam', 'spam', 'eggs', 'spam']
>>> breakfast_counter = Counter(breakfast)
>>> breakfast_counter
Counter({'spam': 3, 'eggs': 1})
```

The `most_common()` function returns all elements in descending order, or just the top count elements if given a count:

```
>>> breakfast_counter.most_common()
[('spam', 3), ('eggs', 1)]
>>> breakfast_counter.most_common(1)
[('spam', 3)]
```

You can combine counters. First, let's see again what's in `breakfast_counter`:

```
>>> breakfast_counter
>>> Counter({'spam': 3, 'eggs': 1})
```

This time, we make a new list called `lunch`, and a counter called `lunch_counter`:

```
>>> lunch = ['eggs', 'eggs', 'bacon']
>>> lunch_counter = Counter(lunch)
>>> lunch_counter
Counter({'eggs': 2, 'bacon': 1})
```

The first way we combine the two counters is by addition, using +:

```
>>> breakfast_counter + lunch_counter
Counter({'spam': 3, 'eggs': 3, 'bacon': 1})
```

As you might expect, you subtract one counter from another by using -. What's for breakfast but not for lunch?

```
>>> breakfast_counter - lunch_counter
Counter({'spam': 3})
```

Okay, now what can we have for lunch that we can't have for breakfast?

```
>>> lunch_counter - breakfast_counter
Counter({'bacon': 1, 'eggs': 1})
```

Similar to sets in Chapter 8, you can get common items by using the intersection operator &:

```
>>> breakfast_counter & lunch_counter
Counter({'eggs': 1})
```

The intersection chose the common element ('eggs') with the lower count. This makes sense: breakfast offered only one egg, so that's the common count.

Finally, you can get all items by using the union operator |:

```
>>> breakfast_counter | lunch_counter
Counter({'spam': 3, 'eggs': 2, 'bacon': 1})
```

The item 'eggs' was again common to both. Unlike addition, union didn't add their counts, but selected the one with the larger count.

Order by Key with OrderedDict()

This is an example run with the Python 2 interpreter:

```
>>> quotes = {
...     'Moe': 'A wise guy, huh?',
...     'Larry': 'Ow!',
...     'Curly': 'Nyuk nyuk!',
...     }
>>> for stooge in quotes:
...    print(stooge)
...
Larry
Curly
Moe
```

 Starting with Python 3.7, dictionaries retain keys in the order in which they were added. OrderedDict is useful for earlier versions, which have an unpredictable order. The examples in this section are relevant only if you're a version of Python earlier than 3.7.

An OrderedDict() remembers the order of key addition and returns them in the same order from an iterator. Try creating an OrderedDict from a sequence of (*key, value*) tuples:

```
>>> from collections import OrderedDict
>>> quotes = OrderedDict([
...     ('Moe', 'A wise guy, huh?'),
...     ('Larry', 'Ow!'),
...     ('Curly', 'Nyuk nyuk!'),
...     ])
>>>
>>> for stooge in quotes:
...     print(stooge)
...
Moe
Larry
Curly
```

Stack + Queue == deque

A deque (pronounced *deck*) is a double-ended queue, which has features of both a stack and a queue. It's useful when you want to add and delete items from either end of a sequence. Here, we work from both ends of a word to the middle to see whether it's a palindrome. The function popleft() removes the leftmost item from the deque and returns it; pop() removes the rightmost item and returns it. Together, they work from the ends toward the middle. As long as the end characters match, it keeps popping until it reaches the middle:

```
>>> def palindrome(word):
...     from collections import deque
...     dq = deque(word)
...     while len(dq) > 1:
...         if dq.popleft() != dq.pop():
...             return False
...     return True
...
...
>>> palindrome('a')
True
>>> palindrome('racecar')
True
>>> palindrome('')
True
>>> palindrome('radar')
True
>>> palindrome('halibut')
False
```

I used this as a simple illustration of deques. If you really wanted a quick palindrome checker, it would be a lot simpler to just compare a string with its reverse. Python doesn't have a reverse() function for strings, but it does have a way to reverse a string with a slice, as illustrated here:

```
>>> def another_palindrome(word):
...     return word == word[::-1]
...
>>> another_palindrome('radar')
True
>>> another_palindrome('halibut')
False
```

Iterate over Code Structures with itertools

itertools (*http://bit.ly/py-itertools*) contains special-purpose iterator functions. Each returns one item at a time when called within a for ... in loop, and remembers its state between calls.

chain() runs through its arguments as though they were a single iterable:

```
>>> import itertools
>>> for item in itertools.chain([1, 2], ['a', 'b']):
...     print(item)
...
1
2
a
b
```

cycle() is an infinite iterator, cycling through its arguments:

```
>>> import itertools
>>> for item in itertools.cycle([1, 2]):
...     print(item)
...
1
2
1
2
.
.
.
```

And, so on.

`accumulate()` calculates accumulated values. By default, it calculates the sum:

```
>>> import itertools
>>> for item in itertools.accumulate([1, 2, 3, 4]):
...     print(item)
...
1
3
6
10
```

You can provide a function as the second argument to `accumulate()`, and it will be used instead of addition. The function should take two arguments and return a single result. This example calculates an accumulated product:

```
>>> import itertools
>>> def multiply(a, b):
...     return a * b
...
>>> for item in itertools.accumulate([1, 2, 3, 4], multiply):
...     print(item)
...
1
2
6
24
```

The `itertools` module has many more functions, notably some for combinations and permutations that can be time savers when the need arises.

Print Nicely with pprint()

All of our examples have used `print()` (or just the variable name, in the interactive interpreter) to print things. Sometimes, the results are hard to read. We need a *pretty printer* such as `pprint()`:

```
>>> from pprint import pprint
>>> quotes = OrderedDict([
```

```
...      ('Moe', 'A wise guy, huh?'),
...      ('Larry', 'Ow!'),
...      ('Curly', 'Nyuk nyuk!'),
...      ])
>>>
```

Plain old print() just dumps things out there:

```
>>> print(quotes)
OrderedDict([('Moe', 'A wise guy, huh?'), ('Larry', 'Ow!'),
    ('Curly', 'Nyuk nyuk!')])
```

However, pprint() tries to align elements for better readability:

```
>>> pprint(quotes)
{'Moe': 'A wise guy, huh?',
 'Larry': 'Ow!',
 'Curly': 'Nyuk nyuk!'}
```

Get Random

We played with random.choice() at the beginning of this chapter. That returns a
value from the sequence (list, tuple, dictionary, string) argument that it's given:

```
>>> from random import choice
>>> choice([23, 9, 46, 'bacon', 0x123abc])
1194684
>>> choice( ('a', 'one', 'and-a', 'two') )
'one'
>>> choice(range(100))
68
>>> choice('alphabet')
'l'
```

Use the sample() function to get more than one value at a time:

```
>>> from random import sample
>>> sample([23, 9, 46, 'bacon', 0x123abc], 3)
[1194684, 23, 9]
>>> sample(('a', 'one', 'and-a', 'two'), 2)
['two', 'and-a']
>>> sample(range(100), 4)
[54, 82, 10, 78]
>>> sample('alphabet', 7)
['l', 'e', 'a', 't', 'p', 'a', 'b']
```

To get a random integer from any range, you can use choice() or sample() with
range(), or use randint() or randrange():

```
>>> from random import randint
>>> randint(38, 74)
71
>>> randint(38, 74)
60
```

```
>>> randint(38, 74)
61
```

randrange(), like range(), has arguments for the start (inclusive) and end (exclusive) integers, and an optional integer step:

```
>>> from random import randrange
>>> randrange(38, 74)
65
>>> randrange(38, 74, 10)
68
>>> randrange(38, 74, 10)
48
```

Finally, get a random real number (a float) between 0.0 and 1.0:

```
>>> from random import random
>>> random()
0.07193393312692198
>>> random()
0.7403243673826271
>>> random()
0.9716517846775018
```

More Batteries: Get Other Python Code

Sometimes, the standard library doesn't have what you need, or doesn't do it in quite the right way. There's an entire world of open source, third-party Python software. Good resources include the following:

- PyPi (*http://pypi.python.org*) (also known as the Cheese Shop, after an old Monty Python skit)
- GitHub (*https://github.com/Python*)
- readthedocs (*https://readthedocs.org*)

You can find many smaller code examples at activestate (*https://oreil.ly/clMAi*).

Almost all of the Python code in this book uses the standard Python installation on your computer, which includes all the built-ins and the standard library. External packages are featured in some places: I mentioned requests in Chapter 1; I have more details in Chapter 18. Appendix B shows how to install third-party Python software, along with many other nuts-and-bolts development details.

Coming Up

The next chapter is a practical one, covering many aspects of data manipulation in Python. You'll encounter the binary *bytes* and *bytearray* data types, handle Unicode characters in text strings, and search text strings with regular expressions.

Things to Do

11.1 Create a file called *zoo.py*. In it, define a function called hours() that prints the string 'Open 9-5 daily'. Then, use the interactive interpreter to import the zoo module and call its hours() function.

11.2 In the interactive interpreter, import the zoo module as menagerie and call its hours() function.

11.3 Staying in the interpreter, import the hours() function from zoo directly and call it.

11.4 Import the hours() function as info and call it.

11.5 Make a dictionary called plain with the key-value pairs 'a': 1, 'b': 2, and 'c': 3, and then print it.

11.6 Make an OrderedDict called fancy from the same pairs listed in the previous question and print it. Did it print in the same order as plain?

11.7 Make a defaultdict called dict_of_lists and pass it the argument list. Make the list dict_of_lists['a'] and append the value 'something for a' to it in one assignment. Print dict_of_lists['a'].

Python in Practice

PART II

CHAPTER 12

Wrangle and Mangle Data

If you torture the data enough, nature will always confess.

—Ronald Coase

Up to this point, we've talked mainly about the Python language itself—its data types, code structures, syntax, and so on. The rest of this book is about application of these to real-world problems.

In this chapter, you'll learn many practical techniques for taming data. Sometimes, this is called *data munging*, or the more businesslike *ETL* (extract/transform/load) of the database world. Although programming books usually don't cover the topic explicitly, programmers spend a lot of time trying to mold data into the right shape for their purposes.

The specialty called *data science* has become very popular in the past few years. A *Harvard Business Review* article called data scientist the "sexiest job of the 21st century." If this meant in demand and well paying, then okay, but there's also more than enough drudgery. Data science goes beyond the ETL requirements of databases, often involving *machine learning* to unearth insights that were not visible to human eyes.

I'll start with basic data formats and then work up to the most useful new tools for data science.

Data formats fall roughly into two categories: *text* and *binary*. Python *strings* are used for text data, and this chapter includes string information that we've skipped so far:

- *Unicode* characters
- *Regular expression* pattern matching.

Then, we jump to binary data, and two more of Python's built-in types:

- *Bytes* for immutable eight-bit values
- *Bytearrays* for mutable ones

Text Strings: Unicode

You saw the basics of Python strings in Chapter 5. Now it's time to really dig into Unicode.

Python 3 strings are Unicode character sequences, not byte arrays. This is, by far, the single largest language change from Python 2.

All of the text examples in this book thus far have been plain old ASCII (American Standard Code for Information Interchange). ASCII was defined in the 1960s, before mullets roamed the earth. Computers then were the size of refrigerators, and only slightly smarter.

The basic unit of computer storage is the *byte*, which can store 256 unique values in its eight *bits*. For various reasons, ASCII used only seven bits (128 unique values): 26 uppercase letters, 26 lowercase letters, 10 digits, some punctuation symbols, some spacing characters, and some nonprinting control codes.

Unfortunately, the world has more letters than ASCII provides. You could have a hot dog at a diner, but never a Gewürztraminer[1] at a café. Many attempts have been made to cram more letters and symbols into eight bits, and you'll see them at times. Just a couple of those include:

- *Latin-1*, or *ISO 8859-1*
- Windows code page *1252*

Each of these uses all eight bits, but even that's not enough, especially when you need non-European languages. *Unicode* is an ongoing international standard to define the characters of all the world's languages, plus symbols from mathematics and other fields. And emojis!

> Unicode provides a unique number for every character, no matter what the platform, no matter what the program, no matter what the language.
>
> —The Unicode Consortium

The Unicode Code Charts page (*http://www.unicode.org/charts*) has links to all the currently defined character sets with images. The latest version (12.0) defines more

---

1 This wine has an umlaut in Germany, but loses it in Alsace on the way to France.

than 137,000 characters, each with a unique name and identification number. Python 3.8 handles all of these. The characters are divided into eight-bit sets called *planes*. The first 256 planes are the *basic multilingual planes*. See the Wikipedia page about Unicode planes (*http://bit.ly/unicode-plane*) for details.

Python 3 Unicode Strings

If you know the Unicode ID or name for a character, you can use it in a Python string. Here are some examples:

- A \u followed by *four* hex numbers[2] specifies a character in one of Unicode's 256 basic multilingual planes. The first two are the plane number (00 to FF), and the next two are the index of the character within the plane. Plane 00 is good old ASCII, and the character positions within that plane are the same as ASCII.

- For characters in the higher planes, we need more bits. The Python escape sequence for these is \U followed by *eight* hex characters; the leftmost ones need to be 0.

- For all characters, \N{*name*} lets you specify it by its standard *name*. The Unicode Character Name Index page (*http://www.unicode.org/charts/charindex.html*) lists these.

The Python unicodedata module has functions that translate in both directions:

- lookup()—Takes a case-insensitive name and returns a Unicode character

- name()—Takes a Unicode character and returns an uppercase name

In the following example, we'll write a test function that takes a Python Unicode character, looks up its name, and looks up the character again from the name (it should match the original character):

```
>>> def unicode_test(value):
...     import unicodedata
...     name = unicodedata.name(value)
...     value2 = unicodedata.lookup(name)
...     print('value="%s", name="%s", value2="%s"' % (value, name, value2))
...
```

Let's try some characters, beginning with a plain ASCII letter:

```
>>> unicode_test('A')
value="A", name="LATIN CAPITAL LETTER A", value2="A"
```

---

2 Base 16, specified with characters 0-9 and A-F.

ASCII punctuation:

```
>>> unicode_test('$')
value="$", name="DOLLAR SIGN", value2="$"
```

A Unicode currency character:

```
>>> unicode_test('\u00a2')
value="¢", name="CENT SIGN", value2="¢"
```

Another Unicode currency character:

```
>>> unicode_test('\u20ac')
value="€", name="EURO SIGN", value2="€"
```

The only problem you could potentially run into is limitations in the font you're using to display text. Few fonts have images for all Unicode characters, and might display some placeholder character for missing ones. For instance, here's the Unicode symbol for SNOWMAN, like symbols in dingbat fonts:

```
>>> unicode_test('\u2603')
value="☃", name="SNOWMAN", value2="☃"
```

Suppose that we want to save the word café in a Python string. One way is to copy and paste it from a file or website and hope that it works:

```
>>> place = 'café'
>>> place
'café'
```

This worked because I copied and pasted from a source that used UTF-8 encoding (which we look at in a few pages) for its text.

How can we specify that final é character? If you look at the character index for E (*http://bit.ly/e-index*), you see that the name E WITH ACUTE, LATIN SMALL LETTER has the value 00E9. Let's check with the name() and lookup() functions that we were just playing with. First give the code to get the name:

```
>>> unicodedata.name('\u00e9')
'LATIN SMALL LETTER E WITH ACUTE'
```

Next, give the name to look up the code:

```
>>> unicodedata.lookup('E WITH ACUTE, LATIN SMALL LETTER')
Traceback (most recent call last):
  File "<stdin>", line 1, in <module>
KeyError: "undefined character name 'E WITH ACUTE, LATIN SMALL LETTER'"
```

The names listed on the Unicode Character Name Index page were reformatted to make them sort nicely for display. To convert them to their real Unicode names (the ones that Python uses), remove the comma and move the part of the name that was after the comma to the beginning. Accordingly, change E WITH ACUTE, LATIN SMALL LETTER to LATIN SMALL LETTER E WITH ACUTE:

```
>>> unicodedata.lookup('LATIN SMALL LETTER E WITH ACUTE')
'é'
```

Now we can specify the string café by code or by name:

```
>>> place = 'caf\u00e9'
>>> place
'café'
>>> place = 'caf\N{LATIN SMALL LETTER E WITH ACUTE}'
>>> place
'café'
```

In the preceding snippet, we inserted the é directly in the string, but we can also build a string by appending:

```
>>> u_umlaut = '\N{LATIN SMALL LETTER U WITH DIAERESIS}'
>>> u_umlaut
'ü'
>>> drink = 'Gew' + u_umlaut + 'rztraminer'
>>> print('Now I can finally have my', drink, 'in a', place)
Now I can finally have my Gewürztraminer in a café
```

The string len() function counts Unicode *characters*, not bytes:

```
>>> len('$')
1
>>> len('\U0001f47b')
1
```

If you know the Unicode numeric ID, you can use the standard ord() and chr() functions to quickly convert between integer IDs and single-character Unicode strings:

```
>>> chr(233)
'é'
>>> chr(0xe9)
'é'
>>> chr(0x1fc6)
'ῆ'
```

UTF-8

You don't need to worry about how Python stores each Unicode character when you do normal string processing.

However, when you exchange data with the outside world, you need a couple of things:

- A way to *encode* character strings to bytes
- A way to *decode* bytes to character strings

If there were fewer than 65,536 characters in Unicode, we could stuff each Unicode character ID into two bytes. Unfortunately, there are more. We could encode every ID into four bytes, but that would increase the memory and disk storage space needs for common text strings by four times.

Ken Thompson and Rob Pike, whose names will be familiar to Unix developers, designed the *UTF-8* dynamic encoding scheme one night on a placemat in a New Jersey diner. It uses one to four bytes per Unicode character:

- One byte for ASCII
- Two bytes for most Latin-derived (but not Cyrillic) languages
- Three bytes for the rest of the basic multilingual plane
- Four bytes for the rest, including some Asian languages and symbols

UTF-8 is the standard text encoding in Python, Linux, and HTML. It's fast, complete, and works well. If you use UTF-8 encoding throughout your code, life will be much easier than trying to hop in and out of various encodings.

 If you create a Python string by copying and pasting from another source such as a web page, be sure the source is encoded in the UTF-8 format. It's *very* common to see text that was encoded as Latin-1 or Windows 1252 copied into a Python string, which causes an exception later with an invalid byte sequence.

Encode

You *encode* a *string* to *bytes*. The string encode() function's first argument is the encoding name. The choices include those presented in Table 12-1.

Table 12-1. Encodings

Encoding name	Description
'ascii'	Good old seven-bit ASCII
'utf-8'	Eight-bit variable-length encoding, and what you almost always want to use
'latin-1'	Also known as ISO 8859-1
'cp-1252'	A common Windows encoding
'unicode-escape'	Python Unicode literal format, `\u`xxxx or `\U`xxxxxxxx

You can encode anything as UTF-8. Let's assign the Unicode string `'\u2603'` to the name snowman:

```
>>> snowman = '\u2603'
```

snowman is a Python Unicode string with a single character, regardless of how many bytes might be needed to store it internally:

```
>>> len(snowman)
1
```

Next, let's encode this Unicode character to a sequence of bytes:

```
>>> ds = snowman.encode('utf-8')
```

As I mentioned earlier, UTF-8 is a variable-length encoding. In this case, it used three bytes to encode the single snowman Unicode character:

```
>>> len(ds)
3
>>> ds
b'\xe2\x98\x83'
```

Now, `len()` returns the number of bytes (3) because ds is a bytes variable.

You can use encodings other than UTF-8, but you'll get errors if the Unicode string can't be handled by the encoding. For example, if you use the ascii encoding, it will fail unless your Unicode characters happen to be valid ASCII characters, as well:

```
>>> ds = snowman.encode('ascii')
Traceback (most recent call last):
  File "<stdin>", line 1, in <module>
UnicodeEncodeError: 'ascii' codec can't encode character '\u2603'
in position 0: ordinal not in range(128)
```

The `encode()` function takes a second argument to help you avoid encoding exceptions. Its default value, which you can see in the previous example, is `'strict'`; it raises a UnicodeEncodeError if it sees a non-ASCII character. There are other encodings. Use `'ignore'` to throw away anything that won't encode:

```
>>> snowman.encode('ascii', 'ignore')
b''
```

Use `'replace'` to substitute ? for unknown characters:

```
>>> snowman.encode('ascii', 'replace')
b'?'
```

Use `'backslashreplace'` to produce a Python Unicode character string, like unicode-escape:

```
>>> snowman.encode('ascii', 'backslashreplace')
b'\\u2603'
```

You would use this if you needed a printable version of the Unicode escape sequence.

Use 'xmlcharrefreplace' to make HTML-safe strings:

```
>>> snowman.encode('ascii', 'xmlcharrefreplace')
b'&#9731;'
```

I provide more details on HTML conversion in "HTML Entities" on page 227.

Decode

We *decode* byte strings to Unicode text strings. Whenever we get text from some external source (files, databases, websites, network APIs, and so on), it's encoded as byte strings. The tricky part is knowing which encoding was actually used, so we can *run it backward* and get Unicode strings.

The problem is that nothing in the byte string itself says what encoding was used. I mentioned the perils of copying and pasting from websites earlier. You've probably visited websites with odd characters where plain old ASCII characters should be.

Let's create a Unicode string called place with the value 'café':

```
>>> place = 'caf\u00e9'
>>> place
'café'
>>> type(place)
<class 'str'>
```

Encode it in UTF-8 format in a bytes variable called place_bytes:

```
>>> place_bytes = place.encode('utf-8')
>>> place_bytes
b'caf\xc3\xa9'
>>> type(place_bytes)
<class 'bytes'>
```

Notice that place_bytes has five bytes. The first three are the same as ASCII (a strength of UTF-8), and the final two encode the 'é'. Now let's decode that byte string back to a Unicode string:

```
>>> place2 = place_bytes.decode('utf-8')
>>> place2
'café'
```

This worked because we encoded to UTF-8 and decoded from UTF-8. What if we told it to decode from some other encoding?

```
>>> place3 = place_bytes.decode('ascii')
Traceback (most recent call last):
  File "<stdin>", line 1, in <module>
UnicodeDecodeError: 'ascii' codec can't decode byte 0xc3 in position 3:
ordinal not in range(128)
```

The ASCII decoder threw an exception because the byte value 0xc3 is illegal in ASCII. There are some 8-bit character set encodings in which values between 128 (hex 80) and 255 (hex FF) are legal but not the same as UTF-8:

```
>>> place4 = place_bytes.decode('latin-1')
>>> place4
'cafÃ©'
>>> place5 = place_bytes.decode('windows-1252')
>>> place5
'cafÃ©'
```

Urk.

The moral of this story: whenever possible, use UTF-8 encoding. It works, is supported everywhere, can express every Unicode character, and is quickly decoded and encoded.

 Even though you can specify any Unicode character, that doesn't mean that your computer will display all of them. That depends on the *font* that you're using, which may display nothing or some fill-in image for many characters. Apple created the Last Resort Font (*https://oreil.ly/q5EZD*) for the Unicode Consortium, and uses it in its own operating systems. This Wikipedia page (*https://oreil.ly/Zm_uZ*) has a few more details. Another font with everything between \u0000 and \uffff, and a few more, is Unifont (*https://oreil.ly/APKlj*).

HTML Entities

Python 3.4 added another way to convert to and from Unicode but using HTML *character entities*.[3] This may be easier to use than looking up Unicode names, especially if you're working on the web:

```
>>> import html
>>> html.unescape("&egrave;")
'è'
```

This conversion also works with numbered entities, decimal or hex:

```
>>> import html
>>> html.unescape("&#233;")
'é'
>>> html.unescape("&#xe9;")
'é'
```

---

3 See the HTML5 named-character reference chart (*https://oreil.ly/pmBWO*).

You can even import the named entity translations as a dictionary and do the conversion yourself. Drop the initial '&' for the dictionary key (you can also drop the final ';', but it seems to work either way):

```
>>> from html.entities import html5
>>> html5["egrave"]
'è'
>>> html5["egrave;"]
'è'
```

To go the other direction (from a single Python Unicode character to an HTML entity name), first get the decimal value of the character with ord():

```
>>> import html
>>> char = '\u00e9'
>>> dec_value = ord(char)
>>> html.entities.codepoint2name[dec_value]
'eacute'
```

For Unicode strings with more than one character, use this two-step conversion:

```
>>> place = 'caf\u00e9'
>>> byte_value = place.encode('ascii', 'xmlcharrefreplace')
>>> byte_value
b'caf&#233;'
>>> byte_value.decode()
'caf&#233;'
```

The expression place.encode('ascii', 'xmlcharrefreplace') returned ASCII characters but as type bytes (because it *en*coded). The following byte_value.decode() is needed to convert byte_value to an HTML-compatible string.

Normalization

Some Unicode characters can be represented by more than one Unicode encoding. They'll look the same, but won't compare the same because they have different internal byte sequences. For example, take the acute accented 'é' in 'café'. Let's make a single-character 'é' in multiple ways:

```
>>> eacute1 = 'é'                                # UTF-8, pasted
>>> eacute2 = '\u00e9'                           # Unicode code point
>>> eacute3 = \                                  # Unicode name
...     '\N{LATIN SMALL LETTER E WITH ACUTE}'
>>> eacute4 = chr(233)                           # decimal byte value
>>> eacute5 = chr(0xe9)                          # hex byte value
>>> eacute1, eacute2, eacute3, eacute4, eacute5
('é', 'é', 'é', 'é', 'é')
>>> eacute1 == eacute2 == eacute3 == eacute4 == eacute5
True
```

Try a few sanity checks:

```
>>> import unicodedata
>>> unicodedata.name(eacute1)
'LATIN SMALL LETTER E WITH ACUTE'
>>> ord(eacute1)              # as a decimal integer
233
>>> 0xe9                      # Unicode hex integer
233
```

Now let's make an accented e by combining a plain e with an acute accent:

```
>>> eacute_combined1 = "e\u0301"
>>> eacute_combined2 = "e\N{COMBINING ACUTE ACCENT}"
>>> eacute_combined3 = "e" + "\u0301"
>>> eacute_combined1, eacute_combined2, eacute_combined3
('é', 'é', 'é'))
>>> eacute_combined1 == eacute_combined2 == eacute_combined3
True
>>> len(eacute_combined1)
2
```

We built a Unicode character from two characters, and it looks the same as the original 'é'. But as they say on Sesame Street, one of these things is not like the other:

```
>>> eacute1 == eacute_combined1
False
```

If you had two different Unicode text strings from different sources, one using eacute1 and another eacute_combined1, they would appear the same, but would mysteriously not act the same.

You can fix this with the normalize() function in the unicodedata module:

```
>>> import unicodedata
>>> eacute_normalized = unicodedata.normalize('NFC', eacute_combined1)
>>> len(eacute_normalized)
1
>>> eacute_normalized == eacute1
True
>>> unicodedata.name(eacute_normalized)
'LATIN SMALL LETTER E WITH ACUTE'
```

That 'NFC' means *normal form, composed*.

For More Information

If you would like to learn more about Unicode, these links are particularly helpful:

- Unicode HOWTO (*http://bit.ly/unicode-howto*)
- Pragmatic Unicode (*http://bit.ly/pragmatic-uni*)

- The Absolute Minimum Every Software Developer Absolutely, Positively Must Know About Unicode and Character Sets (No Excuses!) (*http://bit.ly/jspolsky*)

Text Strings: Regular Expressions

Chapter 5 discussed simple string operations. Armed with that introductory information, you've probably used simple "wildcard" patterns on the command line, such as the UNIX command ls *.py, which means *list all filenames ending in .py.*

It's time to explore more complex pattern matching by using *regular expressions.* These are provided in the standard module re, which we'll import. You define a string *pattern* that you want to match, and the *source* string to match against. For simple matches, usage looks like this:

```
>>> import re
>>> result = re.match('You', 'Young Frankenstein')
```

Here, 'You' is the *pattern* we're looking for, and 'Young Frankenstein' is the *source* (the string we want to search). match() checks whether the *source* begins with the *pattern.*

For more complex matches, you can *compile* your pattern first to speed up the match later:

```
>>> import re
>>> youpattern = re.compile('You')
```

Then, you can perform your match against the compiled pattern:

```
>>> import re
>>> result = youpattern.match('Young Frankenstein')
```

 Because this is a common Python gotcha, I'll say it again here: match() only matches a pattern starting at the *beginning* of the source. search() matches a pattern *anywhere* in the source.

match() is not the only way to compare the pattern and source. Here are several other methods you can use (we discuss each in the following sections):

- search() returns the first match, if any.
- findall() returns a list of all non-overlapping matches, if any.
- split() splits *source* at matches with *pattern* and returns a list of the string pieces.

- sub() takes another *replacement* argument, and changes all parts of *source* that are matched by *pattern* to *replacement*.

 Most of the regular expression examples here use ASCII, but Python's string functions, including regular expressions, work with any Python string and any Unicode characters.

Find Exact Beginning Match with match()

Does the string 'Young Frankenstein' begin with the word 'You'? Here's some code with comments:

```
>>> import re
>>> source = 'Young Frankenstein'
>>> m = re.match('You', source)  # match starts at the beginning of source
>>> if m:   # match returns an object; do this to see what matched
...     print(m.group())
...
You
>>> m = re.match('^You', source) # start anchor does the same
>>> if m:
...     print(m.group())
...
You
```

How about 'Frank'?

```
>>> import re
>>> source = 'Young Frankenstein'
>>> m = re.match('Frank', source)
>>> if m:
...     print(m.group())
...
```

This time, match() returned nothing, so the if did not run the print statement.

As I mentioned in "New: I Am the Walrus" on page 60, in Python 3.8 you can shorten this example with the so-called *walrus operator*:

```
>>> import re
>>> source = 'Young Frankenstein'
>>> if m := re.match('Frank', source):
...     print(m.group())
...
```

Okay, now let's use search() to see whether 'Frank' is anywhere in the source string:

```
>>> import re
>>> source = 'Young Frankenstein'
```

```
>>> m = re.search('Frank', source)
>>> if m:
...     print(m.group())
...
Frank
```

Let's change the pattern and try a beginning match with match() again:

```
>>> import re
>>> source = 'Young Frankenstein'
>>> m = re.match('.*Frank', source)
>>> if m:  # match returns an object
...     print(m.group())
...
Young Frank
```

Here's a brief explanation of how our new '.*Frank' pattern works:

- . means *any single character*.
- * means *zero or more of the preceding thing*. Together, .* mean *any number of characters* (even zero).
- Frank is the phrase that we wanted to match, somewhere.

match() returned the string that matched .*Frank: 'Young Frank'.

Find First Match with search()

You can use search() to find the pattern 'Frank' anywhere in the source string 'Young Frankenstein', without the need for the .* wildcards:

```
>>> import re
>>> source = 'Young Frankenstein'
>>> m = re.search('Frank', source)
>>> if m:  # search returns an object
...     print(m.group())
...
Frank
```

Find All Matches with findall()

The preceding examples looked for one match only. But what if you want to know how many instances of the single-letter string 'n' are in the string?

```
>>> import re
>>> source = 'Young Frankenstein'
>>> m = re.findall('n', source)
>>> m    # findall returns a list
['n', 'n', 'n', 'n']
>>> print('Found', len(m), 'matches')
Found 4 matches
```

How about 'n' followed by any character?

```
>>> import re
>>> source = 'Young Frankenstein'
>>> m = re.findall('n.', source)
>>> m
['ng', 'nk', 'ns']
```

Notice that it did not match that final 'n'. We need to say that the character after 'n' is optional, with ?:

```
>>> import re
>>> source = 'Young Frankenstein'
>>> m = re.findall('n.?', source)
>>> m
['ng', 'nk', 'ns', 'n']
```

Split at Matches with split()

The next example shows you how to split a string into a list by a pattern rather than a simple string (as the normal string split() method would do):

```
>>> import re
>>> source = 'Young Frankenstein'
>>> m = re.split('n', source)
>>> m    # split returns a list
['You', 'g Fra', 'ke', 'stei', '']
```

Replace at Matches with sub()

This is like the string replace() method, but for patterns rather than literal strings:

```
>>> import re
>>> source = 'Young Frankenstein'
>>> m = re.sub('n', '?', source)
>>> m    # sub returns a string
'You?g Fra?ke?stei?'
```

Patterns: Special Characters

Many descriptions of regular expressions start with all the details of how to define them. I think that's a mistake. Regular expressions are a not-so-little language in their own right, with too many details to fit in your head at once. They use so much punctuation that they look like cartoon characters swearing.

With these expressions (match(), search(), findall(), and sub()) under your belt, let's get into the details of building them. The patterns you make apply to any of these functions.

You've seen the basics:

- Literal matches with any nonspecial characters
- Any single character except \n with .
- Any number of the preceding character (including zero) with *
- Optional (zero or one) of the preceding character with ?

First, special characters are shown in Table 12-2.

Table 12-2. Special characters

Pattern	Matches
\d	A single digit
\D	A single nondigit
\w	An alphanumeric character
\W	A non-alphanumeric character
\s	A whitespace character
\S	A nonwhitespace character
\b	A word boundary (between a \w and a \W, in either order)
\B	A nonword boundary

The Python `string` module has predefined string constants that we can use for testing. Let's use `printable`, which contains 100 printable ASCII characters, including letters in both cases, digits, space characters, and punctuation:

```
>>> import string
>>> printable = string.printable
>>> len(printable)
100
>>> printable[0:50]
'0123456789abcdefghijklmnopqrstuvwxyzABCDEFGHIJKLMN'
>>> printable[50:]
'OPQRSTUVWXYZ!"#$%&\'()*+,-./:;<=>?@[\\]^_`{|}~ \t\n\r\x0b\x0c'
```

Which characters in `printable` are digits?

```
>>> re.findall('\d', printable)
['0', '1', '2', '3', '4', '5', '6', '7', '8', '9']
```

Which characters are digits, letters, or an underscore?

```
>>> re.findall('\w', printable)
['0', '1', '2', '3', '4', '5', '6', '7', '8', '9', 'a', 'b',
'c', 'd', 'e', 'f', 'g', 'h', 'i', 'j', 'k', 'l', 'm', 'n',
'o', 'p', 'q', 'r', 's', 't', 'u', 'v', 'w', 'x', 'y', 'z',
'A', 'B', 'C', 'D', 'E', 'F', 'G', 'H', 'I', 'J', 'K', 'L',
'M', 'N', 'O', 'P', 'Q', 'R', 'S', 'T', 'U', 'V', 'W', 'X',
'Y', 'Z', '_']
```

Which are spaces?

```
>>> re.findall('\s', printable)
[' ', '\t', '\n', '\r', '\x0b', '\x0c']
```

In order, those were: plain old space, tab, newline, carriage return, vertical tab, and form feed.

Regular expressions are not confined to ASCII. A \d will match whatever Unicode calls a digit, not just ASCII characters '0' through '9'. Let's add two non-ASCII lowercase letters from FileFormat.info (*http://bit.ly/unicode-letter*):

In this test, we'll throw in the following:

- Three ASCII letters
- Three punctuation symbols that should *not* match a \w
- A Unicode *LATIN SMALL LETTER E WITH CIRCUMFLEX* (\u00ea)
- A Unicode *LATIN SMALL LETTER E WITH BREVE* (\u0115)

```
>>> x = 'abc' + '-/*' + '\u00ea' + '\u0115'
```

As expected, this pattern found only the letters:

```
>>> re.findall('\w', x)
['a', 'b', 'c', 'ê', 'ĕ']
```

Patterns: Using Specifiers

Now let's make "punctuation pizza," using the main pattern specifiers for regular expressions, which are presented in Table 12-3.

In the table, *expr* and the other italicized words mean any valid regular expression.

Table 12-3. Pattern specifiers

Pattern	Matches
abc	Literal abc
(*expr*)	*expr*
expr1 | *expr2*	*expr1* or *expr2*
.	Any character except \n
^	Start of source string
$	End of source string
prev ?	Zero or one *prev*
prev *	Zero or more *prev*, as many as possible
prev *?	Zero or more *prev*, as few as possible
prev +	One or more *prev*, as many as possible

Pattern	Matches
prev +?	One or more *prev*, as few as possible
prev { *m* }	*m* consecutive *prev*
prev { *m*, *n* }	*m* to *n* consecutive *prev*, as many as possible
prev { *m*, *n* }?	*m* to *n* consecutive *prev*, as few as possible
[*abc*]	a or b or c (same as a|b|c)
[^ *abc*]	*not* (a or b or c)
prev (?= *next*)	*prev* if followed by *next*
prev (?! *next*)	*prev* if *not* followed by *next*
(?<= *prev*) *next*	*next* if preceded by *prev*
(?<! *prev*) *next*	*next* if *not* preceded by *prev*

Your eyes might cross permanently when trying to read these examples. First, let's define our source string:

```
>>> source = '''I wish I may, I wish I might
... Have a dish of fish tonight.'''
```

Now we apply different regular expression pattern strings to try to match something in the source string.

 In the following examples, I use plain quoted strings for the patterns. A little later in this section I show how a raw pattern string (r before the initial quote) helps avoid some conflicts between Python's normal string escapes and regular expression ones. So, to be safest, the first argument in all the following examples should actually be a raw string.

First, find wish anywhere:

```
>>> re.findall('wish', source)
['wish', 'wish']
```

Next, find wish or fish anywhere:

```
>>> re.findall('wish|fish', source)
['wish', 'wish', 'fish']
```

Find wish at the beginning:

```
>>> re.findall('^wish', source)
[]
```

Find I wish at the beginning:

```
>>> re.findall('^I wish', source)
['I wish']
```

Find `fish` at the end:

```
>>> re.findall('fish$', source)
[]
```

Finally, find `fish tonight.` at the end:

```
>>> re.findall('fish tonight.$', source)
['fish tonight.']
```

The characters ^ and $ are called *anchors*: ^ anchors the search to the beginning of the search string, and $ anchors it to the end. `.$` matches any character at the end of the line, including a period, so that worked. To be more precise, we should escape the dot to match it literally:

```
>>> re.findall('fish tonight\.$', source)
['fish tonight.']
```

Begin by finding `w` or `f` followed by `ish`:

```
>>> re.findall('[wf]ish', source)
['wish', 'wish', 'fish']
```

Find one or more runs of `w`, `s`, or `h`:

```
>>> re.findall('[wsh]+', source)
['w', 'sh', 'w', 'sh', 'h', 'sh', 'sh', 'h']
```

Find `ght` followed by a non-alphanumeric:

```
>>> re.findall('ght\W', source)
['ght\n', 'ght.']
```

Find `I` followed by `wish`:

```
>>> re.findall('I (?=wish)', source)
['I ', 'I ']
```

And last, `wish` preceded by `I`:

```
>>> re.findall('(?<=I) wish', source)
[' wish', ' wish']
```

I mentioned earlier that there are a few cases in which the regular expression pattern rules conflict with the Python string rules. The following pattern should match any word that begins with `fish`:

```
>>> re.findall('\bfish', source)
[]
```

Why doesn't it? As is discussed in Chapter 5, Python employs a few special *escape characters* for strings. For example, \b means backspace in strings, but in the mini-language of regular expressions it means the beginning of a word. Avoid the accidental use of escape characters by using Python's *raw strings* when you define your regular expression string. Always put an r character before your regular expression pattern string, and Python escape characters will be disabled, as demonstrated here:

```
>>> re.findall(r'\bfish', source)
['fish']
```

Patterns: Specifying match() Output

When using match() or search(), all matches are returned from the result object m as m.group(). If you enclose a pattern in parentheses, the match will be saved to its own group, and a tuple of them will be available as m.groups(), as shown here:

```
>>> m = re.search(r'(. dish\b).*(\bfish)', source)
>>> m.group()
'a dish of fish'
>>> m.groups()
('a dish', 'fish')
```

If you use this pattern (?P< *name* > *expr*), it will match *expr*, saving the match in group *name*:

```
>>> m = re.search(r'(?P<DISH>. dish\b).*(?P<FISH>\bfish)', source)
>>> m.group()
'a dish of fish'
>>> m.groups()
('a dish', 'fish')
>>> m.group('DISH')
'a dish'
>>> m.group('FISH')
'fish'
```

Binary Data

Text data can be challenging, but binary data can be, well, interesting. You need to know about concepts such as *endianness* (how your computer's processor breaks data into bytes) and *sign bits* for integers. You might need to delve into binary file formats or network packets to extract or even change data. This section shows you the basics of binary data wrangling in Python.

bytes and bytearray

Python 3 introduced the following sequences of eight-bit integers, with possible values from 0 to 255, in two types:

- *bytes* is immutable, like a tuple of bytes
- *bytearray* is mutable, like a list of bytes

Beginning with a list called `blist`, this next example creates a `bytes` variable called `the_bytes` and a `bytearray` variable called `the_byte_array`:

```
>>> blist = [1, 2, 3, 255]
>>> the_bytes = bytes(blist)
>>> the_bytes
b'\x01\x02\x03\xff'
>>> the_byte_array = bytearray(blist)
>>> the_byte_array
bytearray(b'\x01\x02\x03\xff')
```

 The representation of a `bytes` value begins with a `b` and a quote character, followed by hex sequences such as `\x02` or ASCII characters, and ends with a matching quote character. Python converts the hex sequences or ASCII characters to little integers, but shows byte values that are also valid ASCII encodings as ASCII characters:

```
>>> b'\x61'
b'a'
>>> b'\x01abc\xff'
b'\x01abc\xff'
```

This next example demonstrates that you can't change a `bytes` variable:

```
>>> blist = [1, 2, 3, 255]
>>> the_bytes = bytes(blist)
>>> the_bytes[1] = 127
Traceback (most recent call last):
  File "<stdin>", line 1, in <module>
TypeError: 'bytes' object does not support item assignment
```

But a `bytearray` variable is mellow and mutable:

```
>>> blist = [1, 2, 3, 255]
>>> the_byte_array = bytearray(blist)
>>> the_byte_array
bytearray(b'\x01\x02\x03\xff')
>>> the_byte_array[1] = 127
>>> the_byte_array
bytearray(b'\x01\x7f\x03\xff')
```

Each of these would create a 256-element result, with values from 0 to 255:

```
>>> the_bytes = bytes(range(0, 256))
>>> the_byte_array = bytearray(range(0, 256))
```

When printing `bytes` or `bytearray` data, Python uses `\xxx` for nonprintable bytes and their ASCII equivalents for printable ones (plus some common escape characters, such as `\n` instead of `\x0a`). Here's the printed representation of `the_bytes` (manually reformatted to show 16 bytes per line):

```
>>> the_bytes
b'\x00\x01\x02\x03\x04\x05\x06\x07\x08\t\n\x0b\x0c\r\x0e\x0f
\x10\x11\x12\x13\x14\x15\x16\x17\x18\x19\x1a\x1b\x1c\x1d\x1e\x1f
!"#$%&\'()*+,-./
0123456789:;<=>?
@ABCDEFGHIJKLMNO
PQRSTUVWXYZ[\\]^_
`abcdefghijklmno
pqrstuvwxyz{|}~\x7f
\x80\x81\x82\x83\x84\x85\x86\x87\x88\x89\x8a\x8b\x8c\x8d\x8e\x8f
\x90\x91\x92\x93\x94\x95\x96\x97\x98\x99\x9a\x9b\x9c\x9d\x9e\x9f
\xa0\xa1\xa2\xa3\xa4\xa5\xa6\xa7\xa8\xa9\xaa\xab\xac\xad\xae\xaf
\xb0\xb1\xb2\xb3\xb4\xb5\xb6\xb7\xb8\xb9\xba\xbb\xbc\xbd\xbe\xbf
\xc0\xc1\xc2\xc3\xc4\xc5\xc6\xc7\xc8\xc9\xca\xcb\xcc\xcd\xce\xcf
\xd0\xd1\xd2\xd3\xd4\xd5\xd6\xd7\xd8\xd9\xda\xdb\xdc\xdd\xde\xdf
\xe0\xe1\xe2\xe3\xe4\xe5\xe6\xe7\xe8\xe9\xea\xeb\xec\xed\xee\xef
\xf0\xf1\xf2\xf3\xf4\xf5\xf6\xf7\xf8\xf9\xfa\xfb\xfc\xfd\xfe\xff'
```

This can be confusing, because they're bytes (teeny integers), not characters.

Convert Binary Data with struct

As you've seen, Python has many tools for manipulating text. Tools for binary data are much less prevalent. The standard library contains the struct module, which handles data similar to *structs* in C and C++. Using struct, you can convert binary data to and from Python data structures.

Let's see how this works with data from a PNG file—a common image format that you'll see along with GIF and JPEG files. We'll write a small program that extracts the width and height of an image from some PNG data.

We'll use the O'Reilly logo—the little bug-eyed tarsier shown in Figure 12-1.

Figure 12-1. The O'Reilly tarsier

The PNG file for this image is available on Wikipedia (*http://bit.ly/orm-logo*). I don't show how to read files until Chapter 14, so I downloaded this file, wrote a little program to print its values as bytes, and just typed the values of the first 30 bytes into a Python bytes variable called data for the example that follows. (The PNG format specification says that the width and height are stored within the first 24 bytes, so we don't need more than that for now.)

```
>>> import struct
>>> valid_png_header = b'\x89PNG\r\n\x1a\n'
>>> data = b'\x89PNG\r\n\x1a\n\x00\x00\x00\rIHDR' + \
...     b'\x00\x00\x00\x9a\x00\x00\x00\x8d\x08\x02\x00\x00\x00\xc0'
>>> if data[:8] == valid_png_header:
...     width, height = struct.unpack('>LL', data[16:24])
...     print('Valid PNG, width', width, 'height', height)
... else:
...     print('Not a valid PNG')
...
Valid PNG, width 154 height 141
```

Here's what this code does:

- data contains the first 30 bytes from the PNG file. To fit on the page, I joined two byte strings with + and the continuation character (\).

- valid_png_header contains the eight-byte sequence that marks the start of a valid PNG file.

- width is extracted from bytes 16–19, and height from bytes 20–23.

The >LL is the format string that instructs unpack() how to interpret its input byte sequences and assemble them into Python data types. Here's the breakdown:

- The > means that integers are stored in *big-endian* format.

- Each L specifies a four-byte unsigned long integer.

You can examine each four-byte value directly:

```
>>> data[16:20]
b'\x00\x00\x00\x9a'
>>> data[20:24]0x9a
b'\x00\x00\x00\x8d'
```

Big-endian integers have the most significant bytes to the left. Because the width and height are each less than 255, they fit into the last byte of each sequence. You can verify that these hex values match the expected decimal values:

```
>>> 0x9a
154
>>> 0x8d
141
```

When you want to go in the other direction and convert Python data to bytes, use the struct pack() function:

```
>>> import struct
>>> struct.pack('>L', 154)
b'\x00\x00\x00\x9a'
```

```
>>> struct.pack('>L', 141)
b'\x00\x00\x00\x8d'
```

Tables 12-4 and 12-5 show the format specifiers for pack() and unpack().

The endian specifiers go first in the format string.

Table 12-4. Endian specifiers

Specifier	Byte order
<	Little endian
>	Big endian

Table 12-5. Format specifiers

Specifier	Description	Bytes
x	Skip a byte	1
b	Signed byte	1
B	Unsigned byte	1
h	Signed short integer	2
H	Unsigned short integer	2
i	Signed integer	4
I	Unsigned integer	4
l	Signed long integer	4
L	Unsigned long integer	4
Q	Unsigned long long integer	8
f	Single-precision float	4
d	Double-precision float	8
p	*count* and characters	1 + *count*
s	Characters	*count*

The type specifiers follow the endian character. Any specifier may be preceded by a number that indicates the *count*; 5B is the same as BBBBB.

You can use a *count* prefix instead of >LL:

```
>>> struct.unpack('>2L', data[16:24])
(154, 141)
```

We used the slice data[16:24] to grab the interesting bytes directly. We could also use the x specifier to skip the uninteresting parts:

```
>>> struct.unpack('>16x2L6x', data)
(154, 141)
```

This means:

- Use big-endian integer format (>)
- Skip 16 bytes (16x)
- Read eight bytes—two unsigned long integers (2L)
- Skip the final six bytes (6x)

Other Binary Data Tools

Some third-party open source packages offer the following, more-declarative ways of defining and extracting binary data:

- bitstring (*http://bit.ly/py-bitstring*)
- construct (*http://bit.ly/py-construct*)
- hachoir (*https://pypi.org/project/hachoir*)
- binio (*http://spika.net/py/binio*)
- kaitai struct (*http://kaitai.io*)

Appendix B has details on how to download and install external packages such as these. For the next example, you need to install construct. Here's all you need to do:

```
$ pip install construct
```

Here's how to extract the PNG dimensions from our data bytestring by using construct:

```
>>> from construct import Struct, Magic, UBInt32, Const, String
>>> # adapted from code at https://github.com/construct
>>> fmt = Struct('png',
...     Magic(b'\x89PNG\r\n\x1a\n'),
...     UBInt32('length'),
...     Const(String('type', 4), b'IHDR'),
...     UBInt32('width'),
...     UBInt32('height')
...     )
>>> data = b'\x89PNG\r\n\x1a\n\x00\x00\x00\rIHDR' + \
...     b'\x00\x00\x00\x9a\x00\x00\x00\x8d\x08\x02\x00\x00\x00\xc0'
>>> result = fmt.parse(data)
>>> print(result)
Container:
    length = 13
    type = b'IHDR'
    width = 154
    height = 141
>>> print(result.width, result.height)
154, 141
```

Convert Bytes/Strings with binascii()

The standard `binascii` module has functions to convert between binary data and various string representations: hex (base 16), base 64, uuencoded, and others. For example, in the next snippet, let's print that eight-byte PNG header as a sequence of hex values, instead of the mixture of ASCII and \x *xx* escapes that Python uses to display *bytes* variables:

```
>>> import binascii
>>> valid_png_header = b'\x89PNG\r\n\x1a\n'
>>> print(binascii.hexlify(valid_png_header))
b'89504e470d0a1a0a'
```

Hey, this thing works backward, too:

```
>>> print(binascii.unhexlify(b'89504e470d0a1a0a'))
b'\x89PNG\r\n\x1a\n'
```

Bit Operators

Python provides bit-level integer operators, similar to those in the C language. Table 12-6 summarizes them and includes examples with the integer variables x (decimal 5, binary `0b0101`) and y (decimal 1, binary `0b0001`).

Table 12-6. Bit-level integer operators

Operator	Description	Example	Decimal result	Binary result
&	And	x & y	1	0b0001
|	Or	x | y	5	0b0101
^	Exclusive or	x ^ y	4	0b0100
~	Flip bits	~x	-6	*binary representation depends on int size*
<<	Left shift	x << 1	10	0b1010
>>	Right shift	x >> 1	2	0b0010

These operators work something like the set operators in Chapter 8. The & operator returns bits that are the same in both arguments, and | returns bits that are set in either of them. The ^ operator returns bits that are in one or the other, but not both. The ~ operator reverses all the bits in its single argument; this also reverses the sign because an integer's highest bit indicates its sign (1 = negative) in *two's complement* arithmetic, used in all modern computers. The << and >> operators just move bits to the left or right. A left shift of one bit is the same as multiplying by two, and a right shift is the same as dividing by two.

A Jewelry Analogy

Unicode strings are like charm bracelets, and bytes are like strands of beads.

Coming Up

Next is another practical chapter: how to handle dates and times.

Things to Do

12.1 Create a Unicode string called mystery and assign it the value '\U0001f984'. Print mystery and its Unicode name.

12.2 Encode mystery, this time using UTF-8, into the bytes variable pop_bytes. Print pop_bytes.

12.3 Using UTF-8, decode pop_bytes into the string variable pop_string. Print pop_string. Is pop_string equal to mystery?

12.4 When you're working with text, regular expressions come in very handy. We'll apply them in a number of ways to our featured text sample. It's a poem titled "Ode on the Mammoth Cheese," written by James McIntyre in 1866 in homage to a seven-thousand-pound cheese that was crafted in Ontario and sent on an international tour. If you'd rather not type all of it, use your favorite search engine and cut and paste the words into your Python program, or just grab it from Project Gutenberg (*http://bit.ly/mcintyre-poetry*). Call the text string mammoth.

Example 12-1. mammoth.txt

```
We have seen thee, queen of cheese,
Lying quietly at your ease,
Gently fanned by evening breeze,
Thy fair form no flies dare seize.

All gaily dressed soon you'll go
To the great Provincial show,
To be admired by many a beau
In the city of Toronto.

Cows numerous as a swarm of bees,
Or as the leaves upon the trees,
It did require to make thee please,
And stand unrivalled, queen of cheese.

May you not receive a scar as
We have heard that Mr. Harris
Intends to send you off as far as
```

```
The great world's show at Paris.

Of the youth beware of these,
For some of them might rudely squeeze
And bite your cheek, then songs or glees
We could not sing, oh! queen of cheese.

We'rt thou suspended from balloon,
You'd cast a shade even at noon,
Folks would think it was the moon
About to fall and crush them soon.
```

12.5 Import the re module to use Python's regular expression functions. Use the re.findall() to print all the words that begin with c.

12.6 Find all four-letter words that begin with c.

12.7 Find all the words that end with r.

12.8 Find all words that contain exactly three vowels in a row.

12.9 Use unhexlify to convert this hex string (combined from two strings to fit on a page) to a bytes variable called gif:

```
'47494638396101000100800000000000ffffff21f9' +
'0401000000002c00000000010001000020144003b'
```

12.10 The bytes in gif define a one-pixel transparent GIF file, one of the most common graphics file formats. A legal GIF starts with the ASCII characters *GIF89a*. Does gif match this?

12.11 The pixel width of a GIF is a 16-bit little-endian integer beginning at byte offset 6, and the height is the same size, starting at offset 8. Extract and print these values for gif. Are they both 1?

CHAPTER 13

Calendars and Clocks

"One!" strikes the clock in the belfry tower,
Which but sixty minutes ago
Sounded twelve for the midnight hour.

　　—Frederick B. Needham, *The Round of the Clock*

I've been on a calendar but I have never been on time.

　　—Marilyn Monroe

Programmers devote a surprising amount of effort to dates and times. Let's talk about some of the problems they encounter and then get to some best practices and tricks to make the situation a little less messy.

Dates can be represented in many ways—too many ways, actually. Even in English with the Roman calendar, you'll see many variants of a simple date:

- July 21 1987
- 21 Jul 1987
- 21/7/1987
- 7/21/1987

Among other problems, date representations can be ambiguous. In the previous examples, it's easy to determine that 7 stands for the month and 21 is the day of the month, because months don't go to 21. But how about 1/6/2012? Is that referring to January 6 or June 1?

The month name varies by language within the Roman calendar. Even the year and month can have a different definition in other cultures.

Times have their own sources of grief, especially because of time zones and daylight savings time. If you look at a time zone map, the zones follow political and historic boundaries rather than crisp lines every 15 degrees (360 degrees / 24) of longitude. And countries start and end daylight savings times on different days of the year. Southern hemisphere countries advance their clocks as their northern friends are winding theirs back, and vice versa.

Python's standard library has many date and time modules, including: `datetime`, `time`, `calendar`, `dateutil`, and others. There's some overlap, and it's a bit confusing.

Leap Year

Leap years are a special wrinkle in time. You probably know that every four years is a leap year (and the summer Olympics and the American presidential election). Did you also know that every 100 years is not a leap year, but that every 400 years is? Here's code to test various years for leapiness:

```
>>> import calendar
>>> calendar.isleap(1900)
False
>>> calendar.isleap(1996)
True
>>> calendar.isleap(1999)
False
>>> calendar.isleap(2000)
True
>>> calendar.isleap(2002)
False
>>> calendar.isleap(2004)
True
```

For the curious:

- A year has 365.242196 days (after one spin around the sun, the earth is about a quarter-turn on its axis from where it started).
- Add one day every four years. Now an average year has 365.242196 − 0.25 = 364.992196 days
- Subtract a day every 100 years. Now an average year has 364.992196 + 0.01 = 365.002196 days
- Add a day every 400 years. Now an average year has 365.002196 − 0.0025 = 364.999696 days

Close enough for now! We will not speak of leap seconds (*https://oreil.ly/aJ32N*).

The datetime Module

The standard `datetime` module handles (which should not be a surprise) dates and times. It defines four main object classes, each with many methods:

- `date` for years, months, and days
- `time` for hours, minutes, seconds, and fractions
- `datetime` for dates and times together
- `timedelta` for date and/or time intervals

You can make a `date` object by specifying a year, month, and day. Those values are then available as attributes:

```
>>> from datetime import date
>>> halloween = date(2019, 10, 31)
>>> halloween
datetime.date(2019, 10, 31)
>>> halloween.day
31
>>> halloween.month
10
>>> halloween.year
2019
```

You can print a `date` with its `isoformat()` method:

```
>>> halloween.isoformat()
'2019-10-31'
```

The `iso` refers to ISO 8601, an international standard for representing dates and times. It goes from most general (year) to most specific (day). Because of this, it also sorts correctly: by year, then month, then day. I usually choose this format for date representation in programs, and for filenames that save data by date. The next section describes the more complex `strptime()` and `strftime()` methods for parsing and formatting dates.

This example uses the `today()` method to generate today's date:

```
>>> from datetime import date
>>> now = date.today()
>>> now
datetime.date(2019, 4, 5)
```

This one makes use of a `timedelta` object to add some time interval to a `date`:

```
>>> from datetime import timedelta
>>> one_day = timedelta(days=1)
>>> tomorrow = now + one_day
>>> tomorrow
```

```
datetime.date(2019, 4, 6)
>>> now + 17*one_day
datetime.date(2019, 4, 22)
>>> yesterday = now - one_day
>>> yesterday
datetime.date(2019, 4, 4)
```

The range of date is from date.min (year=1, month=1, day=1) to date.max (year=9999, month=12, day=31). As a result, you can't use it for historic or astronomical calculations.

The datetime module's time object is used to represent a time of day:

```
>>> from datetime import time
>>> noon = time(12, 0, 0)
>>> noon
datetime.time(12, 0)
>>> noon.hour
12
>>> noon.minute
0
>>> noon.second
0
>>> noon.microsecond
0
```

The arguments go from the largest time unit (hours) to the smallest (microseconds). If you don't provide all the arguments, time assumes all the rest are zero. By the way, just because you can store and retrieve microseconds doesn't mean you can retrieve time from your computer to the exact microsecond. The accuracy of subsecond measurements depends on many factors in the hardware and operating system.

The datetime object includes both the date and time of day. You can create one directly, such as the one that follows, which is for January 2, 2019, at 3:04 A.M., plus 5 seconds and 6 microseconds:

```
>>> from datetime import datetime
>>> some_day = datetime(2019, 1, 2, 3, 4, 5, 6)
>>> some_day
datetime.datetime(2019, 1, 2, 3, 4, 5, 6)
```

The datetime object also has an isoformat() method:

```
>>> some_day.isoformat()
'2019-01-02T03:04:05.000006'
```

That middle T separates the date and time parts.

datetime has a now() method to return the current date and time:

```
>>> from datetime import datetime
>>> now = datetime.now()
>>> now
```

```
datetime.datetime(2019, 4, 5, 19, 53, 7, 580562)
>>> now.year
2019
>>> now.month
4
>>> now.day
5
>>> now.hour
19
>>> now.minute
53
>>> now.second
7
>>> now.microsecond
580562
```

You can combine() a date object and a time object into a datetime:

```
>>> from datetime import datetime, time, date
>>> noon = time(12)
>>> this_day = date.today()
>>> noon_today = datetime.combine(this_day, noon)
>>> noon_today
datetime.datetime(2019, 4, 5, 12, 0)
```

You can yank the date and time from a datetime by using the date() and time() methods:

```
>>> noon_today.date()
datetime.date(2019, 4, 5)
>>> noon_today.time()
datetime.time(12, 0)
```

Using the time Module

It is confusing that Python has a datetime module with a time object, and a separate time module. Furthermore, the time module has a function called—wait for it—time().

One way to represent an absolute time is to count the number of seconds since some starting point. *Unix time* uses the number of seconds since midnight on January 1, 1970.[1] This value is often called the *epoch*, and it is often the simplest way to exchange dates and times among systems.

The time module's time() function returns the current time as an epoch value:

```
>>> import time
>>> now = time.time()
```

---

[1] This starting point is roughly when Unix was born, ignoring those pesky leap seconds.

```
>>> now
1554512132.778233
```

More than one billion seconds have ticked by since New Year's, 1970. Where did the time go?

You can convert an epoch value to a string by using ctime():

```
>>> time.ctime(now)
'Fri Apr  5 19:55:32 2019'
```

In the next section, you'll see how to produce more attractive formats for dates and times.

Epoch values are a useful least-common denominator for date and time exchange with different systems, such as JavaScript. Sometimes, though, you need actual days, hours, and so forth, which time provides as struct_time objects. localtime() provides the time in your system's time zone, and gmtime() provides it in UTC:

```
>>> time.localtime(now)
time.struct_time(tm_year=2019, tm_mon=4, tm_mday=5, tm_hour=19,
tm_min=55, tm_sec=32, tm_wday=4, tm_yday=95, tm_isdst=1)
>>> time.gmtime(now)
time.struct_time(tm_year=2019, tm_mon=4, tm_mday=6, tm_hour=0,
tm_min=55, tm_sec=32, tm_wday=5, tm_yday=96, tm_isdst=0)
```

My 19:55 (Central time zone, Daylight Savings) was 00:55 in the next day in UTC (formerly called *Greenwich time* or *Zulu time*). If you omit the argument to local time() or gmtime(), they assume the current time.

Some of the tm_... values in struct_time are a bit ambiguous, so take a look at Table 13-1 for more details.

Table 13-1. struct_time values

Index	Name	Meaning	Values
0	tm_year	Year	0000 to 9999
1	tm_mon	Month	1 to 12
2	tm_mday	Day of month	1 to 31
3	tm_hour	Hour	0 to 23
4	tm_min	Minute	0 to 59
5	tm_sec	Second	0 to 61
6	tm_wday	Day of week	0 (Monday) to 6 (Sunday)
7	tm_yday	Day of year	1 to 366
8	tm_isdst	Daylight savings?	0 = no, 1 = yes, -1 = unknown

If you don't want to type all those tm_... names, struct_time also acts like a named tuple (see "Named Tuples" on page 195), so you can use the indexes from the previous table:

```
>>> import time
>>> now = time.localtime()
>>> now
time.struct_time(tm_year=2019, tm_mon=6, tm_mday=23, tm_hour=12,
tm_min=12, tm_sec=24, tm_wday=6, tm_yday=174, tm_isdst=1)
>>> now[0]
2019
print(list(now[x] for x in range(9)))
[2019, 6, 23, 12, 12, 24, 6, 174, 1]
```

mktime() goes in the other direction, converting a struct_time object to epoch seconds:

```
>>> tm = time.localtime(now)
>>> time.mktime(tm)
1554512132.0
```

This doesn't exactly match our earlier epoch value of now() because the struct_time object preserves time only to the second.

Some advice: wherever possible, *use UTC* instead of time zones. UTC is an absolute time, independent of time zones. If you have a server, *set its time to UTC*; do not use local time.

More advice: *never use daylight savings time* if you can avoid it. If you use daylight savings time, an hour disappears at one time of year ("spring ahead") and occurs twice at another time ("fall back"). For some reason, many organizations use local time with daylight savings in their computer systems, but are mystified twice every year by that spooky hour.

Read and Write Dates and Times

isoformat() is not the only way to write dates and times. You already saw the ctime() function in the time module, which you can use to convert epochs to strings:

```
>>> import time
>>> now = time.time()
>>> time.ctime(now)
'Fri Apr  5 19:58:23 2019'
```

You can also convert dates and times to strings by using strftime(). This is provided as a method in the datetime, date, and time objects, and as a function in the time module. strftime() uses format strings to specify the output, which you can see in Table 13-2.

Table 13-2. Output specifiers for `strftime()`

Format string	Date/time unit	Range
%Y	year	1900-...
%m	month	01-12
%B	month name	January, ...
%b	month abbrev	Jan, ...
%d	day of month	01-31
%A	weekday name	Sunday, ...
a	weekday abbrev	Sun, ...
%H	hour (24 hr)	00-23
%I	hour (12 hr)	01-12
%p	AM/PM	AM, PM
%M	minute	00-59
%S	second	00-59

Numbers are zero-padded on the left.

Here's the `strftime()` function provided by the `time` module. It converts a `struct_time` object to a string. We'll first define the format string `fmt` and use it again later:

```
>>> import time
>>> fmt = "It's %A, %B %d, %Y, local time %I:%M:%S%p"
>>> t = time.localtime()
>>> t
time.struct_time(tm_year=2019, tm_mon=3, tm_mday=13, tm_hour=15,
tm_min=23, tm_sec=46, tm_wday=2, tm_yday=72, tm_isdst=1)
>>> time.strftime(fmt, t)
"It's Wednesday, March 13, 2019, local time 03:23:46PM"
```

If we try this with a `date` object, only the date parts will work, and the time defaults to midnight:

```
>>> from datetime import date
>>> some_day = date(2019, 7, 4)
>>> fmt = "It's %A, %B %d, %Y, local time %I:%M:%S%p"
>>> some_day.strftime(fmt)
"It's Thursday, July 04, 2019, local time 12:00:00AM"
```

For a `time` object, only the time parts are converted:

```
>>> from datetime import time
>>> fmt = "It's %A, %B %d, %Y, local time %I:%M:%S%p"
>>> some_time = time(10, 35)
>>> some_time.strftime(fmt)
"It's Monday, January 01, 1900, local time 10:35:00AM"
```

You won't want to use the day parts from a time object, because they're meaningless.

To go the other way and convert a string to a date or time, use strptime() with the same format string. There's no regular expression pattern matching; the nonformat parts of the string (without %) need to match exactly. Let's specify a format that matches *year-month-day*, such as 2019-01-29. What happens if the date string you want to parse has spaces instead of dashes?

```
>>> import time
>>> fmt = "%Y-%m-%d"
>>> time.strptime("2019 01 29", fmt)
Traceback (most recent call last):
  File "<stdin>",
    line 1, in <module>
  File "/Library/Frameworks/Python.framework/Versions/3.7/lib/python3.7/_strptime.py",
    line 571, in _strptime_time
    tt = _strptime(data_string, format)[0]
  File "/Library/Frameworks/Python.framework/Versions/3.7/lib/python3.7/_strptime.py",
    line 359, in _strptime(data_string, format))
ValueError: time data '2019 01 29' does not match format '%Y-%m-%d
```

If we feed strptime() some dashes, is it happy now?

```
>>> import time
>>> fmt = "%Y-%m-%d"
>>> time.strptime("2019-01-29", fmt)
time.struct_time(tm_year=2019, tm_mon=1, tm_mday=29, tm_hour=0,
tm_min=0, tm_sec=0, tm_wday=1, tm_yday=29, tm_isdst=-1)
```

Or fix the fmt string to match the date string:

```
>>> import time
>>> fmt = "%Y %m %d"
>>> time.strptime("2019 01 29", fmt)
time.struct_time(tm_year=2019, tm_mon=1, tm_mday=29, tm_hour=0,
tm_min=0, tm_sec=0, tm_wday=1, tm_yday=29, tm_isdst=-1)
```

Even if the string seems to match its format, an exception is raised if a value is out of range (file names truncated for space):

```
>>> time.strptime("2019-13-29", fmt)
Traceback (most recent call last):
  File "<stdin>",
    line 1, in <module>
  File ".../3.7/lib/python3.7/_strptime.py",
    line 571, in _strptime_time
    tt = _strptime(data_string, format)[0]
  File ".../3.7/lib/python3.7/_strptime.py",
    line 359, in _strptime(data_string, format))
ValueError: time data '2019-13-29' does not match format '%Y-%m-%d
```

Names are specific to your *locale*—internationalization settings for your operating system. If you need to print different month and day names, change your locale by using setlocale(); its first argument is locale.LC_TIME for dates and times, and the second is a string combining the language and country abbreviation. Let's invite some international friends to a Halloween party. We'll print the month, day, and day of week in US English, French, German, Spanish, and Icelandic (Icelanders have real elves):

```
>>> import locale
>>> from datetime import date
>>> halloween = date(2019, 10, 31)
>>> for lang_country in ['en_us', 'fr_fr', 'de_de', 'es_es', 'is_is',]:
...     locale.setlocale(locale.LC_TIME, lang_country)
...     halloween.strftime('%A, %B %d')
...
'en_us'
'Thursday, October 31'
'fr_fr'
'Jeudi, octobre 31'
'de_de'
'Donnerstag, Oktober 31'
'es_es'
'jueves, octubre 31'
'is_is'
'fimmtudagur, október 31'
>>>
```

Where do you find these magic values for lang_country? This is a bit wonky, but you can try this to get all of them (there are a few hundred):

```
>>> import locale
>>> names = locale.locale_alias.keys()
```

From names, let's get just locale names that seem to work with setlocale(), such as the ones we used in the preceding example—a two-character language code (*http://bit.ly/iso-639-1*) followed by an underscore and a two-character country code (*http://bit.ly/iso-3166-1*):

```
>>> good_names = [name for name in names if \
len(name) == 5 and name[2] == '_']
```

What do the first five look like?

```
>>> good_names[:5]
['sr_cs', 'de_at', 'nl_nl', 'es_ni', 'sp_yu']
```

So, if you wanted all the German language locales, try this:

```
>>> de = [name for name in good_names if name.startswith('de')]
>>> de
['de_at', 'de_de', 'de_ch', 'de_lu', 'de_be']
```

If you run set_locale() and get the error

> locale.Error: unsupported locale setting

that locale is not supported by your operating system. You'll need to figure out what your operating system needs to add it. This can happen even if Python told you (using locale.locale_alias.keys()) that it was a good locale. I had this error when testing on macOS with the locale cy_gb (Welsh, Great Britain), even though it had accepted is_is (Icelandic) in the preceding example.

All the Conversions

Figure 13-1 (from the Python wiki (*https://oreil.ly/C_39k*)) summarizes all the standard Python time interconversions.

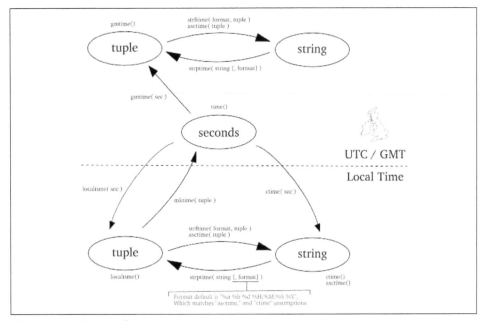

Figure 13-1. Date and time conversions

Alternative Modules

If you find the standard library modules confusing, or lacking a particular conversion that you want, there are many third-party alternatives. Here are just a few of them:

arrow *(https://arrow.readthedocs.io)*
    Combines many date and time functions with a simple API

dateutil *(http://labix.org/python-dateutil)*
    Parses almost any date format and handles relative dates and times well

iso8601 *(https://pypi.python.org/pypi/iso8601)*
    Fills in gaps in the standard library for the ISO8601 format

fleming *(https://github.com/ambitioninc/fleming)*
    Many time zone functions

maya *(https://github.com/kennethreitz/maya)*
    Intuitive interface to dates, times, and intervals

dateinfer *(https://github.com/jeffreystarr/dateinfer)*
    Guesses the right format strings from date/time strings

Coming Up

Files and directories need love, too.

Things to Do

13.1 Write the current date as a string to the text file *today.txt*.

13.2 Read the text file *today.txt* into the string today_string.

13.3 Parse the date from today_string.

13.4 Create a date object of your day of birth.

13.5 What day of the week was your day of birth?

13.6 When will you be (or when were you) 10,000 days old?

CHAPTER 14

Files and Directories

I have files, I have computer files and, you know, files on paper. But most of it is really in my head. So God help me if anything ever happens to my head!

—George R. R. Martin

When you first start programming, you hear some words over and over but aren't sure whether they have a specific technical meaning or are just handwaving. The terms *file* and *directory* are such words, and they do have actual technical meanings. A *file* is a sequence of bytes, stored in some *filesystem*, and accessed by a *filename*. A *directory* is a collection of files, and possibly other directories. The term *folder* is a synonym for directory. It turned up when computers gained graphical user interfaces, and mimicked office concepts to make things seem more familiar.

Many filesystems are hierarchical, and often referred to as being like a tree. Real offices don't tend to have trees in them, and the folder analogy only works if you visualize subfolders all the way down.

File Input and Output

The simplest kind of persistence is a plain old file, sometimes called a *flat file*. You *read* from a file into memory and *write* from memory to a file. Python makes these jobs easy. As with many languages, its file operations were largely modeled on the familiar and popular Unix equivalents.

Create or Open with open()

You need to call the open function before you do the following:

- Read an existing file

- Write to a new file
- Append to an existing file
- Overwrite an existing file

```
fileobj = open( filename, mode )
```

Here's a brief explanation of the pieces of this call:

- *fileobj* is the file object returned by open()
- *filename* is the string name of the file
- *mode* is a string indicating the file's type and what you want to do with it

The first letter of *mode* indicates the *operation*:

- r means read.
- w means write. If the file doesn't exist, it's created. If the file does exist, it's over-written.
- x means write, but only if the file does *not* already exist.
- a means append (write after the end) if the file exists.

The second letter of *mode* is the file's *type*:

- t (or nothing) means text.
- b means binary.

After opening the file, you call functions to read or write data; these will be shown in the examples that follow.

Last, you need to *close* the file to ensure that any writes complete, and that memory is freed. Later, you'll see how to use with to automate this for you.

This program opens a file called *oops.txt* and closes it without writing anything. This would create an empty file:

```
>>> fout = open('oops.txt', 'wt')
>>> fout.close()
```

Write a Text File with print()

Let's re-create *oops.txt*, but now write a line to it and then close it:

```
>>> fout = open('oops.txt', 'wt')
>>> print('Oops, I created a file.', file=fout)
>>> fout.close()
```

We created an empty *oops.txt* file in the previous section, so this just overwrites it.

We used the `file` argument to `print`. Without it, `print` writes to *standard output*, which is your terminal (unless you've told your shell program to redirect output to a file with > or piped it to another program with |).

Write a Text File with write()

We just used `print` to write a line to a file. We can also use `write`.

For our multiline data source, let's use this limerick about special relativity:[1]

```
>>> poem = '''There was a young lady named Bright,
... Whose speed was far faster than light;
... She started one day
... In a relative way,
... And returned on the previous night.'''
>>> len(poem)
150
```

The following code writes the entire poem to the file `'relativity'` in one call:

```
>>> fout = open('relativity', 'wt')
>>> fout.write(poem)
150
>>> fout.close()
```

The `write` function returns the number of bytes written. It does not add any spaces or newlines, as `print` does. As before, you can also `print` a multiline string to a text file:

```
>>> fout = open('relativity', 'wt')
>>> print(poem, file=fout)
>>> fout.close()
```

So, should you use `write` or `print`? As you've seen, by default `print` adds a space after each argument and a newline at the end. In the previous example, it appended a newline to the `relativity` file. To make `print` work like `write`, pass it the following two arguments:

- `sep` (separator, which defaults to a space, ' ')
- `end` (end string, which defaults to a newline, '\n')

---

1 In the first manuscript of this book, I said *general* relativity, and was kindly corrected by a physicist reviewer.

We'll use empty strings to replace these defaults:

```
>>> fout = open('relativity', 'wt')
>>> print(poem, file=fout, sep='', end='')
>>> fout.close()
```

If you have a large source string, you can also write chunks (using slices) until the source is done:

```
>>> fout = open('relativity', 'wt')
>>> size = len(poem)
>>> offset = 0
>>> chunk = 100
>>> while True:
...      if offset > size:
...           break
...      fout.write(poem[offset:offset+chunk])
...      offset += chunk
...
100
50
>>> fout.close()
```

This wrote 100 characters on the first try and the last 50 characters on the next. Slices allow you to "go over the end" without raising an exception.

If the relativity file is precious to us, let's see whether using mode x really protects us from overwriting it:

```
>>> fout = open('relativity', 'xt')
Traceback (most recent call last):
  File "<stdin>", line 1, in <module>
FileExistsError: [Errno 17] File exists: 'relativity'
```

You can use this with an exception handler:

```
>>> try:
...      fout = open('relativity', 'xt')]
...      fout.write('stomp stomp stomp')
... except FileExistsError:
...      print('relativity already exists!. That was a close one.')
...
relativity already exists!. That was a close one.
```

Read a Text File with read(), readline(), or readlines()

You can call read() with no arguments to slurp up the entire file at once, as shown in the example that follows (be careful when doing this with large files; a gigabyte file will consume a gigabyte of memory):

```
>>> fin = open('relativity', 'rt' )
>>> poem = fin.read()
>>> fin.close()
```

```
>>> len(poem)
150
```

You can provide a maximum character count to limit how much `read()` returns at one time. Let's read 100 characters at a time and append each chunk to a `poem` string to rebuild the original:

```
>>> poem = ''
>>> fin = open('relativity', 'rt' )
>>> chunk = 100
>>> while True:
...     fragment = fin.read(chunk)
...     if not fragment:
...         break
...     poem += fragment
...
>>> fin.close()
>>> len(poem)
150
```

After you've read all the way to the end, further calls to `read()` will return an empty string (`''`), which is treated as `False` in `if not fragment`. This breaks out of the `while True` loop.

You can also read the file a line at a time by using `readline()`. In this next example, we append each line to the `poem` string to rebuild the original:

```
>>> poem = ''
>>> fin = open('relativity', 'rt' )
>>> while True:
...     line = fin.readline()
...     if not line:
...         break
...     poem += line
...
>>> fin.close()
>>> len(poem)
150
```

For a text file, even a blank line has a length of one (the newline character), and is evaluated as `True`. When the file has been read, `readline()` (like `read()`) also returns an empty string, which is also evaluated as `False`.

The easiest way to read a text file is by using an *iterator*. This returns one line at a time. It's similar to the previous example but with less code:

```
>>> poem = ''
>>> fin = open('relativity', 'rt' )
>>> for line in fin:
...     poem += line
...
>>> fin.close()
```

```
>>> len(poem)
150
```

All of the preceding examples eventually built the single string poem. The read
lines() call reads a line at a time, and returns a list of one-line strings:

```
>>> fin = open('relativity', 'rt' )
>>> lines = fin.readlines()
>>> fin.close()
>>> print(len(lines), 'lines read')
5 lines read
>>> for line in lines:
...     print(line, end='')
...
There was a young lady named Bright,
Whose speed was far faster than light;
She started one day
In a relative way,
And returned on the previous night.>>>
```

We told print() to suppress the automatic newlines because the first four lines
already had them. The last line did not, causing the interactive prompt >>> to occur
right after the last line.

Write a Binary File with write()

If you include a 'b' in the *mode* string, the file is opened in binary mode. In this case,
you read and write bytes instead of a string.

We don't have a binary poem lying around, so we'll just generate the 256 byte values
from 0 to 255:

```
>>> bdata = bytes(range(0, 256))
>>> len(bdata)
256
```

Open the file for writing in binary mode and write all the data at once:

```
>>> fout = open('bfile', 'wb')
>>> fout.write(bdata)
256
>>> fout.close()
```

Again, write() returns the number of bytes written.

As with text, you can write binary data in chunks:

```
>>> fout = open('bfile', 'wb')
>>> size = len(bdata)
>>> offset = 0
>>> chunk = 100
>>> while True:
...     if offset > size:
```

```
...              break
...          fout.write(bdata[offset:offset+chunk])
...          offset += chunk
...
100
100
56
>>> fout.close()
```

Read a Binary File with read()

This one is simple; all you need to do is just open with `'rb'`:

```
>>> fin = open('bfile', 'rb')
>>> bdata = fin.read()
>>> len(bdata)
256
>>> fin.close()
```

Close Files Automatically by Using with

If you forget to close a file that you've opened, it will be closed by Python after it's no longer referenced. This means that if you open a file within a function and don't close it explicitly, it will be closed automatically when the function ends. But you might have opened the file in a long-running function or the main section of the program. The file should be closed to force any remaining writes to be completed.

Python has *context managers* to clean up things such as open files. You use the form `with` *expression* as *variable*:

```
>>> with open('relativity', 'wt') as fout:
...     fout.write(poem)
...
```

That's it. After the block of code under the context manager (in this case, one line) completes (normally *or* by a raised exception), the file is closed automatically.

Change Position with seek()

As you read and write, Python keeps track of where you are in the file. The `tell()` function returns your current offset from the beginning of the file, in bytes. The `seek()` function lets you jump to another byte offset in the file. This means that you don't have to read every byte in a file to read the last one; you can `seek()` to the last one and just read one byte.

For this example, use the 256-byte binary file `'bfile'` that you wrote earlier:

```
>>> fin = open('bfile', 'rb')
>>> fin.tell()
0
```

Use **seek()** to jump to one byte before the end of the file:

```
>>> fin.seek(255)
255
```

Read until the end of the file:

```
>>> bdata = fin.read()
>>> len(bdata)
1
>>> bdata[0]
255
```

seek() also returns the current offset.

You can call **seek()** with a second argument: seek(*offset, origin*):

- If origin is 0 (the default), go *offset* bytes from the start
- If origin is 1, go *offset* bytes from the current position
- If origin is 2, go *offset* bytes relative to the end

These values are also defined in the standard os module:

```
>>> import os
>>> os.SEEK_SET
0
>>> os.SEEK_CUR
1
>>> os.SEEK_END
2
```

So, we could have read the last byte in different ways:

```
>>> fin = open('bfile', 'rb')
```

One byte before the end of the file:

```
>>> fin.seek(-1, 2)
255
>>> fin.tell()
255
```

Read until the end of the file:

```
>>> bdata = fin.read()
>>> len(bdata)
1
>>> bdata[0]
255
```

You don't need to call tell() for seek() to work. I just wanted to show that they both report the same offset.

Here's an example of seeking from the current position in the file:

```
>>> fin = open('bfile', 'rb')
```

This next example ends up two bytes before the end of the file:

```
>>> fin.seek(254, 0)
254
>>> fin.tell()
254
```

Now go forward one byte:

```
>>> fin.seek(1, 1)
255
>>> fin.tell()
255
```

Finally, read until the end of the file:

```
>>> bdata = fin.read()
>>> len(bdata)
1
>>> bdata[0]
255
```

These functions are most useful for binary files. You can use them with text files, but unless the file is ASCII (one byte per character), you would have a hard time calculating offsets. These would depend on the text encoding, and the most popular encoding (UTF-8) uses varying numbers of bytes per character.

Memory Mapping

An alternative to reading and writing a file is to *memory-map* it with the standard mmap module. This makes the contents of a file look like a bytearray in memory. See the documentation (*https://oreil.ly/GEzkf*) and some examples (*https://oreil.ly/GUtdx*) for more details.

File Operations

Python, like many other languages, patterned its file operations after Unix. Some functions, such as chown() and chmod(), have the same names, but there are a few new ones.

I'll first show how Python handles these tasks with functions from the `os.path` module and then with the newer `pathlib` module.

Check Existence with exists()

To verify whether the file or directory is really there or you just imagined it, you can provide `exists()`, with a relative or absolute pathname, as demonstrated here:

```
>>> import os
>>> os.path.exists('oops.txt')
True
>>> os.path.exists('./oops.txt')
True
>>> os.path.exists('waffles')
False
>>> os.path.exists('.')
True
>>> os.path.exists('..')
True
```

Check Type with isfile()

The functions in this section check whether a name refers to a file, directory, or symbolic link (see the examples that follow for a discussion of links).

The first function we'll look at, `isfile`, asks a simple question: is it a plain old law-abiding file?

```
>>> name = 'oops.txt'
>>> os.path.isfile(name)
True
```

Here's how you determine a directory:

```
>>> os.path.isdir(name)
False
```

A single dot (.) is shorthand for the current directory, and two dots (..) stands for the parent directory. These always exist, so a statement such as the following will always report `True`:

```
>>> os.path.isdir('.')
True
```

The os module contains many functions dealing with *pathnames* (fully qualified filenames, starting with / and including all parents). One such function, `isabs()`, determines whether its argument is an absolute pathname. The argument doesn't need to be the name of a real file:

```
>>> os.path.isabs(name)
False
```

```
>>> os.path.isabs('/big/fake/name')
True
>>> os.path.isabs('big/fake/name/without/a/leading/slash')
False
```

Copy with copy()

The copy() function comes from another module, shutil. This example copies the
file *oops.txt* to the file *ohno.txt*:

```
>>> import shutil
>>> shutil.copy('oops.txt', 'ohno.txt')
```

The shutil.move() function copies a file and then removes the original.

Change Name with rename()

This function does exactly what it says. In the example here, it renames *ohno.txt* to
ohwell.txt:

```
>>> import os
>>> os.rename('ohno.txt', 'ohwell.txt')
```

Link with link() or symlink()

In Unix, a file exists in one place, but it can have multiple names, called *links*. In low-
level *hard links*, it's not easy to find all the names for a given file. A *symbolic link* is an
alternative method that stores the new name as its own file, making it possible for you
to get both the original and new names at once. The link() call creates a hard link,
and symlink() makes a symbolic link. The islink() function checks whether the file
is a symbolic link.

Here's how to make a hard link to the existing file *oops.txt* from the new file *yikes.txt*:

```
>>> os.link('oops.txt', 'yikes.txt')
>>> os.path.isfile('yikes.txt')
True
>>> os.path.islink('yikes.txt')
False
```

To create a symbolic link to the existing file *oops.txt* from the new file *jeepers.txt*, use
the following:

```
>>> os.symlink('oops.txt', 'jeepers.txt')
>>> os.path.islink('jeepers.txt')
True
```

Change Permissions with chmod()

On a Unix system, chmod() changes file permissions. There are read, write, and execute permissions for the user (that's usually you, if you created the file), the main group that the user is in, and the rest of the world. The command takes an intensely compressed octal (base 8) value that combines user, group, and other permissions. For instance, to make *oops.txt* readable only by its owner, type the following:

```
>>> os.chmod('oops.txt', 0o400)
```

If you don't want to deal with cryptic octal values and would rather deal with (slightly less) obscure cryptic symbols, you can import some constants from the stat module and use a statement such as the following:

```
>>> import stat
>>> os.chmod('oops.txt', stat.S_IRUSR)
```

Change Ownership with chown()

This function is also Unix/Linux/Mac–specific. You can change the owner and/or group ownership of a file by specifying the numeric user ID (*uid*) and group ID (*gid*):

```
>>> uid = 5
>>> gid = 22
>>> os.chown('oops', uid, gid)
```

Delete a File with remove()

In this snippet, we use the remove() function and say farewell to *oops.txt*:

```
>>> os.remove('oops.txt')
>>> os.path.exists('oops.txt')
False
```

Directory Operations

In most operating systems, files exist in a hierarchy of *directories* (often called *folders*). The container of all of these files and directories is a *filesystem* (sometimes called a *volume*). The standard os module deals with operating specifics such as these and provides the following functions with which you can manipulate them.

Create with mkdir()

This example shows how to create a directory called poems to store that precious verse:

```
>>> os.mkdir('poems')
>>> os.path.exists('poems')
True
```

Delete with rmdir()

Upon second thought,[2] you decide you don't need that directory after all. Here's how to delete it:

```
>>> os.rmdir('poems')
>>> os.path.exists('poems')
False
```

List Contents with listdir()

OK, take two; let's make poems again, with some contents:

```
>>> os.mkdir('poems')
```

Now get a list of its contents (none so far):

```
>>> os.listdir('poems')
[]
```

Next, make a subdirectory:

```
>>> os.mkdir('poems/mcintyre')
>>> os.listdir('poems')
['mcintyre']
```

Create a file in this subdirectory (don't type all these lines unless you really feel poetic; just make sure you begin and end with matching quotes, either single or tripled):

```
>>> fout = open('poems/mcintyre/the_good_man', 'wt')
>>> fout.write('''Cheerful and happy was his mood,
... He to the poor was kind and good,
... And he oft' times did find them food,
... Also supplies of coal and wood,
... He never spake a word was rude,
... And cheer'd those did o'er sorrows brood,
... He passed away not understood,
... Because no poet in his lays
... Had penned a sonnet in his praise,
... 'Tis sad, but such is world's ways.
... ''')
344
>>> fout.close()
```

Finally, let's see what we have. It had better be there:

```
>>> os.listdir('poems/mcintyre')
['the_good_man']
```

---

2 Why is it never first?

Change Current Directory with chdir()

With this function, you can go from one directory to another. Let's leave the current directory and spend a little time in poems:

```
>>> import os
>>> os.chdir('poems')
>>> os.listdir('.')
['mcintyre']
```

List Matching Files with glob()

The glob() function matches file or directory names by using Unix shell rules rather than the more complete regular expression syntax. Here are those rules:

- `*` matches everything (re would expect `.*`)
- `?` matches a single character
- `[abc]` matches character a, b, or c
- `[!abc]` matches any character *except* a, b, or c

Try getting all files or directories that begin with m:

```
>>> import glob
>>> glob.glob('m*')
['mcintyre']
```

How about any two-letter files or directories?

```
>>> glob.glob('??')
[]
```

I'm thinking of an eight-letter word that begins with m and ends with e:

```
>>> glob.glob('m??????e')
['mcintyre']
```

What about anything that begins with a k, l, or m, and ends with e?

```
>>> glob.glob('[klm]*e')
['mcintyre']
```

Pathnames

Almost all of our computers use hierarchical filesystems, with directories ("folders") containing files and other directories, down to various levels. When you want to refer to a specific file or directory, you need its *pathname*: the sequence of directories needed to get there, either *absolute* from the top (the *root*), or *relative* to your current directory.

You'll often hear people confusing a forward *slash* ('/', not the Guns N' Roses guy) and *backslash* ('\').[3] Unix and Macs (and web URLs) use slash as the *path separator*, and Windows uses backslash.[4]

Python lets you use slash as the path separator when you're specifying names. On Windows, you can use backslash, but you know that backslash is a ubiquitous escape character in Python, so you have to double it everywhere, or use Python's raw strings:

```
>>> win_file = 'eek\\urk\\snort.txt'
>>> win_file2 = r'eek\urk\snort.txt'
>>> win_file
'eek\\urk\\snort.txt'
>>> win_file2
'eek\\urk\\snort.txt'
```

When you're building a pathname, you can do the following:

- Use the appropriate path separation character ('/' or '\')
- Build a pathname (see "Build a Pathname with os.path.join()" on page 274)
- Use pathlib (see "Use pathlib" on page 274)

Get a Pathname with abspath()

This function expands a relative name to an absolute one. If your current directory is */usr/gaberlunzie* and the file *oops.txt* is there, you can type the following:

```
>>> os.path.abspath('oops.txt')
'/usr/gaberlunzie/oops.txt'
```

Get a symlink Pathname with realpath()

In one of the earlier sections, we made a symbolic link to *oops.txt* from the new file *jeepers.txt*. In circumstances such as this, you can get the name of *oops.txt* from *jeepers.txt* by using the realpath() function, as shown here:

```
>>> os.path.realpath('jeepers.txt')
'/usr/gaberlunzie/oops.txt'
```

---

3 One way to remember: forward slash tilts *forward*, backslash tilts *back*.

4 QDOS was the operating system that Bill Gates bought for $50,000 to have "MS-DOS" when IBM came calling about their first PC. It mimicked CP/M, which used slashes for command-line arguments. When MS-DOS later added folders, it had to use backslashes.

Build a Pathname with os.path.join()

When you're constructing a multipart pathname, you can call os.path.join() to combine them pairwise with the proper path separation character for your operating system:

```
>>> import os
>>> win_file = os.path.join("eek", "urk")
>>> win_file = os.path.join(win_file, "snort.txt")
```

If I run this on a Mac or Linux box, I get this:

```
>>> win_file
'eek/urk/snort.txt'
```

Running on Windows would produce this:

```
>>> win_file
'eek\\urk\\snort.txt'
```

But if the same code produces different result depending on where it's run, that could be a problem. The new pathlib module is a portable solution to this.

Use pathlib

Python added the pathlib module in version 3.4. It's an alternative to the os.path modules that I just described. But why do we need another module?

Rather that treating filesystem pathnames as strings, it introduces the Path object to treat them at a little higher level. Create a Path with the Path() class, and then knit your path together with bare slashes (not '/' characters):

```
>>> from pathlib import Path
>>> file_path = Path('eek') / 'urk' / 'snort.txt'
>>> file_path
PosixPath('eek/urk/snort.txt')
>>> print(file_path)
eek/urk/snort.txt
```

This slash trick took advantage of Python's "Magic Methods" on page 190. A Path can tell you a bit about itself:

```
>>> file_path.name
'snort.txt'
>>> file_path.suffix
'.txt'
>>> file_path.stem
'snort'
```

You can feed file_path to open() as you would any filename or pathname string.

You can also see what would happen if you ran this program on another system or if you needed to generate foreign pathnames on your computer:

```
>>> from pathlib import PureWindowsPath
>>> PureWindowsPath(file_path)
PureWindowsPath('eek/urk/snort.txt')
>>> print(PureWindowsPath(file_path))
eek\urk\snort.txt
```

See the docs (*https://oreil.ly/yN87f*) for all the details.

BytesIO and StringIO

You've seen how to modify data in memory and how to get data in and out of files. What do you do if you have in-memory data, but want to call a function that expects a file (or the reverse)? You'd want to modify the data and pass those bytes or characters around, without reading and writing temporary files.

You can use io.BytesIO for binary data (bytes) and io.StringIO for text data (str). Using either of these wraps data as a *file-like object*, suitable to use with all the file functions you've seen in this chapter.

One use case for this is data format conversion. Let's apply this to the PIL library (details coming in "PIL and Pillow" on page 454), which reads and writes image data. The first argument to its Image object's open() and save() methods is a filename *or a file-like object*. The code in Example 14-1 uses BytesIO to read *and* write in-memory data. It reads one or more image files from the command line, converts its image data to three different formats, and prints the length and first 10 bytes of these outputs.

Example 14-1. convert_image.py

```python
from io import BytesIO
from PIL import Image
import sys

def data_to_img(data):
    """Return PIL Image object, with data from in-memory <data>"""
    fp = BytesIO(data)
    return Image.open(fp)      # reads from memory

def img_to_data(img, fmt=None):
    """Return image data from PIL Image <img>, in <fmt> format"""
    fp = BytesIO()
    if not fmt:
        fmt = img.format       # keeps the original format
    img.save(fp, fmt)          # writes to memory
    return fp.getvalue()

def convert_image(data, fmt=None):
    """Convert image <data> to PIL <fmt> image data"""
    img = data_to_img(data)
    return img_to_data(img, fmt)
```

```
def get_file_data(name):
    """Return PIL Image object for image file <name>"""
    img = Image.open(name)
    print("img", img, img.format)
    return img_to_data(img)

if __name__ == "__main__":
    for name in sys.argv[1:]:
        data = get_file_data(name)
        print("in", len(data), data[:10])
        for fmt in ("gif", "png", "jpeg"):
            out_data = convert_image(data, fmt)
            print("out", len(out_data), out_data[:10])
```

 Because it acts like a file, you can seek(), read(), and write() a BytesIO object just like a normal file; if you did a seek() followed by a read(), you would get only the bytes from that seek position to the end. That getvalue() returns all the bytes in the BytesIO object.

Here's the output, using an input image file that you'll see in Chapter 20:

```
$ python convert_image.py ch20_critter.png
img <PIL.PngImagePlugin.PngImageFile image mode=RGB size=154x141 at 0x10340CF28> PNG
in 24941 b'\\x89PNG\\r\\n\\x1a\\n\\x00\\x00'
out 14751 b'GIF87a\\x9a\\x00\\x8d\\x00'
out 24941 b'\\x89PNG\\r\\n\\x1a\\n\\x00\\x00'
out 5914 b'\\xff\xd8\\xff\\xe0\\x00\\x10JFIF'
```

Coming Up

The next chapter is a bit more complex. It deals with *concurrency* (ways of doing multiple things at about the same time) and *processes* (running programs).

Things to Do

14.1 List the files in your current directory.

14.2 List the files in your parent directory.

14.3 Assign the string 'This is a test of the emergency text system' to the variable test1, and write test1 to a file called *test.txt*.

14.4 Open the file *test.txt* and read its contents into the string test2. Are test1 and test2 the same?

CHAPTER 15

Data in Time: Processes and Concurrency

One thing a computer can do that most humans can't is be sealed up in a cardboard box and sit in a warehouse.

—Jack Handey

This chapter and the next two are a bit more challenging than earlier ones. In this one we cover data in time (sequential and concurrent access on a single computer), and following that we look at data in a box (storage and retrieval with special files and databases) in Chapter 16 and then data in space (networking) in Chapter 17.

Programs and Processes

When you run an individual program, your operating system creates a single *process*. It uses system resources (CPU, memory, disk space) and data structures in the operating system's *kernel* (file and network connections, usage statistics, and so on). A process is isolated from other processes—it can't see what other processes are doing or interfere with them.

The operating system keeps track of all the running processes, giving each a little time to run and then switching to another, with the twin goals of spreading the work around fairly and being responsive to the user. You can see the state of your processes with graphical interfaces such as the Mac's Activity Monitor (macOS), Task Manager on Windows-based computers, or the top command in Linux.

You can also access process data from your own programs. The standard library's os module provides a common way of accessing some system information. For instance, the following functions get the *process ID* and the *current working directory* of the running Python interpreter:

```
>>> import os
>>> os.getpid()
```

```
76051
>>> os.getcwd()
'/Users/williamlubanovic'
```

And these get my *user ID* and *group ID*:

```
>>> os.getuid()
501
>>> os.getgid()
20
```

Create a Process with subprocess

All of the programs that you've seen here so far have been individual processes. You can start and stop other existing programs from Python by using the standard library's subprocess module. If you just want to run another program in a shell and grab whatever output it created (both standard output and standard error output), use the getoutput() function. Here, we get the output of the Unix date program:

```
>>> import subprocess
>>> ret = subprocess.getoutput('date')
>>> ret
'Sun Mar 30 22:54:37 CDT 2014'
```

You won't get anything back until the process ends. If you need to call something that might take a lot of time, see the discussion on *concurrency* in "Concurrency" on page 284. Because the argument to getoutput() is a string representing a complete shell command, you can include arguments, pipes, < and > I/O redirection, and so on:

```
>>> ret = subprocess.getoutput('date -u')
>>> ret
'Mon Mar 31 03:55:01 UTC 2014'
```

Piping that output string to the wc command counts one line, six "words," and 29 characters:

```
>>> ret = subprocess.getoutput('date -u | wc')
>>> ret
'       1       6      29'
```

A variant method called check_output() takes a list of the command and arguments. By default it returns standard output only as type bytes rather than a string, and does not use the shell:

```
>>> ret = subprocess.check_output(['date', '-u'])
>>> ret
b'Mon Mar 31 04:01:50 UTC 2014\n'
```

To show the exit status of the other program, `getstatusoutput()` returns a tuple with the status code and output:

```
>>> ret = subprocess.getstatusoutput('date')
>>> ret
(0, 'Sat Jan 18 21:36:23 CST 2014')
```

If you don't want to capture the output but might want to know its exit status, use `call()`:

```
>>> ret = subprocess.call('date')
Sat Jan 18 21:33:11 CST 2014
>>> ret
0
```

(In Unix-like systems, `0` is usually the exit status for success.)

That date and time was printed to output but not captured within our program. So, we saved the return code as `ret`.

You can run programs with arguments in two ways. The first is to specify them in a single string. Our sample command is `date -u`, which prints the current date and time in UTC:

```
>>> ret = subprocess.call('date -u', shell=True)
Tue Jan 21 04:40:04 UTC 2014
```

You need that `shell=True` to recognize the command line `date -u`, splitting it into separate strings and possibly expanding any wildcard characters such as `*` (we didn't use any in this example).

The second method makes a list of the arguments, so it doesn't need to call the shell:

```
>>> ret = subprocess.call(['date', '-u'])
Tue Jan 21 04:41:59 UTC 2014
```

Create a Process with multiprocessing

You can run a Python function as a separate process, or even create multiple independent processes with the `multiprocessing` module. The sample code in Example 15-1 is short and simple; save it as *mp.py* and then run it by typing `python mp.py`:

Example 15-1. mp.py

```
import multiprocessing
import os

def whoami(what):
    print("Process %s says: %s" % (os.getpid(), what))
```

```
if __name__ == "__main__":
    whoami("I'm the main program")
    for n in range(4):
        p = multiprocessing.Process(target=whoami,
            args=("I'm function %s" % n,))
        p.start()
```

When I run this, my output looks like this:

```
Process 6224 says: I'm the main program
Process 6225 says: I'm function 0
Process 6226 says: I'm function 1
Process 6227 says: I'm function 2
Process 6228 says: I'm function 3
```

The Process() function spawned a new process and ran the do_this() function in it. Because we did this in a loop that had four passes, we generated four new processes that executed do_this() and then exited.

The multiprocessing module has more bells and whistles than a clown on a calliope. It's really intended for those times when you need to farm out some task to multiple processes to save overall time; for example, downloading web pages for scraping, resizing images, and so on. It includes ways to queue tasks, enable intercommunication among processes, and wait for all the processes to finish. "Concurrency" on page 284 delves into some of these details.

Kill a Process with terminate()

If you created one or more processes and want to terminate one for some reason (perhaps it's stuck in a loop, or maybe you're bored, or you want to be an evil overlord), use terminate(). In Example 15-2, our process would count to a million, sleeping at each step for a second, and printing an irritating message. However, our main program runs out of patience in five seconds and nukes it from orbit.

Example 15-2. mp2.py

```
import multiprocessing
import time
import os

def whoami(name):
    print("I'm %s, in process %s" % (name, os.getpid()))

def loopy(name):
    whoami(name)
    start = 1
    stop = 1000000
    for num in range(start, stop):
        print("\tNumber %s of %s. Honk!" % (num, stop))
```

```
        time.sleep(1)

if __name__ == "__main__":
    whoami("main")
    p = multiprocessing.Process(target=loopy, args=("loopy",))
    p.start()
    time.sleep(5)
    p.terminate()
```

When I run this program, I get the following:

```
I'm main, in process 97080
I'm loopy, in process 97081
    Number 1 of 1000000. Honk!
    Number 2 of 1000000. Honk!
    Number 3 of 1000000. Honk!
    Number 4 of 1000000. Honk!
    Number 5 of 1000000. Honk!
```

Get System Info with os

The standard os package provides a lot of details on your system, and lets you control
some of it if you run your Python script as a privileged user (root or administrator).
Besides file and directory functions that are covered in Chapter 14, it has informa-
tional functions like these (run on an iMac):

```
>>> import os
>>> os.uname()
posix.uname_result(sysname='Darwin',
nodename='iMac.local',
release='18.5.0',
version='Darwin Kernel Version 18.5.0: Mon Mar 11 20:40:32 PDT 2019;
  root:xnu-4903.251.3~3/RELEASE_X86_64',
machine='x86_64')
>>> os.getloadavg()
(1.794921875, 1.93115234375, 2.2587890625)
>>> os.cpu_count()
4
```

A useful function is system(), which executes a command string as though you typed
it at a terminal:

```
>>> import os
>>> os.system('date -u')
Tue Apr 30 13:10:09 UTC 2019
0
```

It's a grab bag. See the docs (*https://oreil.ly/3r6xN*) for interesting tidbits.

Get Process Info with psutil

The third-party package psutil (*https://oreil.ly/pHpJD*) also provides system and process information for Linux, Unix, macOS, and Windows systems.

You can guess how to install it:

```
$ pip install psutil
```

Coverage includes the following:

System
CPU, memory, disk, network, sensors

Processes
id, parent id, CPU, memory, open files, threads

We already saw (in the previous os discussion) that my computer has four CPUs. How much time (in seconds) have they been using?

```
>>> import psutil
>>> psutil.cpu_times(True)
[scputimes(user=62306.49, nice=0.0, system=19872.71, idle=256097.64),
 scputimes(user=19928.3, nice=0.0, system=6934.29, idle=311407.28),
 scputimes(user=57311.41, nice=0.0, system=15472.99, idle=265485.56),
 scputimes(user=14399.49, nice=0.0, system=4848.84, idle=319017.87)]
```

And how busy are they now?

```
>>> import psutil
>>> psutil.cpu_percent(True)
26.1
>>> psutil.cpu_percent(percpu=True)
[39.7, 16.2, 50.5, 6.0]
```

You might never need this kind of data, but it's good to know where to look if you do.

Command Automation

You often run commands from the shell (either with manually typed commands or shell scripts), but Python has more than one good third-party management tool.

A related topic, *task queues*, is discussed in "Queues" on page 285.

Invoke

Version 1 of the fabric tool let you define local and remote (networked) tasks with Python code. The developers split this original package into fabric2 (remote) and invoke (local).

Install invoke by running the following:

```
$ pip install invoke
```

One use of invoke is to make functions available as command-line arguments. Let's make a *tasks.py* file with the lines shown in Example 15-3.

Example 15-3. tasks.py

```
from invoke import task

@task
def mytime(ctx):
    import time
    now = time.time()
    time_str = time.asctime(time.localtime(now))
    print("Local time is", timestr)
```

(That ctx argument is the first argument for each task function, but it's used only internally by invoke. It doesn't matter what you call it, but an argument needs to be there.)

```
$ invoke mytime
Local time is Thu May  2 13:16:23 2019
```

Use the argument -l or --list to see what tasks are available:

```
$ invoke -l
Available tasks:

  mytime
```

Tasks can have arguments, and you can invoke multiple tasks at one time from the command line (similar to && use in shell scripts).

Other uses include:

- Running local shell commands with the run() function
- Responding to string output patterns of programs

This was a brief glimpse. See the docs (*http://docs.pyinvoke.org*) for all the details.

Other Command Helpers

These Python packages have some similarity to invoke, but one or another may be a better fit when you need it:

- click (*https://click.palletsprojects.com*)
- doit (*http://pydoit.org*)

- sh (*http://amoffat.github.io/sh*)
- delegator (*https://github.com/kennethreitz/delegator.py*)
- pypeln (*https://cgarciae.github.io/pypeln*)

Concurrency

The official Python site discusses concurrency in general and in the standard library (*http://bit.ly/concur-lib*). Those pages have many links to various packages and techniques; in this chapter, we show the most useful ones.

In computers, if you're waiting for something, it's usually for one of two reasons:

I/O bound
> This is by far the most common. Computer CPUs are ridiculously fast—hundreds of times faster than computer memory and many thousands of times faster than disks or networks.

CPU bound
> The CPU keeps busy. This happens with *number crunching* tasks such as scientific or graphic calculations.

Two more terms are related to concurrency:

Synchronous
> One thing follows the other, like a line of goslings behind their parents.

Asynchronous
> Tasks are independent, like random geese splashing down in a pond.

As you progress from simple systems and tasks to real-life problems, you'll need at some point to deal with concurrency. Consider a website, for example. You can usually provide static and dynamic pages to web clients fairly quickly. A fraction of a second is considered interactive, but if the display or interaction takes longer people become impatient. Tests by companies such as Google and Amazon showed that traffic drops off quickly if the page loads even a little slower.

But what if you can't help it when something takes a long time, such as uploading a file, resizing an image, or querying a database? You can't do it within your synchronous web server code anymore, because someone's waiting.

On a single machine, if you want to perform multiple tasks as fast as possible, you want to make them independent. Slow tasks shouldn't block all the others.

This chapter showed earlier how multiprocessing can be used to overlap work on a single machine. If you needed to resize an image, your web server code could call a separate, dedicated-image resizing process to run asynchronously and concurrently. It could scale your application horizontally by invoking multiple resizing processes.

The trick is getting them all to work with one another. Any shared control or state means that there will be bottlenecks. An even bigger trick is dealing with failures, because concurrent computing is harder than regular computing. Many more things can go wrong, and your odds of end-to-end success are lower.

All right. What methods can help you to deal with these complexities? Let's begin with a good way to manage multiple tasks: *queues*.

Queues

A queue is like a list: things are added at one end and taken away from the other. The most common is referred to as *FIFO* (first in, first out).

Suppose that you're washing dishes. If you're stuck with the entire job, you need to wash each dish, dry it, and put it away. You can do this in a number of ways. You might wash the first dish, dry it, and then put it away. You then repeat with the second dish, and so on. Or, you might *batch* operations and wash all the dishes, dry them all, and then put them away; this assumes you have space in your sink and drainer for all the dishes that accumulate at each step. These are all synchronous approaches—one worker, one thing at a time.

As an alternative, you could get a helper or two. If you're the washer, you can hand each cleaned dish to the dryer, who hands each dried dish to the put-away-er. As long as each of you works at the same pace, you should finish much faster than by yourself.

However, what if you wash faster than the dryer dries? Wet dishes either fall on the floor, or you pile them up between you and the dryer, or you just whistle off-key until the dryer is ready. And if the last person is slower than the dryer, dry dishes can end up falling on the floor, or piling up, or the dryer does the whistling. You have multiple workers, but the overall task is still synchronous and can proceed only as fast as the slowest worker.

Many hands make light work, goes the old saying (I always thought it was Amish, because it makes me think of barn building). Adding workers can build a barn or do the dishes, faster. This involves *queues*.

In general, queues transport *messages*, which can be any kind of information. In this case, we're interested in queues for distributed task management, also known as *work queues*, *job queues*, or *task queues*. Each dish in the sink is given to an available washer, who washes and hands it off to the first available dryer, who dries and hands it to a put-away-er. This can be synchronous (workers wait for a dish to handle and another worker to whom to give it), or asynchronous (dishes are stacked between workers with different paces). As long as you have enough workers, and they keep up with the dishes, things move a lot faster.

Processes

You can implement queues in many ways. For a single machine, the standard library's multiprocessing module (which you saw earlier) contains a Queue function. Let's simulate just a single washer and multiple dryer processes (someone can put the dishes away later) and an intermediate dish_queue. Call this program *dishes.py* (Example 15-4).

Example 15-4. dishes.py

```python
import multiprocessing as mp

def washer(dishes, output):
    for dish in dishes:
        print('Washing', dish, 'dish')
        output.put(dish)

def dryer(input):
    while True:
        dish = input.get()
        print('Drying', dish, 'dish')
        input.task_done()

dish_queue = mp.JoinableQueue()
dryer_proc = mp.Process(target=dryer, args=(dish_queue,))
dryer_proc.daemon = True
dryer_proc.start()

dishes = ['salad', 'bread', 'entree', 'dessert']
washer(dishes, dish_queue)
dish_queue.join()
```

Run your new program, thusly:

```
$ python dishes.py
Washing salad dish
Washing bread dish
Washing entree dish
Washing dessert dish
Drying salad dish
Drying bread dish
Drying entree dish
Drying dessert dish
```

This queue looked a lot like a simple Python iterator, producing a series of dishes. It actually started up separate processes along with the communication between the washer and dryer. I used a JoinableQueue and the final join() method to let the washer know that all the dishes have been dried. There are other queue types in the `multiprocessing` module, and you can read the documentation (*http://bit.ly/multi-docs*) for more examples.

Threads

A *thread* runs within a process with access to everything in the process, similar to a multiple personality. The `multiprocessing` module has a cousin called `threading` that uses threads instead of processes (actually, `multiprocessing` was designed later as its process-based counterpart). Let's redo our process example with threads, as shown in Example 15-5.

Example 15-5. thread1.py

```
import threading

def do_this(what):
    whoami(what)

def whoami(what):
    print("Thread %s says: %s" % (threading.current_thread(), what))

if __name__ == "__main__":
    whoami("I'm the main program")
    for n in range(4):
        p = threading.Thread(target=do_this,
          args=("I'm function %s" % n,))
        p.start()
```

Here's what prints for me:

```
Thread <_MainThread(MainThread, started 140735207346960)> says: I'm the main
program
Thread <Thread(Thread-1, started 4326629376)> says: I'm function 0
Thread <Thread(Thread-2, started 4342157312)> says: I'm function 1
Thread <Thread(Thread-3, started 4347412480)> says: I'm function 2
Thread <Thread(Thread-4, started 4342157312)> says: I'm function 3
```

We can reproduce our process-based dish example by using threads, as shown in Example 15-6.

Example 15-6. thread_dishes.py

```
import threading, queue
import time

def washer(dishes, dish_queue):
    for dish in dishes:
        print ("Washing", dish)
```

```
        time.sleep(5)
        dish_queue.put(dish)

def dryer(dish_queue):
    while True:
        dish = dish_queue.get()
        print ("Drying", dish)
        time.sleep(10)
        dish_queue.task_done()


dish_queue = queue.Queue()
for n in range(2):
    dryer_thread = threading.Thread(target=dryer, args=(dish_queue,))
    dryer_thread.start()

dishes = ['salad', 'bread', 'entree', 'dessert']
washer(dishes, dish_queue)
dish_queue.join()
```

One difference between multiprocessing and threading is that threading does not have a terminate() function. There's no easy way to terminate a running thread, because it can cause all sorts of problems in your code, and possibly in the space-time continuum itself.

Threads can be dangerous. Like manual memory management in languages such as C and C++, they can cause bugs that are extremely hard to find, let alone fix. To use threads, all the code in the program (and in external libraries that it uses) must be *thread safe*. In the preceding example code, the threads didn't share any global variables, so they could run independently without breaking anything.

Imagine that you're a paranormal investigator in a haunted house. Ghosts roam the halls, but none are aware of the others, and at any time, any of them can view, add, remove, or move any of the house's contents.

You're walking apprehensively through the house, taking readings with your impressive instruments. Suddenly you notice that the candlestick you passed seconds ago is now missing.

The contents of the house are like the variables in a program. The ghosts are threads in a process (the house). If the ghosts only cast spectral glances at the house's contents, there would be no problem. It's like a thread reading the value of a constant or variable without trying to change it.

Yet, some unseen entity could grab your flashlight, blow cold air down your neck, put marbles on the stairs, or make the fireplace come ablaze. The *really* subtle ghosts would change things in other rooms that you might never notice.

Despite your fancy instruments, you'd have a very hard time figuring out who did what, how, when, and where.

If you used multiple processes instead of threads, it would be like having a number of houses but with only one (living) person in each. If you put your brandy in front of the fireplace, it would still be there an hour later—some lost to evaporation, but in the same place.

Threads can be useful and safe when global data is not involved. In particular, threads are useful for saving time while waiting for some I/O operation to complete. In these cases, they don't have to fight over data, because each has completely separate variables.

But threads do sometimes have good reasons to change global data. In fact, one common reason to launch multiple threads is to let them divide up the work on some data, so a certain degree of change to the data is expected.

The usual way to share data safely is to apply a software *lock* before modifying a variable in a thread. This keeps the other threads out while the change is made. It's like having a Ghostbuster guard the room you want to remain unhaunted. The trick, though, is that you need to remember to unlock it. Plus, locks can be nested: what if another Ghostbuster is also watching the same room, or the house itself? The use of locks is traditional but hard to get right.

 In Python, threads do not speed up CPU-bound tasks because of an implementation detail in the standard Python system called the *Global Interpreter Lock* (GIL). This exists to avoid threading problems in the Python interpreter, and can actually make a multithreaded program slower than its single-threaded counterpart, or even a multi-process version.

So for Python, the recommendations are as follows:

- Use threads for I/O-bound problems
- Use processes, networking, or events (discussed in the next section) for CPU-bound problems

concurrent.futures

As you've just seen, using threads or multiple processes involves a number of details. The concurrent.futures module was added to the Python 3.2 standard library to simplify these. It lets you schedule an asynchronous pool of workers, using threads (when I/O-bound) or processes (when CPU-bound). You get back a *future* to track their state and collect the results.

Example 15-7 contains a test program that you can save as *cf.py*. The task function `calc()` sleeps for one second (our way of faking being busy with something), calculates the square root of its argument, and returns it. The program takes an optional command-line argument of the number of workers to use, which defaults to 3. It starts this number of workers in a thread pool, then a process pool, and then prints the elapsed times. The `values` list contains five numbers, sent to `calc()` one at time in a worker thread or process.

Example 15-7. cf.py

```
from concurrent import futures
import math
import time
import sys

def calc(val):
    time.sleep(1)
    result = math.sqrt(float(val))
    return result

def use_threads(num, values):
    t1 = time.time()
    with futures.ThreadPoolExecutor(num) as tex:
        results = tex.map(calc, values)
    t2 = time.time()
    return t2 - t1

def use_processes(num, values):
    t1 = time.time()
    with futures.ProcessPoolExecutor(num) as pex:
        results = pex.map(calc, values)
    t2 = time.time()
    return t2 - t1

def main(workers, values):
    print(f"Using {workers} workers for {len(values)} values")
    t_sec = use_threads(workers, values)
    print(f"Threads took {t_sec:.4f} seconds")
    p_sec = use_processes(workers, values)
    print(f"Processes took {p_sec:.4f} seconds")

if __name__ == '__main__':
    workers = int(sys.argv[1])
    values = list(range(1, 6)) # 1 .. 5
    main(workers, values)
```

Here are some results that I got:

```
$ python cf.py 1
Using 1 workers for 5 values
```

```
Threads took 5.0736 seconds
Processes took 5.5395 seconds
$ python cf.py 3
Using 3 workers for 5 values
Threads took 2.0040 seconds
Processes took 2.0351 seconds
$ python cf.py 5
Using 5 workers for 5 values
Threads took 1.0052 seconds
Processes took 1.0444 seconds
```

That one-second `sleep()` forced each worker to take a second for each calculation:

- With only one worker at a time, everything was serial, and the total time was more than five seconds.

- Five workers matched the size of the values being tested, so we had an elapsed time just more than a second.

- With three workers, we needed two runs to handle all five values, so two seconds elapsed.

In the program, I ignored the actual `results` (the square roots that we calculated) to emphasize the elapsed times. Also, using `map()` to define the pool causes us to wait for all workers to finish before returning `results`. If you wanted to get each result as it completed, let's try another test (call it *cf2.py*) in which each worker returns the value and its square root as soon as it calculates it (Example 15-8).

Example 15-8. cf2.py

```
from concurrent import futures
import math
import sys

def calc(val):
    result = math.sqrt(float(val))
    return val, result

def use_threads(num, values):
    with futures.ThreadPoolExecutor(num) as tex:
        tasks = [tex.submit(calc, value) for value in values]
        for f in futures.as_completed(tasks):
            yield f.result()

def use_processes(num, values):
    with futures.ProcessPoolExecutor(num) as pex:
        tasks = [pex.submit(calc, value) for value in values]
        for f in futures.as_completed(tasks):
            yield f.result()
```

```python
def main(workers, values):
    print(f"Using {workers} workers for {len(values)} values")
    print("Using threads:")
    for val, result in use_threads(workers, values):
        print(f'{val} {result:.4f}')
    print("Using processes:")
    for val, result in use_processes(workers, values):
        print(f'{val} {result:.4f}')

if __name__ == '__main__':
    workers = 3
    if len(sys.argv) > 1:
        workers = int(sys.argv[1])
    values = list(range(1, 6)) # 1 .. 5
    main(workers, values)
```

Our use_threads() and use_processes() functions are now generator functions that call yield to return on each iteration. From one run on my machine, you can see how the workers don't always finish 1 through 5 in order:

```
$ python cf2.py 5
Using 5 workers for 5 values
Using threads:
3 1.7321
1 1.0000
2 1.4142
4 2.0000
5 2.2361
Using processes:
1 1.0000
2 1.4142
3 1.7321
4 2.0000
5 2.2361
```

You can use concurrent.futures any time you want to launch a bunch of concurrent tasks, such as the following:

- Crawling URLs on the web
- Processing files, such as resizing images
- Calling service APIs

As usual, the docs (*https://oreil.ly/dDdF-*) provide additional details, but are much more technical.

Green Threads and gevent

As you've seen, developers traditionally avoid slow spots in programs by running them in separate threads or processes. The Apache web server is an example of this design.

One alternative is *event-based* programming. An event-based program runs a central *event loop*, doles out any tasks, and repeats the loop. The NGINX web server follows this design, and is generally faster than Apache.

The gevent library is event-based and accomplishes a neat trick: you write normal imperative code, and it magically converts pieces to *coroutines*. These are like generators that can communicate with one another and keep track of where they are. gevent modifies many of Python's standard objects such as socket to use its mechanism instead of blocking. This does not work with Python add-in code that was written in C, as some database drivers are.

You install gevent by using pip:

```
$ pip install gevent
```

Here's a variation of sample code at the gevent website (*http://www.gevent.org*). You'll see the socket module's gethostbyname() function in the upcoming DNS section. This function is synchronous, so you wait (possibly many seconds) while it chases name servers around the world to look up that address. But you could use the gevent version to look up multiple sites independently. Save this as *gevent_test.py* (Example 15-9).

Example 15-9. gevent_test.py

```
import gevent
from gevent import socket
hosts = ['www.crappytaxidermy.com', 'www.walterpottertaxidermy.com',
    'www.antique-taxidermy.com']
jobs = [gevent.spawn(gevent.socket.gethostbyname, host) for host in hosts]
gevent.joinall(jobs, timeout=5)
for job in jobs:
    print(job.value)
```

There's a one-line for-loop in the preceding example. Each hostname is submitted in turn to a gethostbyname() call, but they can run asynchronously because it's the gevent version of gethostbyname().

Run *gevent_test.py*:

```
$ python gevent_test.py
66.6.44.4
74.125.142.121
78.136.12.50
```

gevent.spawn() creates a *greenlet* (also known sometimes as a *green thread* or a *microthread*) to execute each gevent.socket.gethostbyname(url).

The difference from a normal thread is that it doesn't block. If something occurred that would have blocked a normal thread, gevent switches control to one of the other greenlets.

The gevent.joinall() method waits for all the spawned jobs to finish. Finally, we dump the IP addresses that we got for these hostnames.

Instead of the gevent version of socket, you can use its evocatively named *monkey-patching* functions. These modify standard modules such as socket to use greenlets rather than calling the gevent version of the module. This is useful when you want gevent to be applied all the way down, even into code that you might not be able to access.

At the top of your program, add the following call:

```
from gevent import monkey
monkey.patch_socket()
```

This inserts the gevent socket everywhere the normal socket is called, anywhere in your program, even in the standard library. Again, this works only for Python code, not libraries written in C.

Another function monkey-patches even more standard library modules:

```
from gevent import monkey
monkey.patch_all()
```

Use this at the top of your program to get as many gevent speedups as possible.

Save this program as *gevent_monkey.py* (Example 15-9).

Example 15-10. gevent_monkey.py

```
import gevent
from gevent import monkey; monkey.patch_all()
import socket
hosts = ['www.crappytaxidermy.com', 'www.walterpottertaxidermy.com',
    'www.antique-taxidermy.com']
jobs = [gevent.spawn(socket.gethostbyname, host) for host in hosts]
gevent.joinall(jobs, timeout=5)
for job in jobs:
    print(job.value)
```

Again, run the program:

```
$ python gevent_monkey.py
66.6.44.4
```

```
74.125.192.121
78.136.12.50
```

There are potential dangers when using gevent. As with any event-based system, each chunk of code that you execute should be relatively quick. Although it's non-blocking, code that does a lot of work is still slow.

The very idea of monkey-patching makes some people nervous. Yet, many large sites such as Pinterest use gevent to speed up their sites significantly. Like the fine print on a bottle of pills, use gevent as directed.

For more examples, see this thorough gevent tutorial (*https://oreil.ly/BWR_q*).

 You might also want to consider tornado (*http://www.tornado web.org*) or gunicorn (*http://gunicorn.org*), two other popular event-driven frameworks. They provide both the low-level event handling and a fast web server. They're worth a look if you'd like to build a fast website without messing with a traditional web server such as Apache.

twisted

twisted (*http://twistedmatrix.com/trac*) is an asynchronous, event-driven networking framework. You connect functions to events such as data received or connection closed, and those functions are called when those events occur. This is a *callback* design, and if you've written anything in JavaScript, it might seem familiar. If it's new to you, it can seem backwards. For some developers, callback-based code becomes harder to manage as the application grows.

You install it by running the following:

```
$ pip install twisted
```

twisted is a large package, with support for many internet protocols on top of TCP and UDP. To be short and simple, we show a little knock-knock server and client, adapted from twisted examples (*http://bit.ly/twisted-ex*). First, let's look at the server, *knock_server.py*: (Example 15-11).

Example 15-11. knock_server.py

```
from twisted.internet import protocol, reactor

class Knock(protocol.Protocol):
    def dataReceived(self, data):
        print('Client:', data)
        if data.startswith("Knock knock"):
            response = "Who's there?"
        else:
```

```
            response = data + " who?"
        print('Server:', response)
        self.transport.write(response)

class KnockFactory(protocol.Factory):
    def buildProtocol(self, addr):
        return Knock()

reactor.listenTCP(8000, KnockFactory())
reactor.run()
```

Now let's take a glance at its trusty companion, *knock_client.py* (Example 15-12).

Example 15-12. knock_client.py

```
from twisted.internet import reactor, protocol

class KnockClient(protocol.Protocol):
    def connectionMade(self):
        self.transport.write("Knock knock")

    def dataReceived(self, data):
        if data.startswith("Who's there?"):
            response = "Disappearing client"
            self.transport.write(response)
        else:
            self.transport.loseConnection()
            reactor.stop()

class KnockFactory(protocol.ClientFactory):
    protocol = KnockClient

def main():
    f = KnockFactory()
    reactor.connectTCP("localhost", 8000, f)
    reactor.run()

if __name__ == '__main__':
    main()
```

Start the server first:

```
$ python knock_server.py
```

Then, start the client:

```
$ python knock_client.py
```

The server and client exchange messages, and the server prints the conversation:

```
Client: Knock knock
Server: Who's there?
```

```
Client: Disappearing client
Server: Disappearing client who?
```

Our trickster client then ends, keeping the server waiting for the punch line.

If you'd like to enter the twisted passages, try some of the other examples from its documentation.

asyncio

Python added the asyncio library in version 3.4. It's a way of defining concurrent code using the new async and await capabilities. It's a big topic with many details. To avoid overstuffing this chapter, I've moved the discussion of asyncio and related topics to Appendix C.

Redis

Our earlier dishwashing code examples, using processes or threads, were run on a single machine. Let's take another approach to queues that can run on a single machine or across a network. Even with multiple singing processes and dancing threads, sometimes one machine isn't enough, You can treat this section as a bridge between single-box (one machine) and multiple-box concurrency.

To try the examples in this section, you'll need a Redis server and its Python module. You can see where to get them in "Redis" on page 332. In that chapter, Redis's role is that of a database. Here, we're featuring its concurrency personality.

A quick way to make a queue is with a Redis list. A Redis server runs on one machine; this can be the same one as its clients, or another that the clients can access through a network. In either case, clients talk to the server via TCP, so they're networking. One or more provider clients pushes messages onto one end of the list. One or more client workers watches this list with a *blocking pop* operation. If the list is empty, they all just sit around playing cards. As soon as a message arrives, the first eager worker gets it.

Like our earlier process- and thread-based examples, *redis_washer.py* generates a sequence of dishes (Example 15-13).

Example 15-13. redis_washer.py

```
import redis
conn = redis.Redis()
print('Washer is starting')
dishes = ['salad', 'bread', 'entree', 'dessert']
for dish in dishes:
    msg = dish.encode('utf-8')
    conn.rpush('dishes', msg)
```

```
    print('Washed', dish)
conn.rpush('dishes', 'quit')
print('Washer is done')
```

The loop generates four messages containing a dish name, followed by a final message that says "quit." It appends each message to a list called dishes in the Redis server, similar to appending to a Python list.

And as soon as the first dish is ready, *redis_dryer.py* does its work (Example 15-14).

Example 15-14. redis_dryer.py

```
import redis
conn = redis.Redis()
print('Dryer is starting')
while True:
    msg = conn.blpop('dishes')
    if not msg:
        break
    val = msg[1].decode('utf-8')
    if val == 'quit':
        break
    print('Dried', val)
print('Dishes are dried')
```

This code waits for messages whose first token is "dishes" and prints that each one is dried. It obeys the *quit* message by ending the loop.

Start the dryer and then the washer. Using the & at the end puts the first program in the *background*; it keeps running, but doesn't listen to the keyboard anymore. This works on Linux, macOS, and Windows, although you might see different output on the next line. In this case (macOS), it's some information about the background dryer process. Then, we start the washer process normally (in the *foreground*). You'll see the mingled output of the two processes:

```
$ python redis_dryer.py &
[2] 81691
Dryer is starting
$ python redis_washer.py
Washer is starting
Washed salad
Dried salad
Washed bread
Dried bread
Washed entree
Dried entree
Washed dessert
Washer is done
Dried dessert
```

```
Dishes are dried
[2]+  Done                    python redis_dryer.py
```

As soon as dish IDs started arriving at Redis from the washer process, our hard-working dryer process started pulling them back out. Each dish ID was a number, except the final *sentinel* value, the string `'quit'`. When the dryer process read that `quit` dish ID, it quit, and some more background process information printed to the terminal (also system dependent). You can use a sentinel (an otherwise invalid value) to indicate something special from the data stream itself—in this case, that we're done. Otherwise, we'd need to add a lot more program logic, such as the following:

- Agreeing ahead of time on some maximum dish number, which would kind of be a sentinel anyway.
- Doing some special *out-of-band* (not in the data stream) interprocess communication.
- Timing out after some interval with no new data.

Let's make a few last changes:

- Create multiple `dryer` processes.
- Add a timeout to each dryer rather than looking for a sentinel.

The new *redis_dryer2.py* is shown in Example 15-15.

Example 15-15. redis_dryer2.py

```
def dryer():
    import redis
    import os
    import time
    conn = redis.Redis()
    pid = os.getpid()
    timeout = 20
    print('Dryer process %s is starting' % pid)
    while True:
        msg = conn.blpop('dishes', timeout)
        if not msg:
            break
        val = msg[1].decode('utf-8')
        if val == 'quit':
            break
        print('%s: dried %s' % (pid, val))
        time.sleep(0.1)
    print('Dryer process %s is done' % pid)

import multiprocessing
DRYERS=3
```

```
for num in range(DRYERS):
    p = multiprocessing.Process(target=dryer)
    p.start()
```

Start the dryer processes in the background and then the washer process in the foreground:

```
$ python redis_dryer2.py &
Dryer process 44447 is starting
Dryer process 44448 is starting
Dryer process 44446 is starting
$ python redis_washer.py
Washer is starting
Washed salad
44447: dried salad
Washed bread
44448: dried bread
Washed entree
44446: dried entree
Washed dessert
Washer is done
44447: dried dessert
```

One dryer process reads the quit ID and quits:

```
Dryer process 44448 is done
```

After 20 seconds, the other dryer processes get a return value of None from their blpop calls, indicating that they've timed out. They say their last words and exit:

```
Dryer process 44447 is done
Dryer process 44446 is done
```

After the last dryer subprocess quits, the main dryer program ends:

```
[1]+  Done                    python redis_dryer2.py
```

Beyond Queues

With more moving parts, there are more possibilities for our lovely assembly lines to be disrupted. If we need to wash the dishes from a banquet, do we have enough work-ers? What if the dryers get drunk? What if the sink clogs? Worries, worries!

How will you cope with it all? Common techniques include these:

Fire and forget
Just pass things on and don't worry about the consequences, even if no one is there. That's the dishes-on-the-floor approach.

Request-reply
The washer receives an acknowledgment from the dryer, and the dryer from the put-away-er, for each dish in the pipeline.

Back pressure or throttling
> This technique directs a fast worker to take it easy if someone downstream can't keep up.

In real systems, you need to be careful that workers are keeping up with the demand; otherwise, you hear the dishes hitting the floor. You might add new tasks to a *pending* list, while some worker process pops the latest message and adds it to a *working* list. When the message is done, it's removed from the working list and added to a *completed* list. This lets you know what tasks have failed or are taking too long. You can do this with Redis yourself, or use a system that someone else has already written and tested. Some Python-based queue packages that add this extra level of management include:

- `celery` (*http://www.celeryproject.org*) can execute distributed tasks synchronously or asynchronously, using the methods we've discussed: `multiprocessing`, `gevent`, and others.
- rq (*http://python-rq.org*) is a Python library for job queues, also based on Redis.

Queues (*http://queues.io*) offers a discussion of queuing software, Python-based and otherwise.

Coming Up

In this chapter, we flowed data through processes. In the next chapter, you'll see how to store and retrieve data in various file formats and databases.

Things to Do

15.1 Use `multiprocessing` to create three separate processes. Make each one wait a random number of seconds between zero and one, print the current time, and then exit.

CHAPTER 16

Data in a Box: Persistent Storage

It is a capital mistake to theorize before one has data.

—Arthur Conan Doyle

An active program accesses data stored in Random Access Memory, or RAM. RAM is very fast, but it is expensive and requires a constant supply of power; if the power goes out, all the data in memory is lost. Disk drives are slower than RAM but have more capacity, cost less, and retain data even after someone trips over the power cord. Thus, a huge amount of effort in computer systems has been devoted to making the best trade-offs between storing data on disk and RAM. As programmers, we need *persistence*: storing and retrieving data using nonvolatile media such as disks.

This chapter is all about the different flavors of data storage, each optimized for different purposes: flat files, structured files, and databases. File operations other than input and output are covered in Chapter 14.

A *record* is a term for one chunk of related data, consisting of individual *fields*.

Flat Text Files

The simplest persistence is a plain old flat file. This works well if your data has a very simple structure and you exchange all of it between disk and memory. Plain text data might be suitable for this treatment.

Padded Text Files

In this format, each field in a record has a fixed width, and is padded (usually with space characters) to that width in the file, giving each line (record) the same width. A programmer can use seek() to jump around the file and only read and write the records and fields that are needed.

Tabular Text Files

With simple text files, the only level of organization is the line. Sometimes, you want more structure than that. You might want to save data for your program to use later, or send data to another program.

There are many formats, and here's how you can distinguish them:

- A *separator*, or *delimiter*, character like tab ('\t'), comma (','), or vertical bar ('|'). This is an example of the comma-separated values (CSV) format.
- '<' and '>' around *tags*. Examples include XML and HTML.
- Punctuation. An example is JavaScript Object Notation (JSON).
- Indentation. An example is YAML (which is recursively defined as "YAML Ain't Markup Language").
- Miscellaneous, such as configuration files for programs.

Each of these structured file formats can be read and written by at least one Python module.

CSV

Delimited files are often used as an exchange format for spreadsheets and databases. You could read CSV files manually, a line at a time, splitting each line into fields at comma separators, and adding the results to data structures such as lists and dictionaries. But it's better to use the standard csv module, because parsing these files can get more complicated than you think. Following are a few important characteristics to keep in mind when working with CSV:

- Some have alternate delimiters besides a comma: '|' and '\t' (tab) are common.
- Some have *escape sequences*. If the delimiter character can occur within a field, the entire field might be surrounded by quote characters or preceded by some escape character.
- Files have different line-ending characters. Unix uses '\n', Microsoft uses '\r\n', and Apple used to use '\r' but now uses '\n'.
- The first line may contain column names.

First, we see how to read and write a list of rows, each containing a list of columns:

```
>>> import csv
>>> villains = [
...     ['Doctor', 'No'],
...     ['Rosa', 'Klebb'],
```

```
...        ['Mister', 'Big'],
...        ['Auric', 'Goldfinger'],
...        ['Ernst', 'Blofeld'],
...        ]
>>> with open('villains', 'wt') as fout:  # a context manager
...        csvout = csv.writer(fout)
...        csvout.writerows(villains)
```

This creates the file *villains* with these lines:

```
Doctor,No
Rosa,Klebb
Mister,Big
Auric,Goldfinger
Ernst,Blofeld
```

Now, we try to read it back in:

```
>>> import csv
>>> with open('villains', 'rt') as fin:  # context manager
...        cin = csv.reader(fin)
...        villains = [row for row in cin]  # a list comprehension
...
>>> print(villains)
[['Doctor', 'No'], ['Rosa', 'Klebb'], ['Mister', 'Big'],
['Auric', 'Goldfinger'], ['Ernst', 'Blofeld']]
```

We took advantage of the structure created by the reader() function. It created rows in the cin object that we could extract in a for loop.

Using reader() and writer() with their default options, the columns are separated by commas and the rows by line feeds.

The data can be a list of dictionaries rather than a list of lists. Let's read the *villains* file again, this time using the new DictReader() function and specifying the column names:

```
>>> import csv
>>> with open('villains', 'rt') as fin:
...        cin = csv.DictReader(fin, fieldnames=['first', 'last'])
...        villains = [row for row in cin]
...
>>> print(villains)
[OrderedDict([('first', 'Doctor'), ('last', 'No')]),
OrderedDict([('first', 'Rosa'), ('last', 'Klebb')]),
OrderedDict([('first', 'Mister'), ('last', 'Big')]),
OrderedDict([('first', 'Auric'), ('last', 'Goldfinger')]),
OrderedDict([('first', 'Ernst'), ('last', 'Blofeld')])]
```

That OrderedDict is there for compatibility with versions of Python before 3.6, when dictionaries kept their order by default.

Let's rewrite the CSV file by using the new `DictWriter()` function. We also call `write header()` to write an initial line of column names to the CSV file:

```python
import csv
villains = [
    {'first': 'Doctor', 'last': 'No'},
    {'first': 'Rosa', 'last': 'Klebb'},
    {'first': 'Mister', 'last': 'Big'},
    {'first': 'Auric', 'last': 'Goldfinger'},
    {'first': 'Ernst', 'last': 'Blofeld'},
    ]
with open('villains.txt', 'wt') as fout:
    cout = csv.DictWriter(fout, ['first', 'last'])
    cout.writeheader()
    cout.writerows(villains)
```

That creates a *villains.csv* file with a header line (Example 16-1).

Example 16-1. villains.csv

```
first,last
Doctor,No
Rosa,Klebb
Mister,Big
Auric,Goldfinger
Ernst,Blofeld
```

Now, let's read it back. By omitting the `fieldnames` argument in the `DictReader()` call, we tell it to use the values in the first line of the file (`first,last`) as column labels and matching dictionary keys:

```python
>>> import csv
>>> with open('villains.csv', 'rt') as fin:
...     cin = csv.DictReader(fin)
...     villains = [row for row in cin]
...
>>> print(villains)
[OrderedDict([('first', 'Doctor'), ('last', 'No')]),
OrderedDict([('first', 'Rosa'), ('last', 'Klebb')]),
OrderedDict([('first', 'Mister'), ('last', 'Big')]),
OrderedDict([('first', 'Auric'), ('last', 'Goldfinger')]),
OrderedDict([('first', 'Ernst'), ('last', 'Blofeld')])]
```

XML

Delimited files convey only two dimensions: rows (lines) and columns (fields within a line). If you want to exchange data structures among programs, you need a way to encode hierarchies, sequences, sets, and other structures as text.

XML is a prominent *markup* format that does this. It uses *tags* to delimit data, as in this sample *menu.xml* file:

```
<?xml version="1.0"?>
<menu>
  <breakfast hours="7-11">
    <item price="$6.00">breakfast burritos</item>
    <item price="$4.00">pancakes</item>
  </breakfast>
  <lunch hours="11-3">
    <item price="$5.00">hamburger</item>
  </lunch>
  <dinner hours="3-10">
    <item price="8.00">spaghetti</item>
  </dinner>
</menu>
```

Following are a few important characteristics of XML:

- Tags begin with a < character. The tags in this sample were menu, breakfast, lunch, dinner, and item.

- Whitespace is ignored.

- Usually a *start tag* such as <menu> is followed by other content and then a final matching *end tag* such as </menu>.

- Tags can *nest* within other tags to any level. In this example, item tags are children of the breakfast, lunch, and dinner tags; they, in turn, are children of menu.

- Optional *attributes* can occur within the start tag. In this example, price is an attribute of item.

- Tags can contain *values*. In this example, each item has a value, such as pancakes for the second breakfast item.

- If a tag named thing has no values or children, it can be expressed as the single tag by including a forward slash just before the closing angle bracket, such as <thing/>, rather than a start and end tag, like <thing></thing>.

- The choice of where to put data—attributes, values, child tags—is somewhat arbitrary. For instance, we could have written the last item tag as <item price="$8.00" food="spaghetti"/>.

XML is often used for data *feeds* and *messages* and has subformats like RSS and Atom. Some industries have many specialized XML formats, such as the finance field (*http://bit.ly/xml-finance*).

XML's über-flexibility has inspired multiple Python libraries that differ in approach and capabilities.

The simplest way to parse XML in Python is by using the standard `ElementTree` module. Here's a little program to parse the *menu.xml* file and print some tags and attributes:

```
>>> import xml.etree.ElementTree as et
>>> tree = et.ElementTree(file='menu.xml')
>>> root = tree.getroot()
>>> root.tag
'menu'
>>> for child in root:
...     print('tag:', child.tag, 'attributes:', child.attrib)
...     for grandchild in child:
...         print('\ttag:', grandchild.tag, 'attributes:', grandchild.attrib)
...
tag: breakfast attributes: {'hours': '7-11'}
    tag: item attributes: {'price': '$6.00'}
    tag: item attributes: {'price': '$4.00'}
tag: lunch attributes: {'hours': '11-3'}
    tag: item attributes: {'price': '$5.00'}
tag: dinner attributes: {'hours': '3-10'}
    tag: item attributes: {'price': '8.00'}
>>> len(root)      # number of menu sections
3
>>> len(root[0])  # number of breakfast items
2
```

For each element in the nested lists, `tag` is the tag string and `attrib` is a dictionary of its attributes. `ElementTree` has many other ways of searching XML-derived data, modifying it, and even writing XML files. The `ElementTree` documentation (*http://bit.ly/elementtree*) has the details.

Other standard Python XML libraries include the following:

`xml.dom`
> The Document Object Model (DOM), familiar to JavaScript developers, represents web documents as hierarchical structures. This module loads the entire XML file into memory and lets you access all the pieces equally.

`xml.sax`
> Simple API for XML, or SAX, parses XML on the fly, so it does not have to load everything into memory at once. Therefore, it can be a good choice if you need to process very large streams of XML.

An XML Security Note

You can use all the formats described in this chapter to save objects to files and read them back again. It's possible to exploit this process and cause security problems.

For example, the following XML snippet from the billion laughs Wikipedia page defines 10 nested entities, each expanding the lower level 10 times for a total expansion of one billion:

```
<?xml version="1.0"?>
<!DOCTYPE lolz [
 <!ENTITY lol "lol">
 <!ENTITY lol1 "&lol;&lol;&lol;&lol;&lol;&lol;&lol;&lol;&lol;&lol;">
 <!ENTITY lol2 "&lol1;&lol1;&lol1;&lol1;&lol1;&lol1;&lol1;&lol1;&lol1;&lol1;">
 <!ENTITY lol3 "&lol2;&lol2;&lol2;&lol2;&lol2;&lol2;&lol2;&lol2;&lol2;">
 <!ENTITY lol4 "&lol3;&lol3;&lol3;&lol3;&lol3;&lol3;&lol3;&lol3;&lol3;&lol3;">
 <!ENTITY lol5 "&lol4;&lol4;&lol4;&lol4;&lol4;&lol4;&lol4;&lol4;&lol4;&lol4;">
 <!ENTITY lol6 "&lol5;&lol5;&lol5;&lol5;&lol5;&lol5;&lol5;&lol5;&lol5;&lol5;">
 <!ENTITY lol7 "&lol6;&lol6;&lol6;&lol6;&lol6;&lol6;&lol6;&lol6;&lol6;&lol6;">
 <!ENTITY lol8 "&lol7;&lol7;&lol7;&lol7;&lol7;&lol7;&lol7;&lol7;&lol7;&lol7;">
 <!ENTITY lol9 "&lol8;&lol8;&lol8;&lol8;&lol8;&lol8;&lol8;&lol8;&lol8;&lol8;">
]>
<lolz>&lol9;</lolz>
```

The bad news: billion laughs would blow up all of the XML libraries mentioned in the previous sections. Defused XML (*https://bitbucket.org/tiran/defusedxml*) lists this attack and others, along with the vulnerability of Python libraries.

The link shows how to change the settings for many of the libraries to avoid these problems. Also, you can use the defusedxml library as a security frontend for the other libraries:

```
>>> # insecure:
>>> from xml.etree.ElementTree import parse
>>> et = parse(xmlfile)
>>> # protected:
>>> from defusedxml.ElementTree import parse
>>> et = parse(xmlfile)
```

The standard Python site also has its own page on XML vulnerabilities (*https://oreil.ly/Rnsiw*).

HTML

Gigagobs of data are saved as Hypertext Markup Language (HTML), the basic document format of the web. The problem is that much of it doesn't follow the HTML rules, which can make it difficult to parse. HTML is a better display format than a data interchange format. Because this chapter is intended to describe fairly well-defined data formats, I've separated out the discussion about HTML to Chapter 18.

JSON

JavaScript Object Notation (JSON) (*http://www.json.org*) has become a very popular data interchange format, beyond its JavaScript origins. The JSON format is a subset of

JavaScript, and often legal Python syntax, as well. Its close fit to Python makes it a good choice for data interchange among programs. You'll see many examples of JSON for web development in Chapter 18.

Unlike the variety of XML modules, there's one main JSON module, with the unforgettable name `json`. This program encodes (dumps) data to a JSON string and decodes (loads) a JSON string back to data. In this next example, let's build a Python data structure containing the data from the earlier XML example:

```
>>> menu = \
... {
... "breakfast": {
...         "hours": "7-11",
...         "items": {
...                 "breakfast burritos": "$6.00",
...                 "pancakes": "$4.00"
...                 }
...         },
... "lunch" : {
...         "hours": "11-3",
...         "items": {
...                 "hamburger": "$5.00"
...                 }
...         },
... "dinner": {
...         "hours": "3-10",
...         "items": {
...                 "spaghetti": "$8.00"
...                 }
...         }
... }
.
```

Next, encode the data structure (menu) to a JSON string (menu_json) by using `dumps()`:

```
>>> import json
>>> menu_json = json.dumps(menu)
>>> menu_json
'{"dinner": {"items": {"spaghetti": "$8.00"}, "hours": "3-10"},
"lunch": {"items": {"hamburger": "$5.00"}, "hours": "11-3"},
"breakfast": {"items": {"breakfast burritos": "$6.00", "pancakes":
"$4.00"}, "hours": "7-11"}}'
```

And now, let's turn the JSON string `menu_json` back into a Python data structure (menu2) by using `loads()`:

```
>>> menu2 = json.loads(menu_json)
>>> menu2
{'breakfast': {'items': {'breakfast burritos': '$6.00', 'pancakes':
'$4.00'}, 'hours': '7-11'}, 'lunch': {'items': {'hamburger': '$5.00'},
'hours': '11-3'}, 'dinner': {'items': {'spaghetti': '$8.00'}, 'hours': '3-10'}}
```

menu and menu2 are both dictionaries with the same keys and values.

You might get an exception while trying to encode or decode some objects, including objects such as datetime (covered in detail in Chapter 13), as demonstrated here:

```
>>> import datetime
>>> import json
>>> now = datetime.datetime.utcnow()
>>> now
datetime.datetime(2013, 2, 22, 3, 49, 27, 483336)
>>> json.dumps(now)
Traceback (most recent call last):
# ... (deleted stack trace to save trees)
TypeError: datetime.datetime(2013, 2, 22, 3, 49, 27, 483336)
  is not JSON serializable
>>>
```

This can happen because the JSON standard does not define date or time types; it expects you to define how to handle them. You could convert the datetime to something JSON understands, such as a string or an *epoch* value (see Chapter 13):

```
>>> now_str = str(now)
>>> json.dumps(now_str)
'"2013-02-22 03:49:27.483336"'
>>> from time import mktime
>>> now_epoch = int(mktime(now.timetuple()))
>>> json.dumps(now_epoch)
'1361526567'
```

If the datetime value could occur in the middle of normally converted data types, it might be annoying to make these special conversions. You can modify how JSON is encoded by using inheritance, which is described in Chapter 10. Python's JSON documentation (*http://bit.ly/json-docs*) gives an example of this for complex numbers, which also makes JSON play dead. Let's modify it for datetime:

```
>>> import datetime
>>> now = datetime.datetime.utcnow()
>>> class DTEncoder(json.JSONEncoder):
...     def default(self, obj):
...         # isinstance() checks the type of obj
...         if isinstance(obj, datetime.datetime):
...             return int(mktime(obj.timetuple()))
...         # else it's something the normal decoder knows:
...         return json.JSONEncoder.default(self, obj)
...
>>> json.dumps(now, cls=DTEncoder)
'1361526567'
```

The new class DTEncoder is a subclass, or child class, of JSONEncoder. We need to override its only default() method to add datetime handling. Inheritance ensures that everything else will be handled by the parent class.

The `isinstance()` function checks whether the object `obj` is of the class `date time.datetime`. Because everything in Python is an object, `isinstance()` works everywhere:

```
>>> import datetime
>>> now = datetime.datetime.utcnow()
>>> type(now)
<class 'datetime.datetime'>
>>> isinstance(now, datetime.datetime)
True
>>> type(234)
<class 'int'>
>>> isinstance(234, int)
True
>>> type('hey')
<class 'str'>
>>> isinstance('hey', str)
True
```

 For JSON and other structured text formats, you can load from a file into data structures without knowing anything about the structures ahead of time. Then, you can walk through the structures by using `isinstance()` and type-appropriate methods to examine their values. For example, if one of the items is a dictionary, you can extract contents through `keys()`, `values()`, and `items()`.

After making you do it the hard way, it turns out that there's an even easier way to convert `datetime` objects to JSON:

```
>>> import datetime
>>> import json
>>> now = datetime.datetime.utcnow()
>>> json.dumps(now, default=str)
'"2019-04-17 21:54:43.617337"'
```

That `default=str` tells `json.dumps()` to apply the `str()` conversion function for data types that it doesn't understand. This works because the definition of the `date time.datetime` class includes a `__str__()` method.

YAML

Similar to JSON, YAML (*http://www.yaml.org*) has keys and values, but handles more data types such as dates and times. The standard Python library does not yet include YAML handling, so you need to install a third-party library named `yaml` (*http://pyyaml.org/wiki/PyYAML*) to manipulate it. ((("dump() function")))((("load() function")))load() converts a YAML string to Python data, whereas dump() does the opposite.

The following YAML file, *mcintyre.yaml*, contains information on the Canadian poet James McIntyre, including two of his poems:

```
name:
  first: James
  last: McIntyre
dates:
  birth: 1828-05-25
  death: 1906-03-31
details:
  bearded: true
  themes: [cheese, Canada]
books:
  url: http://www.gutenberg.org/files/36068/36068-h/36068-h.htm
poems:
  - title: 'Motto'
    text: |
      Politeness, perseverance and pluck,
      To their possessor will bring good luck.
  - title: 'Canadian Charms'
    text: |
      Here industry is not in vain,
      For we have bounteous crops of grain,
      And you behold on every field
      Of grass and roots abundant yield,
      But after all the greatest charm
      Is the snug home upon the farm,
      And stone walls now keep cattle warm.
```

Values such as `true`, `false`, `on`, and `off` are converted to Python booleans. Integers and strings are converted to their Python equivalents. Other syntax creates lists and dictionaries:

```
>>> import yaml
>>> with open('mcintyre.yaml', 'rt') as fin:
>>>     text = fin.read()
>>> data = yaml.load(text)
>>> data['details']
{'themes': ['cheese', 'Canada'], 'bearded': True}
>>> len(data['poems'])
2
```

The data structures that are created match those in the YAML file, which in this case are more than one level deep in places. You can get the title of the second poem with this dict/list/dict reference:

```
>>> data['poems'][1]['title']
'Canadian Charms'
```

PyYAML can load Python objects from strings, and this is dangerous. Use `safe_load()` instead of `load()` if you're importing YAML
that you don't trust. Better yet, *always* use `safe_load()`. Read Ned
Batchelder's blog post "War is Peace" (*http://bit.ly/war-is-peace*) for
a description of how unprotected YAML loading compromised the
Ruby on Rails platform.

Tablib

After reading all of the previous sections, there's one third-party package that lets you
import, export, and edit tabular data in CSV, JSON, *or* YAML format,[1] as well as
Microsoft Excel, Pandas DataFrame, and a few others. You install it with the familiar
refrain (`pip install tablib`), and peek at the docs (*http://docs.python-tablib.org*).

Pandas

This is as good place as any to introduce pandas (*https://pandas.pydata.org*)—a
Python library for structured data. It's an excellent tool for handling real-life data
issues:

- Read and write many text and binary file formats:
  — Text, with fields separated by commas (CSV), tabs (TSV), or other characters
  — Fixed-width text
  — Excel
  — JSON
  — HTML tables
  — SQL
  — HDF5
  — and others (*https://oreil.ly/EWlgS*).
- Group, split, merge, index, slice, sort, select, label
- Convert data types
- Change size or shape
- Handle missing data
- Generate random values
- Manage time series

---

1 Alas, not XML yet.

The read functions return a `DataFrame` (*https://oreil.ly/zupYI*) object, Pandas' standard representation for two-dimensional data (rows and columns). It's similar in some ways to a spreadsheet or a relational database table. Its one-dimensional little brother is a `Series` (*https://oreil.ly/pISZT*).

Example 16-2 demonstrates a simple application that reads our *villains.csv* file from Example 16-1.

Example 16-2. Read CSV with Pandas

```
>>> import pandas
>>>
>>> data = pandas.read_csv('villains.csv')
>>> print(data)
    first       last
0  Doctor         No
1    Rosa      Klebb
2  Mister        Big
3   Auric  Goldfinger
4   Ernst    Blofeld
```

The variable `data` just shown is a `DataFrame`. which has many more tricks than a basic Python dictionary. It's especially useful for heavy numeric work with NumPy, and data preparation for machine learning.

Refer to the "Getting Started" (*https://oreil.ly/VKSrZ*) section of the documentation for Pandas' features, and "10 Minutes to Pandas" (*https://oreil.ly/CLoVg*) for working examples.

Let's use Pandas for a little calendar example—make a list of the first day of the first three months in 2019:

```
>>> import pandas
>>> dates = pandas.date_range('2019-01-01', periods=3, freq='MS')
>>> dates
DatetimeIndex(['2019-01-01', '2019-02-01', '2019-03-01'],
  dtype='datetime64[ns]', freq='MS')
```

You could write something that does this, using the time and date functions described in Chapter 13, but it would be a lot more work—especially debugging (dates and times are frustrating). Pandas also handles many special date/time details (*https://oreil.ly/vpeTP*), like business months and years.

Pandas will appear again later when I talk about mapping ("Geopandas" on page 479) and scientific applications ("Pandas" on page 498).

Configuration Files

Most programs offer various *options* or *settings*. Dynamic ones can be provided as program arguments, but long-lasting ones need to be kept somewhere. The temptation to define your own quick-and-dirty *config file* format is strong—but resist it. It often turns out to be dirty, but not so quick. You need to maintain both the writer program and the reader program (sometimes called a *parser*). There are good alternatives that you can just drop into your program, including those in the previous sections.

Here, we'll use the standard `configparser` module, which handles Windows-style *.ini* files. Such files have sections of *key* = *value* definitions. Here's a minimal *settings.cfg* file:

```
[english]
greeting = Hello

[french]
greeting = Bonjour

[files]
home = /usr/local
# simple interpolation:
bin = %(home)s/bin
```

Here's the code to read it into Python data structures:

```
>>> import configparser
>>> cfg = configparser.ConfigParser()
>>> cfg.read('settings.cfg')
['settings.cfg']
>>> cfg
<configparser.ConfigParser object at 0x1006be4d0>
>>> cfg['french']
<Section: french>
>>> cfg['french']['greeting']
'Bonjour'
>>> cfg['files']['bin']
'/usr/local/bin'
```

Other options are available, including fancier interpolation. See the `configparser` documentation (*http://bit.ly/configparser*). If you need deeper nesting than two levels, try YAML or JSON.

Binary Files

Some file formats were designed to store particular data structures but are neither relational nor NoSQL databases. The sections that follow present some of them.

Padded Binary Files and Memory Mapping

These are similar to padded text files, but the contents may be binary, and the padding byte may be \x00 instead of a space character. Each record has a fixed size, as does each field within a record. This makes it simpler to seek() throughout the file for the desired records and fields. Every operation on the data is manual, so this approach tends to be used only in very low-level (e.g., close to the hardware) situations.

Data in this form can be *memory mapped* with the standard mmap library. See some examples (*https://pymotw.com/3/mmap*), and the standard documentation (*https://oreil.ly/eI0mv*).

Spreadsheets

Spreadsheets, notably Microsoft Excel, are widespread binary data formats. If you can save your spreadsheet to a CSV file, you can read it by using the standard csv module that was described earlier. This will work for a binary xls file, xlrd (*https://oreil.ly/---YE*), or tablib (mentioned earlier at "Tablib" on page 314).

HDF5

HDF5 (*https://oreil.ly/QTT6x*) is a binary data format for multidimensional or hierarchical numeric data. It's used mainly in science, where fast random access to large datasets (gigabytes to terabytes) is a common requirement. Even though HDF5 could be a good alternative to databases in some cases, for some reason HDF5 is almost unknown in the business world. It's best suited to *WORM* (write once/read many) applications for which database protection against conflicting writes is not needed. Here are some modules that you might find useful:

- h5py is a full-featured low-level interface. Read the documentation (*http://www.h5py.org*) and code (*https://github.com/h5py/h5py*).
- PyTables is a bit higher-level, with database-like features. Read the documentation (*http://www.pytables.org*) and code (*http://pytables.github.com*).

Both of these are discussed in terms of scientific applications of Python in Chapter 22. I'm mentioning HDF5 here in case you have a need to store and retrieve large amounts of data and are willing to consider something outside the box as well as the usual database solutions. A good example is the Million Song dataset (*http://million songdataset.com*), which has downloadable song data in HDF5 and SQLite formats.

TileDB

A recent successor to HDF5 for dense or spare array storage is TileDB (*https:// tiledb.io*). Install the Python interface (*https://github.com/TileDB-Inc/TileDB-Py*) (which includes the TileDB library itself) by running `pip install tiledb`. This is aimed at scientific data and applications.

Relational Databases

Relational databases are only about 40 years old but are ubiquitous in the computing world. You'll almost certainly have to deal with them at one time or another. When you do, you'll appreciate what they provide:

- Access to data by multiple simultaneous users
- Protection from corruption by those users
- Efficient methods to store and retrieve the data
- Data defined by *schemas* and limited by *constraints*
- *Joins* to find relationships across diverse types of data
- A declarative (rather than imperative) query language: *SQL* (Structured Query Language)

These are called *relational* because they show relationships among different kinds of data in the form of rectangular *tables*. For instance, in our menu example earlier, there is a relationship between each item and its price.

A table is a rectangular grid of *columns* (data fields) and *rows* (individual data records), similar to a spreadsheet. The intersection of a row and column is a table *cell*. To create a table, name it and specify the order, names, and types of its columns. Each row has the same columns, although a column may be defined to allow missing data (called *nulls*) in cells. In the menu example, you could create a table with one row for each item being sold. Each item has the same columns, including one for the price.

A column or group of columns is usually the table's *primary key*; its values must be unique in the table. This prevents adding the same data to the table more than once. This key is *indexed* for fast lookups during queries. An index works a little like a book index, making it fast to find a particular row.

Each table lives within a parent *database*, like a file within a directory. Two levels of hierarchy help keep things organized a little better.

Yes, the word *database* is used in multiple ways: as the server, the table container, and the data stored therein. If you'll be referring to all of them at the same time, it might help to call them *database server*, *database*, and *data*.

If you want to find rows by some nonkey column value, define a *secondary index* on that column. Otherwise, the database server must perform a *table scan*—a brute-force search of every row for matching column values.

Tables can be related to each other with *foreign keys*, and column values can be constrained to these keys.

SQL

SQL is not an API or a protocol, but a declarative *language*: you say *what* you want rather than *how* to do it. It's the universal language of relational databases. SQL queries are text strings sent by a client to the database server, which in turn figures out what to do with them.

There have been various SQL standard definitions, and all database vendors have added their own tweaks and extensions, resulting in many SQL *dialects*. If you store your data in a relational database, SQL gives you some portability. Still, dialect and operational differences can make it difficult to move your data to another type of database. There are two main categories of SQL statements:

DDL (data definition language)
Handles creation, deletion, constraints, and permissions for tables, databases, and users.

DML (data manipulation language)
Handles data insertions, selects, updates, and deletions.

Table 16-1 lists the basic SQL DDL commands.

Table 16-1. Basic SQL DDL commands

Operation	SQL pattern	SQL example
Create a database	CREATE DATABASE *dbname*	CREATE DATABASE d
Select current database	USE *dbname*	USE d
Delete a database and its tables	DROP DATABASE *dbname*	DROP DATABASE d
Create a table	CREATE TABLE *tbname* (*coldefs*)	CREATE TABLE t (id INT, count INT)
Delete a table	DROP TABLE *tbname*	DROP TABLE t
Remove all rows from a table	TRUNCATE TABLE *tbname*	TRUNCATE TABLE t

Why all the CAPITAL LETTERS? SQL is case-insensitive, but it's a tradition (don't ask me why) to SHOUT its keywords in code examples to distinguish them from column names.

The main DML operations of a relational database are often known by the acronym CRUD:

- *C*reate by using the SQL INSERT statement
- *R*ead by using SELECT
- *U*pdate by using UPDATE
- *D*elete by using DELETE

Table 16-2 looks at the commands available for SQL DML.

Table 16-2. Basic SQL DML commands

Operation	SQL pattern	SQL example
Add a row	INSERT INTO *tbname* VALUES(...)	INSERT INTO t VALUES(7, 40)
Select all rows and columns	SELECT * FROM *tbname*	SELECT * FROM t
Select all rows, some columns	SELECT *cols* FROM *tbname*	SELECT id, count FROM t
Select some rows, some columns	SELECT *cols* FROM *tbname* WHERE *condition*	SELECT id, count from t WHERE count > 5 AND id = 9
Change some rows in a column	UPDATE *tbname* SET *col = value* WHERE *condition*	UPDATE t SET count=3 WHERE id=5
Delete some rows	DELETE FROM *tbname* WHERE *condition*	DELETE FROM t WHERE count <= 10 OR id = 16

DB-API

An application programming interface (API) is a set of functions that you can call to get access to some service. DB-API (*http://bit.ly/db-api*) is Python's standard API for accessing relational databases. Using it, you can write a single program that works with multiple kinds of relational databases instead of writing a separate program for each one. It's similar to Java's JDBC or Perl's dbi.

Its main functions are the following:

connect()
> Make a connection to the database; this can include arguments such as username, password, server address, and others.

`cursor()`
    Create a *cursor* object to manage queries.

`execute()` *and* `executemany()`
    Run one or more SQL commands against the database.

`fetchone()`, `fetchmany()`, *and* `fetchall()`
    Get the results from `execute()`.

The Python database modules in the coming sections conform to DB-API, often with extensions and some differences in details.

SQLite

SQLite (*http://www.sqlite.org*) is a good, light, open source relational database. It's implemented as a standard Python library, and stores databases in normal files. These files are portable across machines and operating systems, making SQLite a very portable solution for simple relational database applications. It isn't as full featured as MySQL or PostgreSQL, but it does support SQL, and it manages multiple simultaneous users. Web browsers, smartphones, and other applications use SQLite as an embedded database.

You begin with a `connect()` to the local SQLite database file that you want to use or create. This file is the equivalent of the directory-like *database* that parents tables in other servers. The special string `':memory:'` creates the database in memory only; this is fast and useful for testing but will lose data when your program terminates or if your computer goes down.

For the next example, let's make a database called `enterprise.db` and the table `zoo` to manage our thriving roadside petting zoo business. The table columns are as follows:

`critter`
    A variable length string, and our primary key.

`count`
    An integer count of our current inventory for this animal.

`damages`
    The dollar amount of our current losses from animal–human interactions.

```
>>> import sqlite3
>>> conn = sqlite3.connect('enterprise.db')
>>> curs = conn.cursor()
>>> curs.execute('''CREATE TABLE zoo
    (critter VARCHAR(20) PRIMARY KEY,
     count INT,
     damages FLOAT)''')
<sqlite3.Cursor object at 0x1006a22d0>
```

Python's triple quotes are handy when creating long strings such as SQL queries.

Now, add some animals to the zoo:

```
>>> curs.execute('INSERT INTO zoo VALUES("duck", 5, 0.0)')
<sqlite3.Cursor object at 0x1006a22d0>
>>> curs.execute('INSERT INTO zoo VALUES("bear", 2, 1000.0)')
<sqlite3.Cursor object at 0x1006a22d0>
```

There's a safer way to insert data, using a *placeholder*:

```
>>> ins = 'INSERT INTO zoo (critter, count, damages) VALUES(?, ?, ?)'
>>> curs.execute(ins, ('weasel', 1, 2000.0))
<sqlite3.Cursor object at 0x1006a22d0>
```

This time, we used three question marks in the SQL to indicate that we plan to insert three values, and then pass those three values as a tuple to the execute() function. Placeholders handle tedious details such as quoting. They protect you against *SQL injection*, a kind of external attack that inserts malicious SQL commands into the system (and which is common on the web).

Now, let's see if we can get all our animals out again:

```
>>> curs.execute('SELECT * FROM zoo')
<sqlite3.Cursor object at 0x1006a22d0>
>>> rows = curs.fetchall()
>>> print(rows)
[('duck', 5, 0.0), ('bear', 2, 1000.0), ('weasel', 1, 2000.0)]
```

Let's get them again, but ordered by their counts:

```
>>> curs.execute('SELECT * from zoo ORDER BY count')
<sqlite3.Cursor object at 0x1006a22d0>
>>> curs.fetchall()
[('weasel', 1, 2000.0), ('bear', 2, 1000.0), ('duck', 5, 0.0)]
```

Hey, we wanted them in descending order:

```
>>> curs.execute('SELECT * from zoo ORDER BY count DESC')
<sqlite3.Cursor object at 0x1006a22d0>
>>> curs.fetchall()
[('duck', 5, 0.0), ('bear', 2, 1000.0), ('weasel', 1, 2000.0)]
```

Which type of animal is costing us the most?

```
>>> curs.execute('''SELECT * FROM zoo WHERE
...     damages = (SELECT MAX(damages) FROM zoo)''')
<sqlite3.Cursor object at 0x1006a22d0>
>>> curs.fetchall()
[('weasel', 1, 2000.0)]
```

You would have thought it was the bears. It's always best to check the actual data.

Before we leave SQLite, we need to clean up. If we opened a connection and a cursor, we need to close them when we're done:

```
>>> curs.close()
>>> conn.close()
```

MySQL

MySQL (*http://www.mysql.com*) is a very popular open source relational database. Unlike SQLite, it's an actual server, so clients can access it from different devices across the network.

Table 16-3 lists the drivers you can use to access MySQL from Python. For more details on all Python MySQL drivers, see the *python.org* wiki (*https://wiki.python.org/moin/MySQL*).

Table 16-3. MySQL drivers

Name	Link	Pypi package	Import as	Notes
mysqlclient	*https://https:// mysqlclient.readthedocs.io*	mysql-connector-python	`MySQLdb`	
MySQL Connector	*http://bit.ly/mysql-cpdg*	mysql-connector-python	`mysql.connec tor`	
PYMySQL	*https://github.com/petehunt/PyMySQL*	pymysql	`pymysql`	
oursql	*http://pythonhosted.org/oursql*	oursql	`oursql`	Requires the MySQL C client libraries

PostgreSQL

PostgreSQL (*http://www.postgresql.org*) is a full-featured open source relational database. Indeed in many ways, it's more advanced than MySQL. Table 16-4 presents the Python drivers you can use to access it.

Table 16-4. PostgreSQL drivers

Name	Link	Pypi package	Import as	Notes
psycopg2	*http://initd.org/psycopg*	psycopg2	`psycopg2`	Needs `pg_config` from PostgreSQL client tools
py-postgresql	*https://pypi.org/project/py-postgresql*	py-postgresql	postgresql	

The most popular driver is `psycopg2`, but its installation requires the PostgreSQL client libraries.

SQLAlchemy

SQL is not quite the same for all relational databases, and DB-API takes you only so far. Each database implements a particular *dialect* reflecting its features and philosophy. Many libraries try to bridge these differences in one way or another. The most popular cross-database Python library is SQLAlchemy (*http://www.sqlalchemy.org*).

It isn't in the standard library, but it's well known and used by many people. You can install it on your system by using this command:

```
$ pip install sqlalchemy
```

You can use SQLAlchemy on several levels:

- The lowest level manages database connection *pools*, executes SQL commands, and returns results. This is closest to the DB-API.
- Next up is the *SQL expression language*, which lets you express queries in a more Python-oriented way.
- Highest is the ORM (Object Relational Model) layer, which uses the SQL Expression Language and binds application code with relational data structures.

As we go along, you'll understand what the terms mean in those levels. SQLAlchemy works with the database drivers documented in the previous sections. You don't need to import the driver; the initial connection string you provide to SQLAlchemy will determine it. That string looks like this:

```
dialect + driver :// user : password @ host : port / dbname
```

The values you put in this string are as follows:

dialect
> The database type

driver
> The particular driver you want to use for that database

user *and* password
> Your database authentication strings

host *and* port
> The database server's location (: port is needed only if it's not the standard one for this server)

dbname
> The database to initially connect to on the server

Table 16-5 lists the dialects and drivers.

Table 16-5. SQLAlchemy connection

dialect	driver
sqlite	pysqlite (or omit)
mysql	mysqlconnector
mysql	pymysql
mysql	oursql
postgresql	psycopg2
postgresql	pypostgresql

See also the SQLAlchemy details on dialects for MySQL (*https://oreil.ly/yVHy-*), SQLite (*https://oreil.ly/okP9v*), PostgreSQL (*https://oreil.ly/eDddn*), and other databases (*https://oreil.ly/kp5WS*).

The engine layer

First, let's try the lowest level of SQLAlchemy, which does little more than the base DB-API functions.

Let's try it with SQLite, which is already built in to Python. The connection string for SQLite skips the *host*, *port*, *user*, and *password*. The *dbname* tells SQLite what file to use to store your database. If you omit the *dbname*, SQLite builds a database in memory. If the *dbname* starts with a slash (/), it's an absolute filename on your computer (as in Linux and macOS; for example, C:\ on Windows). Otherwise, it's relative to your current directory.

The following segments are all part of one program, separated here for explanation.

To begin, you need to import what we need. The following is an example of an *import alias*, which lets us use the string sa to refer to SQLAlchemy methods. I do this mainly because sa is a lot easier to type than sqlalchemy:

```
>>> import sqlalchemy as sa
```

Connect to the database and create the storage for it in memory (the argument string 'sqlite:///:memory:' also works):

```
>>> conn = sa.create_engine('sqlite://')
```

Create a database table called zoo that comprises three columns:

```
>>> conn.execute('''CREATE TABLE zoo
...     (critter VARCHAR(20) PRIMARY KEY,
...      count INT,
...      damages FLOAT)''')
<sqlalchemy.engine.result.ResultProxy object at 0x1017efb10>
```

Running `conn.execute()` returns a SQLAlchemy object called a `ResultProxy`. You'll soon see what to do with it.

By the way, if you've never made a database table before, congratulations. Check that one off your bucket list.

Now, insert three sets of data into your new empty table:

```
>>> ins = 'INSERT INTO zoo (critter, count, damages) VALUES (?, ?, ?)'
>>> conn.execute(ins, 'duck', 10, 0.0)
<sqlalchemy.engine.result.ResultProxy object at 0x1017efb50>
>>> conn.execute(ins, 'bear', 2, 1000.0)
<sqlalchemy.engine.result.ResultProxy object at 0x1017ef090>
>>> conn.execute(ins, 'weasel', 1, 2000.0)
<sqlalchemy.engine.result.ResultProxy object at 0x1017ef450>
```

Next, ask the database for everything that we just put in:

```
>>> rows = conn.execute('SELECT * FROM zoo')
```

In SQLAlchemy, `rows` is not a list; it's that special `ResultProxy` thing that we can't print directly:

```
>>> print(rows)
<sqlalchemy.engine.result.ResultProxy object at 0x1017ef9d0>
```

However, you can iterate over it like a list, so we can get a row at a time:

```
>>> for row in rows:
...     print(row)
...
('duck', 10, 0.0)
('bear', 2, 1000.0)
('weasel', 1, 2000.0)
```

That was almost the same as the SQLite DB-API example that you saw earlier. The one advantage is that we didn't need to import the database driver at the top; SQL-Alchemy figured that out from the connection string. Just changing the connection string would make this code portable to another type of database. Another plus is SQLAlchemy's *connection pooling*, which you can read about at its documentation site (*http://bit.ly/conn-pooling*).

The SQL Expression Language

The next level up is SQLAlchemy's SQL Expression Language. It introduces functions to create the SQL for various operations. The Expression Language handles more of the SQL dialect differences than the lower-level engine layer does. It can be a handy middle-ground approach for relational database applications.

Here's how to create and populate the zoo table. Again, these are successive fragments of a single program.

The import and connection are the same as before:

```
>>> import sqlalchemy as sa
>>> conn = sa.create_engine('sqlite://')
```

To define the zoo table, we begin using some of the Expression Language instead of SQL:

```
>>> meta = sa.MetaData()
>>> zoo = sa.Table('zoo', meta,
...     sa.Column('critter', sa.String, primary_key=True),
...     sa.Column('count', sa.Integer),
...     sa.Column('damages', sa.Float)
...     )
>>> meta.create_all(conn)
```

Check out the parentheses in that multiline call in the preceding example. The structure of the Table() method matches the structure of the table. Just as our table contains three columns, there are three calls to Column() inside the parentheses of the Table() method call.

Meanwhile, zoo is some magic object that bridges the SQL database world and the Python data structure world.

Insert the data with more Expression Language functions:

```
... conn.execute(zoo.insert(('bear', 2, 1000.0)))
<sqlalchemy.engine.result.ResultProxy object at 0x1017ea910>
>>> conn.execute(zoo.insert(('weasel', 1, 2000.0)))
<sqlalchemy.engine.result.ResultProxy object at 0x1017eab10>
>>> conn.execute(zoo.insert(('duck', 10, 0)))
<sqlalchemy.engine.result.ResultProxy object at 0x1017eac50>
```

Next, create the SELECT statement (zoo.select() selects everything from the table represented by the zoo object, such as SELECT * FROM zoo would do in plain SQL):

```
>>> result = conn.execute(zoo.select())
```

Finally, get the results:

```
>>> rows = result.fetchall()
>>> print(rows)
[('bear', 2, 1000.0), ('weasel', 1, 2000.0), ('duck', 10, 0.0)]
```

The Object-Relational Mapper (ORM)

In the previous section, the zoo object was a mid-level connection between SQL and Python. At the top layer of SQLAlchemy, the Object-Relational Mapper (ORM) uses the SQL Expression Language but tries to make the actual database mechanisms invisible. You define classes, and the ORM handles how to get their data in and out of the database. The basic idea behind that complicated phrase, "object-relational mapper," is that you can refer to objects in your code and thus stay close to the way Python likes to operate while still using a relational database.

We'll define a Zoo class and hook it into the ORM. This time, we make SQLite use the file *zoo.db* so that we can confirm that the ORM worked.

As in the previous two sections, the snippets that follow are actually one program separated by explanations. Don't worry if you don't understand some if it. The SQL-Alchemy documentation has all the details—and this stuff can get complex. I just want you to get an idea of how much work it is to do this, so that you can decide which of the approaches discussed in this chapter suits you.

The initial import is the same, but this time we need another something also:

```
>>> import sqlalchemy as sa
>>> from sqlalchemy.ext.declarative import declarative_base
```

Here, we make the connection:

```
>>> conn = sa.create_engine('sqlite:///zoo.db')
```

Now, we get into SQLAlchemy's ORM. We define the Zoo class and associate its attributes with table columns:

```
>>> Base = declarative_base()
>>> class Zoo(Base):
...     __tablename__ = 'zoo'
...     critter = sa.Column('critter', sa.String, primary_key=True)
...     count = sa.Column('count', sa.Integer)
...     damages = sa.Column('damages', sa.Float)
...     def __init__(self, critter, count, damages):
...         self.critter = critter
...         self.count = count
...         self.damages = damages
...     def __repr__(self):
...         return "<Zoo({}, {}, {})>".format(self.critter, self.count,
...             self.damages)
```

The following line magically creates the database and table:

```
>>> Base.metadata.create_all(conn)
```

You can then insert data by creating Python objects. The ORM manages these internally:

```
>>> first = Zoo('duck', 10, 0.0)
>>> second = Zoo('bear', 2, 1000.0)
>>> third = Zoo('weasel', 1, 2000.0)
>>> first
<Zoo(duck, 10, 0.0)>
```

Next, we get the ORM to take us to SQL land. We create a session to talk to the database:

```
>>> from sqlalchemy.orm import sessionmaker
>>> Session = sessionmaker(bind=conn)
>>> session = Session()
```

Within the session, we write the three objects that we created to the database. The add() function adds one object, and add_all() adds a list:

```
>>> session.add(first)
>>> session.add_all([second, third])
```

Finally, we need to force everything to complete:

```
>>> session.commit()
```

Did it work? Well, it created a *zoo.db* file in the current directory. You can use the command-line sqlite3 program to check it:

```
$ sqlite3 zoo.db
SQLite version 3.6.12
Enter ".help" for instructions
Enter SQL statements terminated with a ";"
sqlite> .tables
zoo
sqlite> select * from zoo;
duck|10|0.0
bear|2|1000.0
weasel|1|2000.0
```

The purpose of this section was to show what an ORM is and how it works at a high level. The author of SQLAlchemy has written a full tutorial (*http://bit.ly/obj-rel-tutorial*). After reading this, decide which of the following levels would best fit your needs:

- Plain DB-API, as in the earlier SQLite section
- The SQLAlchemy engine
- The SQLAlchemy Expression Language
- The SQLAlchemy ORM

It seems like a natural choice to use an ORM to avoid the complexities of SQL. Should you use one? Some people think ORMs should be avoided (*http://bit.ly/obj-rel-map*), but others think the criticism is overdone (*http://bit.ly/fowler-orm*). Whoever's right, an ORM is an abstraction, and all abstractions are leaky (*http://bit.ly/leaky-law*) and break down at some point. When your ORM doesn't do what you want, you must figure out both how it works and how to fix it in SQL. To borrow an internet meme:

> Some people, when confronted with a problem, think, "I know, I'll use an ORM." Now they have two problems.

Use ORMs for simple applications or applications that map data pretty directly to database tables. If the application is that simple, you may consider using straight SQL or the SQL Expression Language.

Other Database Access Packages

If you're looking for Python tools that will handle multiple databases, with more features than the bare db-api but less than SQLAlchemy, these are worth a look:

- `dataset` (*https://dataset.readthedocs.org*) claims the goal "databases for lazy people". It's built on SQLAlchemy and provides a simple ORM for SQL, JSON, and CSV storage.

- `records` (*https://pypi.org/project/records*) bills itself as "SQL for Humans." It supports only SQL queries, using SQLAlchemy internally to handle SQL dialect issues, connection pooling, and other details. Its integration with `tablib` (mentioned at "Tablib" on page 314) lets you export data to CSV, JSON, and other formats.

NoSQL Data Stores

Relational tables are rectangular, but data come in many shapes and may be very difficult to fit without significant effort and contortion. It's a square peg/round hole problem.

Some nonrelational databases have been written to allow more flexible data definitions as well as to process very large data sets or support custom data operations. They've been collectively labeled *NoSQL* (formerly meaning *no SQL*, now the less confrontational *not only SQL*).

The simplest type of NoSQL databases are *key-value stores*. One popularity ranking (*https://oreil.ly/_VCKq*) shows some that I cover in the following sections.

The dbm Family

The dbm formats were around long before the *NoSQL* label was coined. They're simple key-value stores, often embedded in applications such as web browsers to maintain various settings. A dbm database is like a Python dictionary in the following ways:

- You can assign a value to a key, and it's automatically saved to the database on disk.

- You can query a key for its value.

The following is a quick example. The second argument to the following `open()` method is `'r'` to read, `'w'` to write, and `'c'` for both, creating the file if it doesn't exist:

```
>>> import dbm
>>> db = dbm.open('definitions', 'c')
```

To create key-value pairs, just assign a value to a key just as you would a dictionary:

```
>>> db['mustard'] = 'yellow'
>>> db['ketchup'] = 'red'
>>> db['pesto'] = 'green'
```

Let's pause and check what we have so far:

```
>>> len(db)
3
>>> db['pesto']
b'green'
```

Now close, then reopen to see whether it actually saved what we gave it:

```
>>> db.close()
>>> db = dbm.open('definitions', 'r')
>>> db['mustard']
b'yellow'
```

Keys and values are stored as `bytes`. You cannot iterate over the database object `db`, but you can get the number of keys by using `len()`. `get()` and `setdefault()` work as they do for dictionaries.

Memcached

`memcached` (*http://memcached.org*) is a fast in-memory key-value *cache* server. It's often put in front of a database, or used to store web server session data.

You can download versions for Linux and macOS (*https://memcached.org/downloads*) as well as Windows (*http://bit.ly/memcache-win*). If you want to try out this section, you'll need a running memcached server and Python driver.

There are many Python drivers; one that works with Python 3 is `python3-memcached` (*https://oreil.ly/7FA3-*), which you can install by using this command:

```
$ pip install python-memcached
```

To use it, connect to a memcached server, after which you can do the following:

- Set and get values for keys
- Increment or decrement a value
- Delete a key

Data keys and values are *not* persistent, and data that you wrote earlier might disappear. This is inherent in memcached—it's a cache server, not a database, and it avoids running out of memory by discarding old data.

You can connect to multiple memcached servers at the same time. In this next example, we're just talking to one on the same computer:

```
>>> import memcache
>>> db = memcache.Client(['127.0.0.1:11211'])
>>> db.set('marco', 'polo')
True
>>> db.get('marco')
'polo'
>>> db.set('ducks', 0)
True
>>> db.get('ducks')
0
>>> db.incr('ducks', 2)
2
>>> db.get('ducks')
2
```

Redis

Redis (*http://redis.io*) is a *data structure server*. It handles keys and their values, but the values are richer than those in other key-value stores. Like memcached, all of the data in a Redis server should fit in memory. Unlike memcached, Redis can do the following:

- Save data to disk for reliability and restarts
- Keep old data
- Provide more data structures than simple strings

The Redis data types are a close match to Python's, and a Redis server can be a useful intermediary for one or more Python applications to share data. I've found it so useful that it's worth a little extra coverage here.

The Python driver `redis-py` has its source code and tests on GitHub (*https://oreil.ly/aZIbQ*) as well as documentation (*http://bit.ly/redis-py-docs*). You can install it by using this command:

```
$ pip install redis
```

The Redis server (*http://redis.io*) has good documentation. If you install and start the Redis server on your local computer (with the network nickname `localhost`), you can try the programs in the following sections.

Strings

A key with a single value is a Redis *string*. Simple Python data types are automatically converted. Connect to a Redis server at some host (default is `localhost`) and port (default is 6379):

```
>>> import redis
>>> conn = redis.Redis()
```

Connecting to `redis.Redis('localhost')` or `redis.Redis('localhost', 6379)` would have given the same result.

List all keys (none so far):

```
>>> conn.keys('*')
[]
```

Set a simple string (key `'secret'`), integer (key `'carats'`), and float (key `'fever'`):

```
>>> conn.set('secret', 'ni!')
True
>>> conn.set('carats', 24)
True
>>> conn.set('fever', '101.5')
True
```

Get the values back (as Python `byte` values) by key:

```
>>> conn.get('secret')
b'ni!'
>>> conn.get('carats')
b'24'
>>> conn.get('fever')
b'101.5'
```

Here, the `setnx()` method sets a value only if the key does not exist:

```
>>> conn.setnx('secret', 'icky-icky-icky-ptang-zoop-boing!')
False
```

It failed because we had already defined `'secret'`:

```
>>> conn.get('secret')
b'ni!'
```

The `getset()` method returns the old value and sets it to a new one at the same time:

```
>>> conn.getset('secret', 'icky-icky-icky-ptang-zoop-boing!')
b'ni!'
```

Let's not get too far ahead of ourselves. Did it work?

```
>>> conn.get('secret')
b'icky-icky-icky-ptang-zoop-boing!'
```

Now, get a substring by using getrange() (as in Python, offset 0 means start, and -1 means end):

```
>>> conn.getrange('secret', -6, -1)
b'boing!'
```

Replace a substring by using setrange() (using a zero-based offset):

```
>>> conn.setrange('secret', 0, 'ICKY')
32
>>> conn.get('secret')
b'ICKY-icky-icky-ptang-zoop-boing!'
```

Next, set multiple keys at once by using mset():

```
>>> conn.mset({'pie': 'cherry', 'cordial': 'sherry'})
True
```

Get more than one value at once by using mget():

```
>>> conn.mget(['fever', 'carats'])
[b'101.5', b'24']
```

Delete a key by using delete():

```
>>> conn.delete('fever')
True
```

Increment by using the incr() or incrbyfloat() commands, and decrement with decr():

```
>>> conn.incr('carats')
25
>>> conn.incr('carats', 10)
35
>>> conn.decr('carats')
34
>>> conn.decr('carats', 15)
19
>>> conn.set('fever', '101.5')
True
>>> conn.incrbyfloat('fever')
102.5
>>> conn.incrbyfloat('fever', 0.5)
103.0
```

There's no decrbyfloat(). Use a negative increment to reduce the fever:

```
>>> conn.incrbyfloat('fever', -2.0)
101.0
```

Lists

Redis lists can contain only strings. The list is created when you do your first insertion. Insert at the beginning by using lpush():

```
>>> conn.lpush('zoo', 'bear')
1
```

Insert more than one item at the beginning:

```
>>> conn.lpush('zoo', 'alligator', 'duck')
3
```

Insert before or after a value by using linsert():

```
>>> conn.linsert('zoo', 'before', 'bear', 'beaver')
4
>>> conn.linsert('zoo', 'after', 'bear', 'cassowary')
5
```

Insert at an offset by using lset() (the list must exist already):

```
>>> conn.lset('zoo', 2, 'marmoset')
True
```

Insert at the end by using rpush():

```
>>> conn.rpush('zoo', 'yak')
6
```

Get the value at an offset by using lindex():

```
>>> conn.lindex('zoo', 3)
b'bear'
```

Get the values in an offset range by using lrange() (0 to -1 for all):

```
>>> conn.lrange('zoo', 0, 2)
[b'duck', b'alligator', b'marmoset']
```

Trim the list with ltrim(), keeping only those in a range of offsets:

```
>>> conn.ltrim('zoo', 1, 4)
True
```

Get a range of values (use 0 to -1 for all) by using lrange():

```
>>> conn.lrange('zoo', 0, -1)
[b'alligator', b'marmoset', b'bear', b'cassowary']
```

Chapter 15 shows you how you can use Redis lists and *publish-subscribe* to implement job queues.

Hashes

Redis *hashes* are similar to Python dictionaries but can contain only strings. Also, you can go only one level deep, not make deep-nested structures. Here are examples that create and play with a Redis hash called `song`:

Set the fields `do` and `re` in hash `song` at once by using `hmset()`:

```
>>> conn.hmset('song', {'do': 'a deer', 're': 'about a deer'})
True
```

Set a single field value in a hash by using `hset()`:

```
>>> conn.hset('song', 'mi', 'a note to follow re')
1
```

Get one field's value by using `hget()`:

```
>>> conn.hget('song', 'mi')
b'a note to follow re'
```

Get multiple field values by using `hmget()`:

```
>>> conn.hmget('song', 're', 'do')
[b'about a deer', b'a deer']
```

Get all field keys for the hash by using `hkeys()`:

```
>>> conn.hkeys('song')
[b'do', b're', b'mi']
```

Get all field values for the hash by using `hvals()`:

```
>>> conn.hvals('song')
[b'a deer', b'about a deer', b'a note to follow re']
```

Get the number of fields in the hash by using `hlen()`:

```
>>> conn.hlen('song')
3
```

Get all field keys and values in the hash by using `hgetall()`:

```
>>> conn.hgetall('song')
{b'do': b'a deer', b're': b'about a deer', b'mi': b'a note to follow re'}
```

Set a field if its key doesn't exist by using `hsetnx()`:

```
>>> conn.hsetnx('song', 'fa', 'a note that rhymes with la')
1
```

Sets

Redis sets are similar to Python sets, as you'll see in the following examples.

Add one or more values to a set:

```
>>> conn.sadd('zoo', 'duck', 'goat', 'turkey')
3
```

Get the number of values from the set:

```
>>> conn.scard('zoo')
3
```

Get all of the set's values:

```
>>> conn.smembers('zoo')
{b'duck', b'goat', b'turkey'}
```

Remove a value from the set:

```
>>> conn.srem('zoo', 'turkey')
True
```

Let's make a second set to show some set operations:

```
>>> conn.sadd('better_zoo', 'tiger', 'wolf', 'duck')
0
```

Intersect (get the common members of) the zoo and better_zoo sets:

```
>>> conn.sinter('zoo', 'better_zoo')
{b'duck'}
```

Get the intersection of zoo and better_zoo, and store the result in the set fowl_zoo:

```
>>> conn.sinterstore('fowl_zoo', 'zoo', 'better_zoo')
1
```

Who's in there?

```
>>> conn.smembers('fowl_zoo')
{b'duck'}
```

Get the union (all members) of zoo and better_zoo:

```
>>> conn.sunion('zoo', 'better_zoo')
{b'duck', b'goat', b'wolf', b'tiger'}
```

Store that union result in the set fabulous_zoo:

```
>>> conn.sunionstore('fabulous_zoo', 'zoo', 'better_zoo')
4
>>> conn.smembers('fabulous_zoo')
{b'duck', b'goat', b'wolf', b'tiger'}
```

What does zoo have that better_zoo doesn't? Use sdiff() to get the set difference, and sdiffstore() to save it in the zoo_sale set:

```
>>> conn.sdiff('zoo', 'better_zoo')
{b'goat'}
>>> conn.sdiffstore('zoo_sale', 'zoo', 'better_zoo')
```

```
1
>>> conn.smembers('zoo_sale')
{b'goat'}
```

Sorted sets

One of the most versatile Redis data types is the *sorted set*, or *zset*. It's a set of unique
values, but each value has an associated floating-point *score*. You can access each item
by its value or score. Sorted sets have many uses:

- Leader boards
- Secondary indexes
- Timeseries, using timestamps as scores

We show the last use case, tracking user logins via timestamps. We're using the Unix
epoch value (more on this in Chapter 15) that's returned by the Python time()
function:

```
>>> import time
>>> now = time.time()
>>> now
1361857057.576483
```

Let's add our first guest, looking nervous:

```
>>> conn.zadd('logins', 'smeagol', now)
1
```

Five minutes later, another guest:

```
>>> conn.zadd('logins', 'sauron', now+(5*60))
1
```

Two hours later:

```
>>> conn.zadd('logins', 'bilbo', now+(2*60*60))
1
```

One day later, not hasty:

```
>>> conn.zadd('logins', 'treebeard', now+(24*60*60))
1
```

In what order did bilbo arrive?

```
>>> conn.zrank('logins', 'bilbo')
2
```

When was that?

```
>>> conn.zscore('logins', 'bilbo')
1361864257.576483
```

Let's see everyone in login order:

```
>>> conn.zrange('logins', 0, -1)
[b'smeagol', b'sauron', b'bilbo', b'treebeard']
```

With their times, please:

```
>>> conn.zrange('logins', 0, -1, withscores=True)
[(b'smeagol', 1361857057.576483), (b'sauron', 1361857357.576483),
 (b'bilbo', 1361864257.576483), (b'treebeard', 1361943457.576483)]
```

Caches and expiration

All Redis keys have a time-to-live, or *expiration date*. By default, this is forever. We can use the expire() function to instruct Redis how long to keep the key. The value is a number of seconds:

```
>>> import time
>>> key = 'now you see it'
>>> conn.set(key, 'but not for long')
True
>>> conn.expire(key, 5)
True
>>> conn.ttl(key)
5
>>> conn.get(key)
b'but not for long'
>>> time.sleep(6)
>>> conn.get(key)
>>>
```

The expireat() command expires a key at a given epoch time. Key expiration is useful to keep caches fresh and to limit login sessions. An analogy: in the refrigerated room behind the milk racks at your grocery store, store employees yank those gallons as they reach their freshness dates.

Document Databases

A *document database* is a NoSQL database that stores data with varying fields. Compared to a relational table (rectangular, with the same columns in every row) such data is "ragged," with varying fields (columns) per row, and even nested fields. You could handle data like this in memory with Python dictionaries and lists, or store it as JSON files. To store such data in a relational database table, you would need to define every possible column and use nulls for missing data.

ODM can stand for Object Data Manager or Object Document Mapper (at least they agree on the *O* part). An ODM is the document database counterpart of a relational database ORM. Some popular (*https://oreil.ly/5Zpxx*) document databases and tools (drivers and ODMs) are listed in Table 16-6.

Table 16-6. Document databases

Database	Python API
Mongo (*https://www.mongodb.com*)	tools (*https://api.mongodb.com/python/current/tools.html*)
DynamoDB (*https://aws.amazon.com/dynamodb*)	boto3 (*https://docs.aws.amazon.com/amazondynamodb/latest/developerguide/GettingStarted.Python.html*)
CouchDB (*http://couchdb.apache.org*)	couchdb (*https://couchdb-python.readthedocs.io/en/latest/index.html*)

PostgreSQL can do some of the things that document databases do. Some of its extensions allow it to escape relational orthodoxy while keeping features like transactions, data validation, and foreign keys: 1) multidimensional *arrays* (*https://oreil.ly/MkfLY*)—store more than one value in a table cell; 2) *jsonb* (*https://oreil.ly/K_VJg*)—store JSON data in a cell, with full indexing and querying.

Time Series Databases

Time series data may be collected at fixed intervals (such as computer performance metrics) or at random times, which has led to many storage methods. Among many (*https://oreil.ly/CkjC0*) of these (*https://oreil.ly/IbOxQ*), some with Python support are listed in Table 16-7.

Table 16-7. Temporal databases

Database	Python API
InfluxDB (*https://www.influxdata.com*)	influx-client (*https://pypi.org/project/influx-client*)
kdb+ (*https://kx.com*)	PyQ (*https://code.kx.com/v2/interfaces/pyq/*)
Prometheus (*https://prometheus.io*)	prometheus_client (*https://github.com/prometheus/client_python/blob/master/README.md*)
TimescaleDB (*https://www.timescale.com*)	(PostgreSQL clients)
OpenTSDB (*http://opentsdb.net*)	potsdb (*https://pypi.org/project/potsdb*)
PyStore (*https://github.com/ranaroussi/pystore*)	PyStore (*https://pypi.org/project/PyStore*)

Graph Databases

For our last case of data that need its own database category, we have *graphs*: *nodes* (data) connected by *edges* or *vertices* (relationships). An individual Twitter *user* could be a node, with edges to other users like *following* and *followed*.

Graph data has become more visible with the growth of social media, where the value is in the connections as much as the content. Some popular (*https://oreil.ly/MAwMQ*) graph databases are outlined in Table 16-8.

Table 16-8. Graph databases

Database	Python API
Neo4J (*https://neo4j.com*)	py2neo (*https://py2neo.org/v3*)
OrientDB (*https://orientdb.com*)	pyorient (*https://orientdb.com/docs/last/PyOrient.html*)
ArangoDB (*https://www.arangodb.com*)	pyArango (*https://github.com/ArangoDB-Community/pyArango*)

Other NoSQL

The NoSQL servers listed here handle data larger than memory, and many of them use multiple computers. Table 16-9 presents notable servers and their Python libraries.

Table 16-9. NoSQL databases

Database	Python API
Cassandra (*http://cassandra.apache.org*)	pycassa (*https://github.com/pycassa/pycassa*)
CouchDB (*http://couchdb.apache.org*)	couchdb-python (*https://github.com/djc/couchdb-python*)
HBase (*http://hbase.apache.org*)	happybase (*https://github.com/wbolster/happybase*)
Kyoto Cabinet (*http://fallabs.com/kyotocabinet*)	kyotocabinet (*http://bit.ly/kyotocabinet*)
MongoDB (*http://www.mongodb.org*)	mongodb (*http://api.mongodb.org/python/current*)
Pilosa (*https://www.pilosa.com*)	python-pilosa (*https://github.com/pilosa/python-pilosa*)
Riak (*http://basho.com/riak*)	riak-python-client (*https://github.com/basho/riak-python-client*)

Full-Text Databases

Finally, there's a special category of databases for *full-text* search. They index every-thing, so you can find that poem that talks about windmills and giant wheels of cheese. You can see some popular open source examples along with their Python APIs in Table 16-10.

Table 16-10. Full-text databases

Site	Python API
Lucene (*http://lucene.apache.org*)	pylucene (*http://lucene.apache.org/pylucene*)
Solr (*http://lucene.apache.org/solr*)	SolPython (*http://wiki.apache.org/solr/SolPython*)
ElasticSearch (*http://www.elasticsearch.org*)	elasticsearch (*https://elasticsearch-py.readthedocs.io*)
Sphinx (*http://sphinxsearch.com*)	sphinxapi (*http://bit.ly/sphinxapi*)
Xapian (*http://xapian.org*)	xappy (*https://code.google.com/p/xappy*)
Whoosh (*http://bit.ly/mchaput-whoosh*)	(written in Python, includes an API)

Coming Up

The previous chapter was about interleaving code in time (*concurrency*). The next one is about moving data through space (*networking*), which can be used for concurrency and other reasons.

Things to Do

16.1 Save the following text lines to a file called *books.csv* (notice that if the fields are separated by commas, you need to surround a field with quotes if it contains a comma):

```
author,book
J R R Tolkien,The Hobbit
Lynne Truss,"Eats, Shoots & Leaves"
```

16.2 Use the `csv` module and its `DictReader` method to read *books.csv* to the variable books. Print the values in books. Did `DictReader` handle the quotes and commas in the second book's title?

16.3 Create a CSV file called *books2.csv* by using these lines:

```
title,author,year
The Weirdstone of Brisingamen,Alan Garner,1960
Perdido Street Station,China Miéville,2000
Thud!,Terry Pratchett,2005
The Spellman Files,Lisa Lutz,2007
Small Gods,Terry Pratchett,1992
```

16.4 Use the `sqlite3` module to create a SQLite database called *books.db* and a table called books with these fields: `title` (text), `author` (text), and `year` (integer).

16.5 Read *books2.csv* and insert its data into the book table.

16.6 Select and print the `title` column from the book table in alphabetical order.

16.7 Select and print all columns from the book table in order of publication.

16.8 Use the `sqlalchemy` module to connect to the sqlite3 database *books.db* that you just made in exercise 16.4. As in 16.6, select and print the `title` column from the book table in alphabetical order.

16.9 Install the Redis server and the Python `redis` library (`pip install redis`) on your computer. Create a Redis hash called `test` with the fields count (1) and name (`'Fester Bestertester'`). Print all the fields for `test`.

16.10 Increment the count field of `test` and print it.

CHAPTER 17

Data in Space: Networks

> Time is nature's way of keeping everything from happening at once. Space is what pre-
> vents everything from happening to me.
>
> —Quotes About Time (*http://bit.ly/wiki-time*)

In Chapter 15, you read about *concurrency*: how to do more than one thing at a time.
Now we'll try to do things in more than one place: *distributed computing* or *networking*. There are many good reasons to challenge time and space:

Performance
> Your goal is to keep fast components busy, not waiting for slow ones.

Robustness
> There's safety in numbers, so you want to duplicate tasks to work around hard-
> ware and software failures.

Simplicity
> It's best practice to break complex tasks into many little ones that are easier to
> create, understand, and fix.

Scalability
> Increase your servers to handle load, decrease them to save money.

In this chapter, we work our way up from networking primitives to higher-level concepts. Let's start with TCP/IP and sockets.

TCP/IP

The internet is based on rules about how to make connections, exchange data, terminate connections, handle timeouts, and so on. These are called *protocols*, and they are
arranged in *layers*. The purpose of layers is to allow innovation and alternative ways

of doing things; you can do anything you want on one layer as long as you follow the conventions in dealing with the layers above and below you.

The very lowest layer governs aspects such as electrical signals; each higher layer builds on those below. In the middle, more or less, is the IP (Internet Protocol) layer, which specifies how network locations are addressed and how *packets* (chunks) of data flow. In the layer above that, two protocols describe how to move bytes between locations:

UDP (User Datagram Protocol)
> This is used for short exchanges. A *datagram* is a tiny message sent in a single burst, like a note on a postcard.

TCP (Transmission Control Protocol)
> This protocol is used for longer-lived connections. It sends *streams* of bytes and ensures that they arrive in order without duplication.

UDP messages are not acknowledged, so you're never sure whether they arrive at their destination. If you wanted to tell a joke over UDP:

```
Here's a UDP joke. Get it?
```

TCP sets up a secret handshake between sender and receiver to ensure a good connection. A TCP joke would start like this:

```
Do you want to hear a TCP joke?
Yes, I want to hear a TCP joke.
Okay, I'll tell you a TCP joke.
Okay, I'll hear a TCP joke.
Okay, I'll send you a TCP joke now.
Okay, I'll receive the TCP joke now.
... (and so on)
```

Your local machine always has the IP address `127.0.0.1` and the name `localhost`. You might see this called the *loopback interface*. If it's connected to the internet, your machine will also have a *public* IP. If you're just using a home computer, it's behind equipment such as a cable modem or router. You can run internet protocols even between processes on the same machine.

Most of the internet with which we interact—the web, database servers, and so on—is based on the TCP protocol running atop the IP protocol; for brevity, TCP/IP. Let's first look at some basic internet services. After that, we explore general networking patterns.

Sockets

If you like to know how things work, all the way down, this section is for you.

The lowest level of network programming uses a *socket*, borrowed from the C language and the Unix operating system. Socket-level coding is tedious. You'll have more fun using something like ZeroMQ, but it's useful to see what lies beneath. For instance, messages about sockets often turn up when networking errors take place.

Let's write a very simple client-server exchange, once with UDP and once with TCP. In the UDP example, the client sends a string in a UDP datagram to a server, and the server returns a packet of data containing a string. The server needs to listen at a particular address and port—like a post office and a post office box. The client needs to know these two values to deliver its message and receive any reply.

In the following client and server code, `address` is a tuple of (*address*, *port*). The `address` is a string, which can be a name or an *IP address*. When your programs are just talking to one another on the same machine, you can use the name `'localhost'` or the equivalent address string `'127.0.0.1'`.

First, let's send a little data from one process to another and return a little data back to the originator. The first program is the client and the second is the server. In each program, we print the time and open a socket. The server will listen for connections to its socket, and the client will write to its socket, which transmits a message to the server.

Example 17-1 presents the first program, *udp_server.py*.

Example 17-1. udp_server.py

```python
from datetime import datetime
import socket

server_address = ('localhost', 6789)
max_size = 4096

print('Starting the server at', datetime.now())
print('Waiting for a client to call.')
server = socket.socket(socket.AF_INET, socket.SOCK_DGRAM)
server.bind(server_address)

data, client = server.recvfrom(max_size)

print('At', datetime.now(), client, 'said', data)
server.sendto(b'Are you talking to me?', client)
server.close()
```

The server has to set up networking through two methods imported from the socket package. The first method, socket.socket, creates a socket, and the second, bind, *binds* to it (listens to any data arriving at that IP address and port). AF_INET means we'll create an IP socket. (There's another type for *Unix domain sockets*, but those work only on the local machine.) SOCK_DGRAM means we'll send and receive datagrams —in other words, we'll use UDP.

At this point, the server sits and waits for a datagram to come in (recvfrom). When one arrives, the server wakes up and gets both the data and information about the client. The client variable contains the address and port combination needed to reach the client. The server ends by sending a reply and closing its connection.

Let's take a look at *udp_client.py* (Example 17-2).

Example 17-2. udp_client.py

```
import socket
from datetime import datetime

server_address = ('localhost', 6789)
max_size = 4096

print('Starting the client at', datetime.now())
client = socket.socket(socket.AF_INET, socket.SOCK_DGRAM)
client.sendto(b'Hey!', server_address)
data, server = client.recvfrom(max_size)
print('At', datetime.now(), server, 'said', data)
client.close()
```

The client has most of the same methods as the server (with the exception of bind()). The client sends and then receives, whereas the server receives first.

Start the server first, in its own window. It will print its greeting and then wait with an eerie calm until a client sends it some data:

```
$ python udp_server.py
Starting the server at 2014-02-05 21:17:41.945649
Waiting for a client to call.
```

Next, start the client in another window. It will print its greeting, send data (the bytes value 'Hey') to the server, print the reply, and then exit:

```
$ python udp_client.py
Starting the client at 2014-02-05 21:24:56.509682
At 2014-02-05 21:24:56.518670 ('127.0.0.1', 6789) said b'Are you talking to me?'
```

Finally, the server will print the message it received, and exit:

```
At 2014-02-05 21:24:56.518473 ('127.0.0.1', 56267) said b'Hey!'
```

The client needed to know the server's address and port number but didn't need to specify a port number for itself. That was automatically assigned by the system—in this case, it was 56267.

UDP sends data in single chunks. It does not guarantee delivery. If you send multiple messages via UDP, they can arrive out of order, or not at all. It's fast, light, connectionless, and unreliable. UDP is useful when you need to push packets quickly, and can tolerate a lost packet now and then, such as with VoIP (voice over IP).

Which brings us to TCP (Transmission Control Protocol). TCP is used for longer-lived connections, such as the web. TCP delivers data in the order in which you send it. If there were any problems, it tries to send it again. This makes TCP a bit slower than UDP, but usually a better choice when you need all the packets, in the right order.

The first two versions of the web protocol HTTP were based on TCP, but HTTP/3 is based on a protocol called QUIC (*https:// oreil.ly/Y3Jym*), which itself uses UDP. So choosing between UDP and TCP can involve many factors.

Let's shoot a few packets from client to server and back with TCP.

tcp_client.py acts like the previous UDP client, sending only one string to the server, but there are small differences in the socket calls, illustrated in Example 17-3.

Example 17-3. tcp_client.py

```
import socket
from datetime import datetime

address = ('localhost', 6789)
max_size = 1000

print('Starting the client at', datetime.now())
client = socket.socket(socket.AF_INET, socket.SOCK_STREAM)
client.connect(address)
client.sendall(b'Hey!')
data = client.recv(max_size)
print('At', datetime.now(), 'someone replied', data)
client.close()
```

We've replaced SOCK_DGRAM with SOCK_STREAM to get the streaming protocol, TCP. We also added a connect() call to set up the stream. We didn't need that for UDP because each datagram was on its own in the wild, wooly internet.

As Example 17-4 demonstrates, *tcp_server.py* also differs from its UDP cousin.

Example 17-4. tcp_server.py

```
from datetime import datetime
import socket

address = ('localhost', 6789)
max_size = 1000

print('Starting the server at', datetime.now())
print('Waiting for a client to call.')
server = socket.socket(socket.AF_INET, socket.SOCK_STREAM)
server.bind(address)
server.listen(5)

client, addr = server.accept()
data = client.recv(max_size)

print('At', datetime.now(), client, 'said', data)
client.sendall(b'Are you talking to me?')
client.close()
server.close()
```

`server.listen(5)` is configured to queue up to five client connections before refusing new ones. `server.accept()` gets the first available message as it arrives.

The `client.recv(1000)` sets a maximum acceptable message length of 1,000 bytes.

As you did earlier, start the server and then the client, and watch the fun. First, the server:

```
$ python tcp_server.py
Starting the server at 2014-02-06 22:45:13.306971
Waiting for a client to call.
At 2014-02-06 22:45:16.048865 <socket.socket object, fd=6, family=2, type=1,
    proto=0> said b'Hey!'
```

Now, start the client. It will send its message to the server, receive a response, and then exit:

```
$ python tcp_client.py
Starting the client at 2014-02-06 22:45:16.038642
At 2014-02-06 22:45:16.049078 someone replied b'Are you talking to me?'
```

The server collects the message, prints it, responds, and then quits:

```
At 2014-02-06 22:45:16.048865 <socket.socket object, fd=6, family=2, type=1,
    proto=0> said b'Hey!'
```

Notice that the TCP server called `client.sendall()` to respond, and the earlier UDP server called `client.sendto()`. TCP maintains the client-server connection across multiple socket calls and remembers the client's IP address.

This didn't look so bad, but if you try to write anything more complex, you'll see how sockets really operate at a low level:

- UDP sends messages, but their size is limited and they're not guaranteed to reach their destination.

- TCP sends streams of bytes, not messages. You don't know how many bytes the system will send or receive with each call.

- To exchange entire messages with TCP, you need some extra information to reassemble the full message from its segments: a fixed message size (bytes), or the size of the full message, or some delimiting character.

- Because messages are bytes, not Unicode text strings, you need to use the Python `bytes` type. For more information on that, see Chapter 12.

After all of this, if you find yourself interested in socket programming, check out the Python socket programming HOWTO (*http://bit.ly/socket-howto*) for more details.

Scapy

Sometimes you need to dip into the networking stream and watch the bytes swimming by. You may want to debug a web API, or track down some security issue. The `scapy` library and program provide a domain-specific language to create and inspect packets in Python, which is much easier than writing and debugging the equivalent C programs.

A standard install uses `pip install scapy`. The docs (*https://scapy.readthedocs.io*) are extremely thorough. If you use tools like `tcpdump` or `wireshark` to investigate TCP issues, you should look at `scapy`. Finally, don't confuse `scapy` with `scrapy`, which is covered in "Crawl and Scrape" on page 401.

Netcat

Another tool to test networks and ports is Netcat (*https://oreil.ly/K37H2*), often abbreviated to `nc`. Here's an example of an HTTP connnection to Google's website, and requesting some basic information about its home page:

```
$ $ nc www.google.com 80
HEAD / HTTP/1.1

HTTP/1.1 200 OK
Date: Sat, 27 Jul 2019 21:04:02 GMT
...
```

In the next chapter, there's an example that uses "Test with telnet" on page 377 to do the same.

Networking Patterns

You can build networking applications from some basic patterns:

- The most common pattern is *request-reply*, also known as *request-response* or *client-server*. This pattern is synchronous: the client waits until the server responds. You've seen many examples of request-reply in this book. Your web browser is also a client, making an HTTP request to a web server, which returns a reply.

- Another common pattern is *push*, or *fanout*: you send data to any available worker in a pool of processes. An example is a web server behind a load balancer.

- The opposite of push is *pull*, or *fanin*: you accept data from one or more sources. An example would be a logger that takes text messages from multiple processes and writes them to a single log file.

- One pattern is similar to radio or television broadcasting: *publish-subscribe*, or *pub-sub*. With this pattern, a publisher sends out data. In a simple pub-sub system, all subscribers would receive a copy. More often, subscribers can indicate that they're interested only in certain types of data (often called a *topic*), and the publisher will send just those. So, unlike the push pattern, more than one subscriber might receive a given piece of data. If there's no subscriber for a topic, the data are ignored.

Let's show some request-reply examples, and later some pub-sub ones.

The Request-Reply Pattern

This is the most familiar pattern. You request DNS, web, or email data from the appropriate servers, and they reply, or tell you whether there's a problem.

I just showed you how to make some basic requests with UDP or TCP, but it's hard to build a networking application at the socket level. Let's see if ZeroMQ can help.

ZeroMQ

ZeroMQ is a library, not a server. Sometimes described as *sockets on steroids*, ZeroMQ sockets do the things that you sort of expected plain sockets to do:

- Exchange entire messages
- Retry connections

- Buffer data to preserve them when the timing between senders and receivers doesn't line up

The online guide (*http://zguide.zeromq.org*) is well written and witty, and it presents the best description of networking patterns that I've seen. The printed version (*ZeroMQ: Messaging for Many Applications*, by Pieter Hintjens, from that animal house, O'Reilly) has that good code smell and a big fish on the cover, rather than the other way around. All the examples in the printed guide are in the C language, but the online version lets you choose from multiple languages for each code example. The Python examples are also viewable (*http://bit.ly/zeromq-py*). In this chapter, I show you some basic request-reply ZeroMQ examples.

ZeroMQ is like a LEGO set, and we all know that you can build an amazing variety of things from a few Lego shapes. In this case, you construct networks from a few socket types and patterns. The basic "LEGO pieces" presented in the following list are the ZeroMQ socket types, which by some twist of fate look like the network patterns we've already discussed:

- REQ (synchronous request)
- REP (synchronous reply)
- DEALER (asynchronous request)
- ROUTER (asynchronous reply)
- PUB (publish)
- SUB (subscribe)
- PUSH (fanout)
- PULL (fanin)

To try these yourself, you'll need to install the Python ZeroMQ library by typing this command:

```
$ pip install pyzmq
```

The simplest pattern is a single request-reply pair. This is synchronous: one socket makes a request and then the other replies. First, the code for the reply (server), *zmq_server.py*, as shown in Example 17-5.

Example 17-5. zmq_server.py

```
import zmq

host = '127.0.0.1'
port = 6789
context = zmq.Context()
server = context.socket(zmq.REP)
```

```
server.bind("tcp://%s:%s" % (host, port))
while True:
    #  Wait for next request from client
    request_bytes = server.recv()
    request_str = request_bytes.decode('utf-8')
    print("That voice in my head says: %s" % request_str)
    reply_str = "Stop saying: %s" % request_str
    reply_bytes = bytes(reply_str, 'utf-8')
    server.send(reply_bytes)
```

We create a Context object: this is a ZeroMQ object that maintains state. Then, we make a ZeroMQ socket of type REP (for REPly). We call bind() to make it listen on a particular IP address and port. Notice that they're specified in a string such as 'tcp://localhost:6789' rather than a tuple, as in the plain-socket examples.

This example keeps receiving requests from a sender and sending a response. The messages can be very long—ZeroMQ takes care of the details.

Example 17-6 shows the code for the corresponding request (client), *zmq_client.py*. Its type is REQ (for REQuest), and it calls connect() rather than bind().

Example 17-6. zmq_client.py

```
import zmq

host = '127.0.0.1'
port = 6789
context = zmq.Context()
client = context.socket(zmq.REQ)
client.connect("tcp://%s:%s" % (host, port))
for num in range(1, 6):
    request_str = "message #%s" % num
    request_bytes = request_str.encode('utf-8')
    client.send(request_bytes)
    reply_bytes = client.recv()
    reply_str = reply_bytes.decode('utf-8')
    print("Sent %s, received %s" % (request_str, reply_str))
```

Now it's time to start them. One interesting difference from the plain-socket examples is that you can start the server and client in either order. Go ahead and start the server in one window in the background:

> $ **python zmq_server.py &**

Start the client in the same window:

> $ **python zmq_client.py**

You'll see these alternating output lines from the client and server:

```
That voice in my head says 'message #1'
Sent 'message #1', received 'Stop saying message #1'
That voice in my head says 'message #2'
Sent 'message #2', received 'Stop saying message #2'
That voice in my head says 'message #3'
Sent 'message #3', received 'Stop saying message #3'
That voice in my head says 'message #4'
Sent 'message #4', received 'Stop saying message #4'
That voice in my head says 'message #5'
Sent 'message #5', received 'Stop saying message #5'
```

Our client ends after sending its fifth message, but we didn't tell the server to quit, so it sits by the phone, waiting for another message. If you run the client again, it will print the same five lines, and the server will print its five also. If you don't kill the *zmq_server.py* process and try to run another one, Python will complain that the address is already is use:

```
$ python zmq_server.py
[2] 356
Traceback (most recent call last):
  File "zmq_server.py", line 7, in <module>
    server.bind("tcp://%s:%s" % (host, port))
  File "socket.pyx", line 444, in zmq.backend.cython.socket.Socket.bind
      (zmq/backend/cython/socket.c:4076)
  File "checkrc.pxd", line 21, in zmq.backend.cython.checkrc._check_rc
      (zmq/backend/cython/socket.c:6032)
zmq.error.ZMQError: Address already in use
```

The messages need to be sent as byte strings, so we encoded our example's text strings in UTF-8 format. You can send any kind of message you like, as long as you convert it to bytes. We used simple text strings as the source of our messages, so encode() and decode() were enough to convert to and from byte strings. If your messages have other data types, you can use a library such as MessagePack (*http://msgpack.org*).

Even this basic REQ-REP pattern allows for some fancy communication patterns, because any number of REQ clients can connect() to a single REP server. The server handles requests one at a time, synchronously, but doesn't drop other requests that are arriving in the meantime. ZeroMQ buffers messages, up to some specified limit, until they can get through; that's where it earns the Q in its name. The Q stands for Queue, the M stands for Message, and the Zero means there doesn't need to be any broker.

Although ZeroMQ doesn't impose any central brokers (intermediaries), you can build them where needed. For example, use DEALER and ROUTER sockets to connect multiple sources and/or destinations asynchronously.

Multiple REQ sockets connect to a single ROUTER, which passes each request to a DEALER, which then contacts any REP sockets that have connected to it (Figure 17-1). This is similar to a bunch of browsers contacting a proxy server in front of a web server farm. It lets you add multiple clients and servers as needed.

The REQ sockets connect only to the ROUTER socket; the DEALER connects to the multiple REP sockets behind it. ZeroMQ takes care of the nasty details, ensuring that the requests are load balanced and that the replies go back to the right place.

Another networking pattern called the *ventilator* uses PUSH sockets to farm out asynchronous tasks, and PULL sockets to gather the results.

The last notable feature of ZeroMQ is that it scales up *and* down, just by changing the connection type of the socket when it's created:

- `tcp` between processes, on one or more machines
- `ipc` between processes on one machine
- `inproc` between threads in a single process

That last one, `inproc`, is a way to pass data between threads without locks, and an alternative to the `threading` example in "Threads" on page 287.

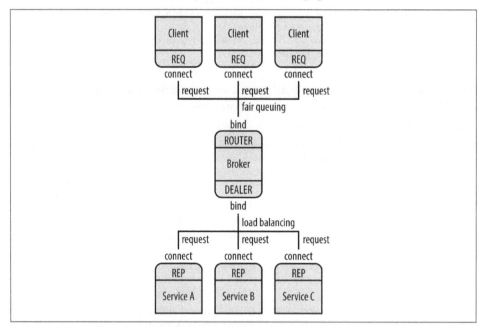

Figure 17-1. Using a broker to connect multiple clients and services

After using ZeroMQ, you may not want to write raw socket code again.

Other Messaging Tools

ZeroMQ is certainly not the only message-passing library that Python supports. Message passing is one of the most popular ideas in networking, and Python keeps up with other languages:

- The Apache project, whose web server we saw in "Apache" on page 386, also maintains the ActiveMQ (*https://activemq.apache.org*) project, including several Python interfaces using the simple-text STOMP (*https://oreil.ly/a3h_M*) protocol.
- RabbitMQ (*http://www.rabbitmq.com*) is also popular, and it has useful online Python tutorials (*http://bit.ly/rabbitmq-tut*).
- NATS (*http://www.nats.io*) is a fast messaging system, written in Go.

The Publish-Subscribe Pattern

Publish-subscribe is not a queue but a broadcast. One or more processes publish messages. Each subscriber process indicates what type of messages it would like to receive. A copy of each message is sent to each subscriber that matched its type. Thus, a given message might be processed once, more than once, or not at all. Like a lonely radio operator, each publisher is just broadcasting and doesn't know who, if anyone, is listening.

Redis

You've seen Redis in Chapter 16, mainly as a data structure server, but it also contains a pub-sub system. The publisher emits messages with a topic and a value, and subscribers say which topics they want to receive.

Example 17-7 contains a publisher, *redis_pub.py*.

Example 17-7. redis_pub.py

```
import redis
import random

conn = redis.Redis()
cats = ['siamese', 'persian', 'maine coon', 'norwegian forest']
hats = ['stovepipe', 'bowler', 'tam-o-shanter', 'fedora']
for msg in range(10):
    cat = random.choice(cats)
    hat = random.choice(hats)
    print('Publish: %s wears a %s' % (cat, hat))
    conn.publish(cat, hat)
```

Each topic is a breed of cat, and the accompanying message is a type of hat.

Example 17-8 shows a single subscriber, *redis_sub.py*.

Example 17-8. redis_sub.py

```python
import redis
conn = redis.Redis()

topics = ['maine coon', 'persian']
sub = conn.pubsub()
sub.subscribe(topics)
for msg in sub.listen():
    if msg['type'] == 'message':
        cat = msg['channel']
        hat = msg['data']
        print('Subscribe: %s wears a %s' % (cat, hat))
```

This subscriber wants all messages for cat types `'maine coon'` and `'persian'`, and no others. The `listen()` method returns a dictionary. If its type is `'message'`, it was sent by the publisher and matches our criteria. The `'channel'` key is the topic (cat), and the `'data'` key contains the message (hat).

If you start the publisher first and no one is listening, it's like a mime falling in the forest (does he make a sound?), so start the subscriber first:

```
$ python redis_sub.py
```

Next, start the publisher. It will send 10 messages and then quit:

```
$ python redis_pub.py
Publish: maine coon wears a stovepipe
Publish: norwegian forest wears a stovepipe
Publish: norwegian forest wears a tam-o-shanter
Publish: maine coon wears a bowler
Publish: siamese wears a stovepipe
Publish: norwegian forest wears a tam-o-shanter
Publish: maine coon wears a bowler
Publish: persian wears a bowler
Publish: norwegian forest wears a bowler
Publish: maine coon wears a stovepipe
```

The subscriber cares about only two types of cat:

```
$ python redis_sub.py
Subscribe: maine coon wears a stovepipe
Subscribe: maine coon wears a bowler
Subscribe: maine coon wears a bowler
Subscribe: persian wears a bowler
Subscribe: maine coon wears a stovepipe
```

We didn't tell the subscriber to quit, so it's still waiting for messages. If you restart the publisher, the subscriber will grab a few more messages and print them.

You can have as many subscribers (and publishers) as you want. If there's no subscriber for a message, it disappears from the Redis server. However, if there are subscribers, the messages stay in the server until all subscribers have retrieved them.

ZeroMQ

ZeroMQ has no central server, so each publisher writes to all subscribers. The publisher, *zmq_pub.py*, is provided in Example 17-9.

Example 17-9. zmq_pub.py

```
import zmq
import random
import time
host = '*'
port = 6789
ctx = zmq.Context()
pub = ctx.socket(zmq.PUB)
pub.bind('tcp://%s:%s' % (host, port))
cats = ['siamese', 'persian', 'maine coon', 'norwegian forest']
hats = ['stovepipe', 'bowler', 'tam-o-shanter', 'fedora']
time.sleep(1)
for msg in range(10):
    cat = random.choice(cats)
    cat_bytes = cat.encode('utf-8')
    hat = random.choice(hats)
    hat_bytes = hat.encode('utf-8')
    print('Publish: %s wears a %s' % (cat, hat))
    pub.send_multipart([cat_bytes, hat_bytes])
```

Notice how this code uses UTF-8 encoding for the topic and value strings.

The file for the subscriber is *zmq_sub.py* (Example 17-10).

Example 17-10. zmq_sub.py

```
import zmq
host = '127.0.0.1'
port = 6789
ctx = zmq.Context()
sub = ctx.socket(zmq.SUB)
sub.connect('tcp://%s:%s' % (host, port))
topics = ['maine coon', 'persian']
for topic in topics:
    sub.setsockopt(zmq.SUBSCRIBE, topic.encode('utf-8'))
while True:
    cat_bytes, hat_bytes = sub.recv_multipart()
    cat = cat_bytes.decode('utf-8')
    hat = hat_bytes.decode('utf-8')
    print('Subscribe: %s wears a %s' % (cat, hat))
```

In this code, we subscribe to two different byte values: the two strings in `topics`, encoded as UTF-8.

 It seems a little backward, but if you want *all* topics, you need to subscribe to the empty bytestring `b''`; if you don't, you'll get nothing.

Notice that we call `send_multipart()` in the publisher and `recv_multipart()` in the subscriber. This makes it possible for us to send multipart messages and use the first part as the topic. We could also send the topic and message as a single string or bytestring, but it seems cleaner to keep cats and hats separate.

Start the subscriber:

```
$ python zmq_sub.py
```

Start the publisher. It immediately sends 10 messages and then quits:

```
$ python zmq_pub.py
Publish: norwegian forest wears a stovepipe
Publish: siamese wears a bowler
Publish: persian wears a stovepipe
Publish: norwegian forest wears a fedora
Publish: maine coon wears a tam-o-shanter
Publish: maine coon wears a stovepipe
Publish: persian wears a stovepipe
Publish: norwegian forest wears a fedora
Publish: norwegian forest wears a bowler
Publish: maine coon wears a bowler
```

The subscriber prints what it requested and received:

```
Subscribe: persian wears a stovepipe
Subscribe: maine coon wears a tam-o-shanter
Subscribe: maine coon wears a stovepipe
Subscribe: persian wears a stovepipe
Subscribe: maine coon wears a bowler
```

Other Pub-Sub Tools

You might like to explore some of these other Python pub-sub links:

- RabbitMQ is a well-known messaging broker, and `pika` is a Python API for it. See the `pika` documentation (*http://pika.readthedocs.org*) and a pub-sub tutorial (*http://bit.ly/pub-sub-tut*).

- Go to the PyPi (*https://pypi.python.org*) search window and type `pubsub` to find Python packages like `pypubsub` (*http://pubsub.sourceforge.net*).

- PubSubHubbub (*https://code.google.com/p/pubsubhubbub*) enables subscribers to register callbacks with publishers.
- NATS (*https://nats.io*) is a fast, open source messaging system that supports pubsub, request-reply, and queuing.

Internet Services

Python has an extensive networking toolset. In the following sections, we look at ways to automate some of the most popular internet services. The official, comprehensive documentation (*http://bit.ly/py-internet*) is available online.

Domain Name System

Computers have numeric IP addresses such as 85.2.101.94, but we remember names better than numbers. The Domain Name System (DNS) is a critical internet service that converts IP addresses to and from names via a distributed database. Whenever you're using a web browser and suddenly see a message like "looking up host," you've probably lost your internet connection, and your first clue is a DNS failure.

Some DNS functions are found in the low-level socket module. gethostbyname() returns the IP address for a domain name, and the extended edition gethostbyname_ex() returns the name, a list of alternative names, and a list of addresses:

```
>>> import socket
>>> socket.gethostbyname('www.crappytaxidermy.com')
'66.6.44.4'
>>> socket.gethostbyname_ex('www.crappytaxidermy.com')
('crappytaxidermy.com', ['www.crappytaxidermy.com'], ['66.6.44.4'])
```

The getaddrinfo() method looks up the IP address, but it also returns enough information to create a socket to connect to it:

```
>>> socket.getaddrinfo('www.crappytaxidermy.com', 80)
[(2, 2, 17, '', ('66.6.44.4', 80)),
 (2, 1, 6, '', ('66.6.44.4', 80))]
```

The preceding call returned two tuples: the first for UDP, and the second for TCP (the 6 in the 2, 1, 6 is the value for TCP).

You can ask for TCP or UDP information only:

```
>>> socket.getaddrinfo('www.crappytaxidermy.com', 80, socket.AF_INET,
socket.SOCK_STREAM)
[(2, 1, 6, '', ('66.6.44.4', 80))]
```

Some TCP and UDP port numbers (*http://bit.ly/tcp-udp-ports*) are reserved for certain services by IANA, and are associated with service names. For example, HTTP is named http and is assigned TCP port 80.

These functions convert between service names and port numbers:

```
>>> import socket
>>> socket.getservbyname('http')
80
>>> socket.getservbyport(80)
'http'
```

Python Email Modules

The standard library contains these email modules:

- smtplib (*https://oreil.ly/_kF6V*) for sending email messages via Simple Mail Transfer Protocol (SMTP)
- email (*https://oreil.ly/WVGbE*) for creating and parsing email messages
- poplib (*https://oreil.ly/xiJT7*) for reading email via Post Office Protocol 3 (POP3)
- imaplib (*https://oreil.ly/wengo*) for reading email via Internet Message Access Protocol (IMAP)

If you want to write your own Python SMTP server, try smtpd (*https://oreil.ly/JkLsD*), or the new asynchronous version aiosmtpd (*https://aiosmtpd.readthedocs.io*).

Other Protocols

Using the standard ftplib module (*http://bit.ly/py-ftplib*), you can push bytes around by using the File Transfer Protocol (FTP). Although it's an old protocol, FTP still performs very well.

You've seen many of these modules in various places in this book, but also try the documentation for standard library support of internet protocols (*http://bit.ly/py-internet*).

Web Services and APIs

Information providers always have a website, but those are targeted for human eyes, not automation. If data is published only on a website, anyone who wants to access and structure the data needs to write scrapers (as shown in "Crawl and Scrape" on page 401), and rewrite them each time a page format changes. This is usually tedious. In contrast, if a website offers an API to its data, the data becomes directly available to client programs. APIs change less often than web page layouts, so client rewrites are less common. A fast, clean data pipeline also makes it easier to build unforeseen but useful combinations.

In many ways, the easiest API is a web interface, but one that provides data in a structured format such as JSON or XML rather than plain text or HTML. The API might be minimal or a full-fledged RESTful API (defined in "Web APIs and REST" on page 400), but it provides another outlet for those restless bytes.

At the very beginning of this book, you saw a web API query the Internet Archive for an old copy of a website.

APIs are especially useful for mining well-known social media sites such as Twitter, Facebook, and LinkedIn. All these sites provide APIs that are free to use, but they require you to register and get a key (a long-generated text string, sometimes also known as a *token*) to use when connecting. The key lets a site determine who's accessing its data. It can also serve as a way to limit request traffic to servers.

Here are some interesting service APIs:

- New York Times (*http://developer.nytimes.com*)
- Twitter (*https://python-twitter.readthedocs.io*)
- Facebook (*https://developers.facebook.com/tools*)
- Weather Underground (*http://www.wunderground.com/weather/api*)
- Marvel Comics (*http://developer.marvel.com*)

You can see examples of APIs for maps in Chapter 21, and others in Chapter 22.

Data Serialization

As you saw in Chapter 16, formats like XML, JSON, and YAML are ways to store structured text data. Networked applications need to exchange data with other programs. The conversion between data in memory and byte sequences "on the wire" is called *serialization* or *marshaling*. JSON is a popular serialization format, especially with web RESTful systems, but it can't express all Python data types directly. Also, as a text format it tends to be more verbose than some binary serialization methods. Let's look at some approaches that you're likely to run into.

Serialize with pickle

Python provides the `pickle` module to save and restore any object in a special binary format.

Remember how JSON lost its mind when encountering a `datetime` object? Not a problem for `pickle`:

```
>>> import pickle
>>> import datetime
>>> now1 = datetime.datetime.utcnow()
>>> pickled = pickle.dumps(now1)
>>> now2 = pickle.loads(pickled)
```

```
>>> now1
datetime.datetime(2014, 6, 22, 23, 24, 19, 195722)
>>> now2
datetime.datetime(2014, 6, 22, 23, 24, 19, 195722)
```

`pickle` works with your own classes and objects, too. Let's define a little class called Tiny that returns the string 'tiny' when treated as a string:

```
>>> import pickle
>>> class Tiny():
...     def __str__(self):
...         return 'tiny'
...
>>> obj1 = Tiny()
>>> obj1
<__main__.Tiny object at 0x10076ed10>
>>> str(obj1)
'tiny'
>>> pickled = pickle.dumps(obj1)
>>> pickled
b'\x80\x03c__main__\nTiny\nq\x00)\x81q\x01.'
>>> obj2 = pickle.loads(pickled)
>>> obj2
<__main__.Tiny object at 0x10076e550>
>>> str(obj2)
'tiny'
```

`pickled` is the pickled binary string made from the object `obj1`. We converted that back to the object `obj2` to make a copy of `obj1`. Use `dump()` to pickle to a file, and `load()` to unpickle from one.

The `multiprocessing` module uses `pickle` to interchange data among processes.

If `pickle` can't serialize your data format, a newer third-party package called `dill` (*https://pypi.org/project/dill*) might.

 Because `pickle` can create Python objects, the same security warnings that were discussed in earlier sections apply. A public service announcement: don't unpickle something that you don't trust.

Other Serialization Formats

These binary data interchange formats are usually more compact and faster than XML or JSON:

- MsgPack (*http://msgpack.org*)
- Protocol Buffers (*https://code.google.com/p/protobuf*)

- Avro (*http://avro.apache.org/docs/current*)
- Thrift (*http://thrift.apache.org*)
- Lima (*https://lima.readthedocs.io*)
- `Serialize` (*https://pypi.org/project/Serialize*) is a Python frontend to other formats, including JSON, YAML, pickle, and MsgPack.
- A benchmark (*https://oreil.ly/S3ESH*) of various Python serialization packages.

Because they are binary, none can be easily edited by a human with a text editor.

Some third-party packages interconvert objects and basic Python data types (allowing further conversion to/from formats like JSON), and provide *validation* of the following:

- Data types
- Value ranges
- Required versus optional data

These include:

- Marshmallow (*https://marshmallow.readthedocs.io/en/3.0*)
- Pydantic (*https://pydantic-docs.helpmanual.io*)—uses type hints, so requires at least Python 3.6
- TypeSystem (*https://www.encode.io/typesystem*)

These are often used with web servers to ensure that the bytes that came over the wire via HTTP end up in the right data structures for further processing.

Remote Procedure Calls

Remote Procedure Calls (RPCs) look like normal functions but execute on remote machines across a network. Instead of calling a RESTful API with arguments encoded in the URL or request body, you call an RPC function on your own machine. Your local machine:

- Serializes your function arguments into bytes.
- Sends the encoded bytes to the remote machine.

The remote machine:

- Receives the encoded request bytes.
- Deserializes the bytes back to data structures.

- Finds and calls the service function with the decoded data.
- Encodes the function results.
- Sends the encoded bytes back to the caller.

And finally, the local machine that started it all:

- Decodes the bytes to return values.

RPC is a popular technique, and people have implemented it in many ways. On the server side, you start a server program, connect it with some byte transport and encoding/decoding method, define some service functions, and light up your *RPC is open for business* sign. The client connects to the server and calls one of its functions via RPC.

XML RPC

The standard library includes one RPC implementation that uses XML as the exchange format: xmlrpc. You define and register functions on the server, and the client calls them as though they were imported. First, let's explore the file *xmlrpc_server.py*, as shown in Example 17-11.

Example 17-11. xmlrpc_server.py

```
from xmlrpc.server import SimpleXMLRPCServer

def double(num):
    return num * 2

server = SimpleXMLRPCServer(("localhost", 6789))
server.register_function(double, "double")
server.serve_forever()
```

The function we're providing on the server is called double(). It expects a number as an argument and returns the value of that number times two. The server starts up on an address and port. We need to *register* the function to make it available to clients via RPC. Finally, start serving and carry on.

Now—you guessed it—*xmlrpc_client.py*, proudly presented in Example 17-12.

Example 17-12. xmlrpc_client.py

```
import xmlrpc.client

proxy = xmlrpc.client.ServerProxy("http://localhost:6789/")
num = 7
```

```
result = proxy.double(num)
print("Double %s is %s" % (num, result))
```

The client connects to the server by using `ServerProxy()`. Then, it calls the function `proxy.double()`. Where did that come from? It was created dynamically by the server. The RPC machinery magically hooks this function name into a call to the remote server.

Give it a try—start the server and then run the client:

```
$ python xmlrpc_server.py
```

Run the client again:

```
$ python xmlrpc_client.py
Double 7 is 14
```

The server then prints the following:

```
127.0.0.1 - - [13/Feb/2014 20:16:23] "POST / HTTP/1.1" 200 -
```

Popular transport methods are HTTP and ZeroMQ.

JSON RPC

JSON-RPC (versions 1.0 (*https://oreil.ly/OklKa*) and 2.0 (*https://oreil.ly/4CS0r*)) is similar to XML-RPC, but with JSON. There are many Python JSON-RPC libraries, but the simplest one I've found comes in two parts: client (*https://oreil.ly/8npxf*) and server (*https://oreil.ly/P_uDr*).

Installation of both is familiar: `pip install jsonrpcserver` and `pip install jsonrpclient`.

These libraries provide many alternative ways to write a client (*https://oreil.ly/fd412*) and server (*https://oreil.ly/SINeg*). In Example 17-13 and Example 17-14, I use this library's built-in server, which uses port 5000 and is the simplest.

First, the server.

Example 17-13. jsonrpc_server.py

```
from jsonrpcserver import method, serve

@method
def double(num):
    return num * 2

if __name__ == "__main__":
    serve()
```

Second, the client.

Example 17-14. jsonrpc_client.py

```
from jsonrpcclient import request

num = 7
response = request("http://localhost:5000", "double", num=num)
print("Double", num, "is", response.data.result)
```

As with most of the client-server examples in this chapter, start the server first (in its own terminal window, or with a following & to put it in the background) and then run the client:

```
$ python jsonrpc_server.py &
[1] 10621
$ python jsonrpc_client.py
127.0.0.1 - - [23/Jun/2019 15:39:24] "POST / HTTP/1.1" 200 -
Double 7 is 14
```

If you put the server in the background, kill it when you're done.

MessagePack RPC

The encoding library MessagePack has its own Python RPC implementation (*http://bit.ly/msgpack-rpc*). Here's how to install it:

```
$ pip install msgpack-rpc-python
```

This will also install `tornado`, a Python event-based web server that this library uses as a transport. As usual, the server (*msgpack_server.py*) comes first (Example 17-15).

Example 17-15. msgpack_server.py

```
from msgpackrpc import Server, Address

class Services():
    def double(self, num):
        return num * 2

server = Server(Services())
server.listen(Address("localhost", 6789))
server.start()
```

The `Services` class exposes its methods as RPC services. Go ahead and start the client, *msgpack_client.py* (Example 17-16).

Example 17-16. msgpack_client.py

```
from msgpackrpc import Client, Address

client = Client(Address("localhost", 6789))
num = 8
result =  client.call('double', num)
print("Double %s is %s" % (num, result))
```

To run these, follow the usual drill—start the server and client in separate terminal windows,[1] and observe the results:

```
$ python msgpack_server.py
```

```
$ python msgpack_client.py
Double 8 is 16
```

Zerorpc

Written by the developers of Docker (when they were called dotCloud), zerorpc (*http://www.zerorpc.io*) uses ZeroMQ and MsgPack to connect clients and servers. It magically exposes functions as RPC endpoints.

Type `pip install zerorpc` to install it. The sample code in Example 17-17 and Example 17-18 shows a request-reply client and server.

Example 17-17. zerorpc_server.py

```
import zerorpc

class RPC():
    def double(self, num):
        return 2 * num

server = zerorpc.Server(RPC())
server.bind("tcp://0.0.0.0:4242")
server.run()
```

Example 17-18. zerorpc_client.py

```
import zerorpc

client = zerorpc.Client()
client.connect("tcp://127.0.0.1:4242")
num = 7
```

---

1 Or put the server in the background with a final &.

```
result = client.double(num)
print("Double", num, "is", result)
```

Notice that the client calls `client.double()`, even though there's no definition of it in there:

```
$ python zerorpc_server &
[1] 55172
$ python zerorpc_client.py
Double 7 is 14
```

The site has many more examples (*https://github.com/0rpc/zerorpc-python*).

gRPC

Google created gRPC (*https://grpc.io*) as a portable and fast way to define and connect services. It encodes data as protocol buffers (*https://oreil.ly/UINlc*).

Install the Python parts:

```
$ pip install grpcio
$ pip install grpcio-tools
```

The Python client docs (*https://grpc.io/docs/quickstart/python*) are very detailed, so I'm giving only a brief overview here. You may also like this separate tutorial (*https://oreil.ly/awnxO*).

To use gRPC, you write a *.proto* file to define a `service` and its `rpc` methods.

An `rpc` method is like a function definition (describing its arguments and return types) and may specify one of these networking patterns:

- Request-response (sync or async)
- Request-streaming response
- Streaming request-response (sync or async)
- Streaming request-streaming response

Single responses can be blocking or asynchronous. Streaming responses are iterated.

Next, you would run the `grpc_tools.protoc` program to create Python code for the client and server. gRPC handles the serialization and network communication; you add your application-specific code to the client and server stubs.

gRPC is a top-level alternative to web REST APIs. It seems to be a better fit than REST for inter-service communication, and REST may be preferred for public APIs.

Twirp

Twirp (*https://oreil.ly/buf4x*) is similar to gRPC, but claims to be simpler. You define a `.proto` file as you would with gRPC, and twirp can generate Python code to handle the client and server ends.

Remote Management Tools

- `Salt` (*http://www.saltstack.com*) is written in Python. It started as a way to implement remote execution, but grew to a full-fledged systems management platform. Based on ZeroMQ rather than SSH, it can scale to thousands of servers.

- `Puppet` (*http://puppetlabs.com*) and `Chef` (*http://www.getchef.com/chef*) are popular and closely tied to Ruby.

- The `Ansible` (*http://www.ansible.com/home*) package, which like Salt is written in Python, is also comparable. It's free to download and use, but support and some add-on packages require a commercial license. It uses SSH by default and does not require any special software to be installed on the machines that it will manage.

`Salt` and `Ansible` are both functional supersets of `Fabric`, handling initial configuration, deployment, and remote execution.

Big Fat Data

As Google and other internet companies grew, they found that traditional computing solutions didn't scale. Software that worked for single machines, or even a few dozen, could not keep up with thousands.

Disk storage for databases and files involved too much *seeking*, which requires mechanical movement of disk heads. (Think of a vinyl record, and the time it takes to move the needle from one track to another manually. And think of the screeching sound it makes when you drop it too hard, not to mention the sounds made by the record's owner.) But you could *stream* consecutive segments of the disk more quickly.

Developers found that it was faster to distribute and analyze data on many networked machines than on individual ones. They could use algorithms that sounded simplistic but actually worked better overall with massively distributed data. One of these is MapReduce, which spreads a calculation across many machines and then gathers the results. It's similar to working with queues.

Hadoop

After Google published its MapReduce results in a paper (*https://oreil.ly/cla0d*), Yahoo followed with an open source Java-based package named *Hadoop* (named after the toy stuffed elephant of the lead programmer's son).

The phrase *big data* applies here. Often it just means "data too big to fit on my machine": data that exceeds the disk, memory, CPU time, or all of the above. To some organizations, if *big data* is mentioned somewhere in a question, the answer is always Hadoop. Hadoop copies data among machines, running them through *map* (scatter) and *reduce* (gather) programs, and saving the results on disk at each step.

This batch process can be slow. A quicker method called *Hadoop streaming* works like Unix pipes, streaming the data through programs without requiring disk writes at each step. You can write Hadoop streaming programs in any language, including Python.

Many Python modules have been written for Hadoop, and some are discussed in the blog post "A Guide to Python Frameworks for Hadoop" (*http://bit.ly/py-hadoop*). Spotify, known for streaming music, open sourced its Python component for Hadoop streaming, Luigi (*https://github.com/spotify/luigi*).

Spark

A rival named Spark (*http://bit.ly/about-spark*) was designed to run 10 to 100 times faster than Hadoop. It can read and process any Hadoop data source and format. Spark includes APIs for Python and other languages. You can find the installation (*http://bit.ly/dl-spark*) documents online.

Disco

Another alternative to Hadoop is Disco (*http://discoproject.org*), which uses Python for MapReduce processing and Erlang for communication. Alas, you can't install it with pip; see the documentation (*http://bit.ly/get-disco*).

Dask

Dask (*https://dask.org*) is similar to Spark, although it's written in Python and is largely used with scientific Python packages like NumPy, Pandas, and scikit-learn. It can spread tasks across thousand-machine clusters.

To get Dask and all of its extra helpers:

```
$ pip install dask[complete]
```

See Chapter 22 for related examples of *parallel programming*, in which a large structured calculation is distributed among many machines.

Clouds

I really don't know clouds at all.

—Joni Mitchell

Not so long ago, you would buy your own servers, bolt them into racks in data centers, and install layers of software on them: operating systems, device drivers, filesystems, databases, web servers, email servers, name servers, load balancers, monitors, and more. Any initial novelty wore off as you tried to keep multiple systems alive and responsive. And you worried constantly about security.

Many hosting services offered to take care of your servers for a fee, but you still leased the physical devices and had to pay for your peak load configuration at all times.

With more individual machines, failures are no longer infrequent: they're very common. You need to scale services horizontally and store data redundantly. You can't assume that the network operates like a single machine. The eight fallacies of distributed computing, according to Peter Deutsch, are as follows:

- The network is reliable.
- Latency is zero.
- Bandwidth is infinite.
- The network is secure.
- Topology doesn't change.
- There is one administrator.
- Transport cost is zero.
- The network is homogeneous.

You can try to build these complex distributed systems, but it's a lot of work, and a different toolset is needed. To borrow an analogy, when you have a handful of servers, you treat them like pets—you give them names, know their personalities, and nurse them back to health when needed. But at scale, you treat servers more like livestock: they look alike, have numbers, and are just replaced if they have any problems.

Instead of building, you can rent servers in the *cloud*. By adopting this model, maintenance is someone else's problem, and you can concentrate on your service, or blog, or whatever you want to show the world. Using web dashboards and APIs, you can spin up servers with whatever configuration you need, quickly and easily—they're *elastic*. You can monitor their status, and be alerted if some metric exceeds a given threshold. Clouds are currently a pretty hot topic, and corporate spending on cloud components has spiked.

The big cloud vendors are:

- Amazon (AWS)
- Google
- Microsoft Azure

Amazon Web Services

As Amazon was growing from hundreds to thousands to millions of servers, developers ran into all the nasty problems of distributed systems. One day in 2002 or thereabouts, CEO Jeff Bezos declared to Amazon employees that, henceforth, all data and functionality needed to be exposed only via network service interfaces—not files, or databases, or local function calls. They had to design these interfaces as though they were being offered to the public. The memo ended with a motivational nugget: *"Anyone who doesn't do this will be fired."*

Not surprisingly, developers got to work, and over time built a huge service-oriented architecture. They borrowed or innovated many solutions, evolving into Amazon Web Services (AWS) (*http://aws.amazon.com*), which now dominates the market. The official Python AWS library is boto3:

- documentation (*https://oreil.ly/y2Baz*)
- SDK (*https://aws.amazon.com/sdk-for-python*) pages

Install it with:

```
$ pip install boto3
```

You can use boto3 as an alternative to AWS's web-based management pages.

Google Cloud

Google uses Python a lot internally, and it employs some prominent Python developers (even Guido van Rossum himself, for some time). From its main (*https://cloud.google.com*) and Python (*https://cloud.google.com/python*) pages, you can find details on its many services.

Microsoft Azure

Microsoft caught up with Amazon and Google with its cloud offering, Azure (*https://azure.microsoft.com*). See Python on Azure (*https://oreil.ly/Yo6Nz*) to learn how to develop and deploy Python applications.

OpenStack

OpenStack (*https://www.openstack.org*) is an open source framework of Python services and REST APIs. Many of the services are similar to those in the commercial clouds.

Docker

The humble standardized shipping container revolutionized international trade. Only a few years ago, Docker applied the *container* name and analogy to a *virtualization* method using some little-known Linux features. Containers are much lighter than virtual machines, and a bit heavier than Python virtualenvs. They allow you to package an application separately from other applications on the same machine, sharing only the operating system kernel.

To install Docker's Python client library (*https://pypi.org/project/docker*):

```
$ pip install docker
```

Kubernetes

Containers caught on and spread through the computing world. Eventually, people needed ways to manage multiple containers and wanted to automate some of the manual steps that have been usually required in large distributed systems:

- Failover
- Load balancing
- Scaling up and down

It looks like Kubernetes (*https://kubernetes.io*) is leading the pack in this new area of *container orchestration*.

To install the Python client library (*https://github.com/kubernetes-client/python*):

```
$ pip install kubernetes
```

Coming Up

As they say on television, our next guest needs no introduction. Learn why Python is one of the best languages to tame the web.

Things to Do

17.1 Use a plain `socket` to implement a current-time-service. When a client sends the string *time* to the server, return the current date and time as an ISO string.

17.2 Use ZeroMQ REQ and REP sockets to do the same thing.

17.3 Try the same with XMLRPC.

17.4 You may have seen the classic *I Love Lucy* television episode in which Lucy and Ethel worked in a chocolate factory. The duo fell behind as the conveyor belt that supplied the confections for them to process began operating at an ever-faster rate. Write a simulation that pushes different types of chocolates to a Redis list, and Lucy is a client doing blocking pops of this list. She needs 0.5 seconds to handle a piece of chocolate. Print the time and type of each chocolate as Lucy gets it, and how many remain to be handled.

17.5 Use ZeroMQ to publish the poem from exercise 12.4 (from Example 12-1), one word at a time. Write a ZeroMQ consumer that prints every word that starts with a vowel, and another that prints every word that contains five letters. Ignore punctuation characters.

CHAPTER 18

The Web, Untangled

Oh, what a tangled web we weave…

—Walter Scott, *Marmion*

Straddling the French–Swiss border is CERN—a particle physics research institute that smashes atoms multiple times, just to make sure.

All that smashing generates a mountain of data. In 1989, the English scientist Tim Berners-Lee first circulated a proposal within CERN to help disseminate information there and across the research community. He called it the *World Wide Web* and distilled its design into three simple ideas:

HTTP (Hypertext Transfer Protocol)
  A protocol for web clients and servers to interchange requests and responses.

HTML (Hypertext Markup Language)
  A presentation format for results.

URL (Uniform Resource Locator)
  A way to uniquely represent a server and a *resource* on that server.

In its simplest usage, a web client (I think Berners-Lee was the first to use the term *browser*) connected to a web server with HTTP, requested a URL, and received HTML.

This was all built on the networking base from the *internet*, which at the time was noncommercial, and known only to a few universities and research organizations.

He wrote the first web browser and server on a NeXT[1] computer. Web awareness really expanded in 1993, when a group of students at the University of Illinois released the Mosaic web browser (for Windows, the Macintosh, and Unix) and the NCSA *httpd* server. When I downloaded Mosaic that summer and started building sites, I had no idea that the web and the internet would soon become part of everyday life. The internet[2] was still officially noncommercial then; there were about 500 known web servers in the world (*http://home.web.cern.ch/about/birth-web*). By the end of 1994, the number of web servers had grown to 10,000. The internet was opened to commercial use, and the authors of Mosaic founded Netscape to write commercial web software. Netscape went public as part of the early internet frenzy, and the web's explosive growth has never stopped.

Almost every computer language has been used to write web clients and web servers. The dynamic languages Perl, PHP, and Ruby have been especially popular. In this chapter, I show why Python is a particularly good language for web work at every level:

- Clients, to access remote sites
- Servers, to provide data for websites and web APIs
- Web APIs and services, to interchange data in other ways than viewable web pages

And while we're at it, we'll build an actual interactive website in the exercises at the end of this chapter.

Web Clients

The low-level network plumbing of the internet is called Transmission Control Protocol/Internet Protocol, or more commonly, simply TCP/IP ("TCP/IP" on page 343 goes into more detail about this). It moves bytes among computers, but doesn't care about what those bytes mean. That's the job of higher-level *protocols*—syntax definitions for specific purposes. HTTP is the standard protocol for web data interchange.

The web is a client-server system. The client makes a *request* to a server: it opens a TCP/IP connection, sends the URL and other information via HTTP, and receives a *response*.

---

1 A company founded by Steve Jobs during his exile from Apple.

2 Let's kill a *zombie lie* here. Senator (and later, Vice President) Al Gore championed bipartisan legislation and cooperation that greatly advanced the early internet, including funding for the group that wrote Mosaic. He never claimed that he "invented the internet"; that phrase was falsely attributed to him by political rivals as he began running for president in 2000.

The format of the response is also defined by HTTP. It includes the status of the request, and (if the request succeeded) the response's data and format.

The most well-known web client is a web *browser*. It can make HTTP requests in a number of ways. You might initiate a request manually by typing a URL into the location bar or clicking a link in a web page. Very often, the data returned is used to display a website —HTML documents, JavaScript files, CSS files, and images—but it can be any type of data, not just that intended for display.

An important aspect of HTTP is that it's *stateless*. Each HTTP connection that you make is independent of all the others. This simplifies basic web operations but complicates others. Here are just a few samples of the challenges:

Caching
Remote content that doesn't change should be saved by the web client and used to avoid downloading from the server again.

Sessions
A shopping website should remember the contents of your shopping cart.

Authentication
Sites that require your username and password should remember them while you're logged in.

Solutions to statelessness include *cookies*, in which the server sends the client enough specific information to be able to identify it uniquely when the client sends the cookie back.

Test with telnet

HTTP is a text-based protocol, so you can actually type it yourself for web testing. The ancient `telnet` program lets you connect to any server and port, and type commands to any service that's running there. For secure (encrypted) connections to other machines, it's been replaced by `ssh`.

Let's ask everyone's favorite test site, Google, some basic information about its home page. Type this:

```
$ telnet www.google.com 80
```

If there is a web server on port 80 (this is where unencrypted `http` usually runs; encrypted `https` uses port 443) at *google.com* (I think that's a safe bet), `telnet` will print some reassuring information, and then display a final blank line that's your cue to type something else:

```
Trying 74.125.225.177...
Connected to www.google.com.
Escape character is '^]'.
```

Now, type an actual HTTP command for `telnet` to send to the Google web server. The most common HTTP command (the one your browser uses when you type a URL in its location bar) is `GET`. This retrieves the contents of the specified resource, such as an HTML file, and returns it to the client. For our first test, we'll use the HTTP command `HEAD`, which just retrieves some basic information *about* the resource:

```
HEAD / HTTP/1.1
```

Add an extra carriage return to send a blank line so the remote server knows you're all done and want a response. That `HEAD /` sends the HTTP `HEAD` *verb* (command) to get information about the home page (/). You'll receive a response such as this (I trimmed some of the long lines using … so they wouldn't stick out of the book):

```
HTTP/1.1 200 OK
Date: Mon, 10 Jun 2019 16:12:13 GMT
Expires: -1
Cache-Control: private, max-age=0
Content-Type: text/html; charset=ISO-8859-1
P3P: CP="This is not a P3P policy! See g.co/p3phelp for more info."
Server: gws
X-XSS-Protection: 0
X-Frame-Options: SAMEORIGIN
Set-Cookie: 1P_JAR=...; expires=... GMT; path=/; domain=.google.com
Set-Cookie: NID=...; expires=... GMT; path=/; domain=.google.com; HttpOnly
Transfer-Encoding: chunked
Accept-Ranges: none
Vary: Accept-Encoding
```

These are HTTP response headers and their values. Some, like `Date` and `Content-Type`, are required. Others, such as `Set-Cookie`, are used to track your activity across multiple visits (we talk about *state management* a little later in this chapter). When you make an HTTP `HEAD` request, you get back only headers. If you had used the HTTP `GET` or `POST` commands, you would also receive data from the home page (a mixture of HTML, CSS, JavaScript, and whatever else Google decided to throw into its home page).

I don't want to leave you stranded in `telnet`. To close `telnet`, type the following:

```
q
```

Test with curl

Using `telnet` is simple, but is a completely manual process. The `curl` (*https://curl.haxx.se*) program is probably the most popular command-line web client. Documentation includes the book *Everything Curl* (*https://curl.haxx.se/book.html*), in HTML, PDF, and ebook formats. A table (*https://oreil.ly/dLR8b*) compares `curl` with similar tools. The download (*https://curl.haxx.se/download.html*) page includes all the major platforms, and many obscure ones.

The simplest use of curl does an implicit GET (output truncated here):

```
$ curl http://www.example.com
<!doctype html>
<html>
<head>
    <title>Example Domain</title>
    ...
```

This uses HEAD:

```
$ curl --head http://www.example.com
HTTP/1.1 200 OK
Content-Encoding: gzip
Accept-Ranges: bytes
Cache-Control: max-age=604800
Content-Type: text/html; charset=UTF-8
Date: Sun, 05 May 2019 16:14:30 GMT
Etag: "1541025663"
Expires: Sun, 12 May 2019 16:14:30 GMT
Last-Modified: Fri, 09 Aug 2013 23:54:35 GMT
Server: ECS (agb/52B1)
X-Cache: HIT
Content-Length: 606
```

If you're passing arguments, you can include them in the command line or a data file. In these examples, I use the following:

- *url* for any website
- data.txt as a text data file with these contents: a=1&b=2
- data.json as a JSON data file with these contents: {"a":1, "b": 2}
- a=1&b=2 as two data arguments

Using default (*form-encoded*) arguments:

```
$ curl -X POST -d "a=1&b=2" url
$ curl -X POST -d "@data.txt" url
```

For JSON-encoded arguments:

```
$ curl -X POST -d "{'a':1,'b':2}" -H "Content-Type: application/json" url
$ curl -X POST -d "@data.json" url
```

Test with httpie

A more Pythonic alternative to curl is httpie (*https://httpie.org*).

```
$ pip install httpie
```

To make a form-encoded POST, similar to the methods for `curl` above (`-f` is a synonym for `--form`):

```
$ http -f POST url a=1 b=2
$ http POST -f url < data.txt
```

The default encoding is JSON:

```
$ http POST url a=1 b=2
$ http POST url < data.json
```

`httpie` also handles HTTP headers, cookies, file uploads, authentication, redirects, SSL, and so on. As usual, see the docs (*https://httpie.org/doc*)

Test with httpbin

You can test your web queries against the site `httpbin` (*https://httpbin.org*), or download and run the site in a local Docker image:

```
$ docker run -p 80:80 kennethreitz/httpbin
```

Python's Standard Web Libraries

In Python 2, web client and server modules were a bit scattered. One of the Python 3 goals was to bundle these modules into two *packages* (remember from Chapter 11 that a package is just a directory containing module files):

- `http` manages all the client-server HTTP details:
  - `client` does the client-side stuff
  - `server` helps you write Python web servers
  - `cookies` and `cookiejar` manage cookies, which save data between site visits
- `urllib` runs on top of `http`:
  - `request` handles the client request
  - `response` handles the server response
  - `parse` cracks the parts of a URL

 If you're trying to write code that's compatible with both Python 2 and Python 3, keep in mind that `urllib` changed a lot (*https://oreil.ly/ww5_R*) between the two versions. For a better alternative, refer to "Beyond the Standard Library: requests" on page 382.

Let's use the standard library to get something from a website. The URL in the following example returns information from a test website:

```
>>> import urllib.request as ur
>>>
>>> url = 'http://www.example.com/'
>>> conn = ur.urlopen(url)
```

This little chunk of Python opened a TCP/IP connection to the remote web server www.example.com, made an HTTP request, and received an HTTP response. The response contained more than just the page data. In the official documentation (*http://bit.ly/httpresponse-docs*), we find that conn is an HTTPResponse object with a number of methods and attributes. One of the most important parts of the response is the HTTP *status code*:

```
>>> print(conn.status)
200
```

A 200 means that everything was peachy. There are dozens of HTTP status codes, grouped into five ranges by their first (hundreds) digit:

1xx (information)
    The server received the request but has some extra information for the client.

2xx (success)
    It worked; every success code other than 200 conveys extra details.

3xx (redirection)
    The resource moved, so the response returns the new URL to the client.

4xx (client error)
    Some problem from the client side, such as the well-known 404 (not found). 418 (*I'm a teapot*) was an April Fool's joke.

5xx (server error)
    500 is the generic whoops; you might see a 502 (bad gateway) if there's some disconnect between a web server and a backend application server.

To get the actual data contents from the web page, use the read() method of the conn variable. This returns a bytes value. Let's get the data and print the first 50 bytes:

```
>>> data = conn.read()
>>> print(data[:50])

b'<!doctype html>\n<html>\n<head>\n    <title>Example D'
```

We can convert these bytes to a string and print its first 50 characters:

```
>>> str_data = data.decode('utf8')
>>> print(str_data[:50])
<!doctype html>
```

```
<html>
<head>
    <title>Example D
>>>
```

The rest is more HTML and CSS.

Out of sheer curiosity, what HTTP headers were sent back to us?

```
>>> for key, value in conn.getheaders():
...     print(key, value)
...
Cache-Control max-age=604800
Content-Type text/html; charset=UTF-8
Date Sun, 05 May 2019 03:09:26 GMT
Etag "1541025663+ident"
Expires Sun, 12 May 2019 03:09:26 GMT
Last-Modified Fri, 09 Aug 2013 23:54:35 GMT
Server ECS (agb/5296)
Vary Accept-Encoding
X-Cache HIT
Content-Length 1270
Connection close
```

Remember that `telnet` example a little earlier? Now, our Python library is parsing all those HTTP response headers and providing them in a dictionary. `Date` and `Server` seem straightforward; some of the others, less so. It's helpful to know that HTTP has a set of standard headers such as `Content-Type`, and many optional ones.

Beyond the Standard Library: requests

At the beginning of Chapter 1, there was a program that accessed a Wayback Machine API by using the standard libraries `urllib.request` and `json`. Following that example is a version that uses the third-party module `requests`. The `requests` version is shorter and easier to understand.

For most purposes, I think web client development with `requests` is easier. You can browse the documentation (*https://oreil.ly/zF8cy*) (which is pretty good) for full details. I'll show the basics of `requests` in this section and use it throughout this book for web client tasks.

First, install the `requests` library:

```
$ pip install requests
```

Now, let's redo our example.com query with `requests`:

```
>>> import requests
>>> resp = requests.get('http://example.com')
>>> resp
<Response [200]>
```

```
>>> resp.status_code
200
>>> resp.text[:50]
'<!doctype html>\n<html>\n<head>\n    <title>Example D'
```

To show a JSON query, here's a minimal version of a program that appears at the end of this chapter. You provide a string, and it uses an Internet Archive search API to look through the titles of billions of multimedia items saved there. Notice that in the `requests.get()` call shown in Example 18-1, you only need to pass a `params` dictionary, and `requests` handles all the query construction and character escaping.

Example 18-1. ia.py

```python
import json
import sys

import requests

def search(title):
    url = "http://archive.org/advancedsearch.php"
    params = {"q": f"title:({title})",
              "output": "json",
              "fields": "identifier,title",
              "rows": 50,
              "page": 1,}
    resp = requests.get(url, params=params)
    return resp.json()

if __name__ == "__main__":
    title = sys.argv[1]
    data = search(title)
    docs = data["response"]["docs"]
    print(f"Found {len(docs)} items, showing first 10")
    print("identifier\ttitle")
    for row in docs[:10]:
        print(row["identifier"], row["title"], sep="\t")
```

How's their stock of wendigo items?

```
$ python ia.py wendigo
Found 24 items, showing first 10
identifier   title
cd_wendigo_penny-sparrow   Wendigo
Wendigo1   Wendigo 1
wendigo_ag_librivox   The Wendigo
thewendigo10897gut   The Wendigo
isbn_9780843944792   Wendigo mountain ; Death camp
jamendo-060508   Wendigo - Audio Leash
fav-lady_wendigo   lady_wendigo Favorites
011bFearTheWendigo   011b Fear The Wendigo
```

```
CharmedChats112 Episode 112 - The Wendigo
jamendo-076964  Wendigo - Tomame o Dejame>
```

The first column (the *identifier*) can be used to actually view the item at the *archive.org* site. You'll see how to do this at the end of this chapter.

Web Servers

Web developers have found Python to be an excellent language for writing web servers and server-side programs. This has led to such a variety of Python-based web *frameworks* that it can be hard to navigate among them and make choices—not to mention deciding what deserves to go into a book.

A web framework provides features with which you can build websites, so it does more than a simple web (HTTP) server. You'll see features such as routing (URL to server function), templates (HTML with dynamic inclusions), debugging, and more.

I'm not going to cover all of the frameworks here—just those that I've found to be relatively simple to use and suitable for real websites. I'll also show how to run the dynamic parts of a website with Python and other parts with a traditional web server.

The Simplest Python Web Server

You can run a simple web server by typing just one line of Python:

```
$ python -m http.server
```

This implements a bare-bones Python HTTP server. If there are no problems, this will print an initial status message:

```
Serving HTTP on 0.0.0.0 port 8000 ...
```

That `0.0.0.0` means *any TCP address*, so web clients can access it no matter what address the server has. There's more low-level details on TCP and other network plumbing for you to read about in Chapter 17.

You can now request files, with paths relative to your current directory, and they will be returned. If you type `http://localhost:8000` in your web browser, you should see a directory listing there, and the server will print access log lines such as this:

```
127.0.0.1 - - [20/Feb/2013 22:02:37] "GET / HTTP/1.1" 200 -
```

`localhost` and `127.0.0.1` are TCP synonyms for *your local computer*, so this works regardless of whether you're connected to the internet. You can interpret this line as follows:

- `127.0.0.1` is the client's IP address
- The first - is the remote username, if found

- The second - is the login username, if required
- `[20/Feb/2013 22:02:37]` is the access date and time
- `"GET / HTTP/1.1"` is the command sent to the web server:
  — The HTTP method (`GET`)
  — The resource requested (`/`, the top)
  — The HTTP version (`HTTP/1.1`)
- The final `200` is the HTTP status code returned by the web server

Click any file. If your browser can recognize the format (HTML, PNG, GIF, JPEG, and so on) it should display it, and the server will log the request. For instance, if you have the file *oreilly.png* in your current directory, a request for *http://localhost:8000/oreilly.png* should return the image of the unsettling fellow in Figure 20-2, and the log should show something such as this:

```
127.0.0.1 - - [20/Feb/2013 22:03:48] "GET /oreilly.png HTTP/1.1" 200 -
```

If you have other files in the same directory on your computer, they should show up in a listing on your display, and you can click any one to download it. If your browser is configured to display that file's format, you'll see the results on your screen; otherwise, your browser will ask you if you want to download and save the file.

The default port number used is 8000, but you can specify another:

```
$ python -m http.server 9999
```

You should see this:

```
Serving HTTP on 0.0.0.0 port 9999 ...
```

This Python-only server is best suited for quick tests. You can stop it by killing its process; in most terminals, press Ctrl+C.

You should not use this basic server for a busy production website. Traditional web servers such as Apache and NGINX are much faster for serving static files. In addition, this simple server has no way to handle dynamic content, which more extensive servers can do by accepting parameters.

Web Server Gateway Interface (WSGI)

All too soon, the allure of serving simple files wears off, and we want a web server that can also run programs dynamically. In the early days of the web, the *Common Gateway Interface* (CGI) was designed for clients to make web servers run external programs and return the results. CGI also handled getting input arguments from the client through the server to the external programs. However, the programs were started anew for *each* client access. This could not scale well, because even small programs have appreciable startup time.

To avoid this startup delay, people began merging the language interpreter into the web server. Apache ran PHP within its `mod_php` module, Perl in `mod_perl`, and Python in `mod_python`. Then, code in these dynamic languages could be executed within the long-running Apache process itself rather than in external programs.

An alternative method was to run the dynamic language within a separate long-running program and have it communicate with the web server. FastCGI and SCGI are examples.

Python web development made a leap with the definition of the *Web Server Gateway Interface* (WSGI), a universal API between Python web applications and web servers. All of the Python web frameworks and web servers in the rest of this chapter use WSGI. You don't normally need to know how WSGI works (there really isn't much to it), but it helps to know what some of the parts under the hood are called. This is a *synchronous* connection—one step follows another.

ASGI

In a few places so far, I've mentioned that Python has been introducing *asynchronous* language features like `async`, `await`, and `asyncio`. ASGI (Asynchronous Server Gateway Interface) is a counterpart of WSGI that uses these new features. In Appendix C, you'll see more discussion, and examples of new web frameworks that use ASGI.

Apache

The `apache` (*http://httpd.apache.org*) web server's best WSGI module is `mod_wsgi` (*https://code.google.com/p/modwsgi*). This can run Python code within the Apache process or in separate processes that communicate with Apache.

You should already have `apache` if your system is Linux or macOS. For Windows, you'll need to install apache (*http://bit.ly/apache-http*).

Finally, install your preferred WSGI-based Python web framework. Let's try `bottle` here. Almost all of the work involves configuring Apache, which can be a dark art.

Create the test file shown in Example 18-2 and save it as */var/www/test/home.wsgi*.

Example 18-2. home.wsgi

```
import bottle

application = bottle.default_app()

@bottle.route('/')
```

```
def home():
    return "apache and wsgi, sitting in a tree"
```

Do not call run() this time, because that starts the built-in Python web server. We need to assign to the variable application because that's what mod_wsgi looks for to marry the web server and the Python code.

If apache and its mod_wsgi module are working correctly, we just need to connect them to our Python script. We want to add one line to the file that defines the default website for this apache server, but finding that file is a task itself. It could be */etc/apache2/httpd.conf*, or */etc/apache2/sites-available/default*, or the Latin name of someone's pet salamander.

Let's assume for now that you understand apache and found that file. Add this line inside the <VirtualHost> section that governs the default website:

```
WSGIScriptAlias / /var/www/test/home.wsgi
```

That section might then look like this:

```
<VirtualHost *:80>
    DocumentRoot /var/www

    WSGIScriptAlias / /var/www/test/home.wsgi

    <Directory /var/www/test>
    Order allow,deny
    Allow from all
    </Directory>
</VirtualHost>
```

Start apache, or restart it if it was running to make it use this new configuration. If you then browse to *http://localhost/*, you should see:

```
apache and wsgi, sitting in a tree
```

This runs mod_wsgi in *embedded mode,* as part of apache itself.

You can also run it in *daemon mode,* as one or more processes, separate from apache. To do this, add two new directive lines to your apache config file:

```
WSGIDaemonProcess domain-name user=user-name group=group-name threads=25
WSGIProcessGroup domain-name
```

In the preceding example, *user-name* and *group-name* are the operating system user and group names, and the *domain-name* is the name of your internet domain. A minimal apache config might look like this:

```
<VirtualHost *:80>
    DocumentRoot /var/www

    WSGIScriptAlias / /var/www/test/home.wsgi
```

```
WSGIDaemonProcess mydomain.com user=myuser group=mygroup threads=25
WSGIProcessGroup mydomain.com

<Directory /var/www/test>
Order allow,deny
Allow from all
</Directory>
</VirtualHost>
```

NGINX

The NGINX (*http://nginx.org*) web server does not have an embedded Python module. Instead, it's a frontend to a separate WSGI server such as uWSGI or gUnicorn. Together they make a very fast and configurable platform for Python web development.

You can install nginx from its website (*http://wiki.nginx.org/Install*). For examples of setting up Flask with NGINX and a WSGI server, see this (*https://oreil.ly/7FTPa*).

Other Python Web Servers

Following are some of the independent Python-based WSGI servers that work like apache or nginx, using multiple processes and/or threads (see "Concurrency" on page 284) to handle simultaneous requests:

- uwsgi (*http://projects.unbit.it/uwsgi*)
- cherrypy (*http://www.cherrypy.org*)
- pylons (*http://www.pylonsproject.org*)

Here are some *event-based* servers, which use a single process but avoid blocking on any single request:

- tornado (*http://www.tornadoweb.org*)
- gevent (*http://gevent.org*)
- gunicorn (*http://gunicorn.org*)

I have more to say about events in the discussion about *concurrency* in Chapter 15.

Web Server Frameworks

Web servers handle the HTTP and WSGI details, but you use web *frameworks* to actually write the Python code that powers the site. So, let's talk about frameworks for a while and then get back to alternative ways of actually serving sites that use them.

If you want to write a website in Python, there are many (some say too many) Python web frameworks. A web framework handles, at a minimum, client requests and server responses. Most major web frameworks include these tasks:

- HTTP protocol handling
- Authentication (*authn*, or who are you?)
- Authorization (*authz*, or what can you do?)
- Establish a session
- Get parameters
- Validate parameters (required/optional, type, range)
- Handle HTTP verbs
- Route (functions/classes)
- Serve static files (HTML, JS, CSS, images)
- Serve dynamic data (databases, services)
- Return values and HTTP status

Optional features include:

- Backend templates
- Database connectivity, ORMs
- Rate limiting
- Asynchronous tasks

In the coming sections, we write example code for two frameworks (`bottle` and `flask`). These are *synchronous*. Later, I talk about alternatives, especially for database-backed websites. You can find a Python framework to power any site that you can think of.

Bottle

Bottle consists of a single Python file, so it's very easy to try out, and it's easy to deploy later. Bottle isn't part of standard Python, so to install it, type the following command:

```
$ pip install bottle
```

Here's code that will run a test web server and return a line of text when your browser accesses the URL *http://localhost:9999/*. Save it as *bottle1.py* (Example 18-3).

Example 18-3. bottle1.py

```python
from bottle import route, run

@route('/')
def home():
  return "It isn't fancy, but it's my home page"

run(host='localhost', port=9999)
```

Bottle uses the `route` decorator to associate a URL with the following function; in this case, / (the home page) is handled by the `home()` function. Make Python run this server script by typing this:

```
$ python bottle1.py
```

You should see this on your browser when you access *http://localhost:9999/*:

```
It isn't fancy, but it's my home page
```

The `run()` function executes `bottle`'s built-in Python test web server. You don't need to use this for `bottle` programs, but it's useful for initial development and testing.

Now, instead of creating text for the home page in code, let's make a separate HTML file called *index.html* that contains this line of text:

```
My <b>new</b> and <i>improved</i> home page!!!
```

Make `bottle` return the contents of this file when the home page is requested. Save this script as *bottle2.py* (Example 18-4).

Example 18-4. bottle2.py

```python
from bottle import route, run, static_file

@route('/')
def main():
    return static_file('index.html', root='.')

run(host='localhost', port=9999)
```

In the call to `static_file()`, we want the file `index.html` in the directory indicated by `root` (in this case, '.', the current directory). If your previous server example code was still running, stop it. Now, run the new server:

```
$ python bottle2.py
```

When you ask your browser to get *http:/localhost:9999/*, you should see this:

```
My new and improved home page!!!
```

Let's add one last example that shows how to pass arguments to a URL and use them. Of course, this will be *bottle3.py*, which you can see in Example 18-5.

Example 18-5. bottle3.py

```
from bottle import route, run, static_file

@route('/')
def home():
    return static_file('index.html', root='.')

@route('/echo/<thing>')
def echo(thing):
    return "Say hello to my little friend: %s!" % thing

run(host='localhost', port=9999)
```

We have a new function called echo() and want to pass it a string argument in a URL. That's what the line @route('/echo/<thing>') in the preceding example does. That <thing> in the route means that whatever was in the URL after /echo/ is assigned to the string argument thing, which is then passed to the echo function. To see what happens, stop the old server if it's still running and then start it with the new code:

```
$ python bottle3.py
```

Then, access *http://localhost:9999/echo/Mothra* in your web browser. You should see the following:

```
Say hello to my little friend: Mothra!
```

Now, leave *bottle3.py* running for a minute so that we can try something else. You've been verifying that these examples work by typing URLs into your browser and looking at the displayed pages. You can also use client libraries such as requests to do your work for you. Save this as *bottle_test.py* (Example 18-6).

Example 18-6. bottle_test.py

```
import requests

resp = requests.get('http://localhost:9999/echo/Mothra')
if resp.status_code == 200 and \
  resp.text == 'Say hello to my little friend: Mothra!':
    print('It worked! That almost never happens!')
else:
    print('Argh, got this:', resp.text)
```

Great! Now, run it:

```
$ python bottle_test.py
```

You should see this in your terminal:

```
It worked! That almost never happens!
```

This is a little example of a *unit test*. Chapter 19 provides more details on why tests are good and how to write them in Python.

There's more to Bottle than I've shown here. In particular, you can try adding these arguments when you call `run()`:

- `debug=True` creates a debugging page if you get an HTTP error;
- `reloader=True` reloads the page in the browser if you change any of the Python code.

It's well documented at the developer site (*http://bottlepy.org/docs/dev*).

Flask

Bottle is a good initial web framework. If you need a few more cowbells and whistles, try Flask. It started in 2010 as an April Fools' joke, but enthusiastic response encouraged the author, Armin Ronacher, to make it a real framework. He named the result Flask as a wordplay on Bottle.

Flask is about as simple to use as Bottle, but it supports many extensions that are useful in professional web development, such as Facebook authentication and database integration. It's my personal favorite among Python web frameworks because it balances ease of use with a rich feature set.

The `flask` package includes the `werkzeug` WSGI library and the `jinja2` template library. You can install it from a terminal:

```
$ pip install flask
```

Let's replicate the final Bottle example code in Flask. First, though, we need to make a few changes:

- Flask's default directory home for static files is `static`, and URLs for files there also begin with `/static`. We change the folder to `'.'` (current directory) and the URL prefix to `''` (empty) to allow the URL / to map to the file *index.html*.
- In the `run()` function, setting `debug=True` also activates the automatic reloader; `bottle` used separate arguments for debugging and reloading.

Save this file to *flask1.py* (Example 18-7).

Example 18-7. flask1.py

```python
from flask import Flask

app = Flask(__name__, static_folder='.', static_url_path='')

@app.route('/')
def home():
    return app.send_static_file('index.html')

@app.route('/echo/<thing>')
def echo(thing):
    return "Say hello to my little friend: %s" % thing

app.run(port=9999, debug=True)
```

Then, run the server from a terminal or window:

```
$ python flask1.py
```

Test the home page by typing this URL into your browser:

```
http://localhost:9999/
```

You should see the following (as you did for `bottle`):

My **new** and *improved* home page!!!

Try the /echo endpoint:

```
http://localhost:9999/echo/Godzilla
```

You should see this:

```
Say hello to my little friend: Godzilla
```

There's another benefit to setting `debug` to `True` when calling `run`. If an exception occurs in the server code, Flask returns a specially formatted page with useful details about what went wrong, and where. Even better, you can type some commands to see the values of variables in the server program.

 Do not set debug = `True` in production web servers. It exposes too much information about your server to potential intruders.

So far, the Flask example just replicates what we did with Bottle. What can Flask do that Bottle can't? Flask includes `jinja2`, a more extensive templating system. Here's a tiny example of how to use `jinja2` and Flask together.

Create a directory called `templates` and a file within it called *flask2.html* (Example 18-8).

Example 18-8. flask2.html

```
<html>
<head>
<title>Flask2 Example</title>
</head>
<body>
Say hello to my little friend: {{ thing }}
</body>
</html>
```

Next, we write the server code to grab this template, fill in the value of *thing* that we passed it, and render it as HTML (I'm dropping the `home()` function here to save space). Save this as *flask2.py* (Example 18-9).

Example 18-9. flask2.py

```
from flask import Flask, render_template

app = Flask(__name__)

@app.route('/echo/<thing>')
def echo(thing):
    return render_template('flask2.html', thing=thing)

app.run(port=9999, debug=True)
```

That `thing = thing` argument means to pass a variable named `thing` to the template, with the value of the string `thing`.

Ensure that *flask1.py* isn't still running and then start *flask2.py*:

```
$ python flask2.py
```

Now, type this URL:

```
http://localhost:9999/echo/Gamera
```

You should see the following:

```
Say hello to my little friend: Gamera
```

Let's modify our template and save it in the *templates* directory as *flask3.html*:

```
<html>
<head>
<title>Flask3 Example</title>
</head>
<body>
```

```
Say hello to my little friend: {{ thing }}.
Alas, it just destroyed {{ place }}!
</body>
</html>
```

You can pass this second argument to the echo URL in many ways.

Pass an argument as part of the URL path

Using this method, you simply extend the URL itself. Save the code shown in Example 18-10 as *flask3a.py*.

Example 18-10. flask3a.py

```
from flask import Flask, render_template

app = Flask(__name__)

@app.route('/echo/<thing>/<place>')
def echo(thing, place):
    return render_template('flask3.html', thing=thing, place=place)

app.run(port=9999, debug=True)
```

As usual, stop the previous test server script if it's still running and then try this new one:

```
$ python flask3a.py
```

The URL would look like this:

```
http://localhost:9999/echo/Rodan/McKeesport
```

And you should see the following:

```
Say hello to my little friend: Rodan. Alas, it just destroyed McKeesport!
```

Or, you can provide the arguments as GET parameters, as shown in Example 18-11; save this as *flask3b.py*.

Example 18-11. flask3b.py

```
from flask import Flask, render_template, request

app = Flask(__name__)

@app.route('/echo/')
def echo():
    thing = request.args.get('thing')
    place = request.args.get('place')
    return render_template('flask3.html', thing=thing, place=place)
```

```
app.run(port=9999, debug=True)
```

Run the new server script:

```
$ python flask3b.py
```

This time, use this URL:

```
http://localhost:9999/echo?thing=Gorgo&place=Wilmerding
```

You should get back what you see here:

```
Say hello to my little friend: Gorgo. Alas, it just destroyed Wilmerding!
```

When a GET command is used for a URL, any arguments are passed in the form
&*key1=val1&key2=val2&*...

You can also use the dictionary ** operator to pass multiple arguments to a template
from a single dictionary (call this *flask3c.py*), as shown in Example 18-12.

Example 18-12. flask3c.py

```
from flask import Flask, render_template, request

app = Flask(__name__)

@app.route('/echo/')
def echo():
    kwargs = {}
    kwargs['thing'] = request.args.get('thing')
    kwargs['place'] = request.args.get('place')
    return render_template('flask3.html', **kwargs)

app.run(port=9999, debug=True)
```

That **kwargs acts like thing=thing, place=place. It saves some typing if there are
a lot of input arguments.

The jinja2 templating language does a lot more than this. If you've programmed in
PHP, you'll see many similarities.

Django

Django (*https://www.djangoproject.com*) is a very popular Python web framework, especially for large sites. It's worth learning for many reasons, including frequent requests for django experience in Python job ads. It includes ORM code (we talked about ORMs in "The Object-Relational Mapper (ORM)" on page 327) to create automatic web pages for the typical database *CRUD* functions (create, replace, update, delete) that we looked at in Chapter 16. It also includes some automatic admin pages for these, but they're designed for internal use by programmers rather than public web page use. You don't have to use Django's ORM if you prefer another, such as SQLAlchemy, or direct SQL queries.

Other Frameworks

You can compare the frameworks by viewing this online table (*http://bit.ly/web-frames*):

- fastapi (*https://fastapi.tiangelo.com*) handles both synchronous (WSGI) and asynchronous (ASGI) calls, uses type hints, generates test pages, and is well documented. Recommended.

- web2py (*http://www.web2py.com*) covers much the same ground as django, with a different style.

- pyramid (*https://trypyramid.com*) grew from the earlier pylons project, and is similar to django in scope.

- turbogears (*http://turbogears.org*) supports an ORM, many databases, and multiple template languages.

- wheezy.web (*http://pythonhosted.org/wheezy.web*) is a newer framework optimized for performance. It was faster (*http://bit.ly/wheezyweb*) than the others in a recent test.

- molten (*https://moltenframework.com*) also uses type hints, but only supports WSGI.

- apistar (*https://docs.apistar.com*) is similar to fastapi, but is more of an API validation tool than a web framework.

- masonite (*https://docs.masoniteproject.com*) is a Python version of Ruby on Rails, or PHP's Laravel.

Database Frameworks

The web and databases are the peanut butter and jelly of computing: where you find one, you'll eventually find the other. In real-life Python applications, at some point you'll probably need to provide a web interface (site and/or API) to a relational database.

You could build your own with:

- A web framework like Bottle or Flask
- A database package, like db-api or SQLAlchemy
- A database driver, like pymysql

Instead, you could use a web/database package like one of these:

- connexion (*https://connexion.readthedocs.io*)
- datasette (*https://datasette.readthedocs.io*)
- sandman2 (*https://github.com/jeffknupp/sandman2*)
- flask-restless (*https://flask-restless.readthedocs.io*)

Or, you could use a framework with built-in database support, like Django.

Your database may not be a relational one. If your data schema varies significantly—columns that differ markedly across rows—it might be worthwhile to consider a *schemaless* database, such as one of the *NoSQL* databases discussed in Chapter 16. I once worked on a site that initially stored its data in a NoSQL database, switched to a relational one, on to another relational one, to a different NoSQL one, and then finally back to one of the relational ones.

Web Services and Automation

We've just looked at traditional web client and server applications, consuming and generating HTML pages. Yet the web has turned out to be a powerful way to glue applications and data in many more formats than HTML.

webbrowser

Let's start begin a little surprise. Start a Python session in a terminal window and type the following:

```
>>> import antigravity
```

This secretly calls the standard library's `webbrowser` module and directs your browser to an enlightening Python link.[3]

You can use this module directly. This program loads the main Python site's page in your browser:

```
>>> import webbrowser
>>> url = 'http://www.python.org/'
>>> webbrowser.open(url)
True
```

This opens it in a new window:

```
>>> webbrowser.open_new(url)
True
```

And this opens it in a new tab, if your browser supports tabs:

```
>>> webbrowser.open_new_tab('http://www.python.org/')
True
```

The `webbrowser` makes your browser do all the work.

webview

Rather than calling your browser as `webbrowser` does, `webview` displays the page in its own window, using your machine's native GUI. To install on Linux or macOS:

```
$ pip install pywebview[qt]
```

For Windows:

```
$ pip install pywebview[cef]
```

See the installation notes (*https://oreil.ly/NiYD7*) if you have problems.

Here's an example in which I gave it the official US government current time site:

```
>>> import webview
>>> url = input("URL? ")
URL? http://time.gov
>>> webview.create_window(f"webview display of {url}", url)
```

Figure 18-1 shows the result I got back.

---

3 If you don't see it for some reason, visit xkcd (*http://xkcd.com/353*).

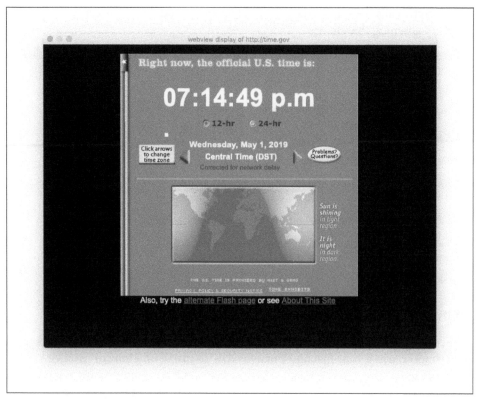

Figure 18-1. webview display window

To stop the program, kill the display window.

Web APIs and REST

Often, data is available only within web pages. If you want to access it, you need to access the pages through a web browser and read it. If the authors of the website made any changes since the last time you visited, the location and style of the data might have changed.

Instead of publishing web pages, you can provide data through a web *application programming interface* (API). Clients access your service by making requests to URLs and getting back responses containing status and data. Instead of HTML pages, the data is in formats that are easier for programs to consume, such as JSON or XML (refer to Chapter 16 for more about these formats).

Representational State Transfer (REST) was defined by Roy Fielding in his doctoral thesis. Many products claim to have a *REST interface* or a *RESTful interface*. In practice, this often only means that they have a *web* interface—definitions of URLs to access a web service.

A *RESTful* service uses the HTTP *verbs* in specific ways:

- HEAD gets information about the resource, but not its data.
- GET retrieves the resource's data from the server. This is the standard method used by your browser. GET should not be used to create, change, or delete data.
- POST creates a new resource.
- PUT replaces an existing resource, creating it if it doesn't exist.
- PATCH partially updates a resource.
- DELETE deletes. Truth in advertising!

A RESTful client can also request one or more content types from the server by using HTTP request headers. For example, a complex service with a REST interface might prefer its input and output to be JSON strings.

Crawl and Scrape

Sometimes, you might want a little bit of information—a movie rating, stock price, or product availability—but what you need is available only in HTML pages, surrounded by ads and extraneous content.

You could extract what you're looking for manually by doing the following:

1. Type the URL into your browser.
2. Wait for the remote page to load.
3. Look through the displayed page for the information you want.
4. Write it down somewhere.
5. Possibly repeat the process for related URLs.

However, it's much more satisfying to automate some or all of these steps. An automated web fetcher is called a *crawler* or *spider*.[4] After the contents have been retrieved from the remote web servers, a *scraper* parses it to find the needle in the haystack.

---

4 Unappealing terms to arachnophobes.

Scrapy

If you need an industrial-strength combined crawler *and* scraper, Scrapy (*http://scrapy.org*) is worth downloading:

```
$ pip install scrapy
```

This installs the module and a standalone command-line `scrapy` program.

Scrapy is a framework, not just a module such as `BeautifulSoup`. It does more, but it's more complex to set up. To learn more about Scrapy, read "Scrapy at a Glance" (*https://oreil.ly/8IYoe*) and the tutorial (*https://oreil.ly/4H_AW*).

BeautifulSoup

If you already have the HTML data from a website and just want to extract data from it, `BeautifulSoup` (*https://oreil.ly/c43mV*) is a good choice. HTML parsing is harder than it sounds. This is because much of the HTML on public web pages is technically invalid: unclosed tags, incorrect nesting, and other complications. If you try to write your own HTML parser by using regular expressions (discussed in "Text Strings: Regular Expressions" on page 230) you'll soon encounter these messes.

To install `BeautifulSoup`, type the following command (don't forget the final 4, or `pip` will try to install an older version and probably fail):

```
$ pip install beautifulsoup4
```

Now, let's use it to get all the links from a web page. The HTML `a` element represents a link, and `href` is its attribute representing the link destination. In Example 18-13, we'll define the function `get_links()` to do the grunt work, and a main program to get one or more URLs as command-line arguments.

Example 18-13. links.py

```python
def get_links(url):
    import requests
    from bs4 import BeautifulSoup as soup
    result = requests.get(url)
    page = result.text
    doc = soup(page)
    links = [element.get('href') for element in doc.find_all('a')]
    return links

if __name__ == '__main__':
    import sys
    for url in sys.argv[1:]:
        print('Links in', url)
        for num, link in enumerate(get_links(url), start=1):
```

```
        print(num, link)
    print()
```

I saved this program as *links.py* and then ran this command:

```
$ python links.py http://boingboing.net
```

Here are the first few lines that it printed:

```
Links in http://boingboing.net/
1 http://boingboing.net/suggest.html
2 http://boingboing.net/category/feature/
3 http://boingboing.net/category/review/
4 http://boingboing.net/category/podcasts
5 http://boingboing.net/category/video/
6 http://bbs.boingboing.net/
7 javascript:void(0)
8 http://shop.boingboing.net/
9 http://boingboing.net/about
10 http://boingboing.net/contact
```

Requests-HTML

Kenneth Reitz, the author of the popular web client package `requests`, has written a new scraping library called requests-html (*http://html.python-requests.org*) (for Python 3.6 and newer versions).

It gets a page and processes its elements, so you can find, for example, all of its links, or all the contents or attributes of any HTML element.

It has a clean design, similar to `requests` and other packages by the same author. Overall, it may be easier to use than `beautifulsoup` or Scrapy.

Let's Watch a Movie

Let's build a full program.

It searches for videos using an API at the Internet Archive.[5] This is one of the few APIs that allows anonymous access *and* should still be around after this book is printed.

 Most web APIs require you to first get an *API key*, and provide it every time you access that API. Why? It's the tragedy of the commons: free resources with anonymous access are often overused or abused. That's why we can't have nice things.

---

5 If you remember, I used another Archive API in the main example program we looked at in Chapter 1.

The following program shown in Example 18-14 does the following:

- Prompts you for part of a movie or video title
- Searches for it at the Internet Archive
- Returns a list of identifiers, names, and descriptions
- Lists them and asks you to select one
- Displays that video in your web browser

Save this as *iamovies.py*.

The `search()` function uses `requests` to access the URL, get the results, and convert them to JSON. The other functions handle everything else. You'll see usage of list comprehensions, string slices, and other things that you've seen in previous chapters. (The line numbers are not part of the source; they'll be used in the exercises to locate code pieces.)

Example 18-14. iamovies.py

```
1 """Find a video at the Internet Archive
2 by a partial title match and display it."""
3
4 import sys
5 import webbrowser
6 import requests
7
8 def search(title):
9     """Return a list of 3-item tuples (identifier,
10        title, description) about videos
11        whose titles partially match :title."""
12     search_url = "https://archive.org/advancedsearch.php"
13     params = {
14         "q": "title:({}) AND mediatype:(movies)".format(title),
15         "fl": "identifier,title,description",
16         "output": "json",
17         "rows": 10,
18         "page": 1,
19         }
20     resp = requests.get(search_url, params=params)
21     data = resp.json()
22     docs = [(doc["identifier"], doc["title"], doc["description"])
23             for doc in data["response"]["docs"]]
24     return docs
25
26 def choose(docs):
27     """Print line number, title and truncated description for
28        each tuple in :docs. Get the user to pick a line
29        number. If it's valid, return the first item in the
30        chosen tuple (the "identifier"). Otherwise, return None."""
```

```
31      last = len(docs) - 1
32      for num, doc in enumerate(docs):
33          print(f"{num}: ({doc[1]}) {doc[2][:30]}...")
34      index = input(f"Which would you like to see (0 to {last})? ")
35      try:
36          return docs[int(index)][0]
37      except:
38          return None
39
40  def display(identifier):
41      """Display the Archive video with :identifier in the browser"""
42      details_url = "https://archive.org/details/{}".format(identifier)
43      print("Loading", details_url)
44      webbrowser.open(details_url)
45
46  def main(title):
47      """Find any movies that match :title.
48         Get the user's choice and display it in the browser."""
49      identifiers = search(title)
50      if identifiers:
51          identifier = choose(identifiers)
52          if identifier:
53              display(identifier)
54          else:
55              print("Nothing selected")
56      else:
57          print("Nothing found for", title)
58
59  if __name__ == "__main__":
60      main(sys.argv[1])
```

Here's what I got when I ran this program and searched for **eegah**:[6]

```
$ python iamovies.py eegah
0: (Eegah) From IMDb : While driving thro...
1: (Eegah) This film has fallen into the ...
2: (Eegah) A caveman is discovered out in...
3: (Eegah (1962)) While driving through the dese...
4: (It's "Eegah" - Part 2) Wait till you see how this end...
5: (EEGAH trailer) The infamous modern-day cavema...
6: (It's "Eegah" - Part 1) Count Gore De Vol shares some ...
7: (Midnight Movie show: eegah) Arch Hall Jr...
Which would you like to see (0 to 7)? 2
Loading https://archive.org/details/Eegah
```

---

6 With Richard Kiel as the caveman, years before he was Jaws in a Bond movie.

It displayed the page in my browser, ready to run (Figure 18-2).

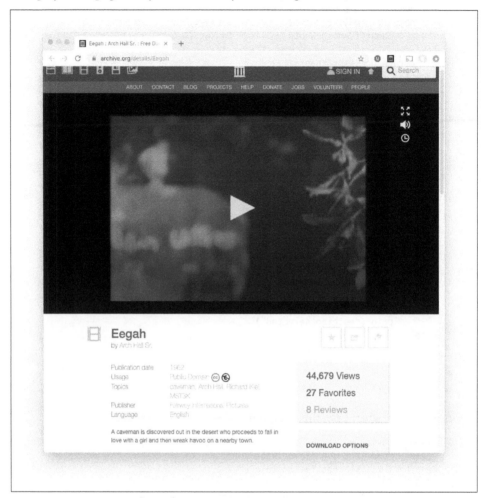

Figure 18-2. Movie search result

Coming Up

The next chapter is an extremely practical one, covering the nuts and bolts of modern Python development. Learn how to become a steely-eyed, card-carrying Pythonista.

Things to Do

18.1 If you haven't installed `flask` yet, do so now. This will also install `werkzeug`, `jinja2`, and possibly other packages.

18.2 Build a skeleton website, using Flask's debug/reload development web server. Ensure that the server starts up for hostname `localhost` on default port `5000`. If your computer is already using port 5000 for something else, use another port number.

18.3 Add a `home()` function to handle requests for the home page. Set it up to return the string `It's alive!`.

18.4 Create a Jinja2 template file called *home.html* with the following contents:

```
<html>
<head>
<title>It's alive!</title>
<body>
I'm of course referring to {{thing}}, which is {{height}} feet tall and {{color}}.
</body>
</html>
```

18.5 Modify your server's `home()` function to use the *home.html* template. Provide it with three GET parameters: `thing`, `height`, and `color`.

CHAPTER 19

Be a Pythonista

Always wanted to travel back in time to try fighting a younger version of yourself? Software development is the career for you!

—Elliot Loh (*http://bit.ly/loh-tweet*)

This chapter is devoted to the art and science of Python development, with "best practice" recommendations. Absorb them, and you too can be a card-carrying Pythonista.

About Programming

First, a few notes about programming, based on personal experience.

My original career path was science, and I taught myself programming to analyze and display experimental data. I expected computer programming to be like my impression of accounting—precise but dull. I was surprised to find that I enjoyed it. Part of the fun was its logical aspects—like solving puzzles—but part was creative. You had to write your program correctly to get the right results, but you had the freedom to write it any way you wanted. It was an unusual balance of right-brain and left-brain thinking.

After I wandered off into a career in programming, I also learned that the field had many niches, with very different tasks and types of people. You could delve into computer graphics, operating systems, business applications—even science.

If you're a programmer, you might have had a similar experience yourself. If you're not, you might try programming a bit to see if it fits your personality, or at least helps you to get something done. As I may have mentioned much earlier in this book, math skills are not so important. It seems that the ability to think logically is most important and that an aptitude for languages seems to help. Finally, patience also helps, especially when you're tracking down an elusive bug in your code.

Find Python Code

When you need to develop some code, the fastest solution is to steal it...from a source that allows it.

The Python standard library (*http://docs.python.org/3/library*) is wide, deep, and mostly clear. Dive in and look for those pearls.

Like the halls of fame for various sports, it takes time for a module to get into the standard library. New packages are appearing outside constantly, and throughout this book, I've highlighted some that either do something new or do something old better. Python is advertised as *batteries included*, but you might need a new kind of battery.

So where, outside the standard library, should you look for good Python code?

The first place to look is the Python Package Index (PyPI) (*https://pypi.org*). Formerly named the *Cheese Shop* after a Monty Python skit, this site is constantly updated with Python packages—more than 113,000 as I write this. When you use `pip` (see the next section), it searches PyPI. The main PyPI page shows the most recently added packages. You can also conduct a direct search by typing something into the search box in the middle of the PyPI home page. For example, `genealogy` yields 21 matches, and `movies` yields 528.

Another popular repository is GitHub. See what Python packages are currently trending (*https://github.com/trending?l=python*).

Popular Python recipes (*http://bit.ly/popular-recipes*) has more than four thousand short Python programs, on every subject.

Install Packages

There are many ways to install Python packages:

- Use `pip` if you can. It's the most common method by far. You can install most of the Python packages you're likely to encounter with `pip`.
- Use `pipenv`, which combines `pip` and `virtualenv`
- Sometimes, you can use a package manager for your operating system.
- Use `conda` if you do a lot of scientific work and want to use the Anaconda distribution of Python. See "Install Anaconda" on page 518 for details.
- Install from source.

If you're interested in several packages in the same area, you might find a Python distribution that already includes them. For instance, in Chapter 22, you can try out a number of numeric and scientific programs that would be tedious to install individually but are included with distributions such as Anaconda.

Use pip

Python packaging has had some limitations. An earlier installation tool called `easy_install` has been replaced by one called `pip`, but neither had been in the standard Python installation. If you're supposed to install things by using `pip`, from where did you get `pip`? Starting with Python 3.4, `pip` will finally be included with the rest of Python to avoid such existential crises. If you're using an earlier version of Python 3 and don't have `pip`, you can get it from *http://www.pip-installer.org*.

The simplest use of `pip` is to install the latest version of a single package by using the following command:

```
$ pip install flask
```

You will see details on what it's doing, just so you don't think it's goofing off: downloading, running *setup.py*, installing files on your disk, and other details.

You can also ask `pip` to install a specific version:

```
$ pip install flask==0.9.0
```

Or, a minimum version (this is useful when some feature that you can't live without turns up in a particular version):

```
$ pip install 'flask≥0.9.0'
```

In the preceding example, those single quotes prevent the > from being interpreted by the shell to redirect output to a file called =0.9.0.

If you want to install more than one Python package, you can use a requirements file (*http://bit.ly/pip-require*). Although it has many options, the simplest use is a list of packages, one per line, optionally with a specific or relative version:

```
$ pip -r requirements.txt
```

Your sample *requirements.txt* file might contain this:

```
flask==0.9.0
django
psycopg2
```

A few more examples:

- Install the latest version: `pip install --upgrade` *package*
- Delete a package: `pip uninstall` *package*

Use virtualenv

The standard way of installing third-party Python packages is to use `pip` and `virtualenv`. I show how to install `virtualenv` in "Install virtualenv" on page 517.

A *virtual environment* is just a directory that contains the Python interpreter, some other programs like `pip`, and some packages. You *activate* it by running the shell script `activate` that's in the `bin` directory of that virtual environment. This sets the environment variable `$PATH` that your shell uses to find programs. By activating a virtual enviroment, you put its `bin` directory ahead of the usual directories in your `$PATH`. The result is that when you type a command like `pip` or `python`, your shell first finds the one in your virtual environment, instead of system directories like `/bin`, `/usr/bin`, or `/usr/local/bin`.

You don't want to install software into those system directories anyhow, because:

- You don't have permission to write to them.
- Even if you could, overwriting your system's standard programs (like `python`) could cause problems.

Use pipenv

A recent package called pipenv (*http://docs.pipenv.org*) combines our friends `pip` and `virtualenv`. It also addresses dependency issues that can arise when using `pip` in different environments (such as your local development machine, versus staging, versus production):

```
$ pip install pipenv
```

Its use is recommended by the Python Packaging Authority (*https://www.pypa.io*)—a working group trying to improve Python's packaging workflow. This is not the same as the group that defines core Python itself, so `pipenv` is not a part of the standard library.

Use a Package Manager

Apple's macOS includes the third-party packagers homebrew (*http://brew.sh*) (brew) and ports (*http://www.macports.org*). They work a little like pip, but aren't restricted to Python packages.

Linux has a different manager for each distribution. The most popular are apt-get, yum, dpkg, and zypper.

Windows has the Windows Installer and package files with a *.msi* suffix. If you installed Python for Windows, it was probably in the MSI format.

Install from Source

Occasionally, a Python package is new, or the author hasn't managed to make it available with pip. To build the package, you generally do the following:

- Download the code.
- Extract the files by using zip, tar, or another appropriate tool if they're archived or compressed.
- Run python setup.py install in the directory containing a *setup.py* file.

As always, be careful what you download and install. It's a little harder to hide malware in Python programs, which are readable text, but it has happened.

Integrated Development Environments

I've used a plain-text interface for programs in this book, but that doesn't mean that you need to run everything in a console or text window. There are many free and commercial integrated development environments (IDEs), which are GUIs with support for such tools as text editors, debuggers, library searching, and so on.

IDLE

IDLE (*http://bit.ly/py-idle*) is the only Python IDE that's included with the standard distribution. It's based on tkinter, and its GUI is plain.

PyCharm

PyCharm (*http://www.jetbrains.com/pycharm*) is a recent graphic IDE with many features. The community edition is free, and you can get a free license for the

---

professional edition to use in a classroom or an open source project. Figure 19-1 shows its initial display.

Figure 19-1. Startup screen for PyCharm

IPython

iPython (*http://ipython.org*) started as an enhanced terminal (text) Python IDE, but evolved a graphical interface with the metaphor of a *notebook*. It integrated many packages that are discussed in this book, including Matplotlib and NumPy, and became a popular tool in scientific computing.

You install the basic text version with (you guessed it) `pip install ipython`. When you start it, you'll see something like this:

```
$ ipython
Python 3.7.3 (v3.7.3:ef4ec6ed12, Mar 25 2019, 16:39:00)
Type 'copyright', 'credits' or 'license' for more information
IPython 7.3.0 -- An enhanced Interactive Python. Type '?' for help.

In [1]:
```

As you know, the standard Python interpreter uses the input prompts >>> and ... to indicate where and when you should type code. IPython tracks everything you type in a list called In, and all your output in Out. Each input can be more than one line, so you submit it by holding the Shift key while pressing Enter.

Here's a one-line example:

```
In [1]: print("Hello? World?")
Hello? World?

In [2]:
```

In and Out are automatically numbered lists, letting you access any of the inputs you typed or outputs you received.

If you type ? after a variable, IPython tells you its type, value, ways of making a variable of that type, and some explanation:

```
In [4]: answer = 42

In [5]: answer?
Type:        int
String Form:42
Docstring:
int(x=0) -> integer
int(x, base=10) -> integer

Convert a number or string to an integer, or return 0 if no arguments
are given.  If x is a number, return x.__int__().  For floating point
numbers, this truncates towards zero.

If x is not a number or if base is given, then x must be a string,
bytes, or bytearray instance representing an integer literal in the
given base.  The literal can be preceded by '+' or '-' and be surrounded
by whitespace.  The base defaults to 10.  Valid bases are 0 and 2-36.
Base 0 means to interpret the base from the string as an integer literal.
>>> int('0b100', base=0)
4
```

Name lookup is a popular feature of IDEs such as IPython. If you press the Tab key right after some characters, IPython shows all variables, keywords, and functions that begin with those characters. Let's define some variables and then find everything that begins with the letter f:

```
In [6]: fee = 1

In [7]: fie = 2

In [8]: fo = 3

In [9]: fum = 4

In [10]: ftab
%%file    fie      finally   fo       format     frozenset
fee       filter   float     for      from       fum
```

If you type `fe` followed by the Tab key, it expands to the variable `fee`, which, in this program, is the only thing that starts with `fe`:

```
In [11]: fee
Out[11]: 1
```

There's much more to IPython. Take a look at its tutorial (*https://oreil.ly/PIvVK*) to get a feel for its features.

Jupyter Notebook

Jupyter (*https://jupyter.org*) is an evolution of IPython. The name combines the languages Julia, Python, and R—all of which are popular in data science and scientific computing. Jupyter Notebooks are a modern way to develop and publish your code with documentation for any of these languages.

If you'd like to play with it first before installing anything on your computer, you can first try it out (*https://jupyter.org/try*) in your web browser.

To install Jupyter Notebook locally, type `pip install jupyter`. Run it with `jupyter notebook`.

JupyterLab

JupyterLab is the next generation of Jupyter Notebook and will eventually replace it. As with the Notebook, you can first try out (*https://jupyter.org/try*) JupyterLab in your browser. You install it locally with `pip install jupyterlab` and then run it with `jupyter lab`.

Name and Document

You won't remember what you wrote. Sometimes, I look at code that I wrote even recently and wonder where on earth it came from. That's why it helps to document your code. Documentation can include comments and docstrings, but it can also incorporate informative naming of variables, functions, modules, and classes. Don't be obsessive, as in this example:

```
>>> # I'm going to assign 10 to the variable "num" here:
... num = 10
>>> # I hope that worked
... print(num)
10
>>> # Whew.
```

Instead, say *why* you assigned the value 10. Point out why you called the variable `num`. If you were writing the venerable Fahrenheit-to-Celsius converter, you might name variables to explain what they do rather than a lump of magic code. And a little test code wouldn't hurt (Example 19-1).

Example 19-1. ftoc1.py

```python
def ftoc(f_temp):
    "Convert Fahrenheit temperature <f_temp> to Celsius and return it."
    f_boil_temp = 212.0
    f_freeze_temp = 32.0
    c_boil_temp = 100.0
    c_freeze_temp = 0.0
    f_range = f_boil_temp - f_freeze_temp
    c_range = c_boil_temp - c_freeze_temp
    f_c_ratio = c_range / f_range
    c_temp = (f_temp - f_freeze_temp) * f_c_ratio + c_freeze_temp
    return c_temp

if __name__ == '__main__':
    for f_temp in [-40.0, 0.0, 32.0, 100.0, 212.0]:
        c_temp = ftoc(f_temp)
        print('%f F => %f C' % (f_temp, c_temp))
```

Let's run the tests:

```
$ python ftoc1.py
-40.000000 F => -40.000000 C
0.000000 F => -17.777778 C
32.000000 F => 0.000000 C
100.000000 F => 37.777778 C
212.000000 F => 100.000000 C
```

We can make (at least) two improvements:

- Python doesn't have constants, but the PEP8 stylesheet recommends (*http://bit.ly/pep-constant*) using capital letters and underscores (e.g., ALL_CAPS) when naming variables that should be considered constants. Let's rename those constant-y variables in our example.

- Because we precompute values based on constant values, let's move them to the top level of the module. Then, they'll be calculated only once rather than in every call to the ftoc() function.

Example 19-2 shows the result of our rework.

Example 19-2. ftoc2.py

```python
F_BOIL_TEMP = 212.0
F_FREEZE_TEMP = 32.0
C_BOIL_TEMP = 100.0
```

```
C_FREEZE_TEMP = 0.0
F_RANGE = F_BOIL_TEMP - F_FREEZE_TEMP
C_RANGE = C_BOIL_TEMP - C_FREEZE_TEMP
F_C_RATIO = C_RANGE / F_RANGE

def ftoc(f_temp):
    "Convert Fahrenheit temperature <f_temp> to Celsius and return it."
    c_temp = (f_temp - F_FREEZE_TEMP) * F_C_RATIO + C_FREEZE_TEMP
    return c_temp

if __name__ == '__main__':
    for f_temp in [-40.0, 0.0, 32.0, 100.0, 212.0]:
        c_temp = ftoc(f_temp)
        print('%f F => %f C' % (f_temp, c_temp))
```

Add Type Hints

Static languages require you to define the types of your variables, and they can catch some errors at compile time. As you know, Python doesn't do this, and you can encounter bugs only when the code is run. Python variables are names and only refer to actual objects. Objects have strict types, but names can point to any object at any time.

Yet in real code (in Python and other languages), a name tends to refer to a particular object. It would help, at least in documentation, if we could annotate things (variables, function returns, and so on) with the object types we expect them to be referencing. Then, developers would not need to look through as much code to see how a particular variable is supposed to act.

Python 3.x added *type hints* (or *type annotations*) to address this. It's completely optional, and does not force types on variables. It helps developers who are used to static languages, where variable types *must* be declared.

Hints for a function that converts a number to a string would look like this:

```
def num_to_str(num: int) -> str:
    return str(num)
```

These are only hints, and they don't change how Python works. Their main use is for documentation, but people are finding more uses. For example, the FastAPI (*https:// fastapi.tiangolo.com*) web framework uses hints to generate web documentation with live forms for testing.

Test

You probably already know this, but if not: even trivial code changes can break your program. Python lacks the type-checking of static languages, which makes some things easier but also lets undesirable results through the door. Testing is essential.

The very simplest way to test Python programs is to add `print()` statements. The Python interactive interpreter's Read-Evaluate-Print Loop (REPL) lets you edit and test changes quickly. However, you don't want `print()` statements in production code, so you need to remember to remove them all.

Check with pylint, pyflakes, flake8, or pep8

The next step, before creating actual test programs, is to run a Python code checker. The most popular are `pylint` (*http://www.pylint.org*) and `pyflakes` (*http://bit.ly/ pyflakes*). You can install either or both by using `pip`:

```
$ pip install pylint
$ pip install pyflakes
```

These check for actual code errors (such as referring to a variable before assigning it a value) and style faux pas (the code equivalent of wearing plaids and stripes). Example 19-3 is a fairly meaningless program with a bug and style issue.

Example 19-3. style1.py

```
a = 1
b = 2
print(a)
print(b)
print(c)
```

Here's the initial output of `pylint`:

```
$ pylint style1.py
No config file found, using default configuration
************* Module style1
C:  1,0: Missing docstring
C:  1,0: Invalid name "a" for type constant
    (should match (([A-Z_][A-Z0-9_]*)|(__.*__))$)
C:  2,0: Invalid name "b" for type constant
    (should match (([A-Z_][A-Z0-9_]*)|(__.*__))$)
E:  5,6: Undefined variable 'c'
```

Much further down, under `Global evaluation`, is our score (10.0 is perfect):

```
Your code has been rated at -3.33/10
```

Ouch. Let's fix the bug first. That `pylint` output line starting with an E indicates an `Error`, which occurred because we didn't assign a value to c before we printed it. Take a look at Example 19-4 to see how we can fix that.

Example 19-4. style2.py

```
a = 1
b = 2
c = 3
print(a)
print(b)
print(c)
```

```
$ pylint style2.py
No config file found, using default configuration
************* Module style2
C:  1,0: Missing docstring
C:  1,0: Invalid name "a" for type constant
    (should match (([A-Z_][A-Z0-9_]*)|(__.*__))$)
C:  2,0: Invalid name "b" for type constant
    (should match (([A-Z_][A-Z0-9_]*)|(__.*__))$)
C:  3,0: Invalid name "c" for type constant
    (should match (([A-Z_][A-Z0-9_]*)|(__.*__))$)
```

Good, no more E lines. And our score jumped from -3.33 to 4.29:

```
Your code has been rated at 4.29/10
```

pylint wants a docstring (a short text at the top of a module or function, describing the code), and it thinks short variable names such as a, b, and c are tacky. Let's make pylint happier and improve *style2.py* to *style3.py* (Example 19-5).

Example 19-5. style3.py

```
"Module docstring goes here"

def func():
    "Function docstring goes here. Hi, Mom!"
    first = 1
    second = 2
    third = 3
    print(first)
    print(second)
    print(third)

func()
```

```
$ pylint style3.py
No config file found, using default configuration
```

Hey, no complaints. And our score?

```
Your code has been rated at 10.00/10
```

And there was much rejoicing.

Another style checker is pep8 (*https://pypi.python.org/pypi/pep8*), which you can install in your sleep by now:

```
$ pip install pep8
```

What does it say about our style makeover?

```
$ pep8 style3.py
style3.py:3:1: E302 expected 2 blank lines, found 1
```

To be really stylish, it's recommending that I add a blank line after the initial module docstring.

Test with unittest

We've verified that we're no longer insulting the style senses of the code gods, so let's move on to actual tests of the logic in your program.

It's a good practice to write independent test programs first, to ensure that they all pass before you commit your code to any source control system. Writing tests can seem tedious at first, but they really do help you find problems faster—especially *regressions* (breaking something that used to work). Painful experience teaches all developers that even the teeniest change, which they swear could not possibly affect anything else, actually does. If you look at well-written Python packages, they always include a test suite.

The standard library contains not one, but two test packages. Let's start with uni ttest (*https://oreil.ly/ImFmE*). We'll write a module that capitalizes words. Our first version just uses the standard string function capitalize(), with some unexpected results as we'll see. Save this as *cap.py* (Example 19-6).

Example 19-6. cap.py

```
def just_do_it(text):
    return text.capitalize()
```

The basis of testing is to decide what outcome you want from a certain input (here, you want the capitalized version of whatever text you input), submit the input to the function you're testing, and then check whether it returned the expected results. The expected result is called an *assertion*, so in unittest you check your results by using methods with names that begin with assert, like the assertEqual method shown in Example 19-7.

Save this test script as *test_cap.py*.

Example 19-7. test_cap.py

```python
import unittest
import cap

class TestCap(unittest.TestCase):

    def setUp(self):
        pass

    def tearDown(self):
        pass

    def test_one_word(self):
        text = 'duck'
        result = cap.just_do_it(text)
        self.assertEqual(result, 'Duck')

    def test_multiple_words(self):
        text = 'a veritable flock of ducks'
        result = cap.just_do_it(text)
        self.assertEqual(result, 'A Veritable Flock Of Ducks')


if __name__ == '__main__':
    unittest.main()
```

The setUp() method is called before each test method, and the tearDown() method is called after each. Their purpose is to allocate and free external resources needed by the tests, such as a database connection or some test data. In this case, our tests are self-contained, and we wouldn't even need to define setUp() and tearDown(), but it doesn't hurt to have empty versions there. At the heart of our test are the two functions named test_one_word() and test_multiple_words(). Each runs the just_do_it() function we defined with different input and checks whether we got back what we expect. Okay, let's run it. This will call our two test methods:

```
$ python test_cap.py
F.
=======================================================================
FAIL: test_multiple_words (__main__.TestCap)
-----------------------------------------------------------------------
Traceback (most recent call last):
  File "test_cap.py", line 20, in test_multiple_words
  self.assertEqual(result, 'A Veritable Flock Of Ducks')
AssertionError: 'A veritable flock of ducks' != 'A Veritable Flock Of Ducks'
- A veritable flock of ducks
?   ^         ^    ^  ^
+ A Veritable Flock Of Ducks
?   ^         ^    ^  ^
```

```
    --------------------------------------------------------------
    Ran 2 tests in 0.001s

    FAILED (failures=1)
```

It liked the first test (test_one_word), but not the second (test_multiple_words). The up arrows (^) show where the strings actually differed.

What's special about multiple words? Reading the documentation for the string capi talize (*https://oreil.ly/x1IV8*) function yields an important clue: it capitalizes only the first letter of the first word. Maybe we should have read that first.

Consequently, we need another function. Gazing down that page a bit, we find title() (*https://oreil.ly/CNKNl*). So, let's change *cap.py* to use title() instead of cap italize() (Example 19-8).

Example 19-8. cap.py, revised

```python
def just_do_it(text):
    return text.title()
```

Rerun the tests, and let's see what happens:

```
$ python test_cap.py

..
--------------------------------------------------------------------
Ran 2 tests in 0.000s

OK
```

Everything is great. Well, actually, they're not. We need to add at least one more method to *test_cap.py* (Example 19-9).

Example 19-9. test_cap.py, revised

```python
    def test_words_with_apostrophes(self):
        text = "I'm fresh out of ideas"
        result = cap.just_do_it(text)
        self.assertEqual(result, "I'm Fresh Out Of Ideas")
```

Go ahead and try it again:

```
$ python test_cap.py

..F
============================================================================
FAIL: test_words_with_apostrophes (__main__.TestCap)
----------------------------------------------------------------------------
Traceback (most recent call last):
```

```
    File "test_cap.py", line 25, in test_words_with_apostrophes
      self.assertEqual(result, "I'm Fresh Out Of Ideas")
AssertionError: "I'M Fresh Out Of Ideas" != "I'm Fresh Out Of Ideas"
- I'M Fresh Out Of Ideas
?   ^
+ I'm Fresh Out Of Ideas
?   ^


----------------------------------------------------------------
Ran 3 tests in 0.001s

FAILED (failures=1)
```

Our function capitalized the m in I'm. A quick run back to the documentation for title() shows that it doesn't handle apostrophes well. We *really* should have read the entire text first.

At the bottom of the standard library's string documentation is another candidate: a helper function called capwords(). Let's use it in *cap.py* (Example 19-10).

Example 19-10. cap.py, re-revised

```
def just_do_it(text):
    from string import capwords
    return capwords(text)
```

```
$ python test_cap.py

...
-----------------------------------------------------------------
Ran 3 tests in 0.004s

OK
```

At last, we're finally done! Uh, no. We have one more test to add to *test_cap.py* (Example 19-11).

Example 19-11. test_cap.py, re-revised

```
def test_words_with_quotes(self):
    text = "\"You're despicable,\" said Daffy Duck"
    result = cap.just_do_it(text)
    self.assertEqual(result, "\"You're Despicable,\" Said Daffy Duck")
```

Did it work?

```
$ python test_cap.py

...F
================================================================
```

```
FAIL: test_words_with_quotes (__main__.TestCap)
-------------------------------------------------------------------------
Traceback (most recent call last):
  File "test_cap.py", line 30, in test_words_with_quotes
    self.assertEqual(result, "\"You're
    Despicable,\" Said Daffy Duck") AssertionError: '"you\'re Despicable,"
        Said Daffy Duck'
 != '"You\'re Despicable," Said Daffy Duck' - "you're Despicable,"
        Said Daffy Duck
 ?   ^ + "You're Despicable," Said Daffy Duck
 ?   ^
-------------------------------------------------------------------------
Ran 4 tests in 0.004s

FAILED (failures=1)
```

It looks like that first double quote confused even capwords, our favorite capitalizer thus far. It tried to capitalize the ", and lowercased the rest (You're). We should have also tested that our capitalizer left the rest of the string untouched.

People who do testing for a living have a knack for spotting these edge cases, but developers often have blind spots when it comes to their own code.

unittest provides a small but powerful set of assertions, letting you check values, confirm whether you have the class you want, determine whether an error was raised, and so on.

Test with doctest

The second test package in the standard library is doctest (*http://bit.ly/py-doctest*). With this package, you can write tests within the docstring itself, also serving as documentation. It looks like the interactive interpreter: the characters >>>, followed by the call, and then the results on the following line. You can run some tests in the interactive interpreter and just paste the results into your test file. Let's modify our old *cap.py* as *cap2.py* (without that troublesome last test with quotes), as shown in Example 19-12.

Example 19-12. cap2.py

```
def just_do_it(text):
    """
    >>> just_do_it('duck')
    'Duck'
    >>> just_do_it('a veritable flock of ducks')
    'A Veritable Flock Of Ducks'
    >>> just_do_it("I'm fresh out of ideas")
    "I'm Fresh Out Of Ideas"
    """
    from string import capwords
```

```
    return capwords(text)

if __name__ == '__main__':
    import doctest
    doctest.testmod()
```

When you run it, it doesn't print anything if all tests passed:

```
$ python cap2.py
```

Give it the verbose (-v) option to see what actually happened:

```
$ python cap2.py -v
Trying:
    just_do_it('duck')
Expecting:
    'Duck'
ok
Trying:
    just_do_it('a veritable flock of ducks')
Expecting:
    'A Veritable Flock Of Ducks'
ok
Trying:
    just_do_it("I'm fresh out of ideas")
Expecting:
    "I'm Fresh Out Of Ideas"
ok
1 items had no tests:
    __main__
1 items passed all tests:
    3 tests in __main__.just_do_it
3 tests in 2 items.
3 passed and 0 failed.
Test passed.
```

Test with nose

The third-party package called nose (*https://oreil.ly/gWK6r*) is another alternative to
unittest. Here's the command to install it:

```
$ pip install nose
```

You don't need to create a class that includes test methods, as we did with unittest.
Any function with a name matching test somewhere in its name will be run. Let's
modify our last version of our unittest tester and save it as *test_cap_nose.py*
(Example 19-13).

Example 19-13. test_cap_nose.py

```
import cap2
from nose.tools import eq_

def test_one_word():
    text = 'duck'
    result = cap.just_do_it(text)
    eq_(result, 'Duck')

def test_multiple_words():
    text = 'a veritable flock of ducks'
    result = cap.just_do_it(text)
    eq_(result, 'A Veritable Flock Of Ducks')

def test_words_with_apostrophes():
    text = "I'm fresh out of ideas"
    result = cap.just_do_it(text)
    eq_(result, "I'm Fresh Out Of Ideas")

def test_words_with_quotes():
    text = "\"You're despicable,\" said Daffy Duck"
    result = cap.just_do_it(text)
    eq_(result, "\"You're Despicable,\" Said Daffy Duck")
```

Run the tests:

```
$ nosetests test_cap_nose.py
...F
======================================================================
FAIL: test_cap_nose.test_words_with_quotes
----------------------------------------------------------------------
Traceback (most recent call last):
  File "/Users/.../site-packages/nose/case.py", line 198, in runTest
    self.test(*self.arg)
  File "/Users/.../book/test_cap_nose.py", line 23, in test_words_with_quotes
    eq_(result, "\"You're Despicable,\" Said Daffy Duck")
AssertionError: '"you\'re Despicable," Said Daffy Duck'        !=
'"You\'re Despicable," Said Daffy Duck'
----------------------------------------------------------------------
Ran 4 tests in 0.005s

FAILED (failures=1)
```

This is the same bug we found when we used `unittest` for testing; fortunately, there's an exercise to fix it at the end of this chapter.

Other Test Frameworks

For some reason, people like to write Python test frameworks. If you're curious, you can check out some other popular ones:

- `tox` (*http://tox.readthedocs.org*)
- `py.test` (*https://pytest.org*)
- `green` (*https://github.com/CleanCut/green*)

Continuous Integration

When your group is cranking out a lot of code daily, it helps to automate tests as soon as changes arrive. You can automate source control systems to run tests on all code as it's checked in. This way, everyone knows whether someone *broke the build* and just disappeared for an early lunch—or a new job.

These are big systems, and I'm not going into installation and usage details here. In case you need them someday, you'll know where to find them:

`buildbot` (*http://buildbot.net*)
> Written in Python, this source control system automates building, testing, and releasing.

`jenkins` (*http://jenkins-ci.org*)
> This is written in Java, and seems to be the preferred CI tool of the moment.

`travis-ci` (*http://travis-ci.com*)
> This automates projects hosted at GitHub, and is free for open source projects.

`circleci` (*https://circleci.com*)
> This one is commercial but free for open source and private projects.

Debug Python Code

> Debugging is like being the detective in a crime movie where you are also the murderer.
>
> —Filipe Fortes

> Everyone knows that debugging is twice as hard as writing a program in the first place. So if you're as clever as you can be when you write it, how will you ever debug it?
>
> —Brian Kernighan

Test first. The better your tests are, the less you'll have to fix later. Yet, bugs happen and need to be fixed when they're found later.

When code breaks, it's usually because of something you just did. So you typically debug "from the bottom up," starting with your most recent changes.[1]

But sometimes the cause is elsewhere, in something that you trusted and thought worked. You would think that if there were problems in something that many people use, someone would have noticed by now. That is not always what happens. The trickiest bugs that I've encountered, that each took more than a week to fix, had external causes. So after blaming the person in the mirror, question your assumptions. This is a "top-down" approach, and it takes longer.

The following are some debugging techniques, from quick and dirty to slower, but often just as dirty.

Use print()

The simplest way to debug in Python is to print out strings. Some useful things to print include `vars()`, which extracts the values of your local variables, including function arguments:

```
>>> def func(*args, **kwargs):
...     print(vars())
...
>>> func(1, 2, 3)
{'args': (1, 2, 3), 'kwargs': {}}
>>> func(['a', 'b', 'argh'])
{'args': (['a', 'b', 'argh'],), 'kwargs': {}}
```

Other things that are often worth printing are `locals()` and `globals()`.

If your code also includes normal prints to standard output, you can write your debugging messages to standard error output with `print(`*stuff,*` file=sys.stderr)`.

Use Decorators

As you read in "Decorators" on page 159, a decorator can call code before or after a function without modifying the code within the function itself. This means that you can use a decorator to do something before or after any Python function, not just ones that you wrote. Let's define the decorator `dump` to print the input arguments and output values of any function as it's called (designers know that a dump often needs decorating), as shown in Example 19-14.

---

1 You, as the detective: "I know I'm in there! And if I don't come out with my hands up, I'm coming in after me!"

Example 19-14. dump.py

```
def dump(func):
    "Print input arguments and output value(s)"
    def wrapped(*args, **kwargs):
        print("Function name:", func.__name__)
        print("Input arguments:", ' '.join(map(str, args)))
        print("Input keyword arguments:", kwargs.items())
        output = func(*args, **kwargs)
        print("Output:", output)
        return output
    return wrapped
```

Now the decoratee. This is a function called double() that expects numeric arguments, either named or unnamed, and returns them in a list with their values doubled (Example 19-15).

Example 19-15. test_dump.py

```
from dump import dump

@dump
def double(*args, **kwargs):
    "Double every argument"
    output_list = [ 2 * arg for arg in args ]
    output_dict =  { k:2*v for k,v in kwargs.items() }
    return output_list, output_dict

if __name__ == '__main__':
    output = double(3, 5, first=100, next=98.6, last=-40)
```

Take a moment to run it:

```
$ python test_dump.py
Function name: double
Input arguments: 3 5
Input keyword arguments: dict_items([('first', 100), ('next', 98.6),
    ('last', -40)])
Output: ([6, 10], {'first': 200, 'next': 197.2, 'last': -80})
```

Use pdb

These techniques help, but sometimes there's no substitute for a real debugger. Most IDEs include a debugger, with varying features and user interfaces. Here, I describe use of the standard Python debugger, pdb (*https://oreil.ly/IIN4y*).

If you run your program with the -i flag, Python will drop you into its interactive interpreter if the program fails.

Here's a program with a bug that depends on data—the kind of bug that can be particularly hard to find. This is a real bug from the early days of computing, and it baffled programmers for quite a while.

We're going to read a file of countries and their capital cities, separated by a comma, and write them out as *capital, country*. They might be capitalized incorrectly, so we should fix that also when we print. Oh, and there might be extra spaces here and there, and you'll want to get rid of those, too. Finally, although it would make sense for the program to just read to the end of the file, for some reason our manager told us to stop when we encounter the word quit (in any mixture of uppercase and lowercase characters). Example 19-16 shows a sample data file.

Example 19-16. cities.csv

```
France, Paris
venuzuela,caracas
  LithuaniA,vilnius
     quit
```

Let's design our *algorithm* (method for solving the problem). This is *pseudocode*—it looks like a program, but is just a way to explain the logic in normal language before converting it to an actual program. One reason programmers like Python is because it *looks a lot like pseudocode*, so there's less work involved when it's time to convert it to a working program:

```
for each line in the text file:
    read the line
    strip leading and trailing spaces
    if `quit` occurs in the lower-case copy of the line:
        stop
    else:
        split the country and capital by the comma character
        trim any leading and trailing spaces
        convert the country and capital to titlecase
        print the capital, a comma, and the country
```

We need to strip initial and trailing spaces from the names because that was a requirement. Likewise for the lowercase comparison with quit and converting the city and country names to title case. That being the case, let's whip out *capitals.py*, which is sure to work perfectly (Example 19-17).

Example 19-17. capitals.py

```python
def process_cities(filename):
    with open(filename, 'rt') as file:
        for line in file:
            line = line.strip()
            if 'quit' in line.lower():
                return
            country, city = line.split(',')
            city = city.strip()
            country = country.strip()
            print(city.title(), country.title(), sep=',')

if __name__ == '__main__':
    import sys
    process_cities(sys.argv[1])
```

Let's try it with that sample data file we made earlier. Ready, fire, aim:

```
$ python capitals.py cities.csv
Paris,France
Caracas,Venuzuela
Vilnius,Lithuania
```

Looks great! It passed one test, so let's put it in production, processing capitals and countries from around the world—until it fails, but only for this data file (Example 19-18).

Example 19-18. cities2.csv

```
argentina,buenos aires
bolivia,la paz
brazil,brasilia
chile,santiago
colombia,Bogotá
ecuador,quito
falkland islands,stanley
french guiana,cayenne
guyana,georgetown
paraguay,Asunción
peru,lima
suriname,paramaribo
uruguay,montevideo
venezuela,caracas
quit
```

The program ends after printing only 5 lines of the 15 in the data file, as demonstrated here:

```
$ python capitals.py cities2.csv
Buenos Aires,Argentina
```

```
La Paz,Bolivia
Brazilia,Brazil
Santiago,Chile
Bogotá,Colombia
```

What happened? We can keep editing *capitals.py*, putting `print()` statements in likely places, but let's see if the debugger can help us.

To use the debugger, import the `pdb` module from the command line by typing `-m` **pdb**, like so:

```
$ python -m pdb capitals.py cities2.csv
> /Users/williamlubanovic/book/capitals.py(1)<module>()
-> def process_cities(filename):
(Pdb)
```

This starts the program and places you at the first line. If you type **c** (*continue*), the program will run until it ends, either normally or with an error:

```
(Pdb) c
Buenos Aires,Argentina
La Paz,Bolivia
Brazilia,Brazil
Santiago,Chile
Bogotá,Colombia
The program finished and will be restarted
> /Users/williamlubanovic/book/capitals.py(1)<module>()
-> def process_cities(filename):
```

It completed normally, just as it did when we ran it earlier outside of the debugger. Let's try again, using some commands to narrow down where the problem lies. It seems to be a *logic error* rather than a syntax problem or exception (which would have printed error messages).

Type **s** (*step*) to single-step through Python lines. This steps through *all* Python code lines: yours, the standard library's, and any other modules you might be using. When you use s, you also go into functions and single-step within them. Type **n** (*next*) to single-step but *not* to go inside functions; when you get to a function, a single n causes the entire function to execute and take you to the next line of your program. Thus, use s when you're not sure where the problem is; use n when you're sure that a particular function isn't the cause, especially if it's a long function. Often you'll single-step through your own code and step over library code, which is presumably well tested. Let's use s to step from the beginning of the program into the function `process_cities()`:

```
(Pdb) s
> /Users/williamlubanovic/book/capitals.py(12)<module>()
  -> if __name__ == '__main__':</pre>
```

```
(Pdb) s

 > /Users/williamlubanovic/book/capitals.py(13)<module>()
 -> import sys

(Pdb) s

 > /Users/williamlubanovic/book/capitals.py(14)<module>()
 -> process_cities(sys.argv[1])

(Pdb) s

 --Call--
 > /Users/williamlubanovic/book/capitals.py(1)process_cities()
 -> def process_cities(filename):

(Pdb) s

 > /Users/williamlubanovic/book/capitals.py(2)process_cities()
 -> with open(filename, 'rt') as file:
```

Type **l** (*list*) to see the next few lines of your program:

```
(Pdb) l
  1        def process_cities(filename):
  2   ->       with open(filename, 'rt') as file:
  3                for line in file:
  4                    line = line.strip()
  5                    if 'quit' in line.lower():
  6                        return
  7                    country, city = line.split(',')
  8                    city = city.strip()
  9                    country = country.strip()
 10                    print(city.title(), country.title(), sep=',')
 11
(Pdb)
```

The arrow (->) denotes the current line.

We could continue using s or n, hoping to spot something, but let's use one of the main features of a debugger: *breakpoints*. A breakpoint stops execution at the line you indicate. In our case, we want to know why process_cities() bails out before it's read all of the input lines. Line 3 (for line in file:) will read every line in the input file, so that seems innocent. The only other place where we could return from the function before reading all of the data is at line 6 (return). Let's set a breakpoint on line 6:

```
(Pdb) b 6

Breakpoint 1 at /Users/williamlubanovic/book/capitals.py:6
```

Next, let's continue the program until it either hits the breakpoint or reads all of the input lines and finishes normally:

```
(Pdb) c
Buenos Aires,Argentina
La Paz,Bolivia
Brasilia,Brazil
Santiago,Chile
Bogotá,Colombia
> /Users/williamlubanovic/book/capitals.py(6)process_cities()
-> return
```

Aha! It stopped at our line 6 breakpoint. This indicates that the program wants to return early after reading the country after Colombia. Let's print the value of line to see what we just read:

```
(Pdb) p line
'ecuador,quito'
```

What's so special about—oh, never mind.

Really? **quit**o? Our manager never expected the string quit to turn up inside normal data, so using it as a *sentinel* (end indicator) value like this was a boneheaded idea. You march right in there and tell him that—while I wait here.

If at this point you still have a job, you can see all your breakpoints by using a plain b command:

```
(Pdb) b
Num Type         Disp Enb   Where
1   breakpoint   keep yes   at /Users/williamlubanovic/book/capitals.py:6
        breakpoint already hit 1 time
```

An l will show your code lines, the current line (->), and any breakpoints (B). A plain l will start listing from the end of your previous call to l, so include the optional starting line (here, let's start from line 1):

```
(Pdb) l 1
  1         def process_cities(filename):
  2             with open(filename, 'rt') as file:
  3                 for line in file:
  4                     line = line.strip()
  5                     if 'quit' in line.lower():
  6 B->                     return
  7                     country, city = line.split(',')
  8                     city = city.strip()
  9                     country = country.strip()
 10                     print(city.title(), country.title(), sep=',')
 11
```

OK, as shown in Example 19-19, let's fix that quit test to match only the full line, not within other characters.

Example 19-19. capitals2.py

```python
def process_cities(filename):
    with open(filename, 'rt') as file:
        for line in file:
            line = line.strip()
            if 'quit' == line.lower():
                return
            country, city = line.split(',')
            city = city.strip()
            country = country.strip()
            print(city.title(), country.title(), sep=',')

if __name__ == '__main__':
    import sys
    process_cities(sys.argv[1])
```

Once more, with feeling:

```
$ python capitals2.py cities2.csv

Buenos Aires,Argentina
La Paz,Bolivia
Brasilia,Brazil
Santiago,Chile
Bogotá,Colombia
Quito,Ecuador
Stanley,Falkland Islands
Cayenne,French Guiana
Georgetown,Guyana
Asunción,Paraguay
Lima,Peru
Paramaribo,Suriname
Montevideo,Uruguay
Caracas,Venezuela
```

That was a skimpy overview of the debugger—just enough to show you what it can do and what commands you'd use most of the time.

Remember: more tests, less debugging.

Use breakpoint()

In Python 3.7, there's a new built-in function called breakpoint(). If you add it to your code, a debugger will automatically start up and pause at each location. Without this, you would need to fire up a debugger like pdb and set breakpoints manually, as you saw earlier.

The default debugger is the one you've just seen (pdb), but this can be changed by setting the environment variable `PYTHONBREAKPOINT`. For example, you could specify use of the web-based remote debugger web-pdb (*https://pypi.org/project/web-pdb*):

```
$ export PYTHONBREAKPOINT='web_pdb.set_trace'
```

The official documentation is a bit dry, but there are good overviews here (*https://oreil.ly/9Q9MZ*) and there (*https://oreil.ly/2LJKy*).

Log Error Messages

At some point you might need to graduate from using `print()` statements to logging messages. A log is usually a system file that accumulates messages, often inserting useful information such as a timestamp or the name of the user who's running the program. Often logs are *rotated* (renamed) daily and compressed; by doing so, they don't fill up your disk and cause problems themselves. When something goes wrong with your program, you can look at the appropriate log file to see what happened. The contents of exceptions are especially useful in logs because they show you the actual line at which your program croaked, and why.

The standard Python library module is `logging` (*http://bit.ly/py-logging*). I've found most descriptions of it somewhat confusing. After a while it makes more sense, but it does seem overly complicated at first. The `logging` module includes these concepts:

- The *message* that you want to save to the log
- Ranked priority *levels* and matching functions: `debug()`, `info()`, `warn()`, `error()`, and `critical()`
- One or more *logger* objects as the main connection with the module
- *Handlers* that direct the message to your terminal, a file, a database, or somewhere else
- *Formatters* that create the output
- *Filters* that make decisions based on the input

For the simplest logging example, just import the module and use some of its functions:

```
>>> import logging
>>> logging.debug("Looks like rain")
>>> logging.info("And hail")
>>> logging.warn("Did I hear thunder?")
WARNING:root:Did I hear thunder?
>>> logging.error("Was that lightning?")
ERROR:root:Was that lightning?
>>> logging.critical("Stop fencing and get inside!")
CRITICAL:root:Stop fencing and get inside!
```

Did you notice that debug() and info() didn't do anything, and the other two printed *LEVEL*:root: before each message? So far, it's like a print() statement with multiple personalities, some of them hostile.

But it is useful. You can scan for a particular value of *LEVEL* in a log file to find particular messages, compare timestamps to see what happened before your server crashed, and so on.

A lot of digging through the documentation answers the first mystery (we get to the second one in a page or two): the default priority *level* is WARNING, and that got locked in as soon as we called the first function (logging.debug()). We can set the default level by using basicConfig(). DEBUG is the lowest level, so this enables it and all the higher levels to flow through:

```
>>> import logging
>>> logging.basicConfig(level=logging.DEBUG)
>>> logging.debug("It's raining again")
DEBUG:root:It's raining again
>>> logging.info("With hail the size of hailstones")
INFO:root:With hail the size of hailstones
```

We did all that with the default logging functions without actually creating a *logger* object. Each logger has a name. Let's make one called bunyan:

```
>>> import logging
>>> logging.basicConfig(level='DEBUG')
>>> logger = logging.getLogger('bunyan')
>>> logger.debug('Timber!')
DEBUG:bunyan:Timber!
```

If the logger name contains any dot characters, they separate levels of a hierarchy of loggers, each with potentially different properties. This means that a logger named quark is higher than one named quark.charmed. The special *root logger* is at the top and is called ' '.

So far, we've just printed messages, which is not a great improvement over print(). We use *handlers* to direct the messages to different places. The most common is a *log file*, and here's how you do it:

```
>>> import logging
>>> logging.basicConfig(level='DEBUG', filename='blue_ox.log')
>>> logger = logging.getLogger('bunyan')
>>> logger.debug("Where's my axe?")
>>> logger.warn("I need my axe")
>>>
```

Aha! The lines aren't on the screen anymore; instead, they're in the file named *blue_ox.log*:

```
DEBUG:bunyan:Where's my axe?
WARNING:bunyan:I need my axe
```

Calling basicConfig() with a filename argument created a FileHandler for you and made it available to your logger. The logging module includes at least 15 handlers to send messages to places such as email and web servers as well as the screen and files.

Finally, you can control the *format* of your logged messages. In our first example, our default gave us something similar to this:

```
WARNING:root:Message...
```

If you provide a format string to basicConfig(), you can change to the format of your preference:

```
>>> import logging
>>> fmt = '%(asctime)s %(levelname)s %(lineno)s %(message)s'
>>> logging.basicConfig(level='DEBUG', format=fmt)
>>> logger = logging.getLogger('bunyan')
>>> logger.error("Where's my other plaid shirt?")
2014-04-08 23:13:59,899 ERROR 1 Where's my other plaid shirt?
```

We let the logger send output to the screen again, but changed the format.

The logging module recognizes a number of variable names in the fmt format string. We used asctime (date and time as an ISO 8601 string), levelname, lineno (line number), and the message itself. There are other built-ins, and you can provide your own variables, as well.

There's much more to logging than this little overview can provide. You can log to more than one place at the same time, with different priorities and formats. The package has a lot of flexibility but sometimes at the cost of simplicity.

Optimize

Python is usually fast enough—until it isn't. In many cases, you can gain speed by using a better algorithm or data structure. The trick is knowing where to do this. Even experienced programmers guess wrong surprisingly often. You need to be like the careful quiltmaker and measure before you cut. And this leads us to *timers*.

Measure Timing

You've seen that the time() function in the time module returns the current epoch time as a floating-point number of seconds. A quick way of timing something is to get the current time, do something, get the new time, and then subtract the original time from the new time. Let's write this up, as presented in Example 19-20, and call it (what else?) *time1.py*.

Example 19-20. time1.py

```
from time import time

t1 = time()
num = 5
num *= 2
print(time() - t1)
```

In this example, we're measuring the time it takes to assign the value 5 to the name num and multiply it by 2. This is *not* a realistic benchmark, just an example of how to measure some arbitrary Python code. Try running it a few times, just to see how much it can vary:

```
$ python time1.py
2.1457672119140625e-06
$ python time1.py
2.1457672119140625e-06
$ python time1.py
2.1457672119140625e-06
$ python time1.py
1.9073486328125e-06
$ python time1.py
3.0994415283203125e-06
```

That was about two or three millionths of a second. Let's try something slower, such as sleep().[2] If we sleep for a second, our timer should take a tiny bit more than a second. Example 19-21 shows the code; save this as *time2.py*.

Example 19-21. time2.py

```
from time import time, sleep

t1 = time()
sleep(1.0)
print(time() - t1)
```

Let's be certain of our results, so run it a few times:

```
$ python time2.py
1.000797986984253
$ python time2.py
1.0010130405426025
$ python time2.py
1.0010390281677246
```

---

2 Many computer books use Fibonacci number calculations in timing examples, but I'd rather sleep than calculate Fibonacci numbers.

As expected, it takes about a second to run. If it didn't, either our timer or `sleep()` should be embarrassed.

There's a handier way to measure code snippets like this: using the standard module `timeit` (*http://bit.ly/py-timeit*). It has a function called (you guessed it) `timeit()`, which will do *count* runs of your test *code* and print some results. The syntax is: `timeit.timeit(`*code*, number=*count*`)`.

In the examples in this section, the `code` needs to be within quotes so that it is not executed after you press the Return key but is executed inside `timeit()`. (In the next section, you'll see how to time a function by passing its name to `timeit()`.) Let's run our previous example just once and time it. Call this file *timeit1.py* (Example 19-22).

Example 19-22. timeit1.py

```
from timeit import timeit
print(timeit('num = 5; num *= 2', number=1))
```

Run it a few times:

```
$ python timeit1.py
2.5600020308047533e-06
$ python timeit1.py
1.9020008039660752e-06
$ python timeit1.py
1.7380007193423808e-06
```

Again, these two code lines ran in about two millionths of a second. We can use the `repeat` argument of the `timeit` module's `repeat()` function to run more sets. Save this as *timeit2.py* (Example 19-23).

Example 19-23. timeit2.py

```
from timeit import repeat
print(repeat('num = 5; num *= 2', number=1, repeat=3))
```

Try running it to see what transpires:

```
$ python timeit2.py
[1.691998477326706e-06, 4.070025170221925e-07, 2.4700057110749185e-07]
```

The first run took two millionths of a second, and the second and third runs were faster. Why? There could be many reasons. For one thing, we're testing a very small piece of code, and its speed could depend on what else the computer was doing in those instants, how the Python system optimizes calculations, and many other things.

Using `timeit()` meant wrapping the code you're trying to measure as a string. What if you have multiple lines of code? You could pass it a triple-quoted multiline string, but that might be hard to read.

Let's define a lazy `snooze()` function that nods off for a second, as we all do occasionally.

First, we can wrap the `snooze()` function itself. We need to include the arguments `globals=globals()` (this helps Python to find snooze) and `number=1` (run it only once; the default is 1000000, and we don't have that much time):

```
>>> import time
>>> from timeit import timeit
>>>
>>> def snooze():
...     time.sleep(1)
...
>>> seconds = timeit('snooze()', globals=globals(), number=1)
>>> print("%.4f" % seconds)
1.0035
```

Or, we can use a decorator:

```
>>> import time
>>>
>>> def snooze():
...     time.sleep(1)
...
>>> def time_decorator(func):
...     def inner(*args, **kwargs):
...         t1 = time.time()
...         result = func(*args, **kwargs)
...         t2 = time.time()
...         print(f"{(t2-t1):.4f}")
...         return result
...     return inner
...
>>> @time_decorator
... def naptime():
...     snooze()
...
>>> naptime()
1.0015
```

Another way is to use a context manager:

```
>>> import time
>>>
>>> def snooze():
...     time.sleep(1)
...
>>> class TimeContextManager:
...     def __enter__(self):
```

```
...              self.t1 = time.time()
...              return self
...       def __exit__(self, type, value, traceback):
...              t2 = time.time()
...              print(f"{(t2-self.t1):.4f}")
...
>>>
>>> with TimeContextManager():
...       snooze()
...
1.0019
```

The __exit()__ method takes three extra arguments that we don't use here; we could
have used *args in their place.

Okay, we've seen many ways to do timing. Now, let's time some code to compare the
efficiency of different algorithms (program logic) and data structures (storage
mechanisms).

Algorithms and Data Structures

The Zen of Python (*http://bit.ly/zen-py*) declares that *There should be one—and pref-
erably only one—obvious way to do it.* Unfortunately, sometimes it isn't obvious, and
you need to compare alternatives. For example, is it better to use a for loop or a list
comprehension to build a list? And what do we mean by *better*? Is it faster, easier to
understand, using less memory, or more "Pythonic"?

In this next exercise, we build a list in different ways, comparing speed, readability,
and Python style. Here's *time_lists.py* (Example 19-24).

Example 19-24. time_lists.py

```
from timeit import timeit

def make_list_1():
    result = []
    for value in range(1000):
        result.append(value)
    return result

def make_list_2():
    result = [value for value in range(1000)]
    return result

print('make_list_1 takes', timeit(make_list_1, number=1000), 'seconds')
print('make_list_2 takes', timeit(make_list_2, number=1000), 'seconds')
```

In each function, we add 1,000 items to a list, and we call each function 1,000 times. Notice that in this test we called `timeit()` with the function name as the first argument rather than code as a string. Let's run it:

```
$ python time_lists.py

make_list_1 takes 0.14117428699682932 seconds
make_list_2 takes 0.06174145900149597 seconds
```

The list comprehension is at least twice as fast as adding items to the list by using `append()`. In general, comprehensions are faster than manual construction.

Use these ideas to make your own code faster.

Cython, NumPy, and C Extensions

If you're pushing Python as hard as you can and still can't get the performance you want, you have yet more options.

Cython (*http://cython.org*) is a hybrid of Python and C, designed to translate Python with some performance annotations to compiled C code. These annotations are fairly small, like declaring the types of some variables, function arguments, or function returns. For scientific-style loops of numeric calculations, adding these hints will make them much faster—as much as a thousand times faster. See the Cython wiki (*https://oreil.ly/MmW_v*) for documentation and examples.

You can read much more about NumPy in Chapter 22. It's a Python math library, written in C for speed.

Many parts of Python and its standard library are written in C for speed and wrapped in Python for convenience. These hooks are available to you for your applications. If you know C and Python and really want to make your code fly, writing a C extension is harder, but the improvements can be worth the trouble.

PyPy

When Java first appeared about 20 years ago, it was as slow as an arthritic Schnauzer. When it started to mean real money to Sun and other companies, though, they put millions into optimizing the Java interpreter and the underlying Java virtual machine (JVM), borrowing techniques from earlier languages like Smalltalk and LISP. Microsoft likewise put great effort into optimizing its rival C# language and .NET VM.

No one owns Python, so no one has pushed that hard to make it faster. You're probably using the standard Python implementation. It's written in C, and often called CPython (not the same as Cython).

Like PHP, Perl, and even Java, Python is not compiled to machine language, but translated to an intermediate language (with names such as *bytecode* or p-code) which is then interpreted in a *virtual machine*.

PyPy (*http://pypy.org*) is a new Python interpreter that applies some of the tricks that sped up Java. Its benchmarks (*http://speed.pypy.org*) show that PyPy is faster than CPython in every test—more than six times faster on average, and up to 20 times faster in some cases. It works with Python 2 and 3. You can download it and use it instead of CPython. PyPy is constantly being improved, and it might even replace CPython some day. Read the latest release notes on the site to see whether it could work for your purposes.

Numba

You can use Numba (*http://numba.pydata.org*) to compile your Python code on the fly to machine code and speed it up.

Install with the usual:

```
$ pip install numba
```

Let's first time a normal Python function that calculates a hypotenuse:

```
>>> import math
>>> from timeit import timeit
>>> from numba import jit
>>>
>>> def hypot(a, b):
...     return math.sqrt(a**2 + b**2)
...
>>> timeit('hypot(5, 6)', globals=globals())
0.6349189280000189
>>> timeit('hypot(5, 6)', globals=globals())
0.6348589239999853
```

Use the @jit decorator to speed up calls after the first:

```
>>> @jit
... def hypot_jit(a, b):
...     return math.sqrt(a**2 + b**2)
...
>>> timeit('hypot_jit(5, 6)', globals=globals())
0.5396156099999985
>>> timeit('hypot_jit(5, 6)', globals=globals())
0.1534771130000081
```

Use @jit(nopython=True) to avoid the overhead of the normal Python interpreter:

```
>>> @jit(nopython=True)
... def hypot_jit_nopy(a, b):
...     return math.sqrt(a**2 + b**2)
...
```

```
>>> timeit('hypot_jit_nopy(5, 6)', globals=globals())
0.18343535700000757
>>> timeit('hypot_jit_nopy(5, 6)', globals=globals())
0.15387067300002855
```

Numba is especially useful with NumPy and other mathematically demanding packages.

Source Control

When you're working on a small group of programs, you can usually keep track of your changes—until you make a boneheaded mistake and clobber a few days of work. Source control systems help protect your code from dangerous forces, like you. If you work with a group of developers, source control becomes a necessity. There are many commercial and open source packages in this area. The most popular in the open source world where Python lives are Mercurial and Git. Both are examples of *distributed* version control systems, which produce multiple copies of code repositories. Earlier systems such as Subversion run on a single server.

Mercurial

Mercurial (*http://mercurial-scm.org*) is written in Python. It's fairly easy to learn, with a handful of subcommands to download code from a Mercurial repository, add files, check in changes, and merge changes from different sources. bitbucket (*https:// bitbucket.org*) and other sites (*http://bit.ly/merc-host*) offer free or commercial hosting.

Git

Git (*http://git-scm.com*) was originally written for Linux kernel development, but now dominates open source in general. It's similar to Mercurial, although some find it slightly trickier to master. GitHub (*http://github.com*) is the largest git host, with more than a million repositories, but there are many other hosts (*http://bit.ly/githost-scm*).

The standalone program examples in this book are available in a public Git repository at GitHub (*https://oreil.ly/U2Rmy*). If you have the `git` program on your computer, you can download these programs by using this command:

```
$ git clone https://github.com/madscheme/introducing-python
```

You can also download the code from the GitHub page:

- Click "Clone in Desktop" to open your computer's version of `git`, if installed.
- Click "Download ZIP" to get a zipped archive of the programs.

If you don't have `git` but would like to try it, read the installation guide (*http://bit.ly/ git-install*). I talk about the command-line version here, but you might be interested in sites such as GitHub that have extra services and might be easier to use in some cases; `git` has many features, but is not always intuitive.

Let's take `git` for a test drive. We won't go far, but the ride will show a few commands and their output.

Make a new directory and change to it:

```
$ mkdir newdir
$ cd newdir
```

Create a local Git repository in your current directory *newdir*:

```
$ git init
```

```
Initialized empty Git repository in /Users/williamlubanovic/newdir/.git/
```

Create a Python file called *test.py*, shown in Example 19-25, with these contents in *newdir*.

Example 19-25. test.py

```
print('Oops')
```

Add the file to the Git repository:

```
$ git add test.py
```

What do you think of that, Mr. Git?

```
$ git status
```

```
On branch master

Initial commit

Changes to be committed:
  (use "git rm --cached <file>..." to unstage)

    new file:   test.py
```

This means that *test.py* is part of the local repository but its changes have not yet been committed. Let's *commit* it:

```
$ git commit -m "simple print program"

 [master (root-commit) 52d60d7] my first commit
  1 file changed, 1 insertion(+)
  create mode 100644 test.py
```

That -m "my first commit" was your *commit message*. If you omitted that, git would pop you into an editor and coax you to enter the message that way. This becomes a part of the git change history for that file.

Let's see what our current status is:

```
$ git status
On branch master
nothing to commit, working directory clean
```

Okay, all current changes have been committed. This means that we can change things and not worry about losing the original version. Make an adjustment now to *test.py*—change Oops to Ops! and save the file (Example 19-26).

Example 19-26. test.py, revised

```
print('Ops!')
```

Let's check to see what git thinks now:

```
$ git status
On branch master
Changes not staged for commit:
  (use "git add <file>..." to update what will be committed)
  (use "git checkout -- <file>..." to discard changes in working directory)

    modified:   test.py

no changes added to commit (use "git add" and/or "git commit -a")
```

Use git diff to see what lines have changed since the last commit:

```
$ git diff
diff --git a/test.py b/test.py
index 76b8c39..62782b2 100644
--- a/test.py
+++ b/test.py
@@ -1 +1 @@
-print('Oops')
+print('Ops!')
```

If you try to commit this change now, git complains:

```
$ git commit -m "change the print string"
On branch master
Changes not staged for commit:
    modified:   test.py

no changes added to commit
```

That `staged for commit` phrase means you need to add the file, which roughly translated means *hey git, look over here*:

```
$ git add test.py
```

You could have also typed `git add .` to add *all* changed files in the current directory; that's handy when you actually have edited multiple files and want to ensure that you check in all their changes. Now we can commit the change:

```
$ git commit -m "my first change"
[master e1e11ec] my first change
  1 file changed, 1 insertion(&plus;), 1 deletion(-)
```

If you'd like to see all the terrible things that you've done to *test.py*, most recent first, use `git log`:

```
$ git log test.py
commit e1e11ecf802ae1a78debe6193c552dcd15ca160a
Author: William Lubanovic <bill@madscheme.com>
Date:   Tue May 13 23:34:59 2014 -0500

    change the print string

commit 52d60d76594a62299f6fd561b2446c8b1227cfe1
Author: William Lubanovic <bill@madscheme.com>
Date:   Tue May 13 23:26:14 2014 -0500

    simple print program
```

Distribute Your Programs

You know that your Python files can be installed in files and directories, and you know that you can run a Python program file with the `python` interpreter.

It's less well known that the Python interpreter can also execute Python code packaged in ZIP files. It's even less well known that special ZIP files known as pex files (*https://pex.readthedocs.io*) can also be used.

Clone This Book

You can get a copy of all the programs in this book. Visit the Git repository (*https://oreil.ly/FbFAE*) and follow the directions to copy it to your local machine. If you have git, run the command `git clone https://github.com/madscheme/introducing-python` to make a Git repository on your computer. You can also download the files in ZIP format.

How You Can Learn More

This is an introduction. It almost certainly says too much about some things that you don't care about and not enough about some things that you do. Let me recommend some Python resources that I've found helpful.

Books

I've found the books in the following list to be especially useful. These range from introductory to advanced, with mixtures of Python 2 and 3:

- Barry, Paul. *Head First Python (2nd Edition)* O'Reilly, 2016.
- Beazley, David M. *Python Essential Reference (5th Edition)*. Addison-Wesley, 2019.
- Beazley, David M. and Brian K. Jones. *Python Cookbook (3rd Edition)*. O'Reilly, 2013.
- Gorelick, Micha and Ian Ozsvald. *High Performance Python*. O'Reilly, 2014.
- Maxwell, Aaron. *Powerful Python*. Powerful Python Press, 2017.
- McKinney, Wes. *Python for Data Analysis: Data Wrangling with Pandas, NumPy, and IPython*. O'Reilly, 2012.
- Ramalho, Luciano. *Fluent Python*. O'Reilly, 2015.
- Reitz, Kenneth and Tanya Schlusser. *The Hitchhiker's Guide to Python*. O'Reilly, 2016.
- Slatkin, Brett. *Effective Python*. Addison-Wesley, 2015.
- Summerfield, Mark. *Python in Practice: Create Better Programs Using Concurrency, Libraries, and Patterns*. Addison-Wesley, 2013.

Of course, there are many more (*https://wiki.python.org/moin/PythonBooks*).

Websites

Here are some websites where you can find helpful tutorials:

- Python for You and Me (*https://pymbook.readthedocs.io*) is an introduction, with good Windows coverage
- Real Python (*http://realpython.com*) by various authors
- Learn Python the Hard Way (*http://learnpythonthehardway.org/book*) by Zed Shaw
- Dive into Python 3 (*https://oreil.ly/UJcGM*) by Mark Pilgrim

- Mouse Vs. Python (*http://www.blog.pythonlibrary.org*) by Michael Driscoll

If you're interested in keeping up with what's going on in the Pythonic world, check out these news websites:

- comp.lang.python (*http://bit.ly/comp-lang-python*)
- comp.lang.python.announce (*http://bit.ly/comp-lang-py-announce*)
- r/python subreddit (*http://www.reddit.com/r/python*)
- Planet Python (*http://planet.python.org/*)

Finally, here are some good websites for finding and downloading packages:

- The Python Package Index (*https://pypi.python.org/pypi*)
- Awesome Python (*https://awesome-python.com*)
- Stack Overflow Python questions (*https://oreil.ly/S1vEL*)
- ActiveState Python recipes (*http://code.activestate.com/recipes/langs/python*)
- Python packages trending on GitHub (*https://github.com/trending?l=python*)

Groups

Computing communities have varied personalities: enthusiastic, argumentative, dull, hipster, button-down, and many others across a broad range. The Python community is friendly and civil. You can find Python groups based on location—meetups (*http://python.meetup.com*) and local user groups around the world (*https://wiki.python.org/moin/LocalUserGroups*). Other groups are distributed and based on common interests. For instance, PyLadies (*http://www.pyladies.com*) is a support network for women who are interested in Python and open source.

Conferences

Of the many conferences (*http://www.pycon.org*) and workshops around the world (*https://www.python.org/community/workshops*), the largest are held annually in North America (*https://us.pycon.org*) and Europe (*https://europython.eu/en*).

Getting a Python Job

Useful search sites include:

- Indeed (*https://www.indeed.com*)
- Stack Overflow (*https://stackoverflow.com/jobs*)
- ZipRecruiter (*https://www.ziprecruiter.com/candidate/suggested-jobs*)

- Simply Hired (*https://www.simplyhired.com*)
- CareerBuilder (*https://www.careerbuilder.com*)
- Google (*https://www.google.com/search?q=jobs*)
- LinkedIn (*https://www.linkedin.com/jobs/search*)

For most of these sites, type `python` in the first box and your location in the other. Good local sites include the Craigslist ones, like this link for Seattle (*https://seattle.craigslist.org/search/jjj*). Simply change the `seattle` part to `sfbay`, `boston`, `nyc`, or other craigslist site prefixes to search those areas. For remote (telecommuting, or "work from home") Python jobs, special sites include:

- Indeed (*https://oreil.ly/pFQwb*)
- Google (*https://oreil.ly/LI529*)
- LinkedIn (*https://oreil.ly/nhV6s*)
- Stack Overflow (*https://oreil.ly/R23Tx*)
- Remote Python (*https://oreil.ly/bPW1I*)
- We Work Remotely (*https://oreil.ly/9c3sC*)
- ZipRecruiter (*https://oreil.ly/ohwAY*)
- Glassdoor (*https://oreil.ly/tK5f5*)
- Remotely Awesome Jobs (*https://oreil.ly/MkMeg*)
- Working Nomads (*https://oreil.ly/uHVE3*)
- GitHub (*https://oreil.ly/smmrZ*)

Coming Up

But wait, there's more! The next three chapters offer tours of Python in the arts, business, and science. You'll find at least one package that you'll want to explore. Bright and shiny objects abound on the net. Only you can tell which are costume jewelry and which are silver bullets. And even if you're not currently pestered by werewolves, you might want some of those silver bullets in your pocket. Just in case.

Finally, we have answers to those annoying end-of-chapter exercises, details on installation of Python and friends, and a few cheat sheets for things that I always need to look up. Your brain is almost certainly better tuned, but they're there if needed.

Things to Do

(Pythonistas don't have homework today.)

CHAPTER 20

Py Art

Well, art is art, isn't it? Still, on the other hand, water is water! And east is east and west is west, and if you take cranberries and stew them like applesauce, they taste much more like prunes than rhubarb does.

> —Groucho Marx

This chapter and the next two discuss the application of Python to some common human endeavors: art, business, and science. If you're interested in any of these areas, you may get some helpful ideas or the urge to try something new.

2-D Graphics

All computer languages have been applied to computer graphics to some degree. Many of the heavy-duty platforms in this chapter were written in C or C++ for speed, but added Python libraries for productivity. Let's begin by looking at some 2-D imaging libraries.

Standard Library

Only a few image-related modules are in the standard library:

imghdr
    Detects the file type of some image files.

colorsys
    Converts colors between various systems: RGB, YIQ, HSV, and HLS.

If you downloaded the O'Reilly logo to a local file called *oreilly.png*, you could run this:

```
>>> import imghdr
>>> imghdr.what('oreilly.png')
'png'
```

Another standard library is `turtle` (*https://oreil.ly/b9vEz*)—"Turtle graphics," which is sometimes used to teach programming to young people. You can run a demo with this command:

```
$ python -m turtledemo
```

Figure 20-1 shows a screenshot of its *rosette* example.

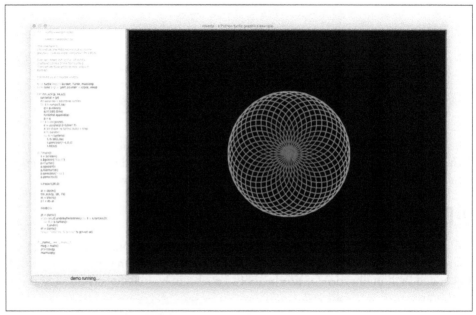

Figure 20-1. Image from turtledemo

To do anything serious with graphics in Python, we need to get some third-party packages. Let's see what's out there.

PIL and Pillow

For many years, the Python Image Library (*http://bit.ly/py-image*) (PIL), although not in the standard library, has been Python's best-known 2-D image processing library. It predated installers such as `pip`, so a "friendly fork" called Pillow (*http://pillow.readthe docs.org*) was created. Pillow's imaging code is backward-compatible with PIL, and its documentation is good, so let's use it here.

Installation is simple; just type the following command:

```
$ pip install Pillow
```

If you've already installed operating system packages such as libjpeg, libfreetype, and zlib, they'll be detected and used by Pillow. See the installation page (*http://bit.ly/pillow-install*) for details on this.

Open an image file:

```
>>> from PIL import Image
>>> img = Image.open('oreilly.png')
>>> img.format
'PNG'
>>> img.size
(154, 141)
>>> img.mode
'RGB'
```

Although the package is called Pillow, you import it as PIL to make it compatible with the older PIL.

To display the image on your screen using the Image object's show() method, you'll first need to install the ImageMagick package described in the next section, and then try this:

```
>>> img.show()
```

The image displayed in Figure 20-2 opens in another window. (This screenshot was captured on a Mac, where the show() function used the Preview application. Your window's appearance might vary.)

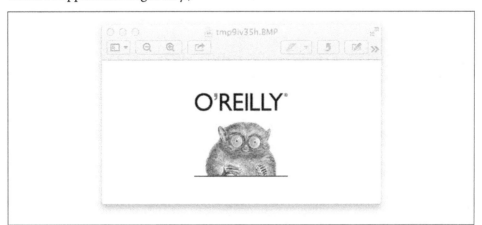

Figure 20-2. Image displayed with the Python Image Library

Let's crop the image in memory, save the result as a new object called img2, and display it. Images are always measured by horizontal (x) values and vertical (y) values, with one corner of the image known as the *origin* and arbitrarily assigned an x and y of 0. In this library, the origin (0, 0) is at the upper left of the image, x increases to the right, and y increases as you move down. We want to give the values of left x (55), top y (70), right x (85), and bottom y (100) to the crop() method, so pass it a tuple with those values in that order:

```
>>> crop = (55, 70, 85, 100)
>>> img2 = img.crop(crop)
>>> img2.show()
```

The results are shown in Figure 20-3.

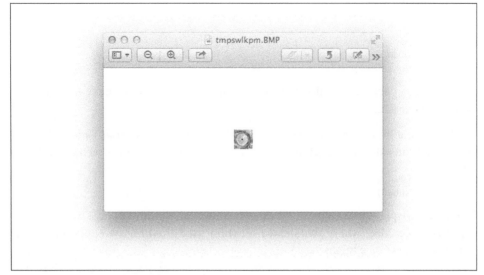

Figure 20-3. The cropped image

Save an image file with the save method. It takes a filename and an optional type. If the filename has a suffix, the library uses that to determine the type. But you can also specify the type explicitly. To save our cropped image as a GIF file, do the following:

```
>>> img2.save('cropped.gif', 'GIF')
>>> img3 = Image.open('cropped.gif')
>>> img3.format
'GIF'
>>> img3.size
(30, 30)
```

For our last example, let's "improve" our little mascot. First download copies of our original critter, shown in Figure 20-4.

Figure 20-4. Beloved ur-critter

He has a sort of scruffy five o'clock shadow, so let's get an image to improve his, um, image; see Figure 20-5.

Figure 20-5. Alien technology

Let's put them together, with some *alpha* channel magic to make the overlap semi-transparent, demonstrated in Example 20-1.

Example 20-1. ch20_critter.py

```
from PIL import Image

critter = Image.open('ch20_critter.png')
stache = Image.open('ch20_stache.png')
stache.putalpha(100)
img = Image.new('RGBA', critter.size, (255, 255, 255, 0))
img.paste(critter, (0, 0))
img.paste(stache, (45, 90), mask=stache)
img.show()
```

Figure 20-6 presents his makeover.

Figure 20-6. Our new, dapper mascot

ImageMagick

ImageMagick (*http://www.imagemagick.org*) is a suite of programs to convert, modify, and display 2-D bitmap images. It's been around for more than 20 years. Various

Python libraries have connected to the ImageMagick C library. A recent one that supports Python 3 is wand (*http://docs.wand-py.org*). To install it, type the following command:

```
$ pip install Wand
```

You can do many of the same things with wand as you can with Pillow:

```
>>> from wand.image import Image
>>> from wand.display import display
>>>
>>> img = Image(filename='oreilly.png')
>>> img.size
(154, 141)
>>> img.format
'PNG'
```

As with Pillow, this displays the image on the screen:

```
>>> display(img)
```

wand includes rotation, resizing, text and line drawing, format conversion, and other features that you can also find in Pillow. Both have good APIs and documentation.

3-D Graphics

Some basic Python packages include the following:

- VPython (*https://vpython.org*) has examples (*https://oreil.ly/J42t0*) that can run in your browser.
- pi3d (*https://pi3d.github.io*) runs on the Raspberry Pi, Windows, Linux, and Android.
- Open3D (*http://www.open3d.org/docs*) is a full-featured 3-D library.

3-D Animation

Watch the long end-credits for almost any contemporary movie, and you'll see mass quantities of people doing special effects and animation. Most of the big studios—Walt Disney Animation, ILM, Weta, Dreamworks, Pixar—hire people with Python experience. Do a web search for "python animation jobs" to see what's available now.

Some Python 3-D packages are:

Panda3D (http://www.panda3d.org)
It's open source and free to use, even for commercial applications. You can download a version from the Panda3D website (*http://bit.ly/dl-panda*).

VPython (https://vpython.org)
> Comes with many examples (*https://oreil.ly/J42t0*).

Blender (http://www.blender.org)
> Blender is a free 3-D animation and game creator. When you download and install (*http://www.blender.org/download*) it, it comes bundled with its own copy of Python 3.

Maya (https://oreil.ly/PhWn-)
> This is a commercial 3-D animation and graphic system. It also comes bundled with a version of Python, currently 2.7. Chad Vernon has written a free downloadable book, *Python Scripting for Maya Artists* (*http://bit.ly/py-maya*). If you search for Python and Maya on the web, you'll find many other resources, both free and commercial, including videos.

Houdini (https://www.sidefx.com)
> Houdini is commercial, although you can download a free version called Apprentice. Like the other animation packages, it comes with a Python binding (*https://oreil.ly/L4C7r*).

Graphical User Interfaces

The name includes the word graphic, but graphical user interfaces (GUIs) concentrate more on the user interface: widgets to present data, input methods, menus, buttons, and windows to frame everything.

The GUI programming (*http://bit.ly/gui-program*) wiki page and FAQ (*http://bit.ly/gui-faq*) list many Python-powered GUIs. Let's begin with the only one that's built in to the standard library: Tkinter (*https://wiki.python.org/moin/TkInter*). It's plain, but it works on all platforms to produce native-looking windows and widgets.

Here's a teeny, tiny Tkinter program to display our favorite googly-eyed mascot in a window:

```
>>> import tkinter
>>> from PIL import Image, ImageTk
>>>
>>> main = tkinter.Tk()
>>> img = Image.open('oreilly.png')
>>> tkimg = ImageTk.PhotoImage(img)
>>> tkinter.Label(main, image=tkimg).pack()
>>> main.mainloop()
```

Notice that it used some modules from PIL/Pillow. You should see the O'Reilly logo again, as shown in Figure 20-7.

Figure 20-7. Image displayed with Tkinter

To make the window go away, click its close button, or leave your Python interpreter.

You can read more about Tkinter at the tkinter wiki (*https://wiki.python.org/moin/TkInter*). Now for the GUIs that are not in the standard library:

Qt (http://qt-project.org)

This is a professional GUI and application toolkit, originated about 20 years ago by Trolltech in Norway. It's been used to help build applications such as Google Earth, Maya, and Skype. It was also used as the base for KDE, a Linux desktop. There are two main Python libraries for Qt: PySide (*http://qt-project.org/wiki/PySide*) is free (LGPL license), and PyQt (*http://bit.ly/pyqt-info*) is licensed either with the GPL or commercially. The Qt folks see these differences (*http://bit.ly/qt-diff*). Download PySide from PyPI (*https://pypi.python.org/pypi/PySide*) or Qt (*http://qt-project.org/wiki/Get-PySide*) and read the tutorial (*http://qt-project.org/wiki/PySide_Tutorials*). You can download Qt for free online (*http://bit.ly/qt-dl*).

GTK+ (http://www.gtk.org)

GTK+ is a competitor of Qt, and it, too, has been used to create many applications, including GIMP and the Gnome desktop for Linux. The Python binding is PyGTK (*http://www.pygtk.org*). To download the code, go to the PyGTK site (*http://bit.ly/pygtk-dl*), where you can also read the documents (*http://bit.ly/py-gtk-docs*).

WxPython (http://www.wxpython.org)

This is the Python binding for WxWidgets (*http://www.wxwidgets.org*). It's another hefty package, free to download online (*http://wxpython.org/download.php*).

Kivy (http://kivy.org)

Kivy is a free modern library for building multimedia user interfaces portably across platforms—desktop (Windows, macOS, Linux), and mobile (Android, iOS). It includes multitouch support. You can download for all the platforms on the Kivy website (*http://kivy.org/#download*). Kivy includes application development tutorials (*http://bit.ly/kivy-intro*).

PySimpleGUI (https://pysimplegui.readthedocs.io)
> Write native or web-based GUIs with one library. PySimpleGUI is a wrapper for some of the other GUIs mentioned in this section, including Tk, Kivy, and Qt.

The web
> Frameworks such as Qt use native components, but some others use the web. After all, the web is a universal GUI, and it has graphics (SVG), text (HTML), and even multimedia now (in HTML5). You can build web applications with any combination of frontend (browser-based) and backend (web server) tools. A *thin client* lets the backend do most of the work. If the frontend dominates, it's a *thick*, or *fat*, or *rich* client; the last adjective sounds more flattering. It's common for the sides to communicate with RESTful APIs, Ajax, and JSON.

Plots, Graphs, and Visualization

Python has become a leading solution for plots, graphs, and data visualization. It's especially popular in science, which is covered in Chapter 22. Useful overviews, with examples, include the official Python wiki (*https://oreil.ly/Wdter*) and the Python Graph Gallery (*https://python-graph-gallery.com*).

Let's look at the most popular ones. In the next chapter, you'll see some of these again, but being used to create maps.

Matplotlib

The Matplotlib (*http://matplotlib.org*) 2-D plotting library can be installed by using the following command:

```
$ pip install matplotlib
```

The examples in the gallery (*http://matplotlib.org/gallery.html*) show the breadth of Matplotlib.

Let's first try the same image display application (with results shown in Figure 20-8), just to see how the code and presentation look:

```
import matplotlib.pyplot as plot
import matplotlib.image as image

img = image.imread('oreilly.png')
plot.imshow(img)
plot.show()
```

Figure 20-8. Image displayed with Matplotlib

The real strength of Matplotlib is in *plot*ting, which is, after all, its middle name. Let's generate two lists of 20 integers, one smoothly increasing from 1 to 20, and another like the first, but with slight wobbles now and then (Example 20-2).

Example 20-2. ch20_matplotlib.py

```python
import matplotlib.pyplot as plt
from random import randint

linear = list(range(1, 21))
wiggly = list(num + randint(-1, 1) for num in linear)

fig, plots = plt.subplots(nrows=1, ncols=3)

ticks = list(range(0, 21, 5))
for plot in plots:
    plot.set_xticks(ticks)
    plot.set_yticks(ticks)

plots[0].scatter(linear, wiggly)
```

```
plots[1].plot(linear, wiggly)
plots[2].plot(linear, wiggly, 'o-')

plt.show()
```

If you run this program, you'll see something like what's shown in Figure 20-9 (not exactly, because the randint() calls make random wiggles).

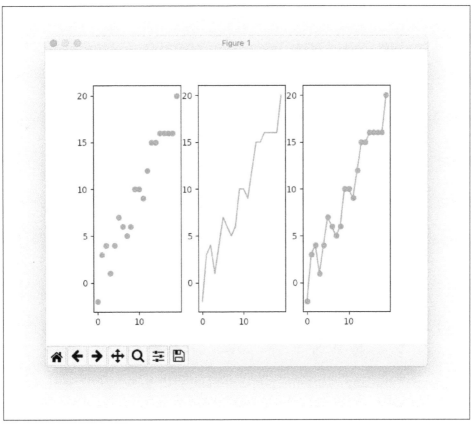

Figure 20-9. Basic Matplotlib scatter and line plots

This example showed a scatterplot, a line plot, and a line plot with data markers. All of the styles and colors used Matplotlib defaults, but they can be customized very extensively. For details, see the Matplotlib site (*https://matplotlib.org*) or an overview like Python Plotting With Matplotlib (Guide) (*https://oreil.ly/T_xdT*).

You can see more of Matplotlib in Chapter 22; it has strong ties to NumPy and other scientific applications.

Seaborn

Seaborn (*https://seaborn.pydata.org*) is a data visualization library (Figure 20-10), built on Matplotlib and with connections to Pandas. The usual installation mantra (`pip install seaborn`) works.

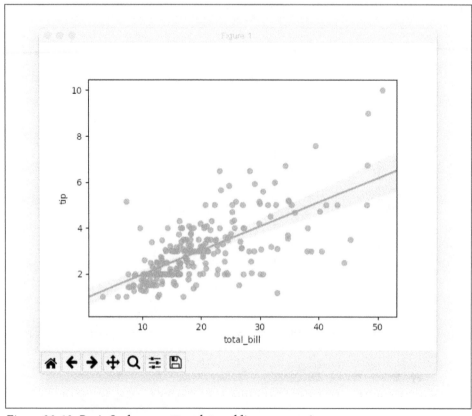

Figure 20-10. Basic Seaborn scatter plot and linear regression

The code in Example 20-3 is based on a Seaborn example (*https://oreil.ly/eBFGi*); it accesses test data on restaurant tipping and plots tips versus total bill amounts with a fitted linear regression line.

Example 20-3. ch20_seaborn.py

```
import seaborn as sns
import matplotlib.pyplot as plt

tips = sns.load_dataset("tips")
sns.regplot(x="total_bill", y="tip", data=tips);
```

```
plt.show()
```

 If you run the preceding code with the standard Python interpreter, you need that initial import line (`import matplotlib.pyplot as plt`) and final line (`plt.show()`), as shown in Example 20-3, or else the plot just won't display. If you're using Jupyter, Matplotlib is built in and you don't need to type them. Remember this when you read code examples of Python mapping tools.

Like Matplotlib, Seaborn has a vast number of options for data handling and display.

Bokeh

In the old web days, developers would generate graphics on the server and give the web browser some URL to access them. More recently, JavaScript has gained performance and client-side graphics generation tools like D3. A page or two ago, I mentioned the possibility of using Python as part of a frontend-backend architecture for graphics and GUIs. A new tool called Bokeh (*http://bokeh.pydata.org*) combines the strengths of Python (large data sets, ease of use) and JavaScript (interactivity, less graphics latency). Its emphasis is quick visualization of large data sets.

If you've already installed its prerequisites (NumPy, Pandas, and Redis), you can install Bokeh by typing this command:

```
$ pip install bokeh
```

(You can see NumPy and Pandas in action in Chapter 22.)

Or, install everything at once from the Bokeh website (*https://oreil.ly/1Fy-L*). Although Matplotlib runs on the server, Bokeh runs mainly in the browser and can take advantage of recent advances on the client side. Click any image in the gallery (*https://oreil.ly/DWN-d*) for an interactive view of the display and its Python code.

Games

Python is such a good game development platform that people have written books about it:

- *Invent Your Own Computer Games with Python* (*http://inventwithpython.com*) by Al Sweigart
- *The Python Game Book* (*http://thepythongamebook.com*) by Horst Jens (a docuwiki book)

There's a general discussion at the Python wiki (*https://wiki.python.org/moin/Python Games*) with even more links.

The best known Python game platform is probably pygame (*http://pygame.org*). You can download an executable installer for your platform from the Pygame website (*http://pygame.org/download.shtml*), and read a line-by-line example of a "pummel the chimp" game (*https://oreil.ly/l-swp*).

Audio and Music

> I sought the serif
> But that did not suit Claude Debussy.
>
> —Deservedly Anonymous

What about sound, and music, and cats singing "Jingle Bells"? Well, as Meatloaf says, two out of three ain't bad.

It's hard to represent sound in a printed book, so here are some up-to-date links to Python packages for sound and music, but Google has many more:

- Standard library audio (*http://docs.python.org/3/library/mm.html*) modules
- Third-party audio (*https://wiki.python.org/moin/Audio*) tools
- Dozens of third-party music (*https://wiki.python.org/moin/PythonInMusic*) applications: graphic and CLI players, converters, notation, analysis, playlists, MIDI, and more

Finally, how about some online sources of music? You've seen code examples throughout this book that access the Internet Archive. Here are links to some of its audio archives:

- Audio recordings (*https://archive.org/details/audio*) (>5 million)
- Live music (*https://archive.org/details/etree*) (>200,000)
- Live Grateful Dead shows (*https://archive.org/details/GratefulDead*) (>13,000)

Coming Up

Act busy! It's Python in business.

Things to Do

20.1 Install `matplotlib`. Draw a scatter diagram of these (x, y) pairs: ((0, 0), (3, 5), (6, 2), (9, 8), (14, 10)).

20.2 Draw a line graph of the same data.

20.3 Draw a plot (a line graph with markers) of the same data.

CHAPTER 21

Py at Work

"Business!" cried the Ghost, wringing its hands again. "Mankind was my business…"

—Charles Dickens, *A Christmas Carol*

The businessman's uniform is a suit and tie. But before he can *get down to business*, he tosses his jacket over a chair, loosens his tie, rolls up his sleeves, and pours some coffee. Meanwhile, the business woman has already been getting work done. Maybe with a latte.

In business and government, we use all of the technologies from the earlier chapters —databases, the web, systems, and networks. Python's productivity is making it more popular in the enterprise (*http://bit.ly/py-enterprise*) and with startups (*http://bit.ly/py-startups*).

Organizations have long fought incompatible file formats, arcane network protocols, language lock-in, and the universal lack of accurate documentation. They can create faster, cheaper, stretchier applications by using with tools such as these:

- Dynamic languages like Python
- The web as a universal graphical user interface
- RESTful APIs as language-independent service interfaces
- Relational and NoSQL databases
- "Big data" and analytics
- Clouds for deployment and capital savings

The Microsoft Office Suite

Business is heavily dependent on Microsoft Office applications and file formats. Although they are not well known, and in some cases poorly documented, there are some Python libraries that can help. Here are some that process Microsoft Office documents:

docx (https://pypi.python.org/pypi/docx)
> This library creates, reads, and writes Microsoft Office Word 2007 *.docx* files.

python-excel (http://www.python-excel.org)
> This one discusses the xlrd, xlwt, and xlutils modules via a PDF tutorial (*http://bit.ly/py-excel*). Excel can also read and write comma-separated values (CSV) files, which you know how to process by using the standard csv module.

oletools (http://bit.ly/oletools)
> This library extracts data from Office formats.

OpenOffice (*http://openoffice.org*) is an open source alternative to Office. It runs on Linux, Unix, Windows, and macOS, and reads and writes Office file formats, It also installs a version of Python 3 for its own use. You can program OpenOffice in Python (*https://oreil.ly/mLiCr*) with the PyUNO (*https://oreil.ly/FASNB*) library.

OpenOffice was owned by Sun Microsystems, and when Oracle acquired Sun, some people feared for its future availability. LibreOffice (*https://www.libreoffice.org*) was spun off as a result. DocumentHacker (*http://bit.ly/docu-hacker*) describes using the Python UNO library with LibreOffice.

OpenOffice and LibreOffice had to reverse engineer the Microsoft file formats, which is not easy. The Universal Office Converter (*http://dag.wiee.rs/home-made/unoconv*) module depends on the UNO library in OpenOffice or LibreOffice. It can convert many file formats: documents, spreadsheets, graphics, and presentations.

If you have a mystery file, python-magic (*https://github.com/ahupp/python-magic*) can guess its format by analyzing specific byte sequences.

The python open document (*http://appyframework.org/pod.html*) library lets you provide Python code within templates to create dynamic documents.

Although not a Microsoft format, Adobe's PDF is very common in business. ReportLab (*http://www.reportlab.com/opensource*) has open source and commercial versions of its Python-based PDF generator. If you need to edit a PDF, you might find some help at StackOverflow (*http://bit.ly/add-text-pdf*).

Carrying Out Business Tasks

You can find a Python module for almost anything. Visit PyPI (*https://pypi.python.org/pypi*) and type something into the search box. Many modules are interfaces to the public APIs of various services. You might be interested in some examples related to business tasks:

- Ship via Fedex (*https://github.com/gtaylor/python-fedex*) or UPS (*https://github.com/openlabs/PyUPS*).
- Mail with the stamps.com (*https://github.com/jzempel/stamps*) API.
- Read a discussion of *Python for business intelligence* (*http://bit.ly/py-biz*).
- If Aeropresses are flying off the shelves in Anoka, was it customer activity or poltergeists? Cubes (*http://cubes.databrewery.org*) is an Online Analytical Processing (OLAP) web server and data browser.
- OpenERP (*https://www.openerp.com/*) is a large commercial Enterprise Resource Planning (ERP) system written in Python and JavaScript, with thousands of add-on modules.

Processing Business Data

Businesses have a particular fondness for data. Sadly, many of them conjure up perverse ways of making data harder to use.

Spreadsheets were a good invention, and over time businesses became addicted to them. Many nonprogrammers were tricked into programming because they were called *macros* instead of programs. But the universe is expanding and data is trying to keep up. Older versions of Excel were limited to 65,536 rows, and even newer versions choke at a million or so. When an organization's data outgrow the limits of a single computer, it's like headcount growing past a hundred people or so—suddenly you need new layers, intermediaries, and communication.

Excessive data programs aren't caused by the size of data on single desktops; rather, they're the result of the aggregate of data pouring into the business. Relational databases handle millions of rows without exploding, but only so many writes or updates at a time. A plain old text or binary file can grow gigabytes in size, but if you need to process it all at once, you need enough memory. Traditional desktop software isn't designed for all this. Companies such as Google and Amazon had to invent solutions to handle so much data at scale. Netflix (*http://bit.ly/py-netflix*) is an example built on Amazon's AWS cloud, using Python to glue together RESTful APIs, security, deployment, and databases.

Extracting, Transforming, and Loading

The underwater portions of the data icebergs include all the work to get the data in the first place. If you speak enterprise, the common term is extract, transform, load, or *ETL*. Synonyms such as *data munging* or *data wrangling* give the impression of taming an unruly beast, which might be apt metaphors. This would seem to be a solved engineering matter by now, but it remains largely an art. I talked a bit about this in Chapter 12. We address *data science* more broadly in Chapter 22, because this is where most developers spend a large part of their time.

If you've seen *The Wizard of Oz*, you probably remember (besides the flying monkeys) the part at the end—when the good witch told Dorothy that she could always go home to Kansas just by clicking her ruby slippers. Even when I was young I thought, "Now she tells her!" Although, in retrospect, I realize the movie would have been much shorter if she'd shared that tip earlier.

But this isn't a movie; we're talking about the world of business here, where making tasks shorter is a good thing. So, let me share some tips with you now. Most of the tools that you need for day-to-day data work in business are those that you've already read about here. Those include high-level data structures such as dictionaries and objects, thousands of standard and third-party libraries, and an expert community that's just a google away.

If you're a computer programmer working for some business, your workflow almost always includes the following:

1. Extracting data from weird file formats or databases
2. "Cleaning up" the data, which covers a lot of ground, all strewn with pointy objects
3. Converting things like dates, times, and character sets
4. Actually doing something with the data
5. Storing resulting data in a file or database
6. Rolling back to step 1 again; lather, rinse, repeat

Here's an example: you want to move data from a spreadsheet to a database. You can save the spreadsheet in CSV format and use the Python libraries from Chapter 16. Or, you can look for a module that reads the binary spreadsheet format directly. Your fingers know how to type python excel into Google and find sites such as Working with Excel files in Python (*http://www.python-excel.org*). You can install one of the packages by using pip, and locate a Python database driver for the last part of the task. I mentioned SQLAlchemy and the direct low-level database drivers in that same chapter. Now you need some code in the middle, and that's where Python's data structures and libraries can save you time.

Let's try an example here, and then we'll try again with a library that saves a few steps. We'll read a CSV file, aggregate the counts in one column by unique values in another, and print the results. If we did this in SQL, we would use SELECT, JOIN, and GROUP BY.

First, the file, *zoo.csv*, which has columns for the type of animal, how many times it has bitten a visitor, the number of stitches required, and how much we've paid the visitor not to tell local television stations:

```
animal,bites,stitches,hush
bear,1,35,300
marmoset,1,2,250
bear,2,42,500
elk,1,30,100
weasel,4,7,50
duck,2,0,10
```

We want to see which animal is costing us the most, so we aggregate the total hush money by the type of animal. (We'll leave bites and stitches to an intern.) We use the csv module from "CSV" on page 304 and Counter from "Count Items with Counter()" on page 209. Save this code as *zoo_counts.py*:

```
import csv
from collections import Counter

counts = Counter()
with open('zoo.csv', 'rt') as fin:
    cin = csv.reader(fin)
    for num, row in enumerate(cin):
        if num > 0:
            counts[row[0]] += int(row[-1])
for animal, hush in counts.items():
    print("%10s %10s" % (animal, hush))
```

We skipped the first row because it contained only the column names. counts is a Counter object, and takes care of initializing the sum for each animal to zero. We also applied a little formatting to right-align the output. Let's try it:

```
$ python zoo_counts.py
      duck         10
       elk        100
      bear        800
    weasel         50
  marmoset        250
```

Hah! It was the bear. He was our prime suspect all along, but now we have the numbers.

Next, let's replicate this with a data processing toolkit called Bubbles (*http:// bubbles.databrewery.org*). You can install it by typing this command:

```
$ pip install bubbles
```

It requires SQLAlchemy; if you don't have that, `pip install sqlalchemy` will do the trick. Here's the test program (call it *bubbles1.py*), adapted from the documentation (*http://bit.ly/py-bubbles*):

```
import bubbles

p = bubbles.Pipeline()
p.source(bubbles.data_object('csv_source', 'zoo.csv', infer_fields=True))
p.aggregate('animal', 'hush')
p.pretty_print()
```

And now, the moment of truth:

```
$ python bubbles1.py
2014-03-11 19:46:36,806 DEBUG calling aggregate(rows)
2014-03-11 19:46:36,807 INFO called aggregate(rows)
2014-03-11 19:46:36,807 DEBUG calling pretty_print(records)
+--------+--------+------------+
|animal  |hush_sum|record_count|
+--------+--------+------------+
|duck    |     10|           1|
|weasel  |     50|           1|
|bear    |    800|           2|
|elk     |    100|           1|
|marmoset|    250|           1|
+--------+--------+------------+
2014-03-11 19:46:36,807 INFO called pretty_print(records)
```

If you read the documentation, you can avoid those debug print lines, and maybe change the format of the table.

Looking at the two examples, we see that the `bubbles` example used a single function call (`aggregate`) to replace our manual reading and counting of the CSV format. Depending on your needs, data toolkits can save a lot of work.

In a more realistic example, our zoo file might have thousands of rows (it's a dangerous place), with misspellings such as `bare`, commas in numbers, and so on. For good examples of practical data problems with Python code, I'd also recommend the following:

- *Data Crunching: Solve Everyday Problems Using Java, Python, and More* (*http://bit.ly/data_crunching*)—Greg Wilson (Pragmatic Bookshelf).

- *Automate the Boring Stuff* (*https://automatetheboringstuff.com*)—Al Sweigart (No Starch).

Data cleanup tools can save a lot of time, and Python has many of them. For another example, PETL (*http://petl.readthedocs.org*) does row and column extraction and renaming. Its related work (*http://bit.ly/petl-related*) page lists many useful modules and products. Chapter 22 has detailed discussions of some especially useful data tools: Pandas, NumPy, and IPython. Although they're currently best known among scientists, they're becoming popular among financial and data developers. At the 2012 Pydata conference, AppData (*http://bit.ly/py-big-data*) discussed how these three and other Python tools help process 15 terabytes of data daily. Python handles very large real-world data loads.

You may also look back at the data serialization and validation tools discussed in "Data Serialization" on page 361.

Data Validation

When cleaning up data, you'll often need to check:

- Data type, such as integer, float, or string
- Range of values
- Correct values, such as a working phone number or email address
- Duplicates
- Missing data

This is especially common when processing web requests and responses.

Useful Python packages for particular data types include:

- `validate_email` (*https://pypi.org/project/validate_email*)
- `phonenumber` (*https://pypi.org/project/phonenumbers*)

Some useful general tools are:

- `validators` (*https://validators.readthedocs.io*)
- `pydantic` (*https://pydantic-docs.helpmanual.io*)—For Python 3.6 and above; uses type hints
- `marshmallow` (*https://marshmallow.readthedocs.io/en/3.0*)—Also serializes and deserializes
- `cerberus` (*http://docs.python-cerberus.org/en/stable*)
- many others (*https://libraries.io/search?keywords=validation&languages=Python*)

Additional Sources of Information

Sometimes, you need data that originates somewhere else. Some business and government data sources include:

data.gov (https://www.data.gov)
> A gateway to thousands of data sets and tools. Its APIs (*https://www.data.gov/developers/apis*) are built on CKAN (*http://ckan.org*), a Python data management system.

Opening government with Python (http://sunlightfoundation.com)
> See the video (*http://bit.ly/opengov-py*) and slides (*http://goo.gl/8Yh3s*).

python-sunlight (http://bit.ly/py-sun)
> Libraries to access the Sunlight APIs (*http://sunlightfoundation.com/api*).

froide (https://froide.readthedocs.io)
> A Django-based platform for managing freedom of information requests.

30 places to find open data on the web (http://blog.visual.ly/data-sources)
> Some handy links.

Open Source Python Business Packages

Odoo (https://www.odoo.com)
> Extensive ERP platform

Tryton (http://www.tryton.org)
> Another extensive business platform

Oscar (http://oscarcommerce.com)
> Ecommerce framework for Django

Grid Studio (https://gridstudio.io)
> Python-based spreadsheet, runs locally or in the cloud

Python in Finance

Recently, the financial industry has developed a great interest in Python. Adapting software from Chapter 22 as well as some of their own, *quants* are building a new generation of financial tools:

Quantitative economics (http://quant-econ.net)
> A tool for economic modeling, with lots of math and Python code

Python for finance (http://www.python-for-finance.com)
> Features the book *Derivatives Analytics with Python: Data Analytics, Models, Simulation, Calibration, and Hedging* by Yves Hilpisch (Wiley)

Quantopian (https://www.quantopian.com)
> An interactive website on which you can write your own Python code and run it against historic stock data to see how it would have done

---

PyAlgoTrade (http://gbeced.github.io/pyalgotrade)
   Another that you can use for stock backtesting, but on your own computer

Quandl (http://www.quandl.com)
   Search millions of financial datasets

Ultra-finance (https://code.google.com/p/ultra-finance)
   A real-time stock collection library

Python for Finance (http://bit.ly/python-finance) (O'Reilly)
   A book by Yves Hilpisch with Python examples for financial modeling

Business Data Security

Security is a special concern for business. Entire books are devoted to this topic, so we just mention a few Python-related tips here.

- "Scapy" on page 349 discusses `scapy`, a Python-powered language for packet forensics. It has been used to explain some major network attacks.
- The Python Security (*http://www.pythonsecurity.org*) site has discussions of security topics, details on some Python modules, and cheat sheets.
- The book *Violent Python* (*http://bit.ly/violent-python*) (subtitled *A Cookbook for Hackers, Forensic Analysts, Penetration Testers and Security Engineers*) by TJ O'Connor (Syngress) is an extensive review of Python and computer security.

Maps

Maps have become valuable to many businesses. Python is very good at making maps, so we're going to spend a little more time in this area. Managers love graphics, and if you can quickly whip up a nice map for your organization's website it wouldn't hurt.

In the early days of the web, I used to visit an experimental mapmaking website at Xerox. When big sites such as Google Maps came along, they were a revelation (along the lines of "why didn't I think of that and make millions?"). Now mapping and *location-based services* are everywhere, and are particularly useful in mobile devices.

Many terms overlap here: mapping, cartography, GIS (geographic information system), GPS (Global Positioning System), geospatial analysis, and many more. The blog at Geospatial Python (*http://bit.ly/geospatial-py*) has an image of the "800-pound gorilla" systems—GDAL/OGR, GEOS, and PROJ.4 (projections)—and surrounding systems, represented as monkeys. Many of these have Python interfaces. Let's talk about some of these, beginning with the simplest formats.

Formats

The mapping world has lots of formats: vector (lines), raster (images), metadata (words), and various combinations.

Esri, a pioneer of geographic systems, invented the *shapefile* format over 20 years ago. A shapefile actually consists of multiple files, including at the very least the following:

.shp
> The "shape" (vector) information

.shx
> The shape index

.dbf
> An attribute database

Let's grab a shapefile for our next example—visit the Natural Earth 1:110m Cultural Vectors page (*http://bit.ly/cultural-vectors*). Under "Admin 1 - States and Provinces," click the green download states and provinces (*https://oreil.ly/7BR2o*) box to download a zip file. After it downloads to your computer, unzip it; you should see these resulting files:

```
ne_110m_admin_1_states_provinces_shp.README.html
ne_110m_admin_1_states_provinces_shp.sbn
ne_110m_admin_1_states_provinces_shp.VERSION.txt
ne_110m_admin_1_states_provinces_shp.sbx
ne_110m_admin_1_states_provinces_shp.dbf
ne_110m_admin_1_states_provinces_shp.shp
ne_110m_admin_1_states_provinces_shp.prj
ne_110m_admin_1_states_provinces_shp.shx
```

We'll use these for our examples.

Draw a Map from a Shapefile

This section is an overly simplified demonstration of reading and displaying a shapefile. You'll see that the result has problems, and that you'd be better off working with a higher-level mapping package, such as those in the sections that follow.

You'll need this library to read a shapefile:

```
$ pip install pyshp
```

Now for the program, *map1.py*, which I've modified from a Geospatial Python blog post (*http://bit.ly/raster-shape*):

```python
def display_shapefile(name, iwidth=500, iheight=500):
    import shapefile
    from PIL import Image, ImageDraw
    r = shapefile.Reader(name)
```

```
        mleft, mbottom, mright, mtop = r.bbox
        # map units
        mwidth = mright - mleft
        mheight = mtop - mbottom
        # scale map units to image units
        hscale = iwidth/mwidth
        vscale = iheight/mheight
        img = Image.new("RGB", (iwidth, iheight), "white")
        draw = ImageDraw.Draw(img)
        for shape in r.shapes():
            pixels = [
                (int(iwidth - ((mright - x) * hscale)), int((mtop - y) * vscale))
                for x, y in shape.points]
            if shape.shapeType == shapefile.POLYGON:
                draw.polygon(pixels, outline='black')
            elif shape.shapeType == shapefile.POLYLINE:
                draw.line(pixels, fill='black')
        img.show()

if __name__ == '__main__':
    import sys
    display_shapefile(sys.argv[1], 700, 700)
```

This reads the shapefile and iterates through its individual shapes. I'm checking for only two shape types: a polygon, which connects the last point to the first, and a polyline, which doesn't. I've based my logic on the original post and a quick look at the documentation for pyshp, so I'm not really sure how it will work. Sometimes, we just need to make a start and deal with any problems as we find them.

So, let's run it. The argument is the base name of the shapefile files, without any extension:

```
$ python map1.py ne_110m_admin_1_states_provinces_shp
```

You should see something like Figure 21-1.

Well, it drew a map that resembles the United States, but:

- It looks like a cat dragged yarn across Alaska and Hawaii; this is a *bug*.
- The country is squished; I need a *projection*.
- The picture isn't pretty; I need better *style* control.

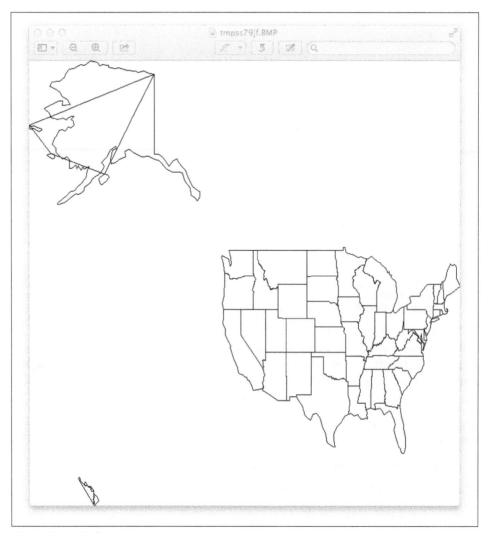

Figure 21-1. Preliminary map

To address the first point: I have a problem somewhere in my logic, but what should I do? Chapter 19 discusses development tips, including debugging, but we can consider other options here. I could write some tests and bear down until I fix this, or I could just try some other mapping library. Maybe something at a higher level would solve all three of my problems (the stray lines, squished appearance, and primitive style).

As far as I can tell, there is no bare-bones pure Python mapping package. Luckily, there are some fancier ones, so let's take a look.

Geopandas

Geopandas (*http://geopandas.org*) integrates `matplotlib`, `pandas`, and other Python libraries into a geospatial data platform.

The base package is installed with the familiar `pip install geopandas`, but it relies on other packages that you will also need to install with `pip` if you don't have them already:

- `numpy`
- `pandas` (version 0.23.4 or later)
- `shapely` (interface to GEOS)
- `fiona` (interface to GDAL)
- `pyproj` (interface to PROJ)
- `six`

Geopandas can read shapefiles (including those from the previous section), and handily includes two from Natural Earth: country/continent outlines, and national capital cities. Example 21-1 is a simple demo that uses both of them.

Example 21-1. geopandas.py

```
import geopandas
import matplotlib.pyplot as plt

world_file = geopandas.datasets.get_path('naturalearth_lowres')
world = geopandas.read_file(world_file)
cities_file = geopandas.datasets.get_path('naturalearth_cities')
cities = geopandas.read_file(cities_file)
base = world.plot(color='orchid')
cities.plot(ax=base, color='black', markersize=2)
plt.show()
```

Run that, and you should get the map shown in Figure 21-2.

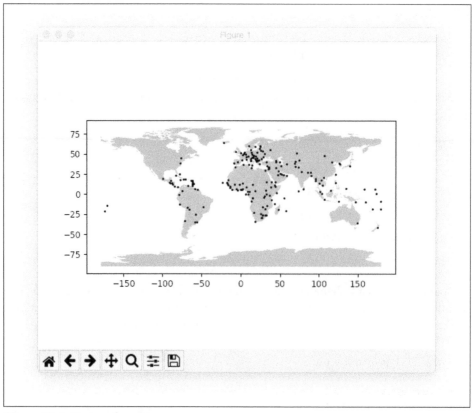

Figure 21-2. Geopandas map

To me, geopandas currently looks like the best combination for geographic data management and display. But there are many worthy contenders, which we look at in the next section.

Other Mapping Packages

Here's a grab bag of links to other Python mapping software; many cannot be installed fully with `pip`, but some can with `conda` (the alternative Python package installer that's especially handy for scientific software):

pyshp (https://pypi.org/project/pyshp)
    A pure-Python shapefile library, mentioned earlier in "Draw a Map from a Shapefile" on page 476.

kartograph (http://kartograph.org)
    Renders shapefiles into SVG maps on the server or client.

---

shapely (https://shapely.readthedocs.io)
> Addresses geometric questions such as, "What buildings in this town are within the 50-year flood contour?"

basemap (http://matplotlib.org/basemap)
> Based on `matplotlib`, draws maps and data overlays. Unfortunately, it has been deprecated in favor of Cartopy.

cartopy (https://scitools.org.uk/cartopy/docs/latest)
> Succeeds Basemap, and does some of the things that `geopandas` does.

folium (https://python-visualization.github.io/folium)
> Works with leaflet.js, used by `geopandas`.

plotly (https://plot.ly/python/maps)
> Another plotting package that includes mapping features.

dash (https://dash.plot.ly)
> Uses Plotly, Flask and JavaScript to create interactive visualizations, including maps.

fiona (https://github.com/Toblerity/Fiona)
> Wraps the OGR library, which handles shapefiles and other vector formats.

Open Street Map (https://oreil.ly/BJeha)
> Accesses the vast OpenStreetMap (*https://www.openstreetmap.org*) world maps.

mapnik (http://mapnik.org)
> A C++ library with Python bindings, for vector (line) and raster (image) maps.

Vincent (http://vincent.readthedocs.org)
> Translates to Vega, a JavaScript visualization tool; see the tutorial: Mapping data in Python with pandas and vincent (*https://oreil.ly/0TbTC*).

Python for ArcGIS (http://bit.ly/py-arcgis)
> Links to Python resources for Esri's commercial ArcGIS product.

Using geospatial data with python (http://bit.ly/geos-py)
> Video presentations.

So you'd like to make a map using Python (http://bit.ly/pythonmap)
> Uses `pandas`, `matplotlib`, `shapely`, and other Python modules to create maps of historic plaque locations.

Python Geospatial Development (http://bit.ly/py-geo-dev) (Packt)
> A book by Eric Westra with examples using `mapnik` and other tools.

Learning Geospatial Analysis with Python (http://bit.ly/learn-geo-py) (Packt)
   Another book by Joel Lawhead reviewing formats and libraries, with geospatial algorithms.

geomancer (https://github.com/thinkingmachines/geomancer)
   Geospatial engineering, such as the distance from a point to the nearest Irish bar.

If you're interested in maps, try downloading and installing one of these packages and see what you can do. Or, you can avoid installing software and try connecting to a remote web service API yourself; Chapter 18 shows you how to connect to web servers and decode JSON responses.

Applications and Data

I've been talking about drawing maps, but you can do a lot more with map data. *Geocoding* converts between addresses and geographic coordinates. There are many geocoding APIs (*https://oreil.ly/ZqwOW*) (see ProgrammableWeb's comparison (*http://bit.ly/free-geo-api*)) and Python libraries:

- geopy (*https://code.google.com/p/geopy*)
- pygeocoder (*https://pypi.python.org/pypi/pygeocoder*)
- googlemaps (*http://py-googlemaps.sourceforge.net*)

If you sign up with Google or another source to get an API key, you can access other services such as step-by-step travel directions or local search.

Here are a few sources of mapping data:

http://www.census.gov/geo/maps-data
   Overview of the US Census Bureau's map files

http://www.census.gov/geo/maps-data/data/tiger.html
   Heaps of geographic and demographic map data

http://wiki.openstreetmap.org/wiki/Potential_Datasources
   Worldwide sources

http://www.naturalearthdata.com
   Vector and raster map data at three scales

I should mention the Data Science Toolkit (*http://www.datasciencetoolkit.org*) here. It includes free bidirectional geocoding, coordinates to political boundaries and statistics, and more. You can also download all the data and software as a virtual machine (VM) and run it self-contained on your own computer.

Coming Up

We go to a Science Fair and see all the Python exhibits.

Things to Do

21.1 Install `geopandas` and run Example 21-1. Try modifying things like colors and marker sizes.

CHAPTER 22

Py Sci

In her reign the power of steam
On land and sea became supreme,
And all now have strong reliance
In fresh victories of science.

—James McIntyre, *Queen's Jubilee Ode 1887*

In the past few years, largely because of the software you'll see in this chapter, Python has become extremely popular with scientists. If you're a scientist or student yourself, you might have used tools like MATLAB and R, or traditional languages such as Java, C, or C++. Now you'll see how Python makes an excellent platform for scientific analysis and publishing.

Math and Statistics in the Standard Library

First, let's take a little trip back to the standard library and visit some features and modules that we've ignored.

Math Functions

Python has a menagerie of math functions in the standard math (*https://oreil.ly/01SHP*) library. Just type `import math` to access them from your programs.

It has a few constants such as `pi` and `e`:

```
>>> import math
>>> math.pi
>>> 3.141592653589793
>>> math.e
2.718281828459045
```

Most of it consists of functions, so let's look at the most useful ones.

`fabs()` returns the absolute value of its argument:

```
>>> math.fabs(98.6)
98.6
>>> math.fabs(-271.1)
271.1
```

Get the integer below (`floor()`) and above (`ceil()`) some number:

```
>>> math.floor(98.6)
98
>>> math.floor(-271.1)
-272
>>> math.ceil(98.6)
99
>>> math.ceil(-271.1)
-271
```

Calculate the factorial (in math, n !) by using `factorial()`:

```
>>> math.factorial(0)
1
>>> math.factorial(1)
1
>>> math.factorial(2)
2
>>> math.factorial(3)
6
>>> math.factorial(10)
3628800
```

Get the logarithm of the argument in base e with `log()`:

```
>>> math.log(1.0)
0.0
>>> math.log(math.e)
1.0
```

If you want a different base for the log, provide it as a second argument:

```
>>> math.log(8, 2)
3.0
```

The function pow() does the opposite, raising a number to a power:

```
>>> math.pow(2, 3)
8.0
```

Python also has the built-in exponentiation operator ** to do the same, but it doesn't automatically convert the result to a float if the base and power are both integers:

```
>>> 2**3
8
>>> 2.0**3
8.0
```

Get a square root with `sqrt()`:

```
>>> math.sqrt(100.0)
10.0
```

Don't try to trick this function; it's seen it all before:

```
>>> math.sqrt(-100.0)
Traceback (most recent call last):
  File "<stdin>", line 1, in <module>
ValueError: math domain error
```

The usual trigonometric functions are all there, and I'll just list their names here: `sin()`, `cos()`, `tan()`, `asin()`, `acos()`, `atan()`, and `atan2()`. If you remember the Pythagorean theorem (or can say it fast three times without spitting), the math library also has a `hypot()` function to calculate the hypotenuse from two sides:

```
>>> x = 3.0
>>> y = 4.0
>>> math.hypot(x, y)
5.0
```

If you don't trust all these fancy functions, you can work it out yourself:

```
>>> math.sqrt(x*x + y*y)
5.0
>>> math.sqrt(x**2 + y**2)
5.0
```

A last set of functions converts angular coordinates:

```
>>> math.radians(180.0)
3.141592653589793
>>> math.degrees(math.pi)
180.0
```

Working with Complex Numbers

Complex numbers are fully supported in the base Python language, with their familiar notation of *real* and *imaginary* parts:

```
>>> # a real number
... 5
5
>>> # an imaginary number
... 8j
8j
>>> # an imaginary number
... 3 + 2j
(3+2j)
```

Because the imaginary number i (1j in Python) is defined as the square root of −1, we can execute the following:

```
>>> 1j * 1j
(-1+0j)
>>> (7 + 1j) * 1j
(-1+7j)
```

Some complex math functions are in the standard cmath (*https://oreil.ly/1EZQ0*) module.

Calculate Accurate Floating Point with decimal

Floating-point numbers in computers are not quite like the real numbers we learned in school:

```
>>> x = 10.0 / 3.0
>>> x
3.3333333333333335
```

Hey, what's that 5 at the end? It should be 3 all the way down. This happens because there are only so many bits in computer CPU registers, and numbers that aren't exact powers of two can't be represented exactly.

With Python's decimal (*https://oreil.ly/o-bmR*) module, you can represent numbers to your desired level of significance. This is especially important for calculations involving money. US currency doesn't go lower than a cent (a hundredth of a dollar), so if we're calculating money amounts as dollars and cents, we want to be accurate to the penny. If we try to represent dollars and cents through floating-point values such as 19.99 and 0.06, we'll lose some significance way down in the end bits before we even begin calculating with them. How do we handle this? Easy. We use the decimal module, instead:

```
>>> from decimal import Decimal
>>> price = Decimal('19.99')
>>> tax = Decimal('0.06')
>>> total = price + (price * tax)
>>> total
Decimal('21.1894')
```

We created the price and tax with string values to preserve their significance. The total calculation maintained all the significant fractions of a cent, but we want to get the nearest cent:

```
>>> penny = Decimal('0.01')
>>> total.quantize(penny)
Decimal('21.19')
```

You might get the same results with plain old floats and rounding, but not always. You could also multiply everything by 100 and use integer cents in your calculations, but that will bite you eventually, too.

Perform Rational Arithmetic with fractions

You can represent numbers as a numerator divided by a denominator through the standard Python fractions (*https://oreil.ly/l286g*) module. Here is a simple operation multiplying one-third by two-thirds:

```
>>> from fractions import Fraction
>>> Fraction(1,  3) * Fraction(2, 3)
Fraction(2, 9)
```

Floating-point arguments can be inexact, so you can use Decimal within Fraction:

```
>>> Fraction(1.0/3.0)
Fraction(6004799503160661, 18014398509481984)
>>> Fraction(Decimal('1.0')/Decimal('3.0'))
Fraction(3333333333333333333333333333, 10000000000000000000000000000)
```

Get the greatest common divisor of two numbers with the gcd function:

```
>>> import fractions
>>> fractions.gcd(24, 16)
8
```

Use Packed Sequences with array

A Python list is more like a linked list than an array. If you want a one-dimensional sequence of the same type, use the array (*https://oreil.ly/VejPU*) type. It uses less space than a list and supports many list methods. Create one with array(*typecode*, *initializer*). The *typecode* specifies the data type (like int or float) and the optional *initializer* contains initial values, which you can specify as a list, string, or iterable.

I've never used this package for real work. It's a low-level data structure, useful for things such as image data. If you actually need an array—especially with more then one dimension—to do numeric calculations, you're much better off with NumPy, which we discuss momentarily.

Handling Simple Stats with statistics

Beginning with Python 3.4, statistics (*https://oreil.ly/DELnM*) is a standard module. It has the usual functions: mean, media, mode, standard deviation, variance, and so on. Input arguments are sequences (lists or tuples) or iterators of various numeric data types: int, float, decimal, and fraction. One function, mode, also accepts strings.

Many more statistical functions are available in packages such as SciPy and Pandas, featured later in this chapter.

Matrix Multiplication

Starting with Python 3.5, you'll see the @ character doing something out of character. It will still be used for decorators, but it will also have a new use for *matrix multiplication (https://oreil.ly/fakoD)*. If you're using an older version of Python, NumPy (coming right up) is your best bet.

Scientific Python

The rest of this chapter covers third-party Python packages for science and math. Although you can install them individually, you should consider downloading all of them at once as part of a scientific Python distribution. Here are your main choices:

Anaconda (https://www.anaconda.com)
    Free, extensive, up-to-the-minute, supports Python 2 and 3, and won't clobber your existing system Python

Enthought Canopy (https://assets.enthought.com/downloads)
    Available in both free and commercial versions

Python(x,y) (https://python-xy.github.io)
    A Windows-only release

Pyzo (http://www.pyzo.org)
    Based on some tools from Anaconda, plus a few others

I recommend installing Anaconda. It's big, but everything in this chapter is in there. The examples in the rest of this chapter will assume that you've installed the required packages, either individually or as part of Anaconda.

NumPy

NumPy (*http://www.numpy.org*) is one of the main reasons for Python's popularity among scientists. You've heard that dynamic languages such as Python are often slower than compiled languages like C, or even other interpreted languages such as Java. NumPy was written to provide fast multidimensional numeric arrays, similar to scientific languages like FORTRAN. You get the speed of C with the developer-friendly nature of Python.

If you've downloaded one of the scientific Python distributions, you already have NumPy. If not, follow the instructions on the NumPy download page (*https://oreil.ly/HcZZi*).

To begin with NumPy, you should understand a core data structure, a multidimensional array called an `ndarray` (for *N-dimensional array*) or just an `array`. Unlike Python's lists and tuples, each element needs to be of the same type. NumPy refers to an array's number of dimensions as its *rank*. A one-dimensional array is like a row of values, a two-dimensional array is like a table of rows and columns, and a three-dimensional array is like a Rubik's Cube. The lengths of the dimensions need not be the same.

> The NumPy array and the standard Python `array` are not the same thing. For the rest of this chapter, when I say *array*, I'm referring to a NumPy array.

But why do you need an array?

- Scientific data often consists of large sequences of data.
- Scientific calculations on this data often use matrix math, regression, simulation, and other techniques that process many data points at a time.
- NumPy handles arrays *much* faster than standard Python lists or tuples.

There are many ways to make a NumPy array.

Make an Array with array()

You can make an array from a normal list or tuple:

```
>>> b = np.array( [2, 4, 6, 8] )
>>> b
array([2, 4, 6, 8])
```

The attribute `ndim` returns the rank:

```
>>> b.ndim
1
```

The total number of values in the array are given by `size`:

```
>>> b.size
4
```

The number of values in each rank are returned by `shape`:

```
>>> b.shape
(4,)
```

Make an Array with arange()

NumPy's `arange()` method is similar to Python's standard `range()`. If you call `arange()` with a single integer argument `num`, it returns an `ndarray` from 0 to `num-1`:

```
>>> import numpy as np
>>> a = np.arange(10)
>>> a
array([0, 1, 2, 3, 4, 5, 6, 7, 8, 9])
>>> a.ndim
1
>>> a.shape
(10,)
>>> a.size
10
```

With two values, it creates an array from the first to the last, minus one:

```
>>> a = np.arange(7, 11)
>>> a
array([ 7,  8,  9, 10])
```

And you can provide a step size to use instead of one as a third argument:

```
>>> a = np.arange(7, 11, 2)
>>> a
array([7, 9])
```

So far, our examples have used integers, but floats work just fine:

```
>>> f = np.arange(2.0, 9.8, 0.3)
>>> f
array([ 2. ,  2.3,  2.6,  2.9,  3.2,  3.5,  3.8,  4.1,  4.4,  4.7,  5. ,
        5.3,  5.6,  5.9,  6.2,  6.5,  6.8,  7.1,  7.4,  7.7,  8. ,  8.3,
        8.6,  8.9,  9.2,  9.5,  9.8])
```

And one last trick: the dtype argument tells `arange` what type of values to produce:

```
>>> g = np.arange(10, 4, -1.5, dtype=np.float)
>>> g
array([ 10. ,   8.5,   7. ,   5.5])
```

Make an Array with zeros(), ones(), or random()

The `zeros()` method returns an array in which all the values are zero. The argument you provide is a tuple with the shape that you want. Here's a one-dimensional array:

```
>>> a = np.zeros((3,))
>>> a
array([ 0.,  0.,  0.])
>>> a.ndim
1
>>> a.shape
(3,)
```

```
>>> a.size
3
```

This one is of rank two:

```
>>> b = np.zeros((2, 4))
>>> b
array([[ 0.,  0.,  0.,  0.],
       [ 0.,  0.,  0.,  0.]])
>>> b.ndim
2
>>> b.shape
(2, 4)
>>> b.size
8
```

The other special function that fills an array with the same value is ones():

```
>>> import numpy as np
>>> k = np.ones((3, 5))
>>> k
array([[ 1.,  1.,  1.,  1.,  1.],
       [ 1.,  1.,  1.,  1.,  1.],
       [ 1.,  1.,  1.,  1.,  1.]])
```

One last initializer creates an array with random values between 0.0 and 1.0:

```
>>> m = np.random.random((3, 5))
>>> m
array([[  1.92415699e-01,   4.43131404e-01,   7.99226773e-01,
          1.14301942e-01,   2.85383430e-04],
       [  6.53705749e-01,   7.48034559e-01,   4.49463241e-01,
          4.87906915e-01,   9.34341118e-01],
       [  9.47575562e-01,   2.21152583e-01,   2.49031209e-01,
          3.46190961e-01,   8.94842676e-01]])
```

Change an Array's Shape with reshape()

So far, an array doesn't seem that different from a list or tuple. One difference is that you can get it to do tricks such as change its shape by using reshape():

```
>>> a = np.arange(10)
>>> a
array([0, 1, 2, 3, 4, 5, 6, 7, 8, 9])
>>> a = a.reshape(2, 5)
>>> a
array([[0, 1, 2, 3, 4],
       [5, 6, 7, 8, 9]])
>>> a.ndim
2
>>> a.shape
(2, 5)
>>> a.size
10
```

You can reshape the same array in different ways:

```
>>> a = a.reshape(5, 2)
>>> a
array([[0, 1],
       [2, 3],
       [4, 5],
       [6, 7],
       [8, 9]])
>>> a.ndim
2
>>> a.shape
(5, 2)
>>> a.size
10
```

Assigning a shapely tuple to shape does the same thing:

```
>>> a.shape = (2, 5)
>>> a
array([[0, 1, 2, 3, 4],
       [5, 6, 7, 8, 9]])
```

The only restriction on a shape is that the product of the rank sizes needs to equal the total number of values (in this case, 10):

```
>>> a = a.reshape(3, 4)
Traceback (most recent call last):
  File "<stdin>", line 1, in <module>
ValueError: total size of new array must be unchanged
```

Get an Element with []

A one-dimensional array works like a list:

```
>>> a = np.arange(10)
>>> a[7]
7
>>> a[-1]
9
```

However, if the array has a different shape, use comma-separated indices within the square brackets:

```
>>> a.shape = (2, 5)
>>> a
array([[0, 1, 2, 3, 4],
       [5, 6, 7, 8, 9]])
>>> a[1,2]
7
```

That's different from a two-dimensional Python list, which has its indexes in separate square brackets:

```
>>> l = [ [0, 1, 2, 3, 4], [5, 6, 7, 8, 9] ]
>>> l
[[0, 1, 2, 3, 4], [5, 6, 7, 8, 9]]
>>> l[1,2]
Traceback (most recent call last):
  File "<stdin>", line 1, in <module>
TypeError: list indices must be integers, not tuple
>>> l[1][2]
7
```

One last thing: slices work, but again, only within one set of square brackets. Let's make our familiar test array again:

```
>>> a = np.arange(10)
>>> a = a.reshape(2, 5)
>>> a
array([[0, 1, 2, 3, 4],
       [5, 6, 7, 8, 9]])
```

Use a slice to get the first row, elements from offset 2 to the end:

```
>>> a[0, 2:]
array([2, 3, 4])
```

Now, get the last row, elements up to the third from the end:

```
>>> a[-1, :3]
array([5, 6, 7])
```

You can also assign a value to more than one element with a slice. The following statement assigns the value 1000 to columns (offsets) 2 and 3 of all rows:

```
>>> a[:, 2:4] = 1000
>>> a
array([[   0,    1, 1000, 1000,    4],
       [   5,    6, 1000, 1000,    9]])
```

Array Math

Making and reshaping arrays was so much fun that we almost forgot to actually *do* something with them. For our first trick, we use NumPy's redefined multiplication (*) operator to multiply all the values in a NumPy array at once:

```
>>> from numpy import *
>>> a = arange(4)
>>> a
array([0, 1, 2, 3])
>>> a *= 3
>>> a
array([0, 3, 6, 9])
```

If you tried to multiply each element in a normal Python list by a number, you'd need a loop or a list comprehension:

```
>>> plain_list = list(range(4))
>>> plain_list
[0, 1, 2, 3]
>>> plain_list = [num * 3 for num in plain_list]
>>> plain_list
[0, 3, 6, 9]
```

This all-at-once behavior also applies to addition, subtraction, division, and other functions in the NumPy library. For example, you can initialize all members of an array to any value by using zeros() and +:

```
>>> from numpy import *
>>> a = zeros((2, 5)) + 17.0
>>> a
array([[ 17.,   17.,   17.,   17.,   17.],
       [ 17.,   17.,   17.,   17.,   17.]])
```

Linear Algebra

NumPy includes many functions for linear algebra. For example, let's define this system of linear equations:

```
4x + 5y = 20
 x + 2y = 13
```

How do we solve for x and y? We build two arrays:

- The *coefficients* (multipliers for x and y)
- The *dependent* variables (right side of the equation)

```
>>> import numpy as np
>>> coefficients = np.array([ [4, 5], [1, 2] ])
>>> dependents = np.array( [20, 13] )
```

Now, use the solve() function in the linalg module:

```
>>> answers = np.linalg.solve(coefficients, dependents)
>>> answers
array([ -8.33333333,  10.66666667])
```

The result says that x is about –8.3 and y is about 10.6. Did these numbers solve the equation?

```
>>> 4 * answers[0] + 5 * answers[1]
20.0
>>> 1 * answers[0] + 2 * answers[1]
13.0
```

How about that. To avoid all that typing, you can also ask NumPy to get the *dot product* of the arrays for you:

```
>>> product = np.dot(coefficients, answers)
>>> product
array([ 20.,  13.])
```

The values in the `product` array should be close to the values in `dependents` if this solution is correct. You can use the `allclose()` function to check whether the arrays are approximately equal (they might not be exactly equal because of floating-point rounding):

```
>>> np.allclose(product, dependents)
True
```

NumPy also has modules for polynomials, Fourier transforms, statistics, and some probability distributions.

SciPy

There's even more in a library of mathematical and statistical functions built on top of NumPy: SciPy (*http://www.scipy.org*). The SciPy release (*https://oreil.ly/Yv7G-*) includes NumPy, SciPy, Pandas (coming later in this chapter), and other libraries.

SciPy includes many modules, including some for the following tasks:

- Optimization
- Statistics
- Interpolation
- Linear regression
- Integration
- Image processing
- Signal processing

If you've worked with other scientific computing tools, you'll find that Python, NumPy, and SciPy cover some of the same ground as the commercial MATLAB (*https://oreil.ly/jOPMO*) or open source R (*http://www.r-project.org*).

SciKit

In the same pattern of building on earlier software, SciKit (*https://scikits.appspot.com*) is a group of scientific packages built on SciPy. SciKit-Learn (*https://scikit-learn.org*) is a prominent *machine learning* package: it supports modeling, classification, clustering, and various algorithms.

Pandas

Recently, the phrase *data science* has become common. Some definitions that I've seen include "statistics done on a Mac," or "statistics done in San Francisco." However you define it, the tools we've talked about in this chapter—NumPy, SciPy, and the subject of this section, Pandas—are components of a growing popular data-science toolkit. (Mac and San Francisco are optional.)

Pandas (*http://pandas.pydata.org*) is a new package for interactive data analysis. It's especially useful for real-world data manipulation, combining the matrix math of NumPy with the processing ability of spreadsheets and relational databases. The book *Python for Data Analysis: Data Wrangling with Pandas, NumPy, and IPython* (*http://bit.ly/python_for_data_analysis*) by Wes McKinney (O'Reilly) covers data wrangling with NumPy, IPython, and Pandas.

NumPy is oriented toward traditional scientific computing, which tends to manipulate multidimensional data sets of a single type, usually floating point. Pandas is more like a database editor, handling multiple data types in groups. In some languages, such groups are called *records* or *structures*. Pandas defines a base data structure called a `DataFrame`. This is an ordered collection of columns with names and types. It has some resemblance to a database table, a Python named tuple, and a Python nested dictionary. Its purpose is to simplify the handling of the kind of data you're likely to encounter not just in science, but also in business. In fact, Pandas was originally designed to manipulate financial data, for which the most common alternative is a spreadsheet.

Pandas is an ETL tool for real-world, messy data—missing values, oddball formats, scattered measurements—of all data types. You can split, join, extend, fill in, convert, reshape, slice, and load and save files. It integrates with the tools we've just discussed —NumPy, SciPy, iPython—to calculate statistics, fit data to models, draw plots, publish, and so on.

Most scientists just want to get their work done, without spending months to become experts in esoteric computer languages or applications. With Python, they can become productive more quickly.

Python and Scientific Areas

We've been looking at Python tools that could be used in almost any area of science. What about software and documentation targeted to specific scientific domains? Here's a small sample of Python's use for specific problems, and some special-purpose libraries:

General
- Python computations in science and engineering (*http://bit.ly/py-comp-sci*)
- A crash course in Python for scientists (*http://bit.ly/pyforsci*)

Physics
- Computational physics (*http://bit.ly/comp-phys-py*)
- Astropy (*https://www.astropy.org*)
- SunPy (*https://sunpy.org*) (solar data analysis)
- MetPy (*https://unidata.github.io/MetPy*) (meteorological data analysis)
- Py-ART (*https://arm-doe.github.io/pyart*) (weather radar)
- Community Intercomparison Suite (*http://www.cistools.net*) (atmospheric sciences)
- Freud (*https://freud.readthedocs.io*) (trajectory analysis)
- Platon (*https://platon.readthedocs.io*) (exoplanet atmospheres)
- PSI4 (*http://psicode.org*) (quantum chemistry)
- OpenQuake Engine (*https://github.com/gem/oq-engine*)
- yt (*https://yt-project.org*) (volumetric data analysis)

Biology and medicine
- Biopython (*https://biopython.org*)
- Python for biologists (*http://pythonforbiologists.com*)
- Introduction to Applied Bioinformatics (*http://readiab.org*)
- Neuroimaging in Python (*http://nipy.org*)
- MNE (*https://www.martinos.org/mne*) (neurophysiological data visualization)
- PyMedPhys (*https://pymedphys.com*)
- Nengo (*https://www.nengo.ai*) (neural simulator)

International conferences on Python and scientific data include the following:

- PyData (*http://pydata.org*)
- SciPy (*http://conference.scipy.org*)
- EuroSciPy (*https://www.euroscipy.org*)

Coming Up

We've reached the end of our observable Python universe, except for the multiverse appendices.

Things to Do

22.1 Install Pandas. Get the CSV file in Example 16-1. Run the program in Example 16-2. Experiment with some of the Pandas commands.

Hardware and Software for Beginning Programmers

Some things make intuitive sense. Some we see in nature, and others are human inventions such as the wheel or pizza.

Others require more of a leap of faith. How does a television convert some invisible wiggles in the air into sounds and moving images?

A computer is one of these hard-to-accept ideas. How can you type something and get a machine to do what you want?

When I was learning to program, it was hard to find answers to some basic questions. For example: some books explain computer memory with the analogy of books on a library shelf. I wondered, if you *read from memory*, the analogy implies you're taking a book from the shelf. So, does that erase it from memory? Actually, no. It's more like getting a *copy* of the book from the shelf.

This appendix is a short review of computer hardware and software, if you're relatively new to programming. I try to explain the things that become "obvious" eventually but may be sticking points at the start.

Hardware

Caveman Computers

When the cavemen Og and Thog returned from hunting, they would each add a rock to their own pile for each mammoth they slew. But they couldn't do much with the piles, other than gain bragging rights if one was noticeably larger than the other.

Distant descendents of Og (Thog got stomped by a mammoth one day, trying to add to his pile) would learn to count, and write, and use an abacus. But some leaps of imagination and technology were needed to get beyond these tools to the concept of a computer. The first necessary technology was electricity.

Electricity

Ben Franklin thought that electricity was a flow of some invisible fluid from a place with more fluid (*positive*) to a place with less (*negative*). He was right, but got the terms backwards. Electrons flow from his "negative" to "positive," but electrons weren't discovered until much later—too late to change the terminology. So, ever since we've needed to remember that electrons flow one way and *current* is defined as flowing the other way.

We're all familiar with natural electrical phenomena like static electricity and lightning. After people discovered how to push electrons through conducting wires to make electrical *circuits*, we got one step closer to making computers.

I used to think that electric current in a wire was caused by jazzed electrons doing laps around the track. It's actually quite different. Electrons jump from one atom to another. They behave a little like ball bearings in a tube (or tapioca balls in a bubble tea straw). When you push a ball at one end, it pushes its neighbor, and so on until the ball at the other end is pushed out. Although an average electron moves slowly (*drift speed* in a wire is only about three inches/hour), this almost-simultaneous bumping causes the generated electromagetic wave to propagate very quickly: 50 to 99% the speed of light, depending on the conductor.

Inventions

We still needed:

- A way to remember things
- A way to do stuff with the things that we remembered

One memory concept was a *switch*: something that's either on or off, and stays as it is until something flips it to the other state. An electrical switch works by opening or closing a circuit, allowing electrons to flow or blocking them. We use switches all the time to control lights and other electrical devices. What was needed was a way to control the switch itself by electricity.

The earliest computers (and televisions) used vacuum tubes for this purpose, but these were big and often burned out. The single key invention that led to modern computers was the *transistor*: smaller, more efficient, and more reliable. The final key step was to make transistors much smaller and connect them in *integrated circuits*.

For many years, computers got faster and ridiculously cheaper as they became smaller and smaller. Signals move faster when the components are closer together.

But there's a limit to how small we can stuff things together. This electron friskiness encounters *resistance*, which generates heat. We reached that lower limit more than 10 years ago, and manufacturers have compensated by putting multiple "chips" on the same board. This has increased the demand for *distributed computing*, which I discuss in a bit.

Regardless of these details, with these inventions we have been able to construct *computers*: machines that can remember things and so something with them.

An Idealized Computer

Real computers have lots of complex features. Let's focus on the essential parts.

A circuit "board" contains the CPU, memory, and wires connecting them to each other and to plugs for external devices.

The CPU

The *CPU* (Central Processing Unit), or "chip," does the actual "computing":

- Mathematical tasks like addition
- Comparing values

Memory and Caches

RAM (Random Access Memory) does the "remembering." It's fast, but *volatile* (loses its data if power is lost).

CPUs have been getting ever faster than memory, so computer designers have been adding *caches*: smaller, faster memory between the CPU and main memory. When your CPU tries to read some bytes from memory, it first tries the closest cache (called an *L1* cache), then the next (*L2*), and eventually to main RAM.

Storage

Because main memory loses its data, we also need *nonvolatile* storage. Such devices are cheaper than memory and hold much more data, but are also much slower.

The traditional storage method has been "spinning rust": *magnetic disks* (or *hard drives* or *HDD*) with movable read-write heads, a little like vinyl records and a stylus.

A hybrid technology called *SSD* (Solid State Drive) is made of semiconductors like RAM, but is nonvolatile like magnetic disks. Price and speed falls between the two.

Inputs

How do you get data into the computer? For people, the main choices are keyboards, mice, and touchscreens.

Outputs

People generally see computer output with displays and printers.

Relative Access Times

The amount of time it takes to get data to and from any of these components varies tremendously. This has big practical implications, For example, software needs to run in memory and access data there, but it also needs to store data safely on nonvolatile devices like disks. The problem is that disks are thousands of times slower, and networks are even slower. This means that programmers spend a lot of time trying to make the best trade-offs between speed and cost.

In Computer Latency at a Human Scale (*https://oreil.ly/G36qD*), David Jeppesen compares them. I've derived Table A-1 from his numbers and others. The last columns—Ratio, Relative Time (CPU = one second) and Relative Distance (CPU = one inch)—are easier for us to relate to than the specific timings.

Table A-1. Relative access times

Location	Time	Ratio	Relative Time	Relative Distance
CPU	0.4 ns	1	1 sec	1 in
L1 cache	0.9 ns	2	2 sec	2 in
L2 cache	2.8 ns	7	7 sec	7 in
L3 cache	28 ns	70	1 min	6 ft
RAM	100 ns	250	4 min	20 ft
SSD	100 μs	250,000	3 days	4 miles
Mag disk	10 ms	25,000,000	9 months	400 miles
Internet: SF→NY	65 ms	162,500,000	5 years	2,500 miles

It's a good thing that a CPU instruction actually takes less than a nanosecond instead of a whole second, or else you could have a baby in the time it takes to access a magnetic disk. Because disk and network times are so much slower than CPU and RAM, it helps to do as much work in memory as you can. And since the CPU itself is so much faster than RAM, it makes sense to keep data contiguous, so the bytes can be served by the faster (but smaller) caches closer to the CPU.

Software

Given all this computer hardware, how would we control it? First, we have both *instructions* (stuff that tells the CPU what to do) and *data* (inputs and outputs for the instructions). In the *stored-program computer*, everything could be treated as data, which simplified the design. But how do you represent instructions and data? What is it that you save in one place and process in another? The far-flung descendants of caveman Og wanted to know.

In the Beginning Was the Bit

Let's go back to the idea of a *switch*: something that maintains one of two values. These could be on or off, high or low voltage, positive or negative—just something that can be set, won't forget, and can later provide its value to anyone who asks. Integrated circuits gave us a way to integrate and connect billions of little switches into small chips.

If a switch can have just two values, it can be used to represent a *bit*, or binary digit. This could be treated as the tiny integers 0 and 1, yes and no, true and false, or anything we want.

However, bits are too small for anything beyond 0 and 1. How can we convince bits to represent bigger things?

For an answer, look at your fingers. We use only 10 digits (0 through 9) in our daily lives, but we make numbers much bigger than 9 by *positional notation*. If I add 1 to the number 38, the 8 becomes a 9 and the whole value is now 39. If I add another 1, the 9 turns into a 0 and I *carry the one* to the left, incrementing the 3 to a 4 and getting the final number 40. The far-right number is in the "one's column," the one to its left is the "ten's column," and so on to the left, multiplying by 10 each time. With three decimal digits, you can represent a thousand (10 * 10 * 10) numbers, from 000 to 999.

We can use positional notation with bits to make larger collections of them. A *byte* has eight bits, with 2^8 (256) possible bit combinations. You can use a byte to store, for example, small integers 0 to 255 (you need to save room for a zero in positional notation).

A byte looks like eight bits in a row, each bit with a value of either 0 (or off, or false) or 1 (or on, or true). The bit on the far right is the *least significant*, and the leftmost one is the *most significant*.

Machine Language

Each computer CPU is designed with an *instruction set* of bit patterns (also called *opcodes*) that it understands. Each opcode performs a certain function, with input values from one place and output values to another place. CPUs have special internal places called *registers* to store these opcodes and values.

Let's use an simplified computer that works only with bytes, and has four byte-sized registers called A, B, C, and D. Assume that:

- The command opcode goes into register A
- The command gets its byte inputs from registers B and C
- The command stores its byte result in register D

(Adding two bytes could *overflow* a single byte result, but I'm ignoring that here to show what happens where.)

Say that:

- Register A contains the opcode for *add two integers*: a decimal 1 (binary 00000001).
- Register B has the decimal value 5 (binary 00000101).
- Register C has the decimal value 3 (binary 00000011).

The CPU sees that an instruction has arrived in register A. It decodes and runs that instruction, reading values from registers B and C and passing them to internal hardware circuits that can add bytes. When it's done, we should see the decimal value 8 (binary 00001000) in register D.

The CPU does addition, and other mathematical functions, using registers in this way. It *decodes* the opcode and directs control to specific circuits within the CPU. It can also compare things, such as "Is the value in B larger than the value in C?" Importantly, it also *fetches* values from memory to CPU and *stores* values from CPU to memory.

The computer stores *programs* (machine-language instructions and data) in memory and handles feeding instructions and data to and from the CPU.

Assembler

It's hard to program in machine language. You have to get specify every bit perfectly, which is very time consuming. So, people came up with a slightly more readable level of languages called *assembly language*, or just *assembler*. These languages are specific to a CPU design and let you use things like variable names to define your instruction flow and data.

Higher-Level Languages

Assembler is still a painstaking endeavor, so people designed *higher-level languages* that were even easier for people to use. These languages would be translated into assembler by a program called a *compiler*, or run directly by an *interpreter*. Among the oldest of these languages are FORTRAN, LISP, and C—wildly different in design and intended use, but similar in their place in computer architecture.

In real jobs you tend to see distinct software "stacks":

Mainframe
　　IBM, COBOL, FORTRAN, and others

Microsoft
　　Windows, ASP, C#, SQL Server

JVM
　　Java, Scala, Groovy

Open source
　　Linux, languages(Python, PHP, Perl, C, C++, Go), databases (MySQL, PostgreSQL), web (apache, nginx)

Programmers tend to stay in one of these worlds, using the languages and tools within it. Some technologies, such as TCP/IP and the web, allow intercommunication between stacks.

Operating Systems

Each innovation was built on those before it, and generally we don't know or care how the lower levels even work. Tools build tools to build even more tools, and we take them for granted.

Tha major operating systems are:

Windows (Microsoft)
　　Commercial, many versions

macOS (Apple)
　　Commercial

Linux
　　Open source

Unix
　　Many commercial versions, largely replaced by Linux

An operating system contains:

A kernel
Schedules and controls programs and I/O

Device drivers
Used by the kernel to access RAM, disk, and other devices

Libraries
Source and binary files for use by developers

Applications
Standalone programs

The same computer hardware can support more than one operating system, but only one at a time. When an operating system starts up, it's called *booting*,[1] so *rebooting* is restarting it. These terms have even appeared in movie marketing, as studios "reboot" previous unsuccessful attempts. You can *dual-boot* your computer by installing more than one operating system, side by side, but only one can be fired up and run at a time.

If you see the phrase *bare metal*, it means a single computer running an operating system. In the next few sections, we step up from bare metal.

Virtual Machines

An operating system is sort of a big program, so eventually someone figured out how to run foreign operating systems as *virtual machines* (guest programs) on *host* machines. So you could have Microsoft Windows running on your PC, but fire up a Linux virtual machine atop it at the same time, without having to buy a second computer or dual-boot it.

Containers

A more recent idea is the *container*—a way to run multiple operating systems at the same time, as long as they share the same kernel. This idea was popularized by Docker (*https://www.docker.com*), which took some little-known Linux kernel features and added useful management features. Their analogy to shipping containers (which revolutionized shipping and saved money for all of us) was clear and appealing. By releasing the code as open-source, Docker enabled containers to be adopted very quickly throughout the computer industry.

---

1 This refers to "Lifting yourself by your own bootstraps," which seems just as improbable as a computer.

Google and other cloud providers had been quietly adding the underlying kernel support to Linux for years, and using containers in their data centers. Containers use fewer resources than virtual machines, letting you pack more programs into each physical computer box.

Distributed Computing and Networks

When businesses first started using personal computers, they needed ways to make them talk to each other as well as to devices like printers. Proprietary networking software, such as Novell's, was originally used, but was eventually replaced by TCP/IP as the internet emerged in the mid- to late 90s. Microsoft grabbed its TCP/IP stack from a free Unix variant called *BSD*.[2]

One effect of the internet boom was a demand for *servers*: machines and software to run all those web, chat, and email services. The old style of *sysadmin* (system administration) was to install and manage all the hardware and software manually. Before long, it became clear to everyone that automation was needed. In 2006, Bill Baker at Microsoft came up with the *pets versus cattle* analogy for server management, and it has since become an industry meme (sometimes as *pets versus livestock*, to be more generic); see Table A-2.

Table A-2. Pets versus livestock

Pets	Livestock
Individually named	Automatically numbered
Customized care	Standardized
Nurse back to health	Replace

You'll often see, as a successor to "sysadmin," the term *DevOps*: development plus operations, a mixture of techniques to support rapid changes to services without blowing them up. Cloud services are extremely large and complex, and even the big companies like Amazon and Google have outages now and then.

The Cloud

People had been building computer *clusters* for a number of years, using many technologies. One early concept was a *Beowulf cluster*: identical commodity computers (Dell or something similar, instead of workstations like Sun or HP), linked by a local network.

---

2 You can still see the copyright notices for the University of California in some Microsoft files.

The term *cloud computing* means using the computers in data centers to perform computing jobs and store data—but not just for the company that owned these back-end resources. The services are provided to anyone, with fees based on CPU time, disk storage amounts, and so on. Amazon and its *AWS* (Amazon Web Services) is the most prominent, but *Azure* (Microsoft) and *Google Cloud* are also biggies.

Behind the scenes, these clouds use bare metal, virtual machines, and containers—all treated as livestock, not pets.

Kubernetes

Companies that needed to manage huge clusters of computers in many data centers—like Google, Amazon, and Facebook—have all borrowed or built solutions to help them scale:

Deployment
> How do you make new computing hardware and software available? How do you replace them when they fail?

Configuration
> How should these systems run? They need things like the names and addresses of other computers, passwords, and security settings.

Orchestration
> How do you manage all these computers, virtual machines, and containers? Can you scale up or down to adjust to load changes?

Service Discovery
> How do you find out who does what, and where it is?

Some competing solutions were built by Docker and others. But just in the past few years, it looks like the battle has been won by Kubernetes (*http://kubernetes.io*).

Google had developed large internal management frameworks, codenamed Borg and Omega. When employees brought up the idea of open sourcing these "crown jewels," management had to think about it a bit, but they took the leap. Google released Kubernetes version 1.0 in 2015, and its ecosystem and influence have grown ever since.

Install Python 3

Most of the examples in this book were written and tested with Python 3.7, the most recent stable version at the time of writing. The What's New in Python page (*https://docs.python.org/3/whatsnew*) presents what was added in each version. There are many sources of Python and many ways to install a new version. In this appendix, I describe a few of these ways:

- A standard installation downloads Python from *python.org*, and adds the helper programs `pip` and `virtualenv`.
- If your work is heavily scientific, you may prefer to get Python bundled with many scientific packages from Anaconda and use its package installer `conda` instead of `pip`.

Windows doesn't have Python at all, and macOS, Linux, and Unix tend to have old versions. Until they catch up, you may need to install Python 3 yourself.

Check Your Python Version

In a terminal or terminal window, type `python -V`:

```
$ python -V
Python 3.7.2
```

Depending on your operating system, if you don't have Python or the operating system can't find it, you'll get some error message like *command not found*.

If you do have Python and it's version 2, you may want to install Python 3—either system wide, or just for yourself in a virtualenv (see "Use virtualenv" on page 412, or "Install virtualenv" on page 517). In this appendix, I show how to install Python 3 system wide.

Install Standard Python

Go to the official Python download page (*https://www.python.org/downloads*) with your web browser. It tries to guess your operating system and present the appropriate choices, but if it guesses wrong, you can use these:

- Python Releases for Windows (*https://www.python.org/downloads/windows*)
- Python Releases for macOS (*https://www.python.org/downloads/mac-osx*)
- Python Source Releases (Linux and Unix) (*https://www.python.org/downloads/source*)

You'll see a page similar to that shown in Figure B-1.

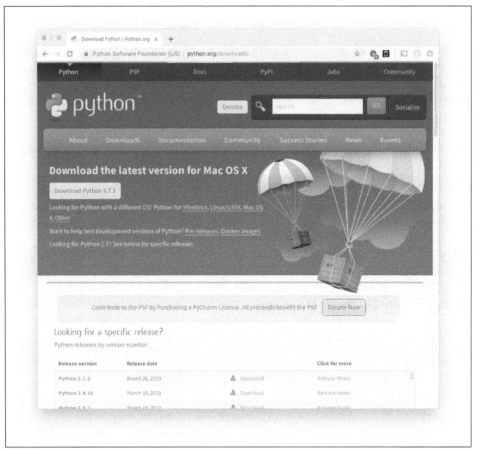

Figure B-1. Sample download page

If you click the yellow Download Python 3.7.3 button, it will download that version for your operating system. If you'd like to learn a little about it first, click the blue link text Python 3.7.3 in the first column of the table at the bottom, under Release version. This takes you to an information page like the one shown in Figure B-2.

Figure B-2. Detail page for download

You need to scroll down the page to see the actual download links (Figure B-3).

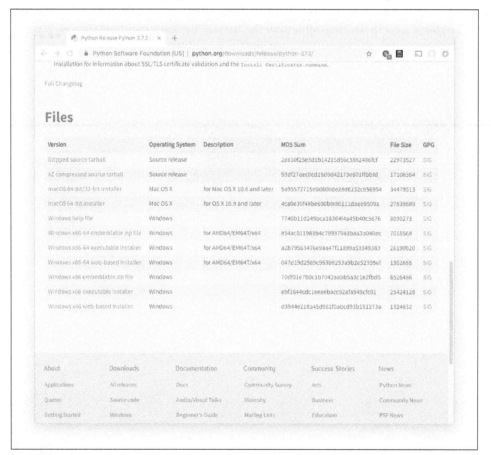

Figure B-3. Bottom of page offering downloads

macOS

Click the macOS 64-bit/32-bit installer (*https://oreil.ly/54lG8*) link to download a Mac *.pkg* file. Double-click it to see an introductory dialog box (Figure B-4).

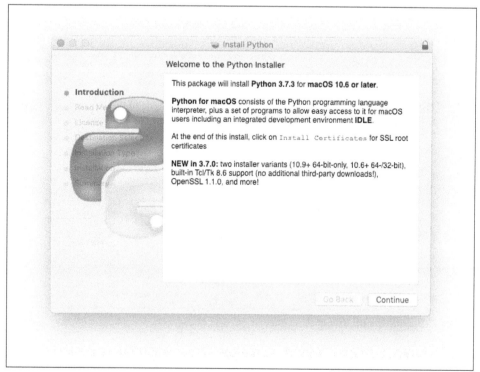

Figure B-4. Mac install dialog 1

Click Continue. You'll go through a succession of other dialog boxes.

When it's all done, you should see the dialog shown in Figure B-5.

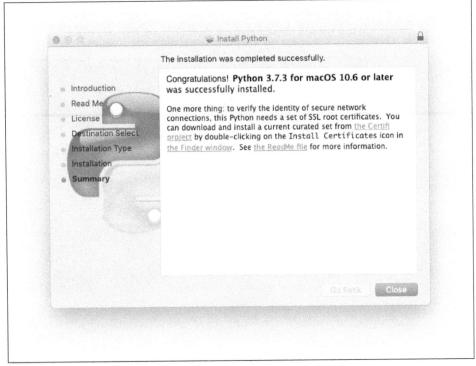

Figure B-5. Mac install dialog 9

Python 3 will be installed as */usr/local/bin/python3*, leaving any existing Python 2 on your computer unchanged.

Windows

Windows has never included Python, but recently made it easier to install. The May 2019 update (*https://oreil.ly/G8Abf*) for Windows 10 includes *python.exe* and *python3.exe* files. These aren't the Python interpreter, but links to a new Python 3.7 page (*https://oreil.ly/Lky_h*) at the Microsoft Store. You can use this link to download and install Python in the same way you get other Windows software.

Or you can download and install Python from the official Python site:

- Windows x86 MSI installer (32-bit) (*http://bit.ly/win-x86*)
- Windows x86-64 MSI installer (64-bit) (*http://bit.ly/win-x86-64*)

To determine whether you have a 32-bit or 64-bit version of Windows:

- Click the Start button.
- Right-click Computer.
- Click Properties and find the bit value.

Click the appropriate installer (*.msi* file). After it's downloaded, double-click it and follow the installer directions.

Linux or Unix

Linux and Unix users get a choice of compressed source formats:

- XZ compressed source tarball (*http://bit.ly/xz-tarball*)
- Gzipped source tarball (*http://bit.ly/gzip-tarball*)

Download either one. Decompress it by using `tar xJ` (*.xz* file) or `tar xz` (*.tgz* file) and then run the resulting shell script.

Install the pip Package Manager

Beyond the standard Python installation, two tools are almost essential for Python development: `pip` and `virtualenv`.

The `pip` package is the most popular way to install third-party (nonstandard) Python packages. It has been annoying that such a useful tool isn't part of standard Python and that you've needed to download and install it yourself. As a friend of mine used to say, it's a cruel hazing ritual. The good news is that `pip` is a standard part of Python, starting with the 3.4 release.

If you have Python 3 but only the Python 2 version of `pip`, here's how to get the Python 3 version on Linux or macOS:

```
$ curl -O http://python-distribute.org/distribute_setup.py
$ sudo python3 distribute_setup.py
$ curl -O https://raw.github.com/pypa/pip/master/contrib/get-pip.py
$ sudo python3 get-pip.py
```

This installs `pip-3.3` in the `bin` directory of your Python 3 installation. Then, use `pip-3.3` to install third-party Python packages rather than Python 2's `pip`.

Install virtualenv

Often used with `pip`, the `virtualenv` program is a way to install Python packages in a specified directory (folder) to avoid interactions with any preexisting system Python packages. This lets you use whatever Python goodies you want, even if you don't have permission to change the existing installation.

Some good guides to `pip` and `virtualenv` are:

- A Non-Magical Introduction to Pip and Virtualenv for Python Beginners (*http://bit.ly/jm-pip-vlenv*)
- The Hitchhiker's Guide to Packaging: Pip (*http://bit.ly/hhgp-pip*)

Other Packaging Solutions

As you've seen, Python's packaging techniques vary, and none work well for every problem. The PyPA (*https://www.pypa.io*) (Python Packaging Authority) is a volunteer working group (not part of the official Python development core group) that's trying to simplify Python packaging. The group wrote the Python Packaging User's Guide (*https://packaging.python.org*), which discusses problems and solutions.

The most popular tools are `pip` and `virtualenv`, and I've used these throughout this book. If they fall short for you, or if you like trying new things, here are some alternatives:

- `pipenv` (*https://pipenv.readthedocs.io*) combines `pip` and `virtualenv` and adds more features. See also some criticism (*https://oreil.ly/NQ3pH*) and threaded discussion (*https://oreil.ly/psWa-*).
- `poetry` (*https://poetry.eustace.io/*) is a rival that addresses some of the problems with `pipenv`.

But the most prominent packaging alternative, especially for scientific and data-heavy applications, is `conda`. You can get it as part of the Anaconda Python distribution, which I talk about next, or by itself ("Install Anaconda's Package Manager conda" on page 519).

Install Anaconda

Anaconda (*https://docs.anaconda.com/anaconda*) is an all-in-one distribution with an emphasis on science. The latest version, Anaconda3, includes Python 3.7 and its standard library as well as the R language for data science. Other goodies include libraries that we've talked about in this book: `beautifulsoup4`, `flask`, `ipython`, `matplotlib`, `nose`, `numpy`, `pandas`, `pillow`, `pip`, `scipy`, `tables`, `zmq`, and many others. It also has a cross-platform installation program called `conda`, which I get to in the next section.

To install Anaconda3, go to the download page (*https://www.anaconda.com/distribu tion*) for the Python 3 versions. Click the appropriate link for your platform (version numbers might have changed since this was written, but you can figure it out):

- The macOS installer will install everything to the *anaconda* directory under your home directory.
- For Windows, double-click the *.exe* file after it downloads.
- For Linux, choose the 32-bit version or the 64-bit version. After it has downloaded, execute it (it's a big shell script).

 Ensure that the name of the file you download starts with *Ana-conda3*. If it starts with just *Anaconda*, that's the Python 2 version.

Anaconda installs everything in its own directory (*anaconda* under your home directory). This means that it won't interfere with any versions of Python that might already be on your computer. It also means that you don't need any special permission (account names like `admin` or `root`) to install it either.

Anaconda now includes more than 1,500 open source packages. Visit the Anaconda docs (*https://docs.anaconda.com/anaconda/packages/pkg-docs*) page and click the link for your platform and Python version.

After installing Anaconda3, you can see what Santa put on your computer by typing the command `conda list`.

Install Anaconda's Package Manager conda

The Anaconda developers built `conda` (*https://docs.conda.io*) to address the problems they've seen with `pip` and other tools. `pip` is a Python package manager, but `conda` works with any software and language. `conda` also avoids the need for something like `virtualenv` to keep installations from stepping on one another.

If you installed the Anaconda distribution, you already have the `conda` program. If not, you can get Python 3 and `conda` from the miniconda (*https://docs.conda.io/en/latest/miniconda.html*) page. As with Anaconda, make sure the file you download starts with `Miniconda3`; if it starts with `Miniconda` alone, it's the Python 2 version.

`conda` works with `pip`. Although it has its own public package repository (*https://anaconda.org/anaconda/repo*), commands like `conda search` will also search the PyPi repository (*http://pypi.python.org*). If you have problems with `pip`, `conda` might be a good alternative.

Something Completely Different: Async

Our first two appendixes were for beginning programmers, but this one is for those who are a bit advanced.

Like most programming languages, Python has been *synchronous*. It runs through code linearly, a line at a time, from top to bottom. When you call a function, Python jumps into its code, and the caller waits until the function returns before resuming what it was doing.

Your CPU can do only one thing at a time, so synchronous execution makes perfect sense. But it turns out that often a program is not actually running any code, but waiting for something, like data from a file or a network service. This is like us staring at a browser screen while waiting for a site to load. If we could avoid this "busy waiting," we might shorten the total time of our programs. This is also called improving *throughput*.

In Chapter 15, you saw that if you want some concurrency, your choices included threads, processes, or a third-party solution like `gevent` or `twisted`. But there are now a growing number of *asynchronous* answers, both built in to Python and third-party solutions. These coexist with the usual synchronous Python code, but, to borrow a Ghostbusters warning, you can't cross the streams. I'll show you how to avoid any ectoplasmic side effects.

Coroutines and Event Loops

In Python 3.4, Python added a standard *asynchronous* module called `asyncio`. Python 3.5 then added the keywords `async` and `await`. These implement some new concepts:

- *Coroutines* are functions that pause at various points
- An *event loop* that schedules and runs coroutines

These let us write asynchronous code that looks something like the normal synchronous code that we're used to. Otherwise, we'd need to use one of the methods mentioned in Chapter 15 and Chapter 17, and summarized later in "Async Versus…" on page 525.

Normal multitasking is what your operating system does to your processes. It decides what's fair, who's being a CPU hog, when to open the I/O spigots, and so on. The event loop, however, provides *cooperative multitasking*, in which coroutines indicate when they're able to start and stop. They run in a single thread, so you don't have the potential issues that I mentioned in "Threads" on page 287.

You *define* a coroutine by putting `async` before its initial `def`. You *call* a coroutine by:

- Putting `await` before it, which quietly adds the coroutine to an existing event loop. You can do this only within another coroutine.
- Or by using `asyncio.run()`, which explicitly starts an event loop.
- Or by using `asyncio.create_task()` or `asyncio.ensure_future()`.

This example uses the first two calling methods:

```
>>> import asyncio
>>>
>>> async def wicked():
...     print("Surrender,")
...     await asyncio.sleep(2)
...     print("Dorothy!")
...
>>> asyncio.run(wicked())
Surrender,
Dorothy!
```

These was a dramatic two-second wait in there that you can't see on a printed page. To prove that we didn't cheat (see Chapter 19 for `timeit` details):

```
>>> from timeit import timeit
>>> timeit("asyncio.run(wicked())", globals=globals(), number=1)
Surrender,
Dorothy!
2.005701574998966
```

That `asyncio.sleep(2)` call was itself a coroutine, just an example here to fake something time consuming like an API call.

The line `asyncio.run(wicked())` is a way of running a coroutine from synchronous Python code (here, the top level of the program).

The difference from a standard synchronous counterpart (using `time.sleep()`) is that the caller of `wicked()` is not blocked for two seconds while it runs.

The third way to run a coroutine is to create a *task* and `await` it. This example shows the task approach along with the previous two methods:

```
>>> import asyncio
>>>
>>> async def say(phrase, seconds):
...     print(phrase)
...     await asyncio.sleep(seconds)
...
>>> async def wicked():
...     task_1 = asyncio.create_task(say("Surrender,", 2))
...     task_2 = asyncio.create_task(say("Dorothy!", 0))
...     await task_1
...     await task_2
...
>>> asyncio.run(wicked())
Surrender,
Dorothy!
```

If you run this, you'll see that there was no delay between the two lines printing this time. That's because they were separate tasks. `task_1` paused two seconds after printing `Surrender`, but that didn't affect `task_2`.

An `await` is similar to a `yield` in a generator, but rather than returning a value, it marks a spot where the event loop can pause it if needed.

There's lots more where this came from in the docs (*https://oreil.ly/Cf_hd*). Synchronous and asynchronous code can coexist in the same program. Just remember to put `async` before the `def` and `await` before the call of your asynchronous function.

Some more information:

- A list (*https://oreil.ly/Vj0yD*) of `asyncio` links.
- Code for an `asyncio` web crawler (*https://oreil.ly/n4FVx*).

Asyncio Alternatives

Although `asyncio` is a standard Python package, you can use `async` and `await` without it. Coroutines and the event loop are independent. The design of `asyncio` is sometimes criticized (*https://oreil.ly/n4FVx*), and third-party alternatives have appeared:

- `curio` (*https://curio.readthedocs.io*)
- `trio` (*https://trio.readthedocs.io*)

Let's show a real example using `trio` and `asks` (*https://asks.readthedocs.io*) (an async web framework, modeled on the `requests` API). Example C-1 shows a concurrent web-crawling example using `trio` and `asks`, adapted from a stackoverflow answer (*https://oreil.ly/CbINS*). To run this, first `pip install` both `trio` and `asks`.

Example C-1. trio_asks_sites.py

```
import time

import asks
import trio

asks.init("trio")

urls = [
    'https://boredomtherapy.com/bad-taxidermy/',
    'http://www.badtaxidermy.com/',
    'https://crappytaxidermy.com/',
    'https://www.ranker.com/list/bad-taxidermy-pictures/ashley-reign',
]

async def get_one(url, t1):
    r = await asks.get(url)
    t2 = time.time()
    print(f"{(t2-t1):.04}\t{len(r.content)}\t{url}")

async def get_sites(sites):
    t1 = time.time()
    async with trio.open_nursery() as nursery:
        for url in sites:
            nursery.start_soon(get_one, url, t1)

if __name__ == "__main__":
    print("seconds\tbytes\turl")
    trio.run(get_sites, urls)
```

Here's what I got:

```
$ python trio_asks_sites.py
seconds bytes   url
0.1287  5735    https://boredomtherapy.com/bad-taxidermy/
0.2134  146082  https://www.ranker.com/list/bad-taxidermy-pictures/ashley-reign
0.215   11029   http://www.badtaxidermy.com/
0.3813  52385   https://crappytaxidermy.com/
```

You'll notice that `trio` did not use `asyncio.run()`, but instead its own `trio.open_nursery()`. If you're curious, you can read an essay (*https://oreil.ly/yp1-r*) and discussion (*https://oreil.ly/P21Ra*) of the design decisions behind `trio`.

A new package called `AnyIO` (*https://anyio.readthedocs.io/en/latest*) provides a single interface to `asyncio`, `curio`, and `trio`.

In the future, you can expect more async approaches, both in standard Python and from third-party developers.

Async Versus...

As you've seen in many places in this book, there are many techniques for concurrency. How does the async stuff compare with them?

Processes
> This is a good solution if you want to use all the CPU cores on your machine, or multiple machines. But processes are heavy, take a while to start, and require serialization for interprocess communication.

Threads
> Although threads were designed as a "lightweight" alternative to processes, each thread uses a good chunk of memory. Coroutines are much lighter than threads; you can create hundreds of thousands of coroutines on a machine that might only support a few thousand threads.

Green threads
> Green threads like `gevent` work well and look like synchronous code, but they require *monkey-patching* standard Python functions, such as socket libraries.

Callbacks
> Libraries like `twisted` rely on *callbacks*: functions that are called when when certain events occur. This is familiar to GUI and JavaScript programmers.

Queues—These tend to be a large-scale solution, when your data or processes really need more than one machine.

Async Frameworks and Servers

The async additions to Python are recent, and it's taking time for developers to create async versions of frameworks like Flask.

The ASGI (*https://asgi.readthedocs.io*) standard is an async version of WSGI, discussed further here (*https://oreil.ly/BnEXT*).

Here are some ASGI web servers:

- hypercorn (*https://pgjones.gitlab.io/hypercorn*)
- sanic (*https://sanic.readthedocs.io*)
- uvicorn (*https://www.uvicorn.org*)

And some async web frameworks:

- aiohttp (*https://aiohttp.readthedocs.io*)—Client *and* server
- api_hour (*https://pythonhosted.org/api_hour*)
- asks (*https://asks.readthedocs.io*)—Like requests
- blacksheep (*https://github.com/RobertoPrevato/BlackSheep*)
- bocadillo (*https://github.com/bocadilloproject/bocadillo*)
- channels (*https://channels.readthedocs.io*)
- fastapi (*https://fastapi.tiangolo.com*)—Uses type annotations
- muffin (*https://muffin.readthedocs.io*)
- quart (*https://gitlab.com/pgjones/quart*)
- responder (*https://python-responder.org*)
- sanic (*https://sanic.readthedocs.io*)
- starlette (*https://www.starlette.io*)
- tornado (*https://www.tornadoweb.org*)
- vibora (*https://vibora.io*)

Finally, some async database interfaces:

- aiomysql (*https://aiomysql.readthedocs.io*)
- aioredis (*https://aioredis.readthedocs.io*)
- asyncpg (*https://github.com/magicstack/asyncpg*)

Answers to Exercises

1. A Taste of Py

1.1 If you don't already have Python 3 installed on your computer, do it now. Read Appendix B for the details for your computer system.

1.2 Start the Python 3 interactive interpreter. Again, details are in Appendix B. It should print a few lines about itself and then a single line starting with >>>. That's your prompt to type Python commands.

Here's what it looks like on my Mac:

```
$ python
Python 3.7.3 (v3.7.3:ef4ec6ed12, Mar 25 2019, 16:39:00)
[GCC 4.2.1 (Apple Inc. build 5666) (dot 3)] on darwin
Type "help", "copyright", "credits" or "license" for more information.
>>>
```

1.3 Play with the interpreter a little. Use it like a calculator and type this: 8 * 9. Press the Enter key to see the result. Python should print 72.

```
>>> 8 * 9
72
```

1.4 Type the number 47 and press the Enter key. Did it print 47 for you on the next line?

```
>>> 47
47
```

1.5 Now type `print(47)` and press Enter. Did that also print 47 for you on the next line?

```
>>> print(47)
47
```

2. Data: Types, Values, Variables, and Names

2.1 Assign the integer value 99 to the variable `prince`, and print it.

```
>>> prince = 99
>>> print(prince)
99
>>>
```

2.2 What type is the value 5?

```
>>> type(5)
<class 'int'>
```

2.3 What type is the value `2.0`?

```
>>> type(2.0)
<class 'float'>
```

2.4 What type is the expression 5 + 2.0?

```
>>> type(5 + 2.0)
<class 'float'>
```

3. Numbers

3.1 How many seconds are in an hour? Use the interactive interpreter as a calculator and multiply the number of seconds in a minute (60) by the number of minutes in an hour (also 60).

```
>>> 60 * 60
3600
```

3.2 Assign the result from the previous task (seconds in an hour) to a variable called seconds_per_hour.

```
>>> seconds_per_hour = 60 * 60
>>> seconds_per_hour
3600
```

3.3 How many seconds are in a day? Use your seconds_per_hour variable.

```
>>> seconds_per_hour * 24
86400
```

3.4 Calculate seconds per day again, but this time save the result in a variable called seconds_per_day.

```
>>> seconds_per_day = seconds_per_hour * 24
>>> seconds_per_day
86400
```

3.5 Divide seconds_per_day by seconds_per_hour. Use floating-point (/) division.

```
>>> seconds_per_day / seconds_per_hour
24.0
```

3.6 Divide seconds_per_day by seconds_per_hour, using integer (//) division. Did this number agree with the floating-point value from the previous question, aside from the final .0?

```
>>> seconds_per_day // seconds_per_hour
24
```

4. Choose with if

4.1 Choose a number between 1 and 10 and assign it to the variable secret. Then, select another number between 1 and 10 and assign it to the variable guess. Next, write the conditional tests (if, else, and elif) to print the string 'too low' if guess is less than secret, 'too high' if greater than secret, and 'just right' if equal to secret.

Did you choose 7 for secret? I bet a lot of people do, because there's something about 7.

```
secret = 7
guess = 5
if guess < secret:
    print('too low')
elif guess > secret:
    print('too high')
else:
    print('just right')
```

Run this program and you should see the following:

```
too low
```

4.2 Assign `True` or `False` to the variables `small` and `green`. Write some `if`/`else` statements to print which of these matches those choices: cherry, pea, watermelon, pumpkin.

```
>>> small = False
>>> green = True
>>> if small:
...     if green:
...         print("pea")
...     else:
...         print("cherry")
... else:
...     if green:
...         print("watermelon")
...     else:
...         print("pumpkin")
...
watermelon
```

5. Text Strings

5.1 Capitalize the word starting with m:

```
>>> song = """When an eel grabs your arm,
... And it causes great harm,
... That's - a moray!"""
```

> Don't forget the space before the m:
>
> ```
> >>> song = """When an eel grabs your arm,
> ... And it causes great harm,
> ... That's - a moray!"""
> >>> song = song.replace(" m", " M")
> >>> print(song)
> When an eel grabs your arm,
> And it causes great harm,
> That's - a Moray!
> ```

5.2 Print each list question with its correctly matching answer, in the form:

Q: *question*
A: *answer*

```
>>> questions = [
...     "We don't serve strings around here. Are you a string?",
...     "What is said on Father's Day in the forest?",
```

```
...        "What makes the sound 'Sis! Boom! Bah!'?"
...        ]
>>> answers = [
...        "An exploding sheep.",
...        "No, I'm a frayed knot.",
...        "'Pop!' goes the weasel."
...        ]
```

You could print each item in questions with its mate from answers in many ways.
Let's try a tuple sandwich (tuples in a tuple) to pair them, and tuple unpacking to
retrieve them for printing:

```
questions = [
    "We don't serve strings around here. Are you a string?",
    "What is said on Father's Day in the forest?",
    "What makes the sound 'Sis! Boom! Bah!'?"
    ]
answers = [
    "An exploding sheep.",
    "No, I'm a frayed knot.",
    "'Pop!' goes the weasel."
    ]

q_a = ( (0, 1), (1,2), (2, 0) )
for q, a in q_a:
    print("Q:", questions[q])
    print("A:", answers[a])
    print()
```

Output:

```
$ python qanda.py
Q: We don't serve strings around here. Are you a string?
A: No, I'm a frayed knot.

Q: What is said on Father's Day in the forest?
A: 'Pop!' goes the weasel.

Q: What makes the sound 'Sis! Boom! Bah!'?
A: An exploding sheep.
```

5.3 Write the following poem by using old-style formatting. Substitute the strings
'roast beef', 'ham', 'head', and 'clam' into this string:

```
My kitty cat likes %s,
My kitty cat likes %s,
My kitty cat fell on his %s
And now thinks he's a %s.
```

```
>>> poem = '''
... My kitty cat likes %s,
... My kitty cat likes %s,
... My kitty cat fell on his %s
... And now thinks he's a %s.
... '''
>>> args = ('roast beef', 'ham', 'head', 'clam')
>>> print(poem % args)

My kitty cat likes roast beef,
My kitty cat likes ham,
My kitty cat fell on his head
And now thinks he's a clam.
```

5.4 Write a form letter by using new-style formatting. Save the following string as letter (you'll use it in the next exercise):

```
Dear {salutation} {name},

Thank you for your letter. We are sorry that our {product}
{verbed} in your {room}. Please note that it should never
be used in a {room}, especially near any {animals}.

Send us your receipt and {amount} for shipping and handling.
We will send you another {product} that, in our tests,
is {percent}% less likely to have {verbed}.

Thank you for your support.

Sincerely,
{spokesman}
{job_title}
```

```
>>> letter = '''
... Dear {salutation} {name},
...
... Thank you for your letter. We are sorry that our {product}
... {verbed} in your {room}. Please note that it should never
... be used in a {room}, especially near any {animals}.
...
... Send us your receipt and {amount} for shipping and handling.
... We will send you another {product} that, in our tests,
... is {percent}% less likely to have {verbed}.
...
... Thank you for your support.
...
... Sincerely,
```

```
... {spokesman}
... {job_title}
... '''
```

5.5 Assign values to variable strings named 'salutation', 'name', 'product', 'ver
bed' (past tense verb), 'room', 'animals', 'percent', 'spokesman', and
'job_title'. Print letter with these values, using letter.format().

```
>>> print (
...     letter.format(salutation='Ambassador',
...                   name='Nibbler',
...                   product='pudding',
...                   verbed='evaporated',
...                   room='gazebo',
...                   animals='octothorpes',
...                   amount='$1.99',
...                   percent=88,
...                   spokesman='Shirley Iugeste',
...                   job_title='I Hate This Job')
...     )

Dear Ambassador Nibbler,

Thank you for your letter. We are sorry that our pudding
evaporated in your gazebo. Please note that it should never
be used in a gazebo, especially near any octothorpes.

Send us your receipt and $1.99 for shipping and handling.
We will send you another pudding that, in our tests,
is 88% less likely to have evaporated.

Thank you for your support.

Sincerely,
Shirley Iugeste
I Hate This Job
```

5.6 After public polls to name things, a pattern emerged: an English submarine (Boaty McBoatface), an Australian racehorse (Horsey McHorseface), and a Swedish train (Trainy McTrainface). Use % formatting to print the winning name at the state fair for a prize duck, gourd, and spitz.

Example D-1. mcnames1.py

```
names = ["duck", "gourd", "spitz"]
for name in names:
    cap_name = name.capitalize()
    print("%sy Mc%sface" % (cap_name, cap_name))
```

Output:

```
Ducky McDuckface
Gourdy McGourdface
Spitzy McSpitzface
```

5.7 Do the same, with `format()` formatting.

Example D-2. mcnames2.py

```
names = ["duck", "gourd", "spitz"]
for name in names:
    cap_name = name.capitalize()
    print("{}y Mc{}face".format(cap_name, cap_name))
```

5.8 Once more, with feeling, and *f strings*.

Example D-3. mcnames3.py

```
names = ["duck", "gourd", "spitz"]
for name in names:
    cap_name = name.capitalize()
    print(f"{cap_name}y Mc{cap_name}face")
```

---

6. Loop with while and for

6.1 Use a for loop to print the values of the list [3, 2, 1, 0].

```
>>> for value in [3, 2, 1, 0]:
...     print(value)
...
3
2
1
0
```

6.2 Assign the value 7 to the variable guess_me, and the value 1 to the variable num
ber. Write a while loop that compares number with guess_me. Print 'too low' if num
ber is less than guess_me. If number equals guess_me, print 'found it!' and then
exit the loop. If number is greater than guess_me, print 'oops' and then exit the loop.
Increment number at the end of the loop.

```
guess_me = 7
number = 1
while True:
    if number < guess_me:
        print('too low')
    elif number == guess_me:
        print('found it!')
        break
    elif number > guess_me:
        print('oops')
        break
    number += 1
```

If you did this right, you should see this:

```
too low
too low
too low
too low
too low
too low
found it!
```

Notice that the elif start > guess_me: line could have been a simple else:,
because if start is not less than or equal to guess_me, it must be greater—at least in
this universe.

6.3 Assign the value 5 to the variable guess_me. Use a for loop to iterate a variable called number over range(10). If number is less than guess_me, print 'too low'. If it equals guess_me, print found it! and then break out of the for loop. If number is greater than guess_me, print 'oops' and then exit the loop.

```
>>> guess_me = 5
>>> for number in range(10):
...     if number < guess_me:
...         print("too low")
...     elif number == guess_me:
...         print("found it!")
...         break
...     else:
...         print("oops")
...         break
...
too low
too low
too low
too low
too low
found it!
```

7. Tuples and Lists

7.1 Create a list called years_list, starting with the year of your birth, and each year thereafter until the year of your fifth birthday. For example, if you were born in 1980, the list would be years_list = [1980, 1981, 1982, 1983, 1984, 1985].

If you were born in 1980, you would type:

```
>>> years_list = [1980, 1981, 1982, 1983, 1984, 1985]
```

7.2 In which of these years was your third birthday? Remember, you were 0 years of age for your first year.

You want offset 3. Thus, if you were born in 1980:

```
>>> years_list[3]
1983
```

7.3 In which year in `years_list` were you the oldest?

> You want the last year, so use offset `-1`. You could also say 5 because you know this list has six items, but `-1` gets the last item from a list of any size. For a 1980-vintage person:
>
> ```
> >>> years_list[-1]
> 1985
> ```

7.4 Make and print a list called `things` with these three strings as elements: `"mozzarella"`, `"cinderella"`, `"salmonella"`.

> ```
> >>> things = ["mozzarella", "cinderella", "salmonella"]
> >>> things
> ['mozzarella', 'cinderella', 'salmonella']
> ```

7.5 Capitalize the element in `things` that refers to a person and then print the list. Did it change the element in the list?

> This capitalizes the word but doesn't change it in the list:
>
> ```
> >>> things[1].capitalize()
> 'Cinderella'
> >>> things
> ['mozzarella', 'cinderella', 'salmonella']
> ```
>
> If you want to change it in the list, you need to assign it back:
>
> ```
> >>> things[1] = things[1].capitalize()
> >>> things
> ['mozzarella', 'Cinderella', 'salmonella']
> ```

7.6 Make the cheesy element of `things` all uppercase and then print the list.

> ```
> >>> things[0] = things[0].upper()
> >>> things
> ['MOZZARELLA', 'Cinderella', 'salmonella']
> ```

7.7 Delete the disease element, collect your Nobel Prize, and then print the list.

This would remove it by value:

```
>>> things.remove("salmonella")
>>> things
['MOZZARELLA', 'Cinderella']
```

Because it was last in the list, the following would have worked also:

```
>>> del things[-1]
```

And you could have deleted by offset from the beginning:

```
>>> del things[2]
```

7.8 Create a list called surprise with the elements "Groucho", "Chico", and "Harpo".

```
>>> surprise = ['Groucho', 'Chico', 'Harpo']
>>> surprise
['Groucho', 'Chico', 'Harpo']
```

7.9 Lowercase the last element of the surprise list, reverse it, and then capitalize it.

```
>>> surprise[-1] = surprise[-1].lower()
>>> surprise[-1] = surprise[-1][::-1]
>>> surprise[-1].capitalize()
'Oprah'
```

7.10 Use a list comprehension to make a list called even of the even numbers in range(10).

```
>>> even = [number for number in range(10) if number % 2 == 0]
>>> even
[0, 2, 4, 6, 8]
```

7.11 Let's create a jumprope rhyme maker. You'll print a series of two-line rhymes. Start with this program fragment:

```
start1 = ["fee", "fie", "foe"]
rhymes = [
    ("flop", "get a mop"),
    ("fope", "turn the rope"),
    ("fa", "get your ma"),
    ("fudge", "call the judge"),
    ("fat", "pet the cat"),
    ("fog", "walk the dog"),
    ("fun", "say we're done"),
    ]
start2 = "Someone better"
```

For each string pair (first, second) in rhymes:

For the first line:

- Print each string in start1, capitalized and followed by an exclamation point and a space.
- Print first, also capitalized and followed by an exclamation point.

For the second line:

- Print start2 and a space.
- Print second and a period.

```
    start1 = ["fee", "fie", "foe"]
    rhymes = [
        ("flop", "get a mop"),
        ("fope", "turn the rope"),
        ("fa", "get your ma"),
        ("fudge", "call the judge"),
        ("fat", "pet the cat"),
        ("fog", "pet the dog"),
        ("fun", "say we're done"),
        ]
    start2 = "Someone better"
    start1_caps = " ".join([word.capitalize() + "!" for word in start1])
    for first, second in rhymes:
        print(f"{start1_caps} {first.capitalize()}!")
        print(f"{start2} {second}.")
```

Output:

```
Fee! Fie! Foe! Flop!
Someone better get a mop.
```

```
Fee! Fie! Foe! Fope!
Someone better turn the rope.
Fee! Fie! Foe! Fa!
Someone better get your ma.
Fee! Fie! Foe! Fudge!
Someone better call the judge.
Fee! Fie! Foe! Fat!
Someone better pet the cat.
Fee! Fie! Foe! Fog!
Someone better walk the dog.
Fee! Fie! Foe! Fun!
Someone better say we're done.
```

8. Dictionaries

8.1 Make an English-to-French dictionary called e2f and print it. Here are your starter words: dog is chien, cat is chat, and walrus is morse.

```
>>> e2f = {'dog': 'chien', 'cat': 'chat', 'walrus': 'morse'}
>>> e2f
{'cat': 'chat', 'walrus': 'morse', 'dog': 'chien'}
```

8.2 Using your three-word dictionary e2f, print the French word for walrus.

```
>>> e2f['walrus']
'morse'
```

8.3 Make a French-to-English dictionary called f2e from e2f. Use the items method.

```
>>> f2e = {}
>>> for english, french in e2f.items():
        f2e[french] = english
>>> f2e
{'morse': 'walrus', 'chien': 'dog', 'chat': 'cat'}
```

8.4 Print the English equivalent of the French word chien.

```
>>> f2e['chien']
'dog'
```

8.5 Print the set of English words from `e2f`.

```
>>> set(e2f.keys())
{'cat', 'walrus', 'dog'}
```

8.6 Make a multilevel dictionary called `life`. Use these strings for the topmost keys: `'animals'`, `'plants'`, and `'other'`. Make the `'animals'` key refer to another dictionary with the keys `'cats'`, `'octopi'`, and `'emus'`. Make the `'cats'` key refer to a list of strings with the values `'Henri'`, `'Grumpy'`, and `'Lucy'`. Make all the other keys refer to empty dictionaries.

```
This is a hard one, so don't feel bad if you peeked here first.
>>> life = {
...       'animals': {
...            'cats': [
...                 'Henri', 'Grumpy', 'Lucy'
...            ],
...            'octopi': {},
...            'emus': {}
...       },
...       'plants': {},
...       'other': {}
...  }
>>>
```

8.7 Print the top-level keys of `life`.

```
>>> print(life.keys())
dict_keys(['animals', 'other', 'plants'])
```
Python 3 includes that `dict_keys` stuff. To print them as a plain list, use this:
```
>>> print(list(life.keys()))
['animals', 'other', 'plants']
```
By the way, you can use spaces to make your code easier to read:
```
>>> print ( list ( life.keys() ) )
['animals', 'other', 'plants']
```

8.8 Print the keys for `life['animals']`.

```
>>> print(life['animals'].keys())
dict_keys(['cats', 'octopi', 'emus'])
```

8.9 Print the values for `life['animals']['cats']`.

```
>>> print(life['animals']['cats'])
['Henri', 'Grumpy', 'Lucy']
```

8.10 Use a dictionary comprehension to create the dictionary squares. Use `range(10)` to return the keys, and use the square of each key as its value.

```
>>> squares = {key: key*key for key in range(10)}
>>> squares
{0: 0, 1: 1, 2: 4, 3: 9, 4: 16, 5: 25, 6: 36, 7: 49, 8: 64, 9: 81}
```

8.11 Use a set comprehension to create the set odd from the odd numbers in `range(10)`.

```
>>> odd = {number for number in range(10) if number % 2 == 1}
>>> odd
{1, 3, 5, 7, 9}
```

8.12 Use a generator comprehension to return the string `'Got '` and a number for the numbers in `range(10)`. Iterate through this by using a `for` loop.

```
>>> for thing in ('Got %s' % number for number in range(10)):
...     print(thing)
...
Got 0
Got 1
Got 2
Got 3
Got 4
Got 5
Got 6
Got 7
```

```
Got 8
Got 9
```

8.13 Use `zip()` to make a dictionary from the key tuple (`'optimist'`, `'pessimist'`, `'troll'`) and the values tuple (`'The glass is half full'`, `'The glass is half empty'`, `'How did you get a glass?'`).

```
>>> keys = ('optimist', 'pessimist', 'troll')
>>> values = ('The glass is half full',
...     'The glass is half empty',
...     'How did you get a glass?')
>>> dict(zip(keys, values))
{'optimist': 'The glass is half full',
 'pessimist': 'The glass is half empty',
 'troll': 'How did you get a glass?'}
```

8.14 Use `zip()` to make a dictionary called `movies` that pairs these lists: `titles = ['Creature of Habit', 'Crewel Fate', 'Sharks On a Plane']` and `plots = ['A nun turns into a monster', 'A haunted yarn shop', 'Check your exits']`

```
>>> titles = ['Creature of Habit',
...     'Crewel Fate',
...     'Sharks On a Plane']
>>> plots = ['A nun turns into a monster',
...     'A haunted yarn shop',
...     'Check your exits']
>>> movies = dict(zip(titles, plots))
>>> movies
{'Creature of Habit': 'A nun turns into a monster',
 'Crewel Fate': 'A haunted yarn shop',
 'Sharks On a Plane': 'Check your exits'}
>>>
```

9. Functions

9.1 Define a function called `good()` that returns the following list: [`'Harry'`, `'Ron'`, `'Hermione'`].

```
>>> def good():
...     return ['Harry', 'Ron', 'Hermione']
...
```

```
>>> good()
['Harry', 'Ron', 'Hermione']
```

9.2 Define a generator function called get_odds() that returns the odd numbers from range(10). Use a for loop to find and print the third value returned.

```
>>> def get_odds():
...     for number in range(1, 10, 2):
...         yield number
...
>>> count = 1
>>> for number in get_odds():
...     if count == 3:
...         print("The third odd number is", number)
...         break
...     count += 1
...
The third odd number is 5
```

9.3 Define a decorator called test that prints 'start' when a function is called, and 'end' when it finishes.

```
>>> def test(func):
...     def new_func(*args, **kwargs):
...         print('start')
...         result = func(*args, **kwargs)
...         print('end')
...         return result
...     return new_func
...
>>>
>>> @test
... def greeting():
...     print("Greetings, Earthling")
...
>>> greeting()
start
Greetings, Earthling
end
```

9.4 Define an exception called OopsException. Raise this exception to see what happens. Then, write the code to catch this exception and print 'Caught an oops'.

```
>>> class OopsException(Exception):
...     pass
...
>>> raise OopsException()
Traceback (most recent call last):
  File "<stdin>", line 1, in <module>
__main__.OopsException
>>>
>>> try:
...     raise OopsException
... except OopsException:
...     print('Caught an oops')
...
Caught an oops
```

10. Oh Oh: Objects and Classes

10.1 Make a class called Thing with no contents and print it. Then, create an object called example from this class and also print it. Are the printed values the same or different?

```
>>> class Thing:
...     pass
...
>>> print(Thing)
<class '__main__.Thing'>
>>> example = Thing()
>>> print(example)
<__main__.Thing object at 0x1006f3fd0>
```

10.2 Make a new class called Thing2 and assign the value 'abc' to a class variable called letters. Print letters.

```
>>> class Thing2:
...     letters = 'abc'
...
>>> print(Thing2.letters)
abc
```

10.3 Make yet another class called (of course) Thing3. This time, assign the value 'xyz' to an instance (object) variable called letters. Print letters. Do you need to make an object from the class to do this?

```
>>> class Thing3:
...     def __init__(self):
...         self.letters = 'xyz'
...
```

The variable letters belongs to any objects made from Thing3, not the Thing3 class itself:

```
>>> print(Thing3.letters)
Traceback (most recent call last):
  File "<stdin>", line 1, in <module>
AttributeError: type object 'Thing3' has no attribute 'letters'
>>> something = Thing3()
>>> print(something.letters)
xyz
```

10.4 Make a class called Element, with instance attributes name, symbol, and number. Create an object called hydrogen of this class with the values 'Hydrogen', 'H', and 1.

```
>>> class Element:
...     def __init__(self, name, symbol, number):
...         self.name = name
...         self.symbol = symbol
...         self.number = number
...
>>> hydrogen = Element('Hydrogen', 'H', 1)
```

10.5 Make a dictionary with these keys and values: 'name': 'Hydrogen', 'symbol': 'H', 'number': 1. Then, create an object called hydrogen from class Element using this dictionary.

Start with the dictionary:

```
>>> el_dict = {'name': 'Hydrogen', 'symbol': 'H', 'number': 1}
```

This works, although it takes a bit of typing:

```
>>> hydrogen = Element(el_dict['name'], el_dict['symbol'], el_dict['number'])
```

Let's check that it worked:

```
>>> hydrogen.name
'Hydrogen'
```

However, you can also initialize the object directly from the dictionary, because its key names match the arguments to __init__ (refer to Chapter 9 for a discussion of keyword arguments):

```
>>> hydrogen = Element(**el_dict)
>>> hydrogen.name
'Hydrogen'
```

10.6 For the Element class, define a method called dump() that prints the values of the object's attributes (name, symbol, and number). Create the hydrogen object from this new definition and use dump() to print its attributes.

```
>>> class Element:
...     def __init__(self, name, symbol, number):
...         self.name = name
...         self.symbol = symbol
...         self.number = number
...     def dump(self):
...         print('name=%s, symbol=%s, number=%s' %
...             (self.name, self.symbol, self.number))
...
>>> hydrogen = Element(**el_dict)
>>> hydrogen.dump()
name=Hydrogen, symbol=H, number=1
```

10.7 Call print(hydrogen). In the definition of Element, change the name of the method dump to __str__, create a new hydrogen object, and call print(hydrogen) again.

```
>>> print(hydrogen)
<__main__.Element object at 0x1006f5310>
>>> class Element:
...     def __init__(self, name, symbol, number):
...         self.name = name
...         self.symbol = symbol
...         self.number = number
...     def __str__(self):
...         return ('name=%s, symbol=%s, number=%s' %
...             (self.name, self.symbol, self.number))
...
>>> hydrogen = Element(**el_dict)
>>> print(hydrogen)
name=Hydrogen, symbol=H, number=1
```

__str__() is one of Python's *magic methods*. The print function calls an object's
__str__() method to get its string representation. If it doesn't have a __str__()
method, it gets the default method from its parent Object class, which returns a
string like <__main__.Element object at 0x1006f5310>.

10.8 Modify Element to make the attributes name, symbol, and number private. Define
a getter property for each to return its value.

```
>>> class Element:
...     def __init__(self, name, symbol, number):
...         self.__name = name
...         self.__symbol = symbol
...         self.__number = number
...     @property
...     def name(self):
...         return self.__name
...     @property
...     def symbol(self):
...         return self.__symbol
...     @property
...     def number(self):
...         return self.__number
...
>>> hydrogen = Element('Hydrogen', 'H', 1)
>>> hydrogen.name
'Hydrogen'
>>> hydrogen.symbol
'H'
>>> hydrogen.number
1
```

10.9 Define three classes: Bear, Rabbit, and Octothorpe. For each, define only one
method: eats(). This should return 'berries' (Bear), 'clover' (Rabbit), and
'campers' (Octothorpe). Create one object from each and print what it eats.

```
>> class Bear:
...     def eats(self):
...         return 'berries'
...
>>> class Rabbit:
...     def eats(self):
...         return 'clover'
...
>>> class Octothorpe:
...     def eats(self):
```

```
...         return 'campers'
...
>>> b = Bear()
>>> r = Rabbit()
>>> o = Octothorpe()
>>> print(b.eats())
berries
>>> print(r.eats())
clover
>>> print(o.eats())
campers
```

10.10 Define these classes: Laser, Claw, and SmartPhone. Each has only one method: does(). This returns 'disintegrate' (Laser), 'crush' (Claw), or 'ring' (Smart Phone). Then, define the class Robot that has one instance (object) of each of these. Define a does() method for the Robot that prints what its component objects do.

```
>>> class Laser:
...     def does(self):
...             return 'disintegrate'
...
>>> class Claw:
...     def does(self):
...             return 'crush'
...
>>> class SmartPhone:
...     def does(self):
...             return 'ring'
...
>>> class Robot:
...     def __init__(self):
...         self.laser = Laser()
...         self.claw = Claw()
...         self.smartphone = SmartPhone()
...     def does(self):
...         return '''I have many attachments:
... My laser, to %s.
... My claw, to %s.
... My smartphone, to %s.''' % (
...         self.laser.does(),
...         self.claw.does(),
...         self.smartphone.does() )
...
>>> robbie = Robot()
>>> print( robbie.does() )
I have many attachments:
My laser, to disintegrate.
```

```
My claw, to crush.
My smartphone, to ring.
```

11. Modules, Packages, and Goodies

11.1 Make a file called *zoo.py*. In it, define a function called hours that prints the string 'Open 9-5 daily'. Then, use the interactive interpreter to import the zoo module and call its hours function.

Here's *zoo.py*:

```
def hours():
    print('Open 9-5 daily')
```

And now, let's import it interactively:

```
>>> import zoo
>>> zoo.hours()
Open 9-5 daily
```

11.2 In the interactive interpreter, import the zoo module as menagerie and call its hours() function.

```
>>> import zoo as menagerie
>>> menagerie.hours()
Open 9-5 daily
```

11.3 Staying in the interpreter, import the hours() function from zoo directly and call it.

```
>>> from zoo import hours
>>> hours()
Open 9-5 daily
```

11.4 Import the hours() function as info and call it.

```
>>> from zoo import hours as info
>>> info()
Open 9-5 daily
```

11.6 Make an OrderedDict called `fancy` from the same pairs and print it. Did it print in the same order as `plain`?

```
>>> from collections import OrderedDict
>>> fancy = OrderedDict([('a', 1), ('b', 2), ('c', 3)])
>>> fancy
OrderedDict([('a', 1), ('b', 2), ('c', 3)])
```

11.7 Make a `defaultdict` called `dict_of_lists` and pass it the argument `list`. Make the list `dict_of_lists['a']` and append the value `'something for a'` to it in one assignment. Print `dict_of_lists['a']`.

```
>>> from collections import defaultdict
>>> dict_of_lists = defaultdict(list)
>>> dict_of_lists['a'].append('something for a')
>>> dict_of_lists['a']
['something for a']
```

12. Wrangle and Mangle Data

12.1 Create a Unicode string called `mystery` and assign it the value `'\U0001f984'`. Print `mystery` and its Unicode name.

```
>>> import unicodedata
>>> mystery = '\U0001f4a9'
>>> mystery
'💩'
>>> unicodedata.name(mystery)
'PILE OF POO'
```

Oh my. What else have they got in there?

12.2 Encode `mystery`, this time using UTF-8, into the bytes variable popbytes. Print `pop_bytes`.

```
>>> pop_bytes = mystery.encode('utf-8')
>>> pop_bytes
b'\xf0\x9f\x92\xa9'
```

12.3 Using UTF-8, decode popbytes into the string variable pop_string. Print pop_string. Is pop_string equal to mystery?

```
>>> pop_string = pop_bytes.decode('utf-8')
>>> pop_string
'💩'
>>> pop_string == mystery
True
```

12.4 When you're working with text, regular expressions come in very handy. We'll apply them in a number of ways to our featured text sample. It's a poem titled "Ode on the Mammoth Cheese," written by James McIntyre in 1866 in homage to a seven-thousand-pound cheese that was crafted in Ontario and sent on an international tour. If you'd rather not type all of it, use your favorite search engine and cut and paste the words into your Python program, or just grab it from Project Gutenberg (*http://bit.ly/mcintyre-poetry*). Call the text string mammoth.

```
>>> mammoth = '''
... We have seen thee, queen of cheese,
... Lying quietly at your ease,
... Gently fanned by evening breeze,
... Thy fair form no flies dare seize.
...
... All gaily dressed soon you'll go
... To the great Provincial show,
... To be admired by many a beau
... In the city of Toronto.
...
... Cows numerous as a swarm of bees,
... Or as the leaves upon the trees,
... It did require to make thee please,
... And stand unrivalled, queen of cheese.
...
... May you not receive a scar as
... We have heard that Mr. Harris
... Intends to send you off as far as
... The great world's show at Paris.
...
... Of the youth beware of these,
... For some of them might rudely squeeze
... And bite your cheek, then songs or glees
... We could not sing, oh! queen of cheese.
...
... We'rt thou suspended from balloon,
... You'd cast a shade even at noon,
... Folks would think it was the moon
```

```
... About to fall and crush them soon.
... '''
```

12.5 Import the `re` module to use Python's regular expression functions. Use the `re.findall()` to print all the words that begin with c.

We'll define the variable `pat` for the pattern and then search for it in `mammoth`:

```
>>> import re
>>> pat = r'\bc\w*'
>>> re.findall(pat, mammoth)
['cheese', 'city', 'cheese', 'cheek', 'could', 'cheese', 'cast', 'crush']
```

The \b means to begin at a boundary between a word and a nonword. Use this to specify either the beginning or end of a word. The literal c is the first letter of the words we're looking for. The \w means any *word character*, which includes letters, digits, and underscores (_). The * means *zero or more* of these word characters. Together, this finds words that begin with c, including 'c' itself. If you didn't use a raw string (with an r right before the starting quote), Python would interpret \b as a backspace and the search would mysteriously fail:

```
>>> pat = '\bc\w*'
>>> re.findall(pat, mammoth)
[]
```

12.6 Find all four-letter words that begin with c.

```
>>> pat = r'\bc\w{3}\b'
>>> re.findall(pat, mammoth)
['city', 'cast']
```

You need that final \b to indicate the end of the word. Otherwise, you'll get the first four letters of all words that begin with c and have at least four letters:

```
>>> pat = r'\bc\w{3}'
>>> re.findall(pat, mammoth)
['chee', 'city', 'chee', 'chee', 'coul', 'chee', 'cast', 'crus']
```

12.7 Find all the words that end with r.

This is a little tricky. We get the right result for words that end with r:

```
>>> pat = r'\b\w*r\b'
>>> re.findall(pat, mammoth)
['your', 'fair', 'Or', 'scar', 'Mr', 'far', 'For', 'your', 'or']
```

However, the results aren't so good for words that end with l:

```
>>> pat = r'\b\w*l\b'
>>> re.findall(pat, mammoth)
['All', 'll', 'Provincial', 'fall']
```

But what's that ll doing there? The \w pattern matches only letters, numbers, and underscores—not ASCII apostrophes. As a result, it grabs the final ll from you'll. We can handle this by adding an apostrophe to the set of characters to match. Our first try fails:

```
>>> pat = r'\b[\w']*l\b'
  File "<stdin>", line 1
    pat = r'\b[\w']*l\b'
```

Python points to the vicinity of the error, but it might take a while to see that the mistake was that the pattern string is surrounded by the same apostrophe/quote character. One way to solve this is to escape it with a backslash:

```
>>> pat = r'\b[\w\']*l\b'
>>> re.findall(pat, mammoth)
['All', "you'll", 'Provincial', 'fall']
```

Another way is to surround the pattern string with double quotes:

```
>>> pat = r"\b[\w']*l\b"
>>> re.findall(pat, mammoth)
['All', "you'll", 'Provincial', 'fall']
```

12.8 Find all the words that contain exactly three vowels in a row.

Begin with a word boundary, any number of *word* characters, three vowels, and then any nonvowel characters to the end of the word:

```
>>> pat = r'\b[^aeiou]*[aeiou]{3}[^aeiou]*\b'
>>> re.findall(pat, mammoth)
['queen', 'quietly', 'beau\nIn', 'queen', 'squeeze', 'queen']
```

This looks right, except for that 'beau\nIn' string. We searched mammoth as a single multiline string. Our [^aeiou] matches any nonvowels, including \n (line feed, which marks the end of a text line). We need to add one more thing to the ignore set: \s matches any space characters, including \n:

```
>>> pat = r'\b\w*[aeiou]{3}[^aeiou\s]\w*\b'
>>> re.findall(pat, mammoth)
['queen', 'quietly', 'queen', 'squeeze', 'queen']
```

We didn't find beau this time, so we need one more tweak to the pattern: match any number (even zero) of nonvowels after the three vowels. Our previous pattern always matched one nonvowel.

```
>>> pat = r'\b\w*[aeiou]{3}[^aeiou\s]*\w*\b'
>>> re.findall(pat, mammoth)
['queen', 'quietly', 'beau', 'queen', 'squeeze', 'queen']
```

What does all of this show? Among other things, that regular expressions can do a lot, but they can be very tricky to get right.

12.9 Use unhexlify() to convert this hex string (combined from two strings to fit on a page) to a bytes variable called gif:

```
'47494638396101000100800000000000ffffff21f9' +
'0401000000002c00000000010001000020144003b'
```

```
>>> import binascii
>>> hex_str = '47494638396101000100800000000000ffffff21f9' + \
...         '0401000000002c00000000010001000020144003b'
>>> gif = binascii.unhexlify(hex_str)
>>> len(gif)
42
```

12.10 The bytes in gif define a one-pixel transparent GIF file, one of the most common graphics file formats. A legal GIF starts with the string *GIF89a*. Does gif match this?

```
>>> gif[:6] == b'GIF89a'
True
```

Notice that we needed to use a b to define a byte string rather than a Unicode character string. You can compare bytes with bytes, but you cannot compare bytes with strings:

```
>>> gif[:6] == 'GIF89a'
False
>>> type(gif)
<class 'bytes'>
>>> type('GIF89a')
<class 'str'>
>>> type(b'GIF89a')
<class 'bytes'>
```

12.11 The pixel width of a GIF is a 16-bit little-endian integer starting at byte offset 6, and the height is the same size, starting at offset 8. Extract and print these values for `gif`. Are they both 1?

```
>>> import struct
>>> width, height = struct.unpack('<HH', gif[6:10])
>>> width, height
(1, 1)
```

13. Calendars and Clocks

13.1 Write the current date as a string to the text file *today.txt*.

```
>>> from datetime import date
>>> now = date.today()
>>> now_str = now.isoformat()
>>> with open('today.txt', 'wt') as output:
...     print(now_str, file=output)
>>>
```

When I ran this, here's what I got in *today.txt*:

```
2019-07-23
```

Instead of `print`, you could have also said something like `output.write(now_str)`. Using `print` adds the final newline.

13.2 Read the text file *today.txt* into the string `today_string`.

```
>>> with open('today.txt', 'rt') as input:
...     today_string = input.read()
...
>>> today_string
'2019-07-23\n'
```

13.3 Parse the date from `today_string`.

```
>>> fmt = '%Y-%m-%d\n'
>>> datetime.strptime(today_string, fmt)
datetime.datetime(2019, 7, 23, 0, 0)
```

> If you wrote that final newline to the file, you need to match it in the format string.

13.4 Create a date object of your day of birth.

> Let's say that you were born on August 14, 1982:
>
> ```
> >>> my_day = date(1982, 8, 14)
> >>> my_day
> datetime.date(1982, 8, 14)
> ```

13.5 What day of the week was your day of birth?

> ```
> >>> my_day.weekday()
> 5
> >>> my_day.isoweekday()
> 6
> ```
>
> With weekday(), Monday is 0 and Sunday is 6. With isoweekday(), Monday is 1 and Sunday is 7. Therefore, this date was a Saturday.

13.6 When will you be (or when were you) 10,000 days old?

> ```
> >>> from datetime import timedelta
> >>> party_day = my_day + timedelta(days=10000)
> >>> party_day
> datetime.date(2009, 12, 30)
> ```
>
> If August 14, 1982 was your birthday, you probably missed an excuse for a party.

14. Files and Directories

14.1 List the files in your current directory.

> If your current directory is *ohmy* and contains three files named after animals, it might look like this:
>
> ```
> >>> import os
> >>> os.listdir('.')
> ['bears', 'lions', 'tigers']
> ```

14.2 List the files in your parent directory.

> If your parent directory contained two files plus the current *ohmy* directory, it might look like this:
>
> ```
> >>> import os
> >>> os.listdir('..')
> ['ohmy', 'paws', 'whiskers']
> ```

14.3 Assign the string 'This is a test of the emergency text system' to the variable test1, nd write test1 to a file called *test.txt*.

> ```
> >>> test1 = 'This is a test of the emergency text system'
> >>> len(test1)
> 43
> ```
>
> Here's how to do it by using open, write, and close:
>
> ```
> >>> outfile = open('test.txt', 'wt')
> >>> outfile.write(test1)
> 43
> >>> outfile.close()
> ```
>
> Or, you can use with and avoid calling close (Python does it for you):
>
> ```
> >>> with open('test.txt', 'wt') as outfile:
> ...     outfile.write(test1)
> ...
> ...
> 43
> ```

14.4 Open the file *test.txt* and read its contents into the string test2. Are test1 and test2 the same?

> ```
> >>> with open('test.txt', 'rt') as infile:
> ...     test2 = infile.read()
> ...
> >>> len(test2)
> 43
> >>> test1 == test2
> True
> ```

15. Data in Time: Processes and Concurrency

15.1 Use `multiprocessing` to create three separate processes. Make each one wait a random number of seconds between zero and one, print the current time, and then exit.

```
import multiprocessing

def now(seconds):
    from datetime import datetime
    from time import sleep
    sleep(seconds)
    print('wait', seconds, 'seconds, time is', datetime.utcnow())

if __name__ == '__main__':
    import random
    for n in range(3):
        seconds = random.random()
        proc = multiprocessing.Process(target=now, args=(seconds,))
        proc.start()
```
```
$ python multi_times.py
wait 0.10720361113059229 seconds, time is 2019-07-24 00:19:23.951594
wait 0.5825144002370065 seconds, time is 2019-07-24 00:19:24.425047
wait 0.6647690569029477 seconds, time is 2019-07-24 00:19:24.509995
```

16. Data in a Box: Persistent Storage

16.1 Save the following text lines to a file called *books.csv* (notice that if the fields are separated by commas, you need to surround a field with quotes if it contains a comma):

```
author,book
J R R Tolkien,The Hobbit
Lynne Truss,"Eats, Shoots & Leaves"
```

```
>>> text = '''author,book
... J R R Tolkien,The Hobbit
... Lynne Truss,"Eats, Shoots & Leaves"
... '''
>>> with open('test.csv', 'wt') as outfile:
...     outfile.write(text)
...
73
```

16.2 Use the csv module and its DictReader method to read *books.csv* to the variable books. Print the values in books. Did DictReader handle the quotes and commas in the second book's title?

```
>>> with open('books.csv', 'rt') as infile:
...     books = csv.DictReader(infile)
...     for book in books:
...         print(book)
...
{'book': 'The Hobbit', 'author': 'J R R Tolkien'}
{'book': 'Eats, Shoots & Leaves', 'author': 'Lynne Truss'}
```

16.3 Create a CSV file called *books2.csv* by using these lines:

```
title,author,year
The Weirdstone of Brisingamen,Alan Garner,1960
Perdido Street Station,China Miéville,2000
Thud!,Terry Pratchett,2005
The Spellman Files,Lisa Lutz,2007
Small Gods,Terry Pratchett,1992
```

```
>>> text = '''title,author,year
... The Weirdstone of Brisingamen,Alan Garner,1960
... Perdido Street Station,China Miéville,2000
... Thud!,Terry Pratchett,2005
... The Spellman Files,Lisa Lutz,2007
... Small Gods,Terry Pratchett,1992
... '''
>>> with open('books2.csv', 'wt') as outfile:
...     outfile.write(text)
...
201
```

16.4 Use the sqlite3 module to create a SQLite database called *books.db* and a table called books with these fields: title (text), author (text), and year (integer).

```
>>> import sqlite3
>>> db = sqlite3.connect('books.db')
>>> curs = db.cursor()
>>> curs.execute('''create table book (title text, author text, year int)''')
<sqlite3.Cursor object at 0x1006e3b90>
>>> db.commit()
```

16.5 Read *books2.csv* and insert its data into the book table.

```
>>> import csv
>>> import sqlite3
>>> ins_str = 'insert into book values(?, ?, ?)'
>>> with open('books.csv', 'rt') as infile:
...     books = csv.DictReader(infile)
...     for book in books:
...         curs.execute(ins_str, (book['title'], book['author'], book['year']))
...
<sqlite3.Cursor object at 0x1007b21f0>
<sqlite3.Cursor object at 0x1007b21f0>
<sqlite3.Cursor object at 0x1007b21f0>
<sqlite3.Cursor object at 0x1007b21f0>
<sqlite3.Cursor object at 0x1007b21f0>
>>> db.commit()
```

16.6 Select and print the `title` column from the book table in alphabetical order.

```
>>> sql = 'select title from book order by title asc'
>>> for row in db.execute(sql):
...     print(row)
...
('Perdido Street Station',)
('Small Gods',)
('The Spellman Files',)
('The Weirdstone of Brisingamen',)
('Thud!',)
```

If you just wanted to print the `title` value without that tuple stuff (parentheses and comma), try this:

```
>>> for row in db.execute(sql):
...     print(row[0])
...
Perdido Street Station
Small Gods
The Spellman Files
The Weirdstone of Brisingamen
Thud!
```

If you want to ignore the initial `'The'` in titles, you need a little extra SQL fairy dust:

```
>>> sql = '''select title from book order by
... case when (title like "The %")
... then substr(title, 5)
... else title end'''
>>> for row in db.execute(sql):
...     print(row[0])
```

```
...
Perdido Street Station
Small Gods
The Spellman Files
Thud!
The Weirdstone of Brisingamen
```

16.7 Select and print all columns from the book table in order of publication.

```
>>> for row in db.execute('select * from book order by year'):
...     print(row)
...
('The Weirdstone of Brisingamen', 'Alan Garner', 1960)
('Small Gods', 'Terry Pratchett', 1992)
('Perdido Street Station', 'China Miéville', 2000)
('Thud!', 'Terry Pratchett', 2005)
('The Spellman Files', 'Lisa Lutz', 2007)
```

To print all the fields in each row, just separate with a comma and space:

```
>>> for row in db.execute('select * from book order by year'):
...     print(*row, sep=', ')
...
The Weirdstone of Brisingamen, Alan Garner, 1960
Small Gods, Terry Pratchett, 1992
Perdido Street Station, China Miéville, 2000
Thud!, Terry Pratchett, 2005
The Spellman Files, Lisa Lutz, 2007
```

16.8 Use the sqlalchemy module to connect to the sqlite3 database *books.db* that you just made in exercise 8.6. As in 8.8, select and print the title column from the book table in alphabetical order.

```
>>> import sqlalchemy
>>> conn = sqlalchemy.create_engine('sqlite:///books.db')
>>> sql = 'select title from book order by title asc'
>>> rows = conn.execute(sql)
>>> for row in rows:
...     print(row)
...
('Perdido Street Station',)
('Small Gods',)
('The Spellman Files',)
('The Weirdstone of Brisingamen',)
('Thud!',)
```

16.9 Install the Redis server (see Appendix B) and the Python `redis` library (`pip install redis`) on your machine. Create a Redis hash called `test` with the fields count (1) and name (`'Fester Bestertester'`). Print all the fields for `test`.

```
>>> import redis
>>> conn = redis.Redis()
>>> conn.delete('test')
1
>>> conn.hmset('test', {'count': 1, 'name': 'Fester Bestertester'})
True
>>> conn.hgetall('test')
{b'name': b'Fester Bestertester', b'count': b'1'}
```

16.10 Increment the count field of `test` and print it.

```
>>> conn.hincrby('test', 'count', 3)
4
>>> conn.hget('test', 'count')
b'4'
```

17. Data in Space: Networks

17.1 Use a plain `socket` to implement a current-time service. When a client sends the string `'time'` to the server, return the current date and time as an ISO string.

Here's one way to write the server, *udp_time_server.py*:

```
from datetime import datetime
import socket

address = ('localhost', 6789)
max_size = 4096

print('Starting the server at', datetime.now())
print('Waiting for a client to call.')
server = socket.socket(socket.AF_INET, socket.SOCK_DGRAM)
server.bind(address)
while True:
    data, client_addr = server.recvfrom(max_size)
    if data == b'time':
        now = str(datetime.utcnow())
        data = now.encode('utf-8')
        server.sendto(data, client_addr)
```

```
            print('Server sent', data)
    server.close()
```

And the client, *udp_time_client.py*:

```
import socket
from datetime import datetime
from time import sleep

address    = ('localhost', 6789)
max_size   = 4096

print('Starting the client at', datetime.now())
client = socket.socket(socket.AF_INET, socket.SOCK_DGRAM)
while True:
    sleep(5)
    client.sendto(b'time', address)
    data, server_addr = client.recvfrom(max_size)
    print('Client read', data)
client.close()
```

I put in a sleep(5) call at the top of the client loop to make the data exchange less supersonic. Start the server in one window:

```
$ python udp_time_server.py
Starting the server at 2014-06-02 20:28:47.415176
Waiting for a client to call.
```

Start the client in another window:

```
$ python udp_time_client.py
Starting the client at 2014-06-02 20:28:51.454805
```

After five seconds, you'll start getting output in both windows. Here are the first three lines from the server:

```
Server sent b'2014-06-03 01:28:56.462565'
Server sent b'2014-06-03 01:29:01.463906'
Server sent b'2014-06-03 01:29:06.465802'
```

And here are the first three from the client:

```
Client read b'2014-06-03 01:28:56.462565'
Client read b'2014-06-03 01:29:01.463906'
Client read b'2014-06-03 01:29:06.465802'
```

Both of these programs run forever, so you'll need to cancel them manually.

17.2. Use ZeroMQ REQ and REP sockets to do the same thing.

```
import zmq
from datetime import datetime
```

```
host = '127.0.0.1'
port = 6789
context = zmq.Context()
server = context.socket(zmq.REP)
server.bind("tcp://%s:%s" % (host, port))
print('Server started at', datetime.utcnow())
while True:
    # Wait for next request from client
    message = server.recv()
    if message == b'time':
        now = datetime.utcnow()
        reply = str(now)
        server.send(bytes(reply, 'utf-8'))
        print('Server sent', reply)

import zmq
from datetime import datetime
from time import sleep

host = '127.0.0.1'
port = 6789
context = zmq.Context()
client = context.socket(zmq.REQ)
client.connect("tcp://%s:%s" % (host, port))
print('Client started at', datetime.utcnow())
while True:
    sleep(5)
    request = b'time'
    client.send(request)
    reply = client.recv()
    print("Client received %s" % reply)
```

With plain sockets, you need to start the server first. With ZeroMQ, you can start either the server or client first.

```
$ python zmq_time_server.py
Server started at 2014-06-03 01:39:36.933532

$ python zmq_time_client.py
Client started at 2014-06-03 01:39:42.538245
```

After 15 seconds or so, you should have some lines from the server:

```
Server sent 2014-06-03 01:39:47.539878
Server sent 2014-06-03 01:39:52.540659
Server sent 2014-06-03 01:39:57.541403
```

Here's what you should see from the client:

```
Client received b'2014-06-03 01:39:47.539878'
Client received b'2014-06-03 01:39:52.540659'
Client received b'2014-06-03 01:39:57.541403'
```

17.3. Try the same with XMLRPC.

From the server:

```
from xmlrpc.server import SimpleXMLRPCServer

def now():
    from datetime import datetime
    data = str(datetime.utcnow())
    print('Server sent', data)
    return data

server = SimpleXMLRPCServer(("localhost", 6789))
server.register_function(now, "now")
server.serve_forever()
```

And from the client:

```
import xmlrpc.client
from time import sleep

proxy = xmlrpc.client.ServerProxy("http://localhost:6789/")
while True:
    sleep(5)
    data = proxy.now()
    print('Client received', data)
```

Start the server:

```
$ python xmlrpc_time_server.py
```

Start the client:

```
$ python xmlrpc_time_client.py
```

Wait 15 seconds or so. Here are the first three lines of server output:

```
Server sent 2014-06-03 02:14:52.299122
127.0.0.1 - - [02/Jun/2014 21:14:52] "POST / HTTP/1.1" 200 -
Server sent 2014-06-03 02:14:57.304741
127.0.0.1 - - [02/Jun/2014 21:14:57] "POST / HTTP/1.1" 200 -
Server sent 2014-06-03 02:15:02.310377
127.0.0.1 - - [02/Jun/2014 21:15:02] "POST / HTTP/1.1" 200 -
```

And here are the first three lines from the client:

```
Client received 2014-06-03 02:14:52.299122
Client received 2014-06-03 02:14:57.304741
Client received 2014-06-03 02:15:02.310377
```

17.4 You may have seen the classic *I Love Lucy* television episode in which Lucy and Ethel worked in a chocolate factory. The duo fell behind as the conveyor belt that supplied the confections for them to process began operating at an ever-faster rate. Write a simulation that pushes different types of chocolates to a Redis list, and Lucy is a client doing blocking pops of this list. She needs 0.5 seconds to handle a piece of chocolate. Print the time and type of each chocolate as Lucy gets it, and how many remain to be handled.

---

redis_choc_supply.py supplies the infinite treats:

```
import redis
import random
from time import sleep

conn = redis.Redis()
varieties = ['truffle', 'cherry', 'caramel', 'nougat']
conveyor = 'chocolates'
while True:
    seconds = random.random()
    sleep(seconds)
    piece = random.choice(varieties)
    conn.rpush(conveyor, piece)
```

redis_lucy.py might look like this:

```
import redis
from datetime import datetime
from time import sleep

conn = redis.Redis()
timeout = 10
conveyor = 'chocolates'
while True:
    sleep(0.5)
    msg = conn.blpop(conveyor, timeout)
    remaining = conn.llen(conveyor)
    if msg:
        piece = msg[1]
        print('Lucy got a', piece, 'at', datetime.utcnow(),
        ', only', remaining, 'left')
```

Start them in either order. Because Lucy takes a half second to handle each, and they're being produced every half second on average, it's a race to keep up. The more of a head start that you give to the conveyor belt, the harder you make Lucy's life.

```
$ python redis_choc_supply.py &

$ python redis_lucy.py
Lucy got a b'nougat' at 2014-06-03 03:15:08.721169 , only 4 left
Lucy got a b'cherry' at 2014-06-03 03:15:09.222816 , only 3 left
Lucy got a b'truffle' at 2014-06-03 03:15:09.723691 , only 5 left
```

```
Lucy got a b'truffle' at 2014-06-03 03:15:10.225008 , only 4 left
Lucy got a b'cherry' at 2014-06-03 03:15:10.727107 , only 4 left
Lucy got a b'cherry' at 2014-06-03 03:15:11.228226 , only 5 left
Lucy got a b'cherry' at 2014-06-03 03:15:11.729735 , only 4 left
Lucy got a b'truffle' at 2014-06-03 03:15:12.230894 , only 6 left
Lucy got a b'caramel' at 2014-06-03 03:15:12.732777 , only 7 left
Lucy got a b'cherry' at 2014-06-03 03:15:13.234785 , only 6 left
Lucy got a b'cherry' at 2014-06-03 03:15:13.736103 , only 7 left
Lucy got a b'caramel' at 2014-06-03 03:15:14.238152 , only 9 left
Lucy got a b'cherry' at 2014-06-03 03:15:14.739561 , only 8 left
```

Poor Lucy.

17.5 Use ZeroMQ to publish the poem from exercise 12.4 (from Example 12-1), one word at a time. Write a ZeroMQ consumer that prints every word that starts with a vowel, and another that prints every word that contains five letters. Ignore punctuation characters.

Here's the server, *poem_pub.py*, which plucks each word from the poem and publishes it to the topic vowels if it starts with a vowel, and the topic five if it has five letters. Some words might be in both topics, some in neither.

```python
import string
import zmq

host = '127.0.0.1'
port = 6789
ctx = zmq.Context()
pub = ctx.socket(zmq.PUB)
pub.bind('tcp://%s:%s' % (host, port))

with open('mammoth.txt', 'rt') as poem:
    words = poem.read()
for word in words.split():
    word = word.strip(string.punctuation)
    data = word.encode('utf-8')
    if word.startswith(('a','e','i','o','u','A','e','i','o','u')):
        pub.send_multipart([b'vowels', data])
    if len(word) == 5:
        pub.send_multipart([b'five', data])
```

The client, *poem_sub.py*, subscribes to the topics vowels and five and prints the topic and word:

```python
import string
import zmq

host = '127.0.0.1'
port = 6789
```

```
ctx = zmq.Context()
sub = ctx.socket(zmq.SUB)
sub.connect('tcp://%s:%s' % (host, port))
sub.setsockopt(zmq.SUBSCRIBE, b'vowels')
sub.setsockopt(zmq.SUBSCRIBE, b'five')
while True:
    topic, word = sub.recv_multipart()
    print(topic, word)
```

If you start these and run them, they *almost* work. Your code looks fine but nothing happens. You need to read the ZeroMQ guide (*http://zguide.zeromq.org/page:all*) to learn about the *slow joiner* problem: even if you start the client before the server, the server begins pushing data immediately after starting, and the client takes a little time to connect to the server. If you're publishing a constant stream of something and don't really care when the subscribers jump in, it's no problem. But in this case, the data stream is so short that it's flown past before the subscriber blinks, like a fastball past a batter.

The easiest way to fix this is to make the publisher sleep a second after it calls bind() and before it starts sending messages. Call this version *poem_pub_sleep.py*:

```
import string
import zmq
from time import sleep

host = '127.0.0.1'
port = 6789
ctx = zmq.Context()
pub = ctx.socket(zmq.PUB)
pub.bind('tcp://%s:%s' % (host, port))

sleep(1)

with open('mammoth.txt', 'rt') as poem:
    words = poem.read()
for word in words.split():
    word = word.strip(string.punctuation)
    data = word.encode('utf-8')
    if word.startswith(('a','e','i','o','u','A','e','i','o','u')):
        print('vowels', data)
        pub.send_multipart([b'vowels', data])
    if len(word) == 5:
        print('five', data)
        pub.send_multipart([b'five', data])
```

Start the subscriber and then the sleepy publisher:

```
$ python poem_sub.py
```

```
$ python poem_pub_sleep.py
```

Now, the subscriber has time to grab its two topics. Here are the first few lines of its output:

```
b'five' b'queen'
b'vowels' b'of'
b'five' b'Lying'
b'vowels' b'at'
b'vowels' b'ease'
b'vowels' b'evening'
b'five' b'flies'
b'five' b'seize'
b'vowels' b'All'
b'five' b'gaily'
b'five' b'great'
b'vowels' b'admired'
```

If you can't add a sleep() to your publisher, you can synchronize publisher and subscriber programs by using REQ and REP sockets. See the *publisher.py* and *subscriber.py* examples on GitHub (*http://bit.ly/pyzmq-gh*).

18. The Web, Untangled

18.1 If you haven't installed flask yet, do so now. This will also install werkzeug, jinja2, and possibly other packages.

18.2 Build a skeleton website, using Flask's debug/reload development web server. Ensure that the server starts up for hostname localhost on default port 5000. If your machine is already using port 5000 for something else, use another port number.

Here's *flask1.py*:

```
from flask import Flask

app = Flask(__name__)

app.run(port=5000, debug=True)
```

Gentlemen, start your engines:

```
$ python flask1.py
 * Running on http://127.0.0.1:5000/
 * Restarting with reloader
```

18.3 Add a home() function to handle requests for the home page. Set it up to return the string It's alive!.

What should we call this one, *flask2.py*?

```
from flask import Flask

app = Flask(__name__)

@app.route('/')
def home():
    return "It's alive!"

app.run(debug=True)
```

Start the server:

```
$ python flask2.py
 * Running on http://127.0.0.1:5000/
 * Restarting with reloader
```

Finally, access the home page via a browser, command-line HTTP program such as
curl or wget, or even telnet:

```
$ curl http://localhost:5000/
It's alive!
```

18.4 Create a Jinja2 template file called *home.html* with the following contents:

```
I'm of course referring to {{thing}},
which is {{height}} feet tall and {{color}}.
```

Make a directory called *templates* and create the file *home.html* with the contents just
shown. If your Flask server is still running from the previous examples, it will detect
the new content and restart itself.

18.5 Modify your server's home() function to use the *home.html* template. Provide it
with three GET parameters: thing, height, and color.

Here comes *flask3.py*:

```
from flask import Flask, request, render_template

app = Flask(__name__)

@app.route('/')
def home():
    thing = request.values.get('thing')
    height = request.values.get('height')
    color = request.values.get('color')
    return render_template('home.html',
        thing=thing, height=height, color=color)

app.run(debug=True)
```

Go to this address in your web client:

```
http://localhost:5000/?thing=Octothorpe&height=7&color=green
```

You should see the following:

```
I'm of course referring to Octothorpe, which is 7 feet tall and green.
```

19. Be a Pythonista

(Pythonistas don't have homework today.)

20. Py Art

20.1 Install `matplotlib`. Draw a scatter diagram of these (x, y) pairs: ((0, 0), (3, 5), (6, 2), (9, 8), (14, 10)).

20.2 Draw a line graph of the same data.

20.3 Draw a plot (a line graph with markers) of the same data

This has all three as subplots:

```
import matplotlib.pyplot as plt

x = (0, 3, 6, 9, 14)
y = (0, 5, 2, 8, 10)
fig, plots = plt.subplots(nrows=1, ncols=3)

plots[0].scatter(x, y)
plots[1].plot(x, y)
plots[2].plot(x, y, 'o-')

plt.show()
```

21. Py at Work

21.1 Install `geopandas` and run Example 21-1. Try modifying things like colors and marker sizes.

22. PySci

22.1 Install Pandas. Get the CSV file in Example 16-1. Run the program in Example 16-2. Experiment with some of the Pandas commands.

Cheat Sheets

I find myself looking up certain things a little too often. Here are some tables that I hope you'll find useful.

Operator Precedence

This table is a remix of the official documentation on precedence in Python 3, with the *highest* precedence operators at the top.

Operator	Description and examples
`[v, …], {v1, …}, {k1:v1, …}, (…)`	List/set/dict/generator creation or comprehension, parenthesized expression
`seq[n]`, `seq[n:m]`, `func(args…)`, `obj.attr`	Index, slice, function call, attribute reference
`**`	Exponentiation
`+n, -n, ~n`	Positive, negative, bitwise `not`
`*, /, //, %`	Multiplication, float division, int division, remainder
`+, -`	Addition, subtraction
`<<, >>`	Bitwise left, right shifts
`&`	Bitwise and
`|`	Bitwise or
`in, not in, is, is not, <, <=, >, >=, !=, ==`	Membership and equality tests
`not x`	Boolean (logical) `not`
`and`	Boolean `and`
`or`	Boolean `or`
`if … else`	Conditional expression
`lambda …`	`lambda` expression

String Methods

Python offers both string *methods* (can be used with any `str` object) and a `string` module with some useful definitions. Let's use these test variables:

```
>>> s = "OH, my paws and whiskers!"
>>> t = "I'm late!"
```

In the following examples, the Python shell prints the result of the method call, but the original variables s and t are not changed.

Change Case

```
>>> s.capitalize()
'Oh, my paws and whiskers!'
>>> s.lower()
'oh, my paws and whiskers!'
>>> s.swapcase()
'oh, MY PAWS AND WHISKERS!'
>>> s.title()
'Oh, My Paws And Whiskers!'
>>> s.upper()
'OH, MY PAWS AND WHISKERS!'
```

Search

```
>>> s.count('w')
2
>>> s.find('w')
9
>>> s.index('w')
9
>>> s.rfind('w')
16
>>> s.rindex('w')
16
>>> s.startswith('OH')
True
```

Modify

```
>>> ''.join(s)
'OH, my paws and whiskers!'
>>> ' '.join(s)
'O H ,   m y   p a w s   a n d   w h i s k e r s !'
>>> ' '.join((s, t))
"OH, my paws and whiskers! I'm late!"
>>> s.lstrip('HO')
', my paws and whiskers!'
>>> s.replace('H', 'MG')
'OMG, my paws and whiskers!'
```

```
>>> s.rsplit()
['OH,', 'my', 'paws', 'and', 'whiskers!']
>>> s.rsplit(' ', 1)
['OH, my paws and', 'whiskers!']
>>> s.split(' ', 1)
['OH,', 'my paws and whiskers!']
>>> s.split(' ')
['OH,', 'my', 'paws', 'and', 'whiskers!']
>>> s.splitlines()
['OH, my paws and whiskers!']
>>> s.strip()
'OH, my paws and whiskers!'
>>> s.strip('s!')
'OH, my paws and whisker'
```

Format

```
>>> s.center(30)
'   OH, my paws and whiskers!   '
>>> s.expandtabs()
'OH, my paws and whiskers!'
>>> s.ljust(30)
'OH, my paws and whiskers!     '
>>> s.rjust(30)
'     OH, my paws and whiskers!'
```

String Type

```
>>> s.isalnum()
False
>>> s.isalpha()
False
>>> s.isprintable()
True
>>> s.istitle()
False
>>> s.isupper()
False
>>> s.isdecimal()
False
>>> s.isnumeric()
False
```

String Module Attributes

These are class attributes that are used as constant definitions.

Attribute	Example
ascii_letters	`'abcdefghijklmnopqrstuvwxyzABCDEFGHIJKLMNOPQRSTUVWXYZ'`
ascii_lowercase	`'abcdefghijklmnopqrstuvwxyz'`
ascii_uppercase	`'ABCDEFGHIJKLMNOPQRSTUVWXYZ'`
digits	`'0123456789'`
hexdigits	`'0123456789abcdefABCDEF'`
octdigits	`'01234567'`
punctuation	`'!"#$%&\'()*+,-./:;<=>?@[\\]^_\{|}~'`
printable	digits + ascii_letters + punctuation + whitespace
whitespace	`' \t\n\r\x0b\x0c'`

Coda

Chester wants to express his appreciation for your diligence. If you need him, he's taking a nap...

Figure E-1. Chester[1]

---

1 He's moved about a foot to the right since Figure 3-1.

…but Lucy is available to answer any questions.

Figure E-2. Lucy

Index

anonymous functions, 156
Ansible, 369
Apache web server, 386
API (application programming interface), 320, 360, 400
append() function, 100
arange() function, 492
arguments, 142-151
    default parameter values for, 146
    defined, 143
    exploding/gathering keyword arguments, 149
    exploding/gathering positional arguments, 147-149
    keyword, 146
    keyword-only, 150
    mutable and immutable, 151
    None, 144
    positional, 145
arithmetic calculations, 489
array() function, 491
arrays, 489
    (see also NumPy)
    changing with reshape(), 493
    getting elements from, 494
    making with arange(), 492
    making with array(), 491
    making with zeros()/ones()/random(), 493
    math functions and, 495
    packed sequences with, 489
art (see graphics)
ASCII, 220
assembly language, 506
assertion, 421
assignment operator (=), 28, 107, 125
assignment, copying versus, 33
asterisk (*)
    duplicating lists with, 101
    duplicating strings with, 68
    duplicating tuples with, 96
    exploding/gathering positional arguments with, 147-149
    multiplication operator, 40
    wildcard, 230
asterisks (**)
    dictionary operator, 122, 396
    exponentiation, 43
    keyword arguments with, 149, 195
asynchronous (term), 284

asynchronous functions, 165
asynchronous tasks, 521-526
    asyncio alternatives, 524-525
    coroutines and event loops, 522-523
    frameworks and servers, 526
    versus other approaches, 525
asyncio library
    about, 297, 522
    alternatives to, 524-525
attributes, 171
    accessing, 181-186
    class and object, 185
    finding with self argument, 180
    getters and setters, 181
    initialization and, 172
    name mangling for privacy, 184
    properties for access, 182-183
    properties for computed values, 184
attrs package, 197
audio, 466
Azure, 372

B

back pressure technique, 301
backslash (\), 54, 66, 67, 273
bare metal, 508
bases, 44
basicConfig() function, 438
BeautifulSoup, 402
Beowulf cluster, 509
best practices
    code, testing, 418-428
    debugging, 428-437
    finding code, 410
    integrated development environments (IDEs), 413-416
    logging, 437-439
    optimizing code, 439-446
    resources, 450-452
    source control, 446-449
big data, 369
binary data, 238-244
    bit-level integer operators, 244
    bytes and bytearrays, 238-240
    converting bytes/strings with binascii(), 244
    converting with struct, 240-244
    practice exercise answers, 552-557
    practice exercises, 245
    reading binary files, 265

W

X

Y

Z

About the Author

Bill Lubanovic has been busy with Unix since 1977, GUIs since 1981, databases since 1990, and the web since 1993:

- 1982–1988 (Intran): Developed MetaForm on the first commercial graphic workstation.
- 1990–1995 (Northwest Airlines): Wrote a graphic yield management system; got the airline on the internet; and wrote its first internet marketing test.
- 1994 (Tela): Cofounded an early ISP.
- 1995–1999 (WAM!NET): Developed web dashboards and 3M Digital Media Repository.
- 1999–2005 (Mad Scheme): Cofounded a web development/hosting company.
- 2005 (O'Reilly): Wrote parts of *Linux Server Security*.
- 2007 (O'Reilly): Coauthored *Linux System Administration*.
- 2010–2013 (Keep): Designed and built Core Services between web frontend and database backends.
- 2014 (O'Reilly): Wrote the first edition of *Introducing Python*.
- 2015–2016 (Internet Archive): Worked on APIs and a Python version of the Wayback Machine.
- 2016–2018 (CrowdStrike): Managed Python-based services processing billions of daily security events.

Bill enjoys life in the Sangre de Sasquatch mountains of Minnesota with his wonderful family: wife Mary; son Tom (and wife Roxie); daughter Karin (and husband Erik); and cats Inga, Chester, and Lucy.

Colophon

The animal on the cover of *Introducing Python* is a python—that is, a member of the *Python* genus, which consists of 10 recognized snake species. Pythons are nonvenomous, constricting snakes native to the tropics and subtropics of the Eastern Hemisphere.

Pythons vary in length, based on species and sex, from approximately 3 feet long (ball python) to reported cases of more than 20 feet long (reticulated python). They are recognizable by their flat triangular-shaped heads and long backward-curving teeth. Generally, they have a combination of brown, tan, and black skin, arranged in diamond or interlocking blotch patterns. Albino pythons are white and yellow, and while at a disadvantage in the wild, are popular in zoos and as pets.

Pythons are strong swimmers, but these snakes almost exclusively ambush prey on land or in trees, attacking with their fangs and then immediately wrapping themselves around the quarry to asphyxiate it. Unlike boas, another well-known group of constrictor snakes, pythons lay eggs rather than birth live young. The female python will brood over the eggs until they hatch, shivering with her large muscular coils to keep the eggs warm.

The Burmese python has become an invasive species in Florida, competing with the American alligator for prey and significantly reducing the number of native birds and small mammals in the Everglades. Along with increased popularity as a pet in the 1990s, it is thought that Hurricane Andrew in 1992 is responsible for allowing captive Burmese pythons into the wild by destroying a zoo and breeding facility.

Most species of python have a conservation status of Least Concern, but the Bermese (native population) and Borneo short-tailed python are currently listed as Vulnerable. Many of the animals on O'Reilly covers are endangered; all of them are important to the world.

The cover illustration is by Jose Marzan, based on a black and white engraving from *Johnson's Natural History*. The cover fonts are Gilroy Semibold and Guardian Sans. The text font is Adobe Minion Pro; the heading font is Adobe Myriad Condensed; and the code font is Dalton Maag's Ubuntu Mono.

O'REILLY®

There's much more where this came from.

Experience books, videos, live online training courses, and more from O'Reilly and our 200+ partners—all in one place.

Learn more at oreilly.com/online-learning